Beyond
That Last
Blue Mountain

Beyond That Last Blue Mountain

published by
Medina Publishing Ltd
310 Ewell Road
Surbiton
Surrey KT6 7AL
medinapublishing.com

ISBN: 978-1-911487-17-3

9 8 7 6 5 4 3 2 1

Edited by Martin Rickerd
Designed by Catherine Perks
Cartography by Martin Lubikowski, ML Design
Printed and bound by Opolgraf SA, Poland

Beyond
That Last
Blue Mountain

Harriet Sandys

Medina Publishing

We are the Pilgrims, master: we shall go
Always a little further: it may be
Beyond that last blue mountan barred with snow
Across that angry or that glimmering sea.

James Elroy Flecker, *Hassan*

We cannot command success but success often
comes to those who dare and act.
It seldom comes to the timid.

Jawaharlal Nehru

for Bryan

Acknowledgements

If I had thought, all those years ago, that one day I would write about my experiences, I would have been more diligent in keeping a journal. At the time my writing was desultory, and I really only put pen to paper to describe an occasional journey. Fortunately, my family kept all my letters and this book is written largely from them. I am grateful to my mother, Anne Sandys, whose own research into her family in India and Afghanistan enabled me to draw upon the lives of my forebears.

My thanks to everyone at Medina Publishing, especially Kitty Carruthers, Rachel Knighton, Kristina Hill, Taslima Begum and Catherine Perks, who guided me through the whole process with great patience. I could not have wished for a better publisher.

My heartfelt thanks to my sister Mary, who proofread the first drafts, corrected my spelling and grammatical errors, cut down the large number of chapters and gave me invaluable advice based on her own long experience in publishing. My thanks too to Martin Rickerd who, on behalf of Medina, edited the final draft and dotted even more 'i's' and crossed even more 't's'.

IT experts Gail Milne and Trisha Sawyers guided me through the complexities of the computer, and many other friends have contributed in some way, shape or form – Amanda Pelham Burn, Joss Graham, Ian James who lent me out-of-print books on military campaigns in 19th-century Afghanistan, Deanna Hodgin, Robert Darr, Julian Gearing, Adrian Quine, my brother Myles Sandys, Jenny KilBride, John Jennings, and Fiona, Michaela and Sandy Gall. Special thanks are due to Jenny Balfour-Paul who suggested I contact Medina, and to Laura Morris who read the first few chapters and gave me kind encouragement.

I am grateful to Helen Saberi for describing the endless variety of Afghan food, and to my Turkmen friend Omar Masom for so patiently answering my questions on Afghan Turkmen culture and language.

I owe a huge debt of gratitude to my husband Bryan for his constant support and encouragement over the many years it took me to write this book, and to my parents, who gave me a wonderful childhood but sadly did not live long enough to read about their wayward daughter's exploits.

To all those who shared my journeys and assisted me in so many ways, I thank you for your support and hope this book will back memories of those extraordinary times. Finally, I will never forget the many people in Pakistan, Afghanistan, Kurdistan and Bosnia who, despite their own lives having been severely blighted by war, extended great hospitality and kindness to a young woman travelling alone.

Contents

List of abbreviations and acronyms

ACAF	Afghan Cultural Assistance Foundation
AP	Associated Press
ARIN	Afghan Refugee Information Network
Dacaar	Danish Sewing Project
FAO	Food and Agriculture Organization (UN)
GAZ	Soviet/Russian make of truck
HALO Trust	Hazardous Area Life-support Organisation, a British de-mining NGO
HTB	Holy Trinity Brompton with St Paul's, Onslow Square and St Augustine's, South Kensington, a church in west London
IKF	Iraqi Kurdistan Front
IRA	Irish Republican Army
KHAD	Khademat-e-Aetla'at-e-Dawlati, the Afghan communist regime's intelligence agency and security police
KRO	Kurdistan Reconstruction Organisation
KWU	Kurdistan Women's Union
MSI	Marie Stopes International
NGO	Non-governmental organisation
NWFP	North-West Frontier Province
PARSA	Physiotherapy and Rehabilitation Support for Afghanistan
PKK	Kurdistan Workers' Party – Kurdish: *Partiya Karkerên Kurdistanê*
PUK	Patriotic Union of Kurdistan
SCA	Swedish Committee for Afghanistan
SGAA	Sandy Gall's Afghanistan Appeal
STC	Save the Children USA
UNESCO	United Nations Educational, Scientific and Cultural Organization
UNHCR	Office of the United Nations High Commissioner for Refugees
UNOCA	United Nations Office for the Coordination of Humanitarian and Economic Assistance Programmes relating to Afghanistan
UNPROFOR	United Nations Protection Force (Former Yugoslavia)

Foreword

Jalalabad, Afghanistan
January 1988

The wide avenue leading from the centre of town to the small walled orchard was lined on either side by gigantic pine trees. Occasional shafts of pale winter sunshine glinted through the boughs, casting pools of yellow light on the thick carpet of needles. But there was no warmth in the rays; the air was dank and chilly. On this January morning in Jalalabad, the second-largest city in eastern Afghanistan and capital of Nangarhar province, hundreds of frontier tribesmen had gathered beneath the trees, waiting patiently for the funeral cortège to arrive. They stood huddled together, their grey woollen *pattus* wrapped tightly around their heads and shoulders for warmth. Scheherezade Faramarzi, Donatella Linari and I stood with them.

Many of the men wore the distinctive red shirts and caps of the Awami National Party, others the traditional silk turbans or flat woollen *pakhols* of the North-West Frontier of Pakistan. Like us, they had entered Afghanistan at dawn just to be present on this particular day, to pay their respects to a much-loved political leader and to offer a final farewell. As the cortège approached, escorted by a small phalanx of elite Afghan Republican guards immaculately dressed in smart khaki uniforms and peaked caps with gold braid, a murmur rippled through the crowd like wind blowing through a field of ripe corn; everyone strained forward, craning their necks for a better view. These men of the Orakzai, Mohmand, Shinwari, Afridi and Waziri tribes – whose forebears a century before had fired long-barrelled jezail muskets at the soldiers of the British Raj – began to weep openly. Tears ran down their fierce, weather-beaten faces as they watched the coffin approach, draped with the red, black and green flag of Afghanistan and decorated with garlands of bright-orange marigolds.

The Republican guards marched past, goose-stepping Russian style and swinging their white-gloved hands across their chests. As the wheels of the cortège crushed the fir cones, the sharp, clean smell of pine resin brought back memories of the great conifer forests of my childhood.

I had no right to be standing amongst the mourners, witnessing their outpouring of grief that January morning. I was no foreign correspondent, journalist or war photographer. While Iranian-born Scheherezade was an accredited journalist with Associated Press, Donatella – who worked for an Italian NGO in Peshawar – and I had come along for the adventure and the opportunity to be present at such an important historic event. Only a few days before, while wandering around the carpet shops in the bazaars of Peshawar buying Afghan rugs and textiles for my shop in London, I had heard that Abdul Ghaffar Khan had died. I knew nothing about him until I read in the local newspapers about his extraordinary life. For days, the streets of Peshawar were crowded with his weeping followers, and word of his death spread like wildfire amongst the expatriate community in Peshawar. When the Afghan government declared a four-day amnesty, halting military action against the Mujahideen, and ordered its consulate in Peshawar to issue entry visas to all government and non-government organisations that wished to attend the funeral, I had applied immediately.

Ghaffar Khan was born into a prosperous Pushtun farming family in 1890. Throughout his life he campaigned tirelessly for 'Pakhtunistan', a homeland for the Pushtuns that would incorporate the tribal territories in the North-West Frontier as well as the traditional lands of the Pushtun tribes in eastern Afghanistan, land that had been divided in two by the Durand Line in 1894. For centuries, the Khyber Pass had provided a natural gateway between India and Afghanistan. Not wishing to lose control of such a strategically important and sensitive area, and with little love lost between the British and the Pushtun tribes who had fought each other for several centuries, the British government gave its support to the Muslim League and a separate Pakistan was born. Ghaffar Khan realised there would be no homeland for the Pushtuns, and felt betrayed by both India and Pakistan. In 1941 the Afghan government made him a gift of the small walled orchard in Jalalabad close to where Scheherezade, Donatella and I were now standing. This was to be his final resting place.

The three of us walked with the tribesmen behind the funeral cortège as it moved slowly down the avenue until we reached a tiny narrow door set into a stone wall. There we turned away from the cortège and followed the mourners through into the orchard.

It was then that we heard the unmistakable *whump-whump-whump* of an approaching helicopter. It was still far away, but my heart raced uncomfortably at the sinister sound. I knew only too well the fearsome reputation of the Soviet *Hind* attack helicopters. The Soviets used them to destroy Afghan villages by pounding the mud walls to rubble in seconds, and to kill refugees fleeing through the mountain passes to Pakistan.

The orchard began to fill with mourners. Afghan soldiers, wearing strange pillbox-style hats, perched precariously in the boughs of the stunted fruit trees, keeping an eye on the crowd and muttering into two-way radios. 'KHAD,' murmured Scheherezade under her breath, referring to Khademat-e-Aetla'at-e-Dawlati, the Afghan communist regime's intelligence agency and security police, trained by the KGB.

During our journey from Pakistan that morning, we had heard that the top leadership of the Soviet-backed Afghan government would be at the funeral, so we knew that security would be tight. A giant of a man with fair hair cropped close to his skull passed by, the front of his full-length chestnut-brown leather coat flapping open to reveal the barrel of an AK-47. 'Spetsnaz, Soviet Special Forces,' Scheherezade whispered.

The helicopter was approaching fast. I nervously scanned the horizon but couldn't see anything. Then, suddenly, from beyond the low wall that surrounded the orchard, and behind the dun-coloured flat-roofed buildings of the city, a small reconnaissance helicopter rose up. To me the pilot's bulbous cockpit window resembled the eye of some malevolent giant prehistoric insect. The machine hovered momentarily before turning on its side and sweeping low over the orchard wall towards us. As it hung in the air above the bare branches of an apricot tree, the noise was quite deafening and the strong downdraught whipped up dead leaves, twigs and grit that stung our faces. I turned my head away, covering my nose and mouth with my *keffiyeh*, and in that brief moment I caught a glimpse of the pilot. He gazed down at us briefly. The helicopter circled once around the cemetery and then, to my relief, swept back over the wall and disappeared towards the town.

As the family and coffin had yet to arrive at the graveside, I took a moment to find myself a good position for photographing the event. I crouched down on the pile of recently excavated earth, as close as possible to the edge of the open grave.

We didn't have long to wait before the family arrived, together with the president of Afghanistan. Dressed in a dark Western-style suit, Dr Najibullah stood beside a small wooden lectern next to the grave, closed his eyes and led the mourners in prayer. Nicknamed 'the Bloody Ox' by the Mujahideen for the atrocities he perpetrated against his own people, he was indeed well built, his chubby face and sallow complexion dominated by a large, very black moustache. Three years later, the Taliban forcibly removed him from the United Nations compound where he had sought refuge, and dragged him through the streets of Kabul tied to the back of a car. Eventually they castrated him, placed a cigarette in his mouth and paper money between his fingers, and hanged him from traffic lights. But on that afternoon in the orchard, if I had stretched out my arm, I could have touched him.

During the prayers I moved to ease the circulation in my cramped legs, but my boot slipped, dislodging a shower of grit and pebbles down into the empty grave.

'Don't bloody move or you'll ruin it for everyone,' an English voice snarled from the far side of the grave. Startled, I looked up to see a young man glaring angrily at me, an impressive array of expensive camera equipment slung about his neck. Stung by his rebuke, I suddenly felt very conscious of my own rather simple camera and lack of journalistic credentials.

Grieving family and tribal leaders now drew near as the coffin was gently lowered on ropes into the ground. Gravediggers began to shovel earth onto the coffin, and the elite Republican Guard fired a volley above the grave.

Suddenly, from beyond the walls, there was a massive explosion. The ground shook, shock waves rippled across the orchard and chaos erupted as panic-stricken mourners ran back towards the car park. I could see clouds of smoke billowing up through the pine trees into the sapphire sky.

'Quick, we've got to get back to the car park!' I shouted, and we raced through the orchard as fast as our legs could carry us. To our relief, our driver and interpreter, who we had left there an hour earlier, had escaped injury, but it was mayhem in the car park. Ramshackle vehicles, buses, cars and vans, which only hours earlier had transported 50,000 mourners from Peshawar to Jalalabad, had been reduced to a mass of twisted metal. Shoes lay scattered everywhere and tattered strips of cloth and body parts festooned the branches of pine trees like detritus caught in brambles beside a fast-flowing stream. The explosion had claimed the lives of 16 people, two of them children.

'I need to file my copy,' announced Scheherezade. It took us an age to find a telephone – we eventually located one in the back room of a Sikh-owned pharmacy – and even longer to get a line to Pakistan. By the time Scheherezade had managed to telephone her copy through to the AP office in Islamabad, the sun was a vast orange disc about to dip below the horizon.

Leaving the city behind us, we started out on the road back to the Pakistan border, but we were stopped at a checkpoint. Soldiers surrounded our small car, pointing their Kalashnikovs through the window. One of them wrenched open the passenger door and jumped in. The barrel of his gun wavered inches from my face, and I hoped he had remembered to apply the safety catch.

'What have we done wrong?' we asked. 'Are we under arrest?'

Curfew was not far off, the soldier replied; it would be unwise for us to travel back to Peshawar across the desert plain in the dark. Besides, the Khyber Pass closed between sunset and sunrise. So for our own safety, he explained, we were being taken to the military barracks, the headquarters of KHAD, for the night. My heart began to thump uncomfortably. At the bottom of my handbag was my Filofax containing the addresses of various Mujahideen groups based in Peshawar. Should we have the misfortune to be searched or, worse still, interrogated, it was bound to be found. No one spoke in the taxi. Possibly they were harbouring similar thoughts.

It wasn't long before we stopped outside a dark, sinister building. The beams of the headlights illuminated the lettering above the front door – Spinghar Hotel. The building and name seemed familiar. Then I realised – I'd been here before! In 1977, I had stayed in this very same hotel as part of a group of tourists visiting archaeological sites in Afghanistan. At the time I was just 23, full of excitement at spending my first night in a country I had longed to visit since I was a teenager. Now, 11 years later, a quirk of fate had brought me back.

In the 1970s the hotel had been a smart watering hole for tourists visiting the Græco-Buddhist site at Hadda, ten miles south of Jalalabad. But after years of war it had been reduced to a dilapidated, run-down shell providing dormitory accommodation for Afghan soldiers. Armed men emerged and gathered around the car. The atmosphere was very tense, and I would be lying if I said I didn't feel anxious and fearful of what might be in store for us.

'They want us to get out of the car. They say we must stay here for the night,' said Mirwais, the young Pakistani student Scheherezade had brought with her from Peshawar as our interpreter.

The soldiers escorted us up a grimy staircase lit by a single bare light bulb. I couldn't speak for Donatella or Scheherezade, but my imagination was working overtime. On the first floor, a soldier unlocked a door to a small room containing three metal-framed beds. Pushing us inside, he left us, and we heard him turn the key in the lock. We sat looking at each other, too cold, hungry and tired to say much, and unsure whether we were guests or prisoners.

As I lay back on the stained pillow and lumpy mattress, my thoughts turned to my home and family in the north of England. It would be about 4pm there, and I visualised my mother and father sitting on either side of the open fire in the library, drinking Earl Grey tea and eating fruit cake. They would be less than pleased if they knew where I was at that precise moment, and I felt a pang of guilt for the worry and disappointment I had caused them over the previous few years. Wandering alone in the narrow streets of the Old City of Peshawar like Kipling's Kim, haggling over the price of carpets, drinking tea and gossiping with Afghan merchants, was not my father's idea of the life he wanted for his youngest daughter. He and my mother had done their utmost to give me a secure and happy childhood and in return I had tried hard to lead the conventional life that they and everyone else expected of me. By the time I reached my mid-20s, though, I had come to the realisation that for years I'd been living a lie, pretending to be someone I wasn't. It was then that I decided the time had come to be true to myself and to break away from it all. So I turned my back on the cocktail and dinner parties of my social life in London, and set out for Peshawar in Pakistan's North-West Frontier. Exploring the narrow dusty streets crammed with rickshaws and horse-drawn tongas, and teeming with Afghan refugees and frontier tribesmen, I experienced an extraordinary sense of freedom and belonging. It was as though, after wandering for years, I had at last arrived home.

PART I
Early Days

Chapter 1

A Cumbrian childhood

One bright and sunny day, I saddled up Ghillie, my grey Connemara cob, and rode out onto the moors. I was 16, happy and carefree. Reaching a tarn in the hills, I turned Ghillie towards a track that meandered up the side of a steep fell. I knew the track well, and cantered through the heather and around the granite outcrops until, reaching the summit, I reined in and sat back in the saddle to enjoy the spectacular panoramic view of the English Lake District. Far below me, just visible between heavily wooded shores, Windermere stretched north, its surface dotted with tiny white sailing dinghies, while far to my left lay the beautiful secluded Rusland valley, dominated by the great dark conifer forest of Grizedale. I loved this view and would ride this way in winter or summer. In winter the dramatic mountains were often covered in snow; in summer, scudding clouds sent deep purple shadows rolling across the peaks and combes. The mountains created a natural amphitheatre enclosing the lakes, tarns, moors and fells; beyond them lay the border with Scotland. This beautiful part of England is often referred to as the roots of Heaven, and I can't think of a better description or a more wonderful place in which to grow up. As I looked out across the mountains that morning, I knew that I loved this land with all my heart. It was in my blood.

My father's roots ran long and deep in this corner of England. His forebears originated from the far north-west corner of Cumberland, close by Hadrian's Wall, where in the 12th century they farmed land north of Burgh-by-Sands along the bleak windswept salt marshes of the Solway Firth, taking their surname del Sandes from a small village called Le Sandes or Sandesfield. It is difficult to understand why anyone should wish to live in such a desolate part of the British Isles, where near-constant Atlantic gales whip up sand from the estuary high into the sky, but the family managed an important ford called the Peatwath that provided a shortcut across the River Eden, used by the kings of England when they wished to cross over into Scotland. Later, the 14th century was a turbulent time on the Border and the crossing points were much used by raiders so, after repeated raids on their cattle by marauding Scots, the family were forced to leave, settling first at Rottington Hall near St Bees before moving to the southern part of the Lake District. This area, once referred to as 'High Furness' or 'Lancashire North of the Sands', is today known by its ancient name of Cumbria, meaning the land of the Celts, and incorporates the former counties of Westmorland, Cumberland and North Lancashire.

The family settled on the shores of Esthwaite Water close to the village of Hawkshead, which in earlier times had been a Viking settlement, Haukar's steading, meaning Haukar's sheiling or summer grazing ground. Here they built a small farmhouse of local Cumbrian green slate with round chimneys and leaded windows. The land was owned by the Cistercian Furness Abbey, which enclosed the land for sheep and managed the woods for making charcoal for smelting iron. Because of its close proximity to the Scottish borders, raids into the Lake District were frequent, and my father's forebears were required to provide soldiers to protect the Abbey lands. After the Dissolution of the Monasteries by Henry VIII in 1537, the family was given the opportunity to purchase the freehold to the land, but continued to provide archers and soldiers for the king's army.

Long before the Lake poets and Beatrix Potter popularised the Lake District, the area was famous for its mineral wealth. Iron ore, copper and lead had been mined in the Lake District since the Iron Age. It is possible that Romans, Anglo-Saxons and Norsemen came to the Lake District to search for the red kidney-shaped iron ore of haematite, for making spears, swords and battleaxes. The heavily wooded fells with fast-flowing becks and abundance of hazel trees provided an ideal environment for processing iron. The family built a bloomsmithy, or water-powered forge, on the edge of Windermere to process haematite, brought across the fells by packhorse from the mine at Roanhead Farm, near Askham-in-Furness, and then taken by boat up Windermere. Charcoal, produced by itinerant charcoal burners who coppiced the hazels and lived all year round in the woods, heated the haematite to a great temperature. This 'smelting' or liquefying of the ore removed impurities and made the iron strong. 'Pig iron' from smelted haematite was much in demand during the Industrial Revolution and was sent south to the factories of Lancashire to be made into ship's boilers and wrought-iron fencing.

Throughout the centuries my father's family managed the land and fells, grazing sheep, smelting iron ore and producing lye from burning bracken and bark peelings to make soap. The sheep's fleeces were washed and taken to Kendal to be dyed and woven into Kendal Green, the cloth used to make the surcoats that England's archers wore over their armour at the Battle of Agincourt.

The Lake District was remote during the 13th and 14th centuries, with access and travel difficult. To the south lay the treacherous quicksands of Morecambe Bay, where the incoming tide flowed faster than a horse could gallop, while to the north lay mountains. Beyond Hadrian's Wall the country was wild and lawless. For generations, therefore, my father's family married locally, the eldest son inheriting Esthwaite while younger sons set up farms of their own on suitable tracts of land nearby. Eventually a second home, Graythwaite, situated in a wooded valley a mile from the shores of Windermere, was occupied by the family. Built originally as a peel tower in the 12th century by the monks of Furness Abbey, its fortified six-foot walls provided protection against the Scots. The name is derived from the Norse *garth*, meaning a stone-walled enclosure for the protection of sheep, and *thwaite*, Old Norse for a clearing in the forest.

I was born on 1 July 1954 in a nursing home on Welbeck Street in London, and spent the first four years of my life with my elder sister and brother being looked after by Nanny Sumner in the nursery wing on the top floor of number 26 Chelsea Park Gardens. Late in the summer of 1958, my parents, who had endured the deprivations, hardships and uncertainty of the Second World War, decided it was time to give their children a country upbringing. Graythwaite had been neglected during the war and my father felt it was time to leave London, where he had been working as a stockbroker, and take on its management. At Euston Station we boarded a steam train and set out on the journey north to the Lake District through England's industrial heartland. It was a long and tedious journey for a small, restless child. With my nose pressed to the grimy window, I gazed out at mile upon mile of back-to-back terraced houses, cobbled streets, railway sidings, allotments and blackened brick factory chimneys.

Our first home was a haunted Elizabethan farmhouse called Low Graythwaite Hall, with whitewashed rendered walls covered in Virginia creeper that turned deep red in the autumn. The interior of the house was all dark wood-panelled walls and low ceilings. Groundsel grew between the kitchen flagstones. The garden was paradise after the pavements of London. Rhododendrons and azaleas grew in profusion around a large, deep pond; they thrived in the peat soil, achieving such massive proportions that during springtime the garden resembled the foothills of the Himalayas. The pond was fed by a beck that had its origins up in the fells. At night I would lie in bed and listen to the thunderous roar as the water passed through a culvert under the road and plummeted over rocks in a spectacular waterfall on its way to the lake.

Once we had settled in, Nanny Sumner, who came from Croydon, felt the north of England was not for her and left us to return south. She found employment at Kensington Palace, looking after Princess Margaret and Lord Snowdon's two children, and was thereafter always referred to as 'the Royal Nanny'. In her wake arrived Marie Holt from Blackpool. One of three unmarried sisters, Marie had worked in a Nabisco biscuit factory and had no previous experience of looking after children. She took on the role of caring for me, took me for long afternoon walks, read me bedtime stories and listened to my prayers. She told me stories of her own childhood growing up in industrial Lancashire between the wars, a world away from my own upbringing.

'Children wore clogs in those days, and would come to school exhausted after a night working in the cotton factories and fall asleep at their desks. The nurse came each week to check our hair for lice,' she told me.

'What did you eat when you were a child, Marie?'

'Pods and bread spread with dripping.'

'What are pods?'

'I'll make them for your tea,' she replied.

Not long after this conversation, I came home from school one day to find a plate of 'pods' waiting for me. Lumps of white bread were bobbing in hot milk, a kind of poor man's bread and butter pudding. I never asked for them again!

When my parents went on holiday to America for six weeks, Marie took me to stay with her sisters to see the Blackpool Illuminations and the Tower Circus. We spent the days walking along the seafront, playing the coin machines in the amusement arcades and enjoying the fairground attractions. And, of course no, visit to Blackpool would be complete without a ride on the donkeys. Marie indulged me by buying candyfloss, toffee apples and sticks of Blackpool rock, treats that were quite forbidden at home, and introduced me to the delights of eating fish and chips, sprinkled with vinegar and accompanied by mushy peas, out of newspaper. Marie remained as part of our family for 20 years, and when she finally retired and moved back to Blackpool to live with her sisters, I felt an immeasurable sense of loss.

The first frosts of autumn brought the red deer down from the moor to the woods around the house. I remember the first time I heard the strange, coughing roars of the stags, an eerie spine-chilling sound to a London child. On one particularly frosty night we stood in the moonlight and watched them fight for possession of a small group of hinds. As the two beasts crashed against each other, the sound of their locking antlers carried to us across the frozen field like the crack of Morris dancers' wooden sticks.

Graythwaite Hall, a mile up the road, was still owned by my grandparents, who lived for 11 months of the year in London. Granny Sandys hated the north, preferring the salons of London or travelling through Europe by chauffeur-driven Rolls-Royce. With its 17 bedrooms, seven bathrooms, a dining room with a wood floor sprung on massive chains for dancing, a wine cellar that ran the length of the house like a catacomb, and an entire wing devoted to laundry, Graythwaite was used as their country cottage. Between the wars, my grandparents employed 17 live-in staff, and 22 gardeners managed the extensive gardens, landscaped by Thomas Mawson. There were endless house parties, balls and outings on the lake in a converted Thames launch called the *Lady Hamilton*.

During my childhood, they would arrive every August by train from London for their annual month's holiday; the chauffeur arrived a few days earlier with my grandmother's lady's maid and the butler in the Rolls. For the rest of the year the house remained shut up, the furniture shrouded under dust sheets. Granny's mother had lost countless babies to stillbirth and miscarriage because, out of vanity, she persisted in wearing stiff whalebone corsets throughout her pregnancy. Finally, she must have taken the advice of doctors to dispense with the corsets if she wanted to have a healthy baby and Granny came into the world, a much-loved, indulged and spoilt only child. Tall, with an hourglass figure, deep chestnut hair, tiny feet and elegant hands, she was considered one of the great beauties of her day, but her nature was arrogant.

I was eight during the bitter winter of 1962 to '63 – the 'Big Freeze' – one of the coldest on record in the United Kingdom. Heavy snow and blizzards swept in from the Arctic, bringing down power lines and creating snowdrifts to a depth of 20 feet. Roads became blocked and villages were cut off. As temperatures fell to minus 19°C, the tarns and Windermere froze solid, and we tobogganed and ice-skated for weeks. The central heating oil turned to jelly in the pipes and refused to flow, so we had no heating. The shippens were full of wintering cattle, so water had to be carried to them from our house, and my parents delivered water in milk churns to cottages with no running water. It was fortunate that our ponies were all hardy native breeds, otherwise I doubt they would have survived. They weren't stabled at night or rugged, as horses are nowadays, and the only fodder available to them was hay thrown out of helicopters. I watched as the bales tumbled out of the sky and landed in our snow-covered fields, after which the helicopters flew on to drop more hay to stock stranded out on the fells.

My siblings and I were so different in character that I once heard my father remark to my mother, 'Really, Anne, one wouldn't think those children all come from the same stable'. Mary, six years older than me, was blessed with all the brains, whereas I was the tomboy, climbing trees, building endless dens in the wood and dams in the beck. In between us came Myles, our parents' much-valued only son and heir. He was fair-haired, handsome, wild and fearless. Danger was not a word he understood. I idolised him and worshipped the ground he stood on, but sadly he saw me only as a deeply irritating younger sister. I looked forward with mounting excitement to the school holidays, when he would return from prep school armed with an inexhaustible supply of rude jokes and naughty limericks, and a backside that was black and blue from repeated canings.

'Mummy, Daddy, Myles has taught me a new rhyme.'

'Well, darling, we'd love to hear it,' said our parents as they arranged themselves on the sofa in the drawing room in anticipation.

There once was a man from Madras
Whose balls were both made of brass.
In stormy weather
They clanged together
And sparks flew out of his arse!'

Myles and I collapsed in giggles. Our parents glared at us in stony silence.

My mother was Scottish on her paternal side. Her grandfather, William Ramsay, came from a farming family in Clackmannanshire. Aged 19, he had set out for Canada, a country that offered great opportunities for a young man at that time. Since Culloden and the Highland Clearances, Scots had been encouraged to settle in America, Canada and Australia, and by the time William arrived in 1854 there would have already been a sizeable Scottish community. The west of Canada was opening up and settlers were moving further in to the hinterlands. He opened a grocery business in Toronto, becoming a provision merchant importing dried foods, wine and spirits from Britain and supplying frontier trading posts in what is now the province of Ontario. His business, particularly the 'liquor' business, thrived, and over the years he amassed a small fortune. From humble beginnings he rose to become one of the founder members of the Imperial Bank of Canada and was actively involved in supporting financially the construction of the Canadian Pacific railway. Married and with eight children, seven of them born in Toronto, he finally returned to Scotland at the age of 47, an exceedingly rich man.

A disciplinarian, he ruled his five boys and three girls with a rod of iron. All his children lived adventurous lives. Four of the boys volunteered to fight in the Boer War and were mentioned in despatches for their bravery. The eldest, William, joined the Pretoria Contingent and in 1894 took part in the suppression of the Malaboch Rising where he was, according to an unidentified newspaper clipping of the time, 'acknowledged to be the pluckiest man at the Front by Boers, British, and Blacks'.

My great-uncle Fred died in police detention after being hit on the head during a drunken brawl in Buffalo, New York. Great-uncle Douglas married Laura Aitken, sister of Lord Beaverbrook, and great-aunt Daisy married Douglas Derry, a Professor of Anatomy at Cairo University who assisted Howard Carter in removing the layers of material wrapped around the mummy of Tutankhamun. Their son, John Derry, was the first Briton to break the sound barrier and was killed in a crash at the Farnborough Airshow in 1952. The youngest, Gordon, was my grandfather, a Cameron Highlander, wounded at Hill 60 at Ypres and invested with the DSO by HRH the Duke of York in 1920. He bought Farleyer, a beautiful house overlooking the River Tay close to Aberfeldy in Perthshire, and this was my mother's home.

My mother brought us up on stories of her maternal forebears in India. Her great-great-great grandfather, Lieutenant-General Joseph Nash, born in Lancashire in 1795, served in India with the 43rd Regiment of Native Infantry during the years of the Great Game. As a young man, on furlough in Cape Town in 1820 he met and married 16-year-old Dina Margaretha Leibrandt, the eldest of ten children of German immigrants. Her brother presented her with an African slave from Simonstown as a wedding present, to accompany her when she sailed to join her husband in India and to help her in her new life. What must her parents have felt as they said goodbye to a daughter who they might never see again, and what courage on the part of Dina Margaretha, leaving her family at such a young age to set out on a perilous voyage to Calcutta. I have a photograph of her and Joseph and one of their sons sitting on the veranda of their home, The Oaks, in the hill station of Mussoorie, their Indian staff lined up behind them. All their children survived the diseases of India and grew to adulthood, a miracle in itself as child mortality at that time was high – the cemeteries of India are filled with the little graves of children who did not live to see their fifth birthday. Throughout their married life in India, Dina Margaretha endured the anxiety of constant separation from her husband, who was engaged in fighting in endless battles. During the Battle of Sobraon in 1846, his horse was shot dead under him.

One day my mother showed us a large uncut ruby, with a hole drilled slightly off-centre, that had been passed down to her through her mother's family. I held it up to the light to admire its size and colour. According to my mother, the ruby had been given to Joseph Nash by Shah Shuja al-Mulk, the ruler of Afghanistan. In 1809 Shah Shuja was defeated at the Battle of Nimla by his enemies the Barakzais and his half-brother, Shah Mahmoud. Leaving Kabul, he took his harem and most of the Afghan royal jewellery (including the Koh-i-Noor diamond, which he wore on his arm) and accepted an offer of asylum by the British East India Company in Ludhiana, a dusty British-controlled garrison in north-west India. The American adventurer, writer, doctor and spy Josiah Hanlon, a Quaker from Pennsylvania who joined the court of the exiled king and later became commander-in-chief of the Afghan army, described Shah Shuja as having 'an unfortunate penchant for removing the ears, tongues, noses and even testicles of those of his courtiers who had offended him'.[1]

When the Tsar of Russia sent Captain Yan Vitkevitch as Russian envoy to the court of Dost Mohammed, the ruler of Kabul, the British, fearful of a Russian incursion into India, moved to reinstate Shah Shuja on the throne of Afghanistan. In 1839 Captain Joseph Nash was appointed Baggage Master for the Bengal Division of the Army of the Indus. Fifteen thousand British and Indian troops, including infantry, cavalry and artillery, a pack of foxhounds, caparisoned elephants, 30,000 camp followers and about the same number of camels to carry officers' baggage, ammunition and suppies, crossed the River Indus at Sukkur and entered Afghanistan via the 80-mile-long Bolan Pass. The officers of one regiment 'commandeered two camels just to carry their cigars. Finally there were several herds of cattle which were to serve as a mobile larder for the task force.'[2] By all accounts the journey in to Afghanistan was a dreadful ordeal.

> We entered the Bolan Pass, a rough and pebbly road between sand hills, studded with flint and limestones, small and large, the space in breadth between the hills varying from 300 to 400 yards to about 30. As the rear guard was coming along, in charge of baggage etc, a number of Belooches fired on them from the hills, about a mile from the ground, and then rolled down stones, but without effect.[3]

So wrote James Atkinson, Superintending Surgeon accompanying the Army of the Indus. The Baluchis daily harassed the army as it made its slow progress through the narrow defile, attacking camp followers and stragglers and carrying off bullocks, horses and camels. At times water and forage were scarce, and the men suffered from the heat in their serge uniforms.

> The road is hemmed in by wild and rugged mountains which afford numerous inaccessible positions for the predatory and murderous Belooches. Their Jezails, the native rifle, with a fixed rest, are formidable weapons, and are said to carry eight hundred yards. A dead camel and camp follower, with his throat cut, and otherwise cruelly mutilated to death, were lying close together on the middle of the road.[4]

After a pause for several weeks at Kandahar to recover from the march through the Bolan Pass, the army moved north and Captain Nash, under the command of Sir John Keane, was present at the storming and capture of the impregnable Afghan fortress of Ghazni, the last bastion to stand in the way of the British army before Kabul. Entering Kabul in 1839, General Nash (as he became) commanded the guards of Shah Shuja and was put in charge of the state prisoners. My mother told us that General Nash was presented with the ruby just before the execution of prisoners, who were to be fired from the end of a cannon. Breaking a cord around his neck on which were strung several large rubies, Shah Shuja handed one to each of the three officers presiding at the execution. Being blown from a gun was a particularly gruesome form of execution, introduced by the Mughals in the 16th century and later adopted by the British as a punishment for native soldiers, particularly during the Indian Mutiny. James Atkinson gives this description of the execution of Afghans of the Ghilzai tribe on 7 July 1839 at Ser-i-asp, a village on the road between Kandahar and Kabul. The men had been found guilty of carrying off camels and wounding and killing *sarwans* (camel-handlers) from Shah Shuja's camp.

> The three men were then tied with ropes to the guns, their backs against the muzzle. The rope, fastened to one of the spokes of the wheel, passed with a knot round the arms, over the muzzle of the gun, round the other arm, and then to the spoke of the opposite wheel, which kept the body fixed. The prisoners, with their wrists tied together, kept crying incessantly, 'There is no God but God, and Mahomet is the Prophet of God!' Just as everything was ready, the prisoner in the middle was let loose, having been pardoned by the Shah, and the noise made the other two turn their heads. At that instant, the priming was fired, and the explosion took place. I could only see the body nearest me, for the thick clouds of smoke. One arm and shoulder blade was driven perpendicularly upwards, at least a hundred feet; the other arm and part of the body were found right forward, thirty yards off, with the hand torn away. The explosion produced a shower of blood and small particles of flesh. On going to the gun, I found the head separate, as if it had been purposely severed from the body, and lying between the wheels: close to it were the lower limbs, trunkless, upturned on the ground, with part of the intestines twisted round one leg.[5]

As I listened to these stories, little did I imagine that, one day far in the future, Afghanistan would become an important part of my life. At times I would walk in the footsteps of Joseph Nash.

Our upbringing was based on my mother's own strict Scottish Presbyterian childhood. She encouraged us to play outdoors in wind, rain, sun and snow, in the belief that sunshine, fresh air and plenty of exercise were important for growing children. 'So your bones grow strong and you don't get rickets,' she explained. To protect us against the Lake District weather, she bought us oilskins and sou'westers, as used by fishermen in the North Atlantic. She taught us how to dance Scottish reels and dressed us in Ramsay tartan kilts; but, most importantly, she taught me to ride. I shall be eternally grateful to her, as riding gave me freedom to roam across the fells without parental supervision. Even the murders of several children on the Yorkshire moors by Myra Hindley and Ian Brady did not deter my parents from allowing us enormous freedom to wander where we wished. It is the aspect of my childhood that I cherish above all others. Riding encouraged me to explore, to take risks and to develop a good sense of direction – in short, to be adventurous and independent. Above all, it was the start of a love affair with horses that has stayed with me throughout my life.

Aged four, seated on an ancient Shetland pony and on the same thick olive-green felt numnah saddle that my mother had used at the same age, I would set off with her across the moors. When I outgrew the Shetland, I graduated to a chestnut Welsh pony and finally to the Connemara.

School holidays were filled with agricultural shows and picnics. Up on the fells above the house was a tarn with a boathouse and two rowing boats for fishing. Dogs and children would pile into the back of the Land Rover along with fishing rods, swimming gear and picnic baskets. Then, with my father at the wheel, we would cling to the overhead roll bar as the vehicle bounced vigorously up a rough stone track. Tartan travelling rugs would be spread out on the heather in preparation for the picnic and we would spend the afternoon swimming in cold, peaty water or fishing for brown trout. Giant dragonflies and bright turquoise damselflies hovered above the water, and swallows skimmed the surface of the tarn in search of midges, swooping in and out of the boathouse where they had their nests. Sometimes, if we were lucky, I might see the barn owl that lived in the loft above the boats. But most of all, I remember lying back in the heather, watching the clouds scudding across the sky and listening to the whirr of the grasshoppers, the twitter of skylarks and the mournful cries of curlews and lapwings.

Without a doubt my childhood was carefree, privileged and secure. I was 11 when we finally moved from Low Graythwaite to Graythwaite. At first, I missed the cosiness of our first home, but my parents had worked miracles on Graythwaite, knocking down a wing, turning other parts of the house into self-contained dwellings and making it a more manageable yet beautiful family home. A 20-foot-high stone wall surrounded our garden and home, and cocooned us from the outside world.

Despite our privileged upbringing, we were definitely not spoilt. My father was a gentle man with a sensitive disposition, but the war years had taken their toll on him. He had an aversion to any sort of upset or confrontation, so the task of disciplining the three of us was largely left to our mother. Her no-nonsense approach to our upbringing was based on Victorian and Edwardian values. Great emphasis was placed upon the values of morality, integrity, punctuality and respect for one's elders and betters. Mary and I were expected to stand up when grown-ups entered the room, and to shake hands and curtsey when introduced. We were not to speak unless we were spoken to first, and we certainly never addressed adults by their Christian names.

In life, my mother weathered all difficulties with extraordinary stoicism and courage and without complaint, prompting her father-in-law to remark, 'Anne, dear, your back is broadened to the burden'. Our parents both believed that expressing emotion in the face of adversity was a weakness, and complaining and whingeing were discouraged. By teaching us self-control, our parents were preparing us for the harsh and real world that lay beyond the walls of Graythwaite but, no matter how hard I tried, I failed spectacularly at keeping a stiff upper lip. I was just too sensitive, and my feelings were always too close to the surface. 'Harriet, you have no backbone. No spine!' my parents would remark with exasperation as I struggled to stop crying after the death of a much-loved pet, a sibling spat or a parental reprimand. It was in such moments that I sought solace in the company of animals, particularly horses. Anyone who has spent time with horses, and come to know, love and understand them, will have experienced their extraordinary ability to bring a sense of healing to a troubled human soul. As Winston Churchill said, 'There's nothing so good for the inside of a man as the outside of a horse'.

Shortly after my fifth birthday, my parents sent me to a school on the outskirts of Bowness-on-Windermere, which involved a twice-daily journey across the lake by steam ferry. Blackwell, a large country house standing high above the lake with spectacular views of the mountains, is one of Britain's finest examples of arts-and-crafts design, with carved panelling, delicate plasterwork, William Morris wallpaper and stained-glass windows. It was here that an event occurred that shaped my destiny.

Miss Mary Burkett was my art teacher at Blackwell but, long before she came to teach nine-year-olds how to print patterns using potato cuts or to apply colourwash as background to a watercolour, she had followed in the steps of Freya Stark and travelled widely in Turkey and Persia. At our weekly art class in a small garret room on the top floor, she would regale us with hilarious stories of adventurous journeys in uncharted territory, visiting Assassins' castles and helping out at an archaeological dig at Qunbad-i-Qabus on the Turkmen steppe. She would bring to our class pottery shards from her digs, Roman glass, fossils and semi-precious stones, and spread them out on the table for us to pick up and examine. Her great sense of humour and her warmth, eccentricity and enthusiasm kept us constantly entertained and enthralled.

One afternoon, she invited me to join her at an archaeological excavation on the site of Galava, a Roman fort at the northern end of Windermere close to the town of Ambleside. It had once been a barracks for 500 soldiers sent to guard the Roman Empire's northernmost outposts. For years I wondered why Mary chose me over all the other little girls in my class. I was about nine years old, very reserved, painfully shy and virtually monosyllabic in the presence of adults. I could hardly have been scintillating company.

I remember, as though it was yesterday, standing on a grassy tussock gazing down into a neatly marked-out square of recently excavated earth.

'Jump down,' instructed Mary.

With a triangular metal trowel, she demonstrated how to use the point carefully to scrape away the layers of mud. We spent a gloriously happy afternoon together unearthing Roman nails encrusted with rust that had lain in the soil since the first century AD. I found something unusual and handed it to her. She rubbed away the mud and held it up to the light for a better look. Then, turning it over and over in her hands, she announced, 'Now, this could be leather. Perhaps part of a centurion's sandal.'

Thinking back all those years, I can see clearly that the visit to Galava was the beginning of a journey that would take me far away from the kind of life I was expected to lead. Perhaps it was *kismet*, the belief amongst Eastern cultures that our fate and path through life are decided before we are born. I could not have known then that, 14 years later, Mary Burkett and I would travel together on a tour of archaeological sites in Afghanistan, a journey that would have far-reaching consequences.

At the age of 12, I followed in my sister's footsteps and went off to Lawnside, a boarding school in the spa town of Malvern in Worcestershire. It was during my time there that I began to harbour romantic ideas of travelling to the East. It all started with a poem we were given to learn by our English mistress, Mrs Scott-Moncrieff, a large lady who dressed from head to foot in Black Watch tartan. She expected us to learn the poem by heart and recite it word-perfect in her next lesson. On a wet November afternoon, as rain hammered against the sheet-glass windows of Lawnside's prefabricated classroom, I opened my *Oxford Book of English Verse*, bent my head over the pages and began to concentrate on the task of committing the poem to memory.

> *Sweet to ride forth at evening from the wells,*
> *When shadows pass gigantic on the sand,*
> *And softly through the silence beat the bells*
> *Along the Golden Road to Samarkand.*
> *We travel not for trafficking alone;*
> *By hotter winds our fiery hearts are fanned:*
> *For lust of knowing what should not be known*
> *We take the Golden Road to Samarkand.*

I gazed out at the thick mist shrouding the Malvern Hills and watched the rain continuing to run in rivulets down the glass. For a moment, I was transported from the drab classroom to another world. In my imagination, I was walking through the desert with camel caravans and nomads. I could almost feel the heat of the sand, smell the sweat of the camels, hear the camel bells, and see the mud-walled caravanserais and the 'palm girt wells' of Flecker's *Hassan*.

My teenage years coincided with the swinging 60s and the hippy era. Young people from all walks of life went travelling overland in buses, Land Rovers and VW camper vans to search for spiritual enlightenment and adventure in India and Nepal. More than anything else, I yearned to set off overland for India. The very thought of driving through Turkey, Iran and Afghanistan seemed so romantic, so exciting – such an *adventure*! At weekends, when we were permitted to change out of school uniform into our own clothes, we would congregate in the common room to listen to records. Sprawled on an ancient sofa covered in faded chintz, wearing flower-patterned bell-bottomed trousers, floppy hats and white lipstick, we would chirp and warble in unison to the songs of The Beatles, Bob Dylan, Leonard Cohen and Cat Stevens. I particularly loved the music of Cat Stevens and would belt out the lyrics of his album 'Lady D'Arbanville' at the top of my voice: 'Kathmandu, I'll soon be seeing you'.

Yes, I thought, more than ready to escape into the real world after five years of pounding the streets of Malvern in a crocodile, *I will soon be seeing you*.

After those years at boarding school I was restless. I couldn't wait to leave and had no desire to stay on a moment longer than I had to. Luckily, Miss Millichamp, the headmistress of Lawnside, agreed. She wrote,

> I do not think that there is a great deal of point in keeping Harriet longer to attempt the two-year Advanced Level course as I think it would be very difficult and rather wearisome for her and not really the best preparation for whatever she does after school days are over.

So I left Lawnside a few days after my 16th birthday. I would not miss the hours of shivering on the hockey pitch in freezing weather, with the wind whipping down from the Malvern Hills, my hands and knees blue with cold, or the early-morning swimming lessons in the public baths in Malvern's Winter Gardens, where the surface of the water was covered in dead flies and cigarette butts. As no woman in my family had ever been to university or followed a profession, I had no expectation of pursuing a career. While this might seem unusual nowadays, I can count on the fingers of one hand the girls from my class at Lawnside who opted to stay on to take A Levels with a view to going to university. The rest of us would go to finishing schools in Switzerland, or 'do the season' in London, combined with a secretarial or Cordon Bleu cookery course. My parents hoped that my sister Mary and I would find happiness and fulfilment in marriage. 'Then,' said my father, 'your husband will look after you.' His advice was to 'find a nice, kind man,' preferably with a large estate and lots of money. In my family, a woman's traditional role was to support her husband, bear children and, in short, be a good wife. Marriage was to be our goal. 'After all,' said our mother, 'you wouldn't want to be left on the shelf to become an Old Maid.'

This attitude was not at all unusual for girls from my background; in fact, it was fairly normal. None of us had any expectations other than doing a 'little job' to earn 'a bit of money' until such time as we met the man we were going to marry. Mary, who had inherited our father's academic brain and was by far the cleverest of the three of us, would have benefited from going to university. Miss Millichamp implored our father to send her, but he was worried she might turn into a bluestocking, 'get odd ideas' and adopt political views different from his own, and thus scupper her chances of finding a husband, so she was sent off to Madame Verlet's establishment in Paris, Les Ambassadrices, to learn French and to be 'finished'.

As an alternative to taking A Levels I was sent to Idbury Manor in the Cotswolds. What an inspired decision by my parents! The year-long course, called 'Look and Learn' and run by two remarkable spinster ladies, Miss Godley and Miss Wood (the latter a large, shy Scotswoman, a brilliant cook and former personal assistant to Sir Winston Churchill during the war), recognised that, at this important stage in their lives, girls were eager to get away from uniforms, class-work and the atmosphere of school discipline and to take part in grown-up activities. They understood that knowledge that has been 'seen' as well as 'learnt' remains a three-dimensional memory, so there were numerous visits to places of interest – Parliament, the Courts of Justice, hospitals and art galleries. This form of learning suited me perfectly. At Lawnside I had struggled to memorise facts for exams but at Idbury I flourished. For the first time I *wanted* to learn. We learnt about the world religions – Hinduism, Buddhism, Confucianism, Islam and Judaism. Margaret Godley, who had spent two years in India – in 1945 she was invited by Lady Mountbatten to make a report on Indian social services – talked to us at length about her frequent meetings with Mahatma Gandhi. Edith Wood, who attended the 1945 Yalta Conference in the Crimea with Churchill, described her meetings with Roosevelt and Stalin.

The shelves in the library on the top floor of the 16th-century manor were packed with interesting books. One wet Sunday afternoon, a bright yellow dust jacket on a shelf caught my eye. I pulled out *Seven Years in Tibet* by Heinrich Harrer. Alongside it was Peter Aufschnaiter's *Eight Years in Tibet*. Both men were mountaineers and joined the German Himalaya expedition to scale the 25,000-foot Nanga Parbat in the summer of 1939. Arrested on the outbreak of war, they were interned in a British POW camp in Dehra Dun as 'enemy aliens'; they eventually escaped, travelling together across the frozen Himalayas to Lhasa in Tibet. When I finished reading both books, I was hooked on the idea of travelling to the Himalayas, and from that moment onwards I read every book about the Dalai Lama, Tibet, India and Afghanistan that I could lay my hands on.

'Life's just a bowl of cherries for you, isn't it?' said my father.

We were driving back together from the village of Hawkshead, where

My paternal grandmother, Mrs George Owen Sandys by de Laszlo in 1915.
(Copyright de Laszlo Foundation.)

My parents before the Coronation of Queen Elizabeth II.

My brother Myles, my sister Mary and me in 1955.

Graythwaite Hall, my family home in Cumbria.

The gardens at Graythwaite Hall.

My mother, aged 19, in her WRNS uniform in 1944.

The market at Tashkurgan (Kholm) in northern Afghanistan.

Children selling fossils and clay whistles at the sacred blue lakes of Band-i-Amir, Bamiyan, in 1977.

Bamiyan Hotel (yurt village) in central Afghanistan in 1977.

Giant Buddha, Bamiyam Valley. The cliffs are pockmarked with hundreds of caves, where more than 5,000 yellow-robed monks once lived.
Right: The colossal yellow-limestone statue of Buddha carved in the 4th century AD in Bamiyam Valley. It was destroyed using explosives by the Taliban in 2001.

At the Afghan orphanage run by Jamiat-i-Islami in Peshwar in 1982.

we had gone to collect the newspapers. I detected the slight criticism in his comment and fell silent, not knowing what exactly he meant. At 18, I was full of the joys of life. My mother, who had been evacuated from her school in Dorset back to Farleyer in Perthshire at the time of Dunkirk, had been home-educated by a French governess and this had left her with the habit of peppering her speech with little French phrases. 'You see your future as *couleur de rose*', she would say, and she was right – I did. I imagined everything in the future would be wonderful and that I would live happily ever after. That morning, I had been recounting some fun event that I had been involved in with friends, and my naive view of life had irked my father. I knew nothing of, let alone understood, the horrors of war that he had experienced. As a young man he attended Eton and Oxford, before joining the 2nd Battalion, Grenadier Guards as an officer at the outbreak of war in 1939. At mealtimes he would sometimes talk about his wartime experiences, but I was too young to really understand much. It was only later that my mother told me how much he had suffered. After being evacuated with his regiment from the beach at Dunkirk, he joined the 3rd Battalion and went on to fight with Montgomery in the Guards Armoured Division against Rommel in North Africa. From Tunisia the battalion was sent to Sicily and Italy. In the battle for Monte Cassino my father spent days holed up in the crypt of a nunnery surrounded by decomposing bodies. He once told me that, while walking up a mountainside in the dark behind a mule train, his foot went through the ribcage of a corpse. The horror of the Italian campaign gave him nightmares for the rest of his life.

One morning, about a year later, my mother asked me what I had decided to do with my life. A sudden squall coming in off the Atlantic had forced me to stay indoors and, with nothing better to do, I had wandered upstairs to look at exhibits displayed in glass showcases brought back by ancestors from various colonial battles. I was busy reading the descriptions carefully written in sepia ink on buff-coloured luggage labels tied to each item by a faded pink ribbon, such as 'Ring taken from a Zulu chief at the Battle of Ulundi 1879' or 'A Russian musket cartridge taken from the pouch of a dead Russian at the battle of Alma. Bloodstains still visible.' If there was one thing guaranteed to irritate my mother, it was finding her children dawdling about the house without purpose. Her question, coming as it did out of the blue, took me completely by surprise. Receiving no reply, she continued briskly, 'Well, you can't stay here forever, you know. It's high time you gave some serious thought to your future.'

Ever since leaving Lawnside, I had been putting off for as long as I could the moment of leaving home and all that I loved. Nothing lasts forever in life and change is inevitable but, while it can open up new opportunities, to me it just meant loss and pain. I wanted everything to remain just as it always had been. But at 19 I was no longer a child, and it was time to move on. However, I had absolutely no idea of what I was actually going to *do.* What *did* a girl from my background do with her life? More importantly, what *could* I do? I was completely unqualified to do anything. Half the time I lived in a fantasy world, my head full of romantic dreams fostered by reading far too many Georgette Heyer novels.

Because I always felt happier in the company of animals than humans, I thought I might become a vet, until my father pointed out the exams that I would be required to pass and the long years of study at university. As I was hopeless at arithmetic and mathematics, I realised that my aspirations were but a pipe dream. The previous year I had done the Season in London, attending Queen Charlotte's Ball, dances and cocktail parties, but being a debutante wasn't my scene. I lacked self-confidence, so making small talk at parties was torture. My sheltered country childhood and conventional upbringing in the north of England had not exactly prepared me for the social life of London. Until that moment it had never occurred to me to wonder whether I was English or Scottish. I just thought of myself as British, but amongst girls brought up in the Home Counties, who seemed so much more mature and sophisticated, I began to feel a cultural and ethnic divide. I was definitely a northerner, and I felt the difference between us. At the numerous coming-out balls, I hated being groped in the discotheques and would find refuge in the ladies' loos until such time as I could decently make my departure.

In the same year, at Winkfield College near Windsor, I learnt how to pluck game, gut fish and sew my own clothes – all skills that my parents felt would stand me in good stead.

'Knowing how to cook will come in handy, darling, when you come to run your own home,' said my father. 'It's very useful to know how to pluck the birds that your husband shoots, or when you go and cook in Scottish lodges.'

Some of my friends were planning to become chalet girls in ski resorts during the winter months. Perhaps I should do the same. For a moment I imagined myself walking through picturesque alpine villages, skiing down pistes in brilliant sunshine, partying in nightclubs and meeting lots of gorgeously tanned young men.

I envied my maternal grandmother, May Ramsay – or Granny Ramsay as we all called her – and my mother. The two world wars occurred in their lives when they were more or less the same age that I was that particular morning. While the Second World War had stolen my mother's teenage years and wrought havoc with her education, war had given opportunities to both women to lead lives far removed from the background they were brought up in. During the First World War, aged just 19, Granny Ramsay became an ambulance driver in London, meeting hospital trains and driving the wounded to hospital. At one hospital they were so short-staffed that she was asked to dress and bandage an amputated stump. At the end of each day she was responsible for scrubbing the blood out of her ambulance. At 18, my mother joined the WRNS (Women's Royal Naval Service) and worked in the signal distribution office, speaking to France on a radio telephone from an office deep inside the white cliffs of Dover. After two years living underground in claustrophobic conditions, she longed for fresh air and sunlight and arranged to be transferred to Immingham Docks. She was demobilised in 1946 at the age of 21. Married at 22, she produced Mary at 23. 'I'd had all three of you by the time I was twenty-nine,' she was fond of telling us. It was certainly an achievement that both Mary and I secretly envied and aspired to.

Since we were children, Mary and I had been brought up to accept that our home was only our home until such time as Myles inherited and married. Primogeniture – the tradition of passing land, money, house and possessions from father to eldest son – had been practised by our family for centuries. Nothing was more important to my father than that the estate and his family name should pass on to the next generation.

'It's how our family has survived,' he would explain, seated at the head of the dining room table surrounded by portraits of his ancestors hanging on panelled walls decorated with Civil War pikes and halberds. 'Not like on the Continent, where everything is divided between all the children. Those families never last longer than a few generations.'

Anyone not brought up in this tradition might think it unfair that the eldest son should inherit everything while younger brothers and sisters get little or nothing, but Mary and I accepted it as just the way things had always been.

My mother's question regarding my future was an uncomfortable reminder that the halcyon days of my childhood were over. There seemed no alternative but to go to London and stay with Mary in our parents' flat on the Brompton Road, which she shared with friends. With a heavy heart I packed a suitcase, cleaned my tack for the last time and said a fond farewell to Ghillie, my Connemara cob. I put my arms around his neck and buried my head in his mane, breathing in his warm, horsey smell. Over the years we had shared some wonderful times together. He had been a loyal and good friend and I would miss him with all my heart.

Later that day, my father drove me to the little Victorian station at Grange-over-Sands to catch the London train. As we rounded the corner on the Newby Bridge road, he decided that the moment had come to impart some fatherly advice to his woefully naive daughter. Now he felt anxious seeing me depart for the Big City, all too aware of my innocence. Anything of a remotely emotional nature, particularly sex, was never discussed openly in our family. We were just expected to pick up the facts of life from observing the farm animals. A shy, reserved man, he found it difficult to talk to his children about anything that really mattered.

'Er, um,' he started hesitantly.

I waited. 'Yes, Daddy?'

'Um, if a young man invites you out to dinner – er – he may ask to be invited in for coffee when he brings you back to the flat. My advice is that you just say goodbye on the doorstep.'

The rest of the journey passed in companionable silence as I ruminated on the meaning of this conversation.

Aboard the train I stood by the open window. Both of us felt constrained searching for things to say to each other as we waited for the train to depart. At last the stationmaster blew his whistle, waved his green flag and the train lurched forward.

'Goodbye, darling.'

As I looked down into my father's face I saw that his eyes had filled with tears. From the train window I could see him standing on the platform, his figure becoming smaller and smaller as he watched the train until it disappeared out of sight. As the train rumbled across the great viaduct spanning the River Kent, I looked out across the vast expanse of mud flats of Morecambe Bay. At that moment I felt like a lamb going towards the jaws of a lion.

In London, I discovered boys and nightclubs. By Christmas I was home again. I had contracted glandular fever and was confined to bed.

'Ah sure, she has the kissing disease,' announced Dr Hill, our Irish GP, who almost knew more about horses than he did about humans.

My conscience pricked me as I detected the looks of disapproval. One morning a few days later, my mother entered my bedroom holding aloft a pale-blue airmail envelope, all crumpled and dusty and covered in beautiful stamps.

I looked at the postmark. The letter had been posted from Lahore. The previous autumn, Myles had set off with three friends for Goa and Trivandrum in southern India, travelling overland via Afghanistan and Kathmandu. Opening the flimsy letter carefully, I read my brother's descriptions of their many hair-raising adventures crossing Iran in a dilapidated Volkswagen camper van and their entry into the wild country of Afghanistan. 'Afghanistan is so primitive, more so than expected, but the people are charming, but ruthless,' Myles wrote.

> The road from the Iranian border to Herat is swarming in bandits with modern rifles which anybody can buy in the bazaar for nothing. Two Americans were shot the same time and place we were, on that road. We were in Afghanistan for four days, and there were no less than seven tourists murdered in that time. Wonderful roads through chasms and gorges and huge craggy rock formations. I can't imagine how the British Army hoped to defeat the Afghans in the nineteenth century in that sort of country and in that heat.

I had just finished reading Wilfred Thesiger's *Desert, Marsh and Mountain*, Rudyard Kipling's *The Man Who Would Be King*, and Eric Newby's *A Short Walk in the Hindu Kush*. Myles's letter, combined with these books, fired my romantic imagination. From that moment, I decided that as soon as circumstances permitted I too would make that journey.

Myles brought me back as a gift a hairy, sleeveless brightly embroidered Afghan sheepskin jacket, bought in the bazaar in Kabul.

'The hide's been cured using camels' urine,' he said as he presented it to me.

I could not have been more overjoyed. Along with patent-leather knee-length boots and mini-skirts, Afghan coats were all the fashion and I couldn't wait to show it off to all my friends. I held it lovingly, even though it smelt absolutely foul – a strong mixture of goat, camel, rancid butter and wood smoke. My mother hung it in a separate cupboard so that my other clothes would not be impregnated with the strong aroma of camels' urine, and there the coat remained, admired but unworn, for several years until finally, attracting moth, it was thrown out. I mourned its departure from the cupboard, as the one tangible link with the country I hoped to visit.

For the next few years I enviously watched friends disappear off to Afghanistan and India while I was stuck in various jobs, trapped and unable to get away.

One morning, quite unexpectedly, I received a letter from Mary Burkett. She reminded me of the afternoon that we had spent together all those years before at Galava, and said she thought I might be interested in joining a small group of tourists visiting the archaeological sites of Afghanistan. The tour would start in the North-West Frontier of Pakistan and continue through the Khyber Pass into Afghanistan. Mary was to be our guest lecturer, taking us round archaeological sites, towns, mosques and bazaars. It was 1977. I was 23 and longing for adventure. Here was the opportunity that I had been waiting for.

'I've seen a felt in a carpet shop that I'm interested in buying,' Mary Burkett announced. 'Would you like to come with me?'

Throughout our journey in Afghanistan, she had been keeping an eye open for interesting felts to add to her collection for a proposed travelling exhibition in England called 'The Art of the Felt Maker'.

We were staying overnight in Pul-i-Khumri, the Bridge of Doves, a small town in the northern province of Baghlan. The town, on the main road from Mazar-i-Sharif to Kabul, overlooked a vast hydroelectric dam that harnessed water from two rivers, the Andarab and its tributary the Pul-i-Khumri, to provide electricity for the north of Afghanistan. It had been a busy day of sightseeing, and the rest of the group had retired to their hotel rooms to recuperate with a whisky before dinner. Earlier in the day we had visited the last great covered bazaar in Central Asia at Khulm, also known by its ancient name of Tashkurgan, which lay south-east of Mazar-i-Sharif. Plaited reed mats laid across poplar beams formed the roof of the bazaar and from time to time holes in the mats enabled shafts of brilliant sunlight to penetrate the dark interior. Tiny shops raised on platforms were set back from the main thoroughfare, and each part of the bazaar was devoted to the sale of a specific item.

A group of eight camels loaded with brown-and-white striped sacks filled with grain were couched outside the covered bazaar. Men wearing the traditional garb of the Turkmen – striped cotton *chapans* (coats), white trousers tucked in to high leather boots, and white turbans – moved amongst the camels, adjusting their loads. The thing that struck me most as I watched the men was their enormous height. Many were well over six feet tall, and some were nearer seven.

As Mary and I wended our way through the narrow, crowded streets of Pul-i-Khumri, past the ice-cream shops and the two-wheeled horse-drawn *gawdi* with harnesses decked out in red wool pompoms, bells and yak-hair whisks, she talked to me about felt.

'It's one of the oldest methods of textile production known to man,' she explained. It was quite possible, she went on, that felt was used at the Neolithic settlement of Çatal Höyük in Turkey as early as 6000 BC. But the finest surviving example of all is the Pazyryk felt, a wall hanging of immense size discovered by Russian archaeologists in 1948. It had been preserved in permafrost in the stone burial chamber of a Scythian nobleman buried in the Altai Mountains sometime in the fifth century BC. She continued, 'Felt has been used for centuries throughout Afghanistan, Turkey, Iran, Iraq and Central Asia, and is highly valued for its qualities as a waterproof covering for floors, roofs of nomads' tents, garments, shepherds' cloaks and numnahs for horses'.

We entered the shop's dark interior, and were soon sitting cross-legged on the floor, drinking green tea and eating *noql-e-badomi*, tiny almonds coated in hard white sugar. The walls were hung with the brightly coloured embroideries used by the nomads of north Afghanistan to decorate their tents, as well as *ikat chapans* and the green, purple and peacock striped silk *chapans* worn by all the men in rural Afghanistan at that time. Ornate silver Turkmen jewellery inlaid with carnelians, lapis lazuli necklaces and 19th-century Russian porcelain 'Gardner' tea-pots and cups were arranged in glass showcases. Piled in neat stacks in one corner were hand-woven carpets, kilims, saddlebags and felts, which the shopkeeper wasted no time in pulling out to show us. One particular kilim camel saddlebag caught my eye. A 'Tartaree', the shopkeeper called it when I asked him where it was from. From the Middle Ages to the 20th century, Europeans called land conquered by Genghis Khan and his

Mongolian hordes 'Tartary', an area that stretched from China to the Caspian Sea. Here lived Turkic-speaking nomadic tribes – Turkmen, Uzbeks, Kazakhs, Kirghiz, Hazara and Uyghur. The saddlebag that I now held would have been used during migration for transporting food and possessions, cooking pots and utensils, even small children. I inhaled the rich aroma of camel, dust and sweat, which so reminded me of the sheepskin coat Myles had brought back for me all those years before, and admired its faded colours, geometric design and intricate weaving. At the top of each pannier were woven slits and loops of brown goat's wool for closing the bags when filled. After some negotiation, I bought it as a souvenir of my visit to Afghanistan and packed it later that evening with loving care and pride at the bottom of my suitcase.

At the far end of the Bamiyan valley, deep in the heart of the Hindu Kush, our small group stood at the foot of a colossal statue of the Buddha, carved out of the yellow sandstone cliff. We marvelled at his enormous size and listened as Mary explained how the carving was once draped with ropes held in place by wooden pegs and covered with a mixture of mud, wheat straw and fine gypsum to create the folds of his robes, illustrating the Greek influence in his dress. It had once been covered with a layer of red paint. A slightly smaller, almost identical statue nearby had been painted blue. Both were carved sometime between the third and fourth centuries AD, during the reign of the Kushan king Kanishka.

The Bamiyan valley formed part of the ancient Silk Route connecting powerful Rome in the west to China and India in the east. The Buddhas, with their brightly coloured robes and gilded hands and faces, must have been a truly magnificent sight to pilgrims and to merchants as they arrived with their string of camels heavily laden with indigo, silks, semi-precious stones, furs and spices at the busy thriving caravanserai in the valley. The cliffs on either side of the Buddhas were pockmarked with hundreds of tiny caves, small cells where more than 5,000 yellow-robed monks once lived, prayed and meditated.

A pathway wound up through the cliff and around the statue. As I groped my way up the dark spiral stairway, I was grateful for the occasional narrow apertures like arrow slits that allowed shafts of sunlight to filter in and illuminate the dust-covered steps hewn from the rock. I thought of the monks and pilgrims who trod these very stairs all those hundreds of years before as they perambulated anti-clockwise around the giant statue intoning their prayers. Each step had been worn smooth by the feet of the devotees.

Reaching the top, I stepped out onto the head of the Buddha to view the fifth-century frescoes painted on the rock ceiling. Nancy Hatch Dupree, in her book *An Historical Guide to Afghanistan*, describes the frescoes as depicting scenes of Paradise, the Buddha and Bodhisattva. Although in a dilapidated state, the delicate pink, blue and gold pigments of the 'flowing scarves, jewelled necklaces' and 'bare-busted female musicians playing cymbals for their dancer companions'[6] were as fresh and bright as though the painting had been done yesterday. Those awe-inspiring statues and the beautiful frescoes sadly no longer exist. In 2001, the Taliban destroyed both statues by detonating explosives placed in the rock face around them, reducing them to rubble.

But that day, across the valley, I gazed out at poplar trees bordering neat emerald-green terraced fields, their bright yellow leaves shimmering and rustling in the warm afternoon breeze signalling the approach of autumn. I peered over the rickety safety rail placed to prevent tourists plummeting 180 feet from the viewing gallery to the ground below and could just identify a few members of our group. They looked like ants as they stood beside the Buddhas' enormous feet. Somewhere in the distance, a flute was being played.

Afghanistan, with its majestic mountains, arid desert, ancient and bustling bazaars filled with nomads, camels and carpets, and myriad archaeological sites illustrating its rich and varied history, was everything I had ever dreamed about. Furthermore, the country and its people were unspoilt, and the traveller was welcomed with warmth, courtesy and enormous hospitality. In the rural areas it was like stepping back in time a thousand years.

On the road leading back to Kabul, the minibus stopped to allow us to photograph a large yellow road sign pointing west to Iran and north to the border with the USSR. As we stood on the road in bright sunshine clicking away with our cameras, none of us could have imagined the terrible tragedy that was about to befall this lovely country. The storm clouds were gathering. Exactly two years and two months later, in December 1979, while families in Britain were enjoying turkey and Christmas pudding, Soviet tanks and armoured vehicles invaded Afghanistan and travelled down this very same road on their way to Kabul.

Chapter 2

London life
1981–1982

Almost overnight, the hawthorn hedge around Regent's Park had burst into leaf. The black spiny twigs had become a mass of lime-green leaves in just a matter of days. It was mid-March, and I was sitting behind a desk at Justerini & Brooks on Cornwall Crescent, typing letters. Or rather, gazing out of the large Georgian windows. Life, I mused, was passing me by. I was bored, very bored. My boss, Derek Plunkett, a charming, quiet, shy chain-smoker, was away in the Far East selling J&B whisky to agents in Tokyo and Hong Kong. After answering his mail each morning, there was nothing else to do. In one week I had read Tolkien's *The Lord of the Rings* and M.M. Kaye's *The Far Pavilions*, and was now sewing up the hem of an evening dress.

Sitting all day behind a desk with little to do except watch the clock until 5 pm was not how I wanted to spend my days. I approached Personnel on the fourth floor.

'Do you think there's a possibility that I might be able to work for someone else while Derek is abroad?' I asked. 'Is there a job going within the company that's a little more managerial than secretarial?'

I didn't think at the time that I was asking too much, but I was taken aback when the personnel manageress replied, 'We don't like to employ girls who want to get on or have a career'. I couldn't believe that J&B still held on to such archaic attitudes, particularly as by then Britain had its first woman prime minister. After this, I felt no desire to stay longer at J&B.

Ever since the purchase of the kilim saddlebag in Pul-i-Khumri I'd wanted to learn more about oriental carpets and textiles, so I wrote to all the auction houses in London to see if there were vacancies in their oriental carpet departments. Sadly, all the replies were the same: there simply weren't any vacancies.

I applied for a course in textile conservation at Hampton Court, but the entry qualification required A Levels in Science and Chemistry, two subjects I knew I would be unlikely to pass. A friend, Lizzie Mann, suggested I study anthropology at the School of Oriental and African Studies, but I would need two A Level passes at A grade. I enrolled on an adult education course at the Working Men's College in Camden, and three nights a week I cycled down the Euston Road to Mornington Crescent after work. At the end of the year I passed A Levels in both Italian and History, but sadly not attaining the A or B grades required by the head of the anthropology department at SOAS.

'You can always try again next year,' Dr Chaudhury said encouragingly, but the thought of having to go through yet another year of trying to hold down a job during the day and studying in the evenings was difficult to contemplate. I had lost enthusiasm and motivation.

Back at my desk at J&B, I scanned the job vacancies on the back page of *The Daily Telegraph*. A small ad caught my eye: 'Part-time secretary required SW5. Non-smoker preferred.' At the end of the week I walked out of the smart offices of J&B for the last time and into a part-time job working every afternoon for film producer David Puttnam in his mews house just off Gloucester Road. The film *Chariots of Fire* was in the post-production stage and David required a secretary for a few months while his long-term secretary, Linda, took a three-month sabbatical in Hollywood. Although I would be working for David in the afternoons, I still needed to find employment during the mornings. Purely by chance, as I cycled home on my last day at J&B, I spied a dramatic Caucasian Chelaberd rug in the front window of a small oriental carpet shop set back from the Brompton Road. I chained my bicycle to a lamp post and went in.

'Do you need a secretary?' I asked the owner, Raymond Benardout.

'No,' he replied, pointing to an elegantly dressed lady seated behind a desk. 'I already have an excellent secretary. But if you really want to learn about oriental carpets, you can work for me as a repairer.'

He led me downstairs to a large basement, where carpets were washed and cleaned before being restored and hung in the gallery on the ground floor. Skeins of coloured wool in various shades hung in rows from hooks on the walls. Next door in a small, quiet and warm room, two young women and an Iranian man were bent over looms in deep concentration, mending carpets.

'You can work here if you like,' said Raymond. 'Yusuf,' pointing to the young Iranian, 'will teach you.'

For the next few weeks I settled happily into the routine of life in Raymond's basement. As an apprentice, my work was unpaid, so I worked mornings only and in the afternoons cycled down the road to David Puttnam's office. One of my first tasks as a carpet repairer was to replace brown wool in the border of a Caucasian soumakh. Yusuf explained that the mordant used in 'fixing' the brown dyes was ferrous oxide, so wool was often soaked in vats containing iron nails. The long-term effect of the ferrous oxide was corrosive, so after many years the brown wool rotted, leaving the warps and wefts exposed.

During the day, Yusuf would listen to cassettes of Iranian fundamentalist

Islamic marching music, which consisted of endless chanting. I was interested to hear about his life in Iran and what had brought him to London. He told me that he had been wanted by SAVAK, the Shah's secret intelligence service, and because of this he had sought and been granted political asylum in Britain. It was 1981, the year after the American hostage crisis, and we talked together about Khomeini and events taking place in Iran at that time. He gloated over the humiliating abortive attempt by the US Delta Force to rescue the American hostages in April 1980, and occasionally he would murmur, 'Shah bad man' or 'Down with USA', all the while singing along to the chanting. After a few weeks, the endless dirge-like music began to grate on my nerves. Irritated, and without thinking through the consequences, I said something along the lines that I didn't think the Shah and Queen Farah were quite as bad as he made out. Yusuf, his face twisted in rage, screamed at me, 'Bladdy woman, bladdy woman! You know nussing!' Taken aback by his vehement outburst, I reached for the glass jug of water sitting on a table behind him, and upended it over his head.

'No one calls *me* a bloody woman!'

He glared at me as water dripped through his thick black hair and off his curly black beard onto the carpet that he was repairing. Suddenly he relaxed, and laughed.

'OK, OK, I sorry. You not bladdy woman,' and we were friends again.

At that moment, Raymond's voice boomed out from the direction of the door.

'Just what is going on in here?'

I was sacked on the spot.

Fortunately for me, Raymond's father, Nissim, owned a carpet shop further down the Brompton Road. He was happy to take me on as a restorer and asked no questions. I started the very next day.

It was around this time that Mary Burkett came to London for some event and invited me to join her for a drink one evening. Knowing of my interest in carpets, she gave me the name of a gallery in Belgravia selling antique oriental textiles. She thought I would find the shop interesting and, following her suggestion, I got in touch with the owner, Joss Graham. I was lucky. Joss told me he needed a 'Saturday girl' to help in the gallery as he was organising an exhibition of Japanese textiles. This suited me perfectly and I accepted his offer.

At the private view of the exhibition I met Elizabeth Winter, who worked as a counsellor at a drop-in centre in Hammersmith mentoring and advising young people. We stood in the basement of Joss's shop clasping glasses of wine and talked about Afghanistan. Like me, Elizabeth had visited the country as a tourist before the Soviet occupation.

'There's a small group of us who travelled in the region before the war,' she said. 'We produce a small quarterly newsletter called Afghan Refugee

Information Network, or ARIN for short, in which we report about the situation in the refugee camps in the North-West Frontier and inside Afghanistan. Why don't you come to my flat for a cup of tea this Sunday and I can tell you more?'

Elizabeth lived on the ground floor of a large red-brick Victorian block of flats at the far end of the Fulham Road. Cycling down Fulham Palace Road to our rendezvous, I thought back over my life. I hadn't achieved any of the things that I or my parents had dreamed of or hoped for. Having spent such a carefree childhood, I found it difficult to sit all day behind a desk in an office. My attention span was limited and I got bored easily.

'The trouble with you, Harriet,' said my mother, 'is that you never stick at anything. You just flit from flower to flower like a butterfly.'

My sister was even more blunt. 'Harriet, you have the attention span of a gnat.'

Both were right, of course. Quite possibly I suffered from what is commonly referred to nowadays as attention deficit syndrome. Over the years I had had a myriad of dead-end jobs: as a mother's help in Norfolk; as an au pair in Italy, where I was more of a success riding the family's horses than looking after their four-year-old daughter; and as a secretary in Edinburgh. I had even spent a summer at a shooting lodge in Sutherland cooking enormous saddles of stag on a temperamental clinker-fuelled range that went out when I forgot to riddle it. Various disastrous relationships along the way meant that I had stood by while friends found husbands, got married and started families. As I chained my bicycle to the railings, I felt like a small boat adrift in a vast ocean without rudder or anchor.

If Elizabeth suspected my feelings of failure, she was far too polite or professional to say. With her background in mentoring, I am sure she detected in me someone who was drifting aimlessly, searching without success to find something with meaning and purpose. As she filled the kettle, her cats arched their backs and rubbed their heads on the chair legs, purring for food and attention. Passing me a cup of tea, she threw me a lifeline with the casual remark, 'Come to the next meeting of ARIN and meet the other members of the group'.

At the meeting Elizabeth introduced me to Gordon Adam, head of the Pushtu department at the BBC World Service, Bush House; Anthony Hyman, journalist and author of several books on the history of Central Asia; Frances D'Souza, a trained anthropologist with a long-standing interest and personal history in Afghanistan (now Baroness D'Souza, Speaker of the House of Lords from 2011 to 2016); Diana Colvin, who had lived for eight months in the Panjshir valley before the war; and ARIN's secretary, Helen Saberi. Originally from Yorkshire, Helen was working at the British Embassy in Kabul when the Soviets invaded. She escaped Afghanistan with her Afghan husband and their small child in March 1980, leaving behind all their material possessions and family.

I felt an affinity straightaway with Helen, perhaps because we were both northerners, albeit from different sides of the Pennines. A year later, when she was expecting her second child, Oliver, I took over her job as secretary of ARIN.

'I'd like to go back to the North-West Frontier and see for myself the situation of Afghan refugees,' I announced at the end of a meeting just before Christmas 1982.

'Well, if you do decide to go, let me know,' said Diana Colvin. 'I've collected some money for an Afghan organisation based in Islamabad working with refugees in the camps. You could take it with you to Pakistan and hand it over.'

At her home in north London, Diana gave me a brown manila envelope containing banknotes.

'When you arrive in Islamabad,' she said, 'just ring the number on the envelope. They know you are coming.'

That evening I telephoned my parents to tell them my plans.

'But Harriet, you've only just come back from India!'

I could hear the dismay, exasperation and anxiety in my father's voice. 'Why can't you just *settle down*?'

Five months earlier, I had trekked with a Cumbrian friend, Diana Washington, in India's most northerly region, Lahoul–Spiti, close to the Tibetan border. With two small ponies to carry our provisions, backpacks and a blue plastic tent bought off the pavement outside a bric-a-brac store on Fulham's Munster Road, we crossed snow bridges and waded through glacial rivers in bare feet, the laces of our walking boots tied around our necks. We scrambled through the remains of glacial moraines, jumping from boulder to boulder amongst flocks of long-haired sheep owned by nomadic *gujars*. Finally, after a gruelling climb, we reached the summit of the 16,000-foot Shingo La pass and entered the hidden kingdom of Zanskar. For two weeks we trekked for ten hours a day above 12,000 feet, passing Buddhist stupas and monasteries, and living on a diet of butter tea, *chang*, rice, chapattis and vegetable curry. When we reached the capital, Padam, we were as lean and fit as racing whippets. From there we hitched a lift out on a Kashmiri truck to Leh in Ladakh.

Now I felt guilty about wanting to go off again so soon.

Nissim Benardout, Raymond's father, was equally horrified when I announced my intention to visit the North-West Frontier.

'You're quite mad. Why do you want to go and be with *those* people?' he demanded.

'I just want to see for myself the situation of the Afghans in the camps.'

'Well,' he said, 'if you're not back within two weeks, I'm coming out to find you!'

PART II
PAKISTAN

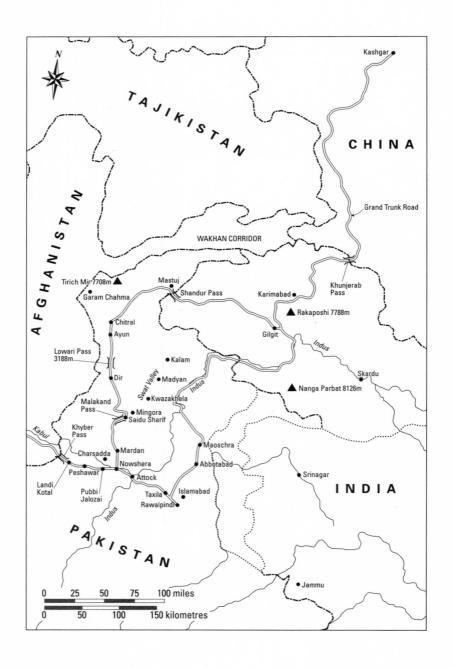

CHAPTER 3

Crossing the border
January 1983

The American pilgrims at the Golden Temple in Amritsar told me that the best way to travel to the Pakistan border was by bus. I had seen them earlier in the day, promenading barefoot across the black-and-white marble tiles around the temple precinct, stopping from time to time to admire the reflection of the gleaming golden dome in the waters of the *tank* (artificial lake). I was intrigued by their strange garb of long, flowing white gowns and tall white hats. Later that evening in the temple's Langar, the Sikh-run hostel where food and accommodation are offered free of charge to all travellers regardless of faith, we finally met. As we sat crossed-legged on *dhurries* eating vegetarian *thali*, the fair-haired, blue-eyed Californians gave me some advice.

'The crossing at Attari is only about 17 miles from Amritsar. A bus will drop you a few miles from the border and then you take a cycle rickshaw right up to customs and immigration on the Indian side. Once you clear customs you just walk across the border to Wagah in Pakistan.'

I woke at dawn. After a night sleeping on the floor of the gurdwara, I wanted to be on the move, anxious to make Lahore before nightfall. The temple was already coming to life. At the main gates, devotees were entering to pray and bathe in the green waters of the *tank*. I stopped for a moment to watch a group of Nihangs sitting by the main door, gossiping and handing out squares of orange cloth to foreigners to cover their heads. They were handsome men with strong aquiline features and long beards, their shalwar kameez and turbans a vibrant kaleidoscope of colours – ochre, crimson, royal blue, orange and yellow. Members of an informal religious army maintained by the gurdwara to defend Sikh faith and traditions, Nihangs are rarely separated from their weapons. Some of them held wooden staffs topped with metal spears, while younger men, resplendent in royal-blue tunics and orange cummerbunds, carried magnificent curved swords that glinted in the early-morning sun as they patrolled the precinct of the temple.

The antiquated bus rattled out through the suburbs of Amritsar covering the roadside vendors in black diesel fumes. It was only a short journey before we arrived at a small depot where the bus terminated. Outside in hot sunshine, I was surrounded by a crowd of cycle rickshaw wallahs all competing to grab my luggage and take me on to the border. I have never liked hiring cycle rickshaws – to my way of thinking, it is a degrading form of transport – but I had no option. There was simply no other way to reach the border. I finally selected one, but I felt uncomfortable as I reclined in the seat and watched the rickshaw wallah wipe rivulets of sweat from his face and neck with a dirty cloth. I couldn't help noticing the veins and muscles of his bulging calves as he stood upright on the pedals, straining to turn the wheels. Looking at his sweat-stained singlet and faded lunghi, I felt the enormity of the gulf between his poverty and my comparative wealth.

Gradually the cacophony of traffic faded as we left behind the shanty dwellings surrounding the bus station and emerged out into the flat Punjabi countryside. We bowled along at a spanking pace in blissful near-silence save for the creak of the wheels. The rickshaw wallah wheeled to a stop outside customs and immigration. Inside, a bored-looking Indian official stamped an exit visa into my passport with a hearty thump and jerked his head towards the door indicating I was free to go.

In brilliant sunshine I set out to walk the hundred yards along the Grand Trunk Road across no-man's-land to the border, dragging my wheeled suitcase along the wide asphalt road beside neatly farmed fields of sugar cane and winter wheat. The silence was extraordinary. No vehicles, pedestrians or animals shared the tarmac with me that afternoon and no voices carried on the cool breeze from neighbouring villages. I stopped to rest for a moment and to breathe in the alpine air blowing down from the snow-capped peaks to the north – so welcome after the dust and petrol and diesel fumes of Amritsar. I checked that the manila envelope was safe in the money belt around my waist and walked on. Apart from a few snow-white egrets standing elegantly in the long grass beside the road, I was utterly and completely alone – a rare experience in a country where, as a *feringee*, I attracted all too much attention.

I gazed across the vast area of farmland that formed a buffer zone between these two great countries, and thought about the terrible barbarity and slaughter of nearly a million Hindus, Muslims and Sikhs after a judge drew a line on a map in 1947 and divided a people. On that afternoon, as I walked through the Punjabi countryside I was struck by the unnatural silence and absence of birdsong. I was reminded of a visit I once made to Theresienstadt concentration camp, outside Prague. No birds sang there, either.

As the border post gradually came into view, the guards watching me approach grew agitated, shouting and gesturing frantically.

'Come on, memsahib. *Hurry! Hurry!*'

I looked at my watch. It was nearly 3.30 pm. In winter, dusk comes early, and the metal border gates would be closing shortly. A porter detached himself from the crowd, ran towards me, took hold of my suitcase and hoisted it up onto his head.

'Quick, memsahib, run!' he said, and the two of us ran side by side towards fluttering green flags emblazoned with a white crescent moon and star. As we burst through the metal gates, handsome grinning border guards in starched khaki fatigues and colourful cravats reached out to shake my hand.

'Hello, memsahib. Welcome to Pakistan. Which country you from?'

At Flashman's hotel in Rawalpindi, I rang the number that Diana Colvin had written on the envelope and arranged a time to visit, explaining that I had brought some money from London.

The taxi dropped me outside a smart house situated in a quiet residential area of Islamabad, surrounded by woods where marijuana grew in the undergrowth and jackals cackled. In answer to my knock, the doors swung open, revealing a large chowkidar sporting a magnificent black beard and armed with an AK-47. Behind him emerged a slightly built man wearing Western-style jacket and trousers.

'I am Doctor Sherahmed Nasri. Welcome to our office.'

I became aware that I had arrived at the headquarters of Jamiat-i-Islami, one of the seven Afghan Mujahideen groups. This was not what I was expecting at all. Diana had said nothing about the money going to the headquarters of a Mujahideen group (the name means 'soldiers of God') when I collected it from her in London. Rather, she had led me to believe that I would be visiting an aid organisation working with refugees.

I followed Dr Nasri up a flight of stairs, the walls of which were decorated with various items captured by the Mujahideen while fighting the Soviets: letters written in Cyrillic script, photographs of young Russian conscripts and identity papers. Many of the letters were bloodstained and I was in no doubt that they had been removed from the dead. Dr Nasri continued his guided tour and running commentary.

'These are plastic butterfly mines. The Soviets scatter them in the mountains and around villages. Sometimes they are in the shape of toys such as small trucks, pens, sweets or dolls. So the children looking after the sheep and goats out on the hillsides pick them up, the mine explodes and they lose a hand. If they step on them they lose a leg.'

Part of the engine from a Soviet helicopter gunship hung at a giddy angle, the grey metal blackened, mangled and distorted by heat. I peered at the inscription written underneath, 'Soviet Hind helicopter destroyed by Mujahideen'. Finally, we stopped in front of a knife with a long blade.

'Ah, this is a Mujahideen knife,' said Dr Nasri. 'It has killed seven Russian soldiers.'

As I glanced nervously at the vicious-looking weapon, I didn't doubt this.

At the top of the staircase we entered a large room. Seated on either side of a long highly polished shisham wood table were eight grey-bearded Afghans wearing the flat woollen *pakhols* more commonly called Chitrali hats. Some wore Western-style grey trousers and pinstriped jackets over pullovers like Dr Nasri, others the traditional *pirhan-tombon*, the Afghan baggy trousers and long shirt with tails that reach to the knee. Pakistani sweet milk tea was served, and formal pleasantries exchanged. Milk tea is served to guests throughout India and Pakistan. The tea leaves are boiled in water for ages to extract the maximum strength and flavour, then the stewed liquid is strained, sweetened with condensed milk and boiled again.

With a lull in conversation, I judged the moment right to hand over the money given to me by Diana. The manila envelope was passed with great ceremony from hand to hand like a game of pass the parcel until it reached Dr Nasri. Slowly he slit open the envelope with a paperknife. The grey beards leaned forward expectantly, eyes fixed on the notes as they fluttered down onto the table. They murmured together and I sensed consternation. Dr Nasri counted the notes.

'Sixty pounds,' he said in Dari, but I knew they had been expecting far more. Why hadn't I thought to ask Diana how much money was in the envelope? By bringing so little I had lost face. I felt mortified. The grey beards recovered their composure. Turning towards me, hands on their hearts, they thanked me with all the grace, dignity and courtesy typical of the Afghan race for bringing the money from England.

As I was leaving, Dr Nasri handed me a card.

'When you reach Peshawar, please telephone this number. This is our representative there. He will look after you.'

I arrived in Peshawar late at night. The rickshaw dropped me outside the only hotel I knew, Dean's, a beautiful bungalow-style building set back from the busy Grand Trunk Road. Dean's Hotel had been built by the British during the days of the Raj and I had last stayed there in 1977, en route to Afghanistan with Mary Burkett. A room there would stretch my small budget but, at night and being a woman alone, I didn't feel confident to start searching for cheaper accommodation. As I stood in the dark, dust and diesel fumes from auto rickshaws swirling around me, I suddenly felt afraid and vulnerable as turbaned tribesmen emerging out of the gloom turned and stared at me. It had all seemed such an adventure when I set out from London, but now I suddenly felt out of my depth. I hurried towards the sanctuary of the hotel gates. In reception I rang the number on the card and arranged to meet the Jamiat-i-Islami representative the following morning.

Masood Khalili spoke near-perfect English with a transatlantic twang.

It was the first thing I noticed about him. The son of Afghanistan's famous poet and Persian poet laureate Ustad Khalilulah Khalili, Masood had spent two years in the United States while his father was serving as ambassador there, hence the American intonation. Following the Soviet invasion, he had returned to Afghanistan in 1980 to join the resistance and had just come back, he told me, from fighting in the mountains of the Panjshir alongside his close friend and Jamiat commander, Ahmad Shah Massoud, 'The Lion of the Panjshir'. He was relaxed and urbane, and I could see why Jamiat-i-Islami had selected him as their spokesperson to meet and greet visiting journalists and war photographers. Years later, on 9 September 2001, just two days before the destruction of the Twin Towers in New York, Masood Khalili was badly injured in a suicide bomb attack. Two Tunisians posing as journalists had arranged to interview Ahmad Shah Massoud at his office in Khoja Bahauddin, his rear headquarters in the far north near the Amu Darya River. Khalili had been invited along to act as interpreter. As they were seated the Tunisians, allegedly belonging to al-Qaeda, detonated a bomb hidden in their video camera. The blast severely injured Ahmad Shah Massoud, who died in the helicopter taking him to hospital. Khalili was badly burnt over much of his body, lost the sight of an eye and part of his hearing, and sustained multiple injuries. Three hundred pieces of shrapnel still remain in his leg. His passport, which Ahmad Shah Massoud suggested he place in his shirt pocket, prevented shrapnel from piercing his heart and probably saved his life.

'I've come to write an article on the situation of Afghan refugees,' I said, handing him a copy of an ARIN newsletter.

'How many days are you staying in Peshawar?'

'Oh, about three, maybe four,' I replied.

'Then I shall make a programme for you. We shall start today by visiting the camps.'

Katchaguri refugee camp, situated close to the entrance to the Khyber Pass, was home to 33,000 refugees. A show camp for visiting foreign journalists and photographers, it was clean and well-organised, and the tents had been replaced by mud huts. It was as though the authorities had come to terms with the fact that the refugees were there to stay as men were busy constructing a mosque, a dispensary and a hospital. Bihar Colony, on the other hand, was a small tented camp typical of so many that had sprung up around Peshawar. The refugees were still living in fields in the tents allocated to them two years previously by UNHCR when they first arrived from Afghanistan. Many of the canvas tents had rotted with gaping holes, and gave little protection against the elements. The drinking water was far from clean.

On day two, Masood took me to the Afghan surgical hospital at Nisherabad. All 40 beds were occupied by Afghan men and boys wounded in the fighting.

Because many of them had travelled for days over the mountains to Pakistan strapped onto donkeys and camels before receiving medical attention, the onset of gangrene meant more amputation than would originally have been necessary. We stopped by the bed of a 14-year-old boy who had lost both legs below the knee, three fingers from his left hand and the ends of all the fingers on his right. Blood and pus had seeped into the gauze bandages and caked hard. I watched while the doctor attempted to re-dress the wounds; the gauze had adhered so firmly to the flesh that he had to pull it away with tweezers. The pain must have been excruciating, but the boy only emitted a gentle whimper. It was my first experience of the extraordinary stoicism of the Afghan people. 'Courage, physical courage, is central to the Afghan character,' writes Brigadier Mohammed Yousaf who, as Director of the Afghan Bureau of Pakistan's ISI (Inter-Services Intelligence), worked closely with the Mujahideen for four years in the 1980s, training them for operations against the Soviets. He describes Afghans as exhibiting 'the ability to suffer pain stoically, without fuss and silently,' adding that 'it is deemed unmanly for an Afghan to cry out, or scream, if gravely injured.'[7]

In the operating theatre the sound of a saw rasping through bone, and the smell of iodine, gangrene, disinfectant and boiled mutton wafting from the hospital kitchen were more than my stomach could cope with. I made a quick exit through a side door into the hospital garden and stood contemplating the roses in the herbaceous border. Behind me, amputees in wheelchairs were lined up in a row, enjoying the winter sunshine. I took deep gulps of fresh air in an attempt to quell the nausea, hoping I wouldn't disgrace myself by being sick in front of them.

'Now I am taking you to see an orphanage for boys,' announced Masood as he collected me from Dean's Hotel on the third morning. We arrived outside a large building dating from the days of the Raj, set back off Sunehri Masjid Road in the Cantonment area of Peshawar.

'There are about a hundred boys here between the ages of four and sixteen,' Masood explained. 'They are well looked after and taught the Qur'an, geography, mathematics, handwriting and public speaking. The Pakistan government charges about seven thousand rupees in rent and the orphanage is run purely by volunteers and by donations received from organisations.'

Most of the boys were away visiting relatives in the neighbouring refugee camps, but a small group took me on a tour of their dormitory to show me where they slept. As I sat on a metal-framed bed almost identical to those at my boarding school, Masood encouraged them to tell me their stories. In a clear, strong voice showing no emotion, a little boy, not more than four or five years of age, described how he had been out on the mountain slopes guarding the sheep and goats when the *Hind* helicopters flew low over his village, dropping bombs and firing rockets directly onto the houses. By the time he had run down the hillside back to his village, his home had been destroyed and his entire family killed. The Mujahideen had found him wandering in the mountains and brought him to the orphanage. As I talked with the boys and listened to their stories, I could see the trauma of their experiences clearly visible in their faces. From now on the boys would grow up in an all-male environment, without mothers, sisters or aunts to provide a female influence in their lives.

In their fragile emotional state the boys were vulnerable to indoctrination. Throughout the 1980s, Afghan boys in orphanages and madrassas in Pakistan were exposed to the teachings of Deobandism, a strict interpretation of Islam that preached a distorted utopia of 'pure' Islam disrespectful of other faiths. The non-violent movement was founded by students in the town of Deoband in India a decade after the Indian Mutiny to unite Muslims in resistance against British colonial rule. Deobandism was reinforced by Wahhabism from Saudia Arabia, introduced by Arab mercenaries who came to fight 'jihad' alongside their Muslim brothers, the Afghan Mujahideen. It was here in the Pakistani refugee camps, madrassas and orphanages that the Taliban movement was spawned.

That evening we travelled by rickshaw to the outskirts of Peshawar for dinner with Abdul Rahim, a young Panjshiri who was responsible for briefing journalists on the situation inside Afghanistan. When I think back on that evening I am sure that, had I asked to travel inside Afghanistan with the Mujahideen, my request might well have been granted, but I was no journalist and I would have been sailing under false colours. As we left the office and stepped out into the dark street, Abdul handed me his Chitrali hat made from the finest camel hair. I treasured it and wore it for years until I sadly lost it.

On my final day in Peshawar, Masood took me to the Old City. We wandered through a labyrinth of narrow alleys to the spice bazaar, with stalls arrayed with woven baskets piled high with coloured pyramids of ground turmeric, cumin, coriander and chillies; and to the nut and grain market of Peepal Mundi, where large hessian sacks were filled with kidney beans, chickpeas, lentils, ginger, dried apricots, rice, raisins, almonds and walnuts. In the Sabzi Mundi, the colourful and busy vegetable market, the quality, freshness and variety of vegetables on offer was awesome – potatoes of all shapes and sizes, fresh coriander, onions, leeks, carrots, tomatoes and turnips.

Pushing our way through the crowds, horse-drawn tongas, donkeys with panniers laden with stone and cement and auto rickshaws belching blue clouds of exhaust, we emerged from the narrow alleys into the plaza of Chowk Yadgar, a wide redeveloped space close to the Bala Hisar Fort dedicated to those who died fighting India in 1965. Nomadic Afghan rugs, camel bags, embroideries and kilims hung from wooden balconies overlooking the plaza, flapping in the breeze. With the knowledge that I had gained while working for Nissim Benardout and Joss Graham, I felt confident enough to buy a few carpets and embroideries with the idea of selling them for a profit once I was back in England.

Back in London I organised a selling exhibition in my house in Fulham and invited friends. I sold all the carpets and embroideries for a small profit, which more than covered my travel expenses to Pakistan. My business was born. But there was something else, too. I had at last found a purpose to my life, a cause to follow and support. The way ahead seemed suddenly clear. From now on I would do something constructive to help the people of Afghanistan. The visit to Peshawar had been a life-changing experience and somehow I knew I would never be quite the same person again.

Joss Graham was organising an exhibition on Afghanistan and for a week I helped him display carpets, kilims and embroideries in his shop. All manner of people interested in Afghanistan came to see the exhibition, not just those who loved textiles but also travellers, journalists, photographers, authors and ex-hippies. It was here that I met Sandy, Peter and Helena. I didn't know it then, but our paths would cross many times in the years ahead.

Six months earlier, ITN newscaster Sandy Gall had walked 150 miles through the mountains and deserts of Afghanistan to make a documentary on the guerrilla war for ITV entitled 'Behind Russian Lines'. He noticed me seated in the corner of Joss's shop, repairing a damaged kilim, and asked if I could repair one that he had been given by an Afghan Mujahideen commander, which required some attention. A few days later, when I had finished mending the kilim, Sandy and his wife Eleanor invited me to Sunday lunch, the first of many such occasions, at their lovely home near Penshurst in Kent. Due to their warm hospitality, I met the rest of the family, in particular two of their three daughters, Fiona and Michaela.

Peter Jouvenal, ex-soldier and freelance cameraman, had also just returned from Afghanistan. He was a bit vague and secretive about what he had been actually doing, which made me all the more intrigued to find out more. Peter was shy and taciturn; he kept his cards very close to his chest. Throughout the 1980s he had been one of a small band of extraordinary and courageous young men who risked their lives to bring back film footage showing what was truly going on inside the country. He travelled on assignments for weeks at a time, gaining extensive knowledge of the war and forging friendships with the Mujahideen groups. He was not afraid to go into battle alongside them with his video camera and, as a result, some of the most daring film footage shown on British television at this time was Peter's. In addition, his great interest in and knowledge of Soviet weaponry, uniforms and insignia were considered most useful in some quarters.

On first acquaintance, Helena Beattie appeared fey and ethereal, but first impressions can be misleading. As I came to know her better, I discovered that behind her mystical countenance lay a strong, feisty character and a sharp brain. One day she mentioned that she was planning to travel to Pakistan to work as a volunteer with the Ockenden Venture, an NGO working with Afghan women embroiderers on the North-West Frontier. I wished her a safe journey but felt concerned about her travelling alone through Pakistan, and wondered how she would manage on the 1,000-mile journey overland from Karachi to Peshawar. As we parted company, I said that I would look forward to meeting her on my next buying trip. A few weeks later I heard that she had arrived safely in Peshawar and was working with the Tibetan couple who ran the Ockenden Venture. Helena invited me to stay with her when I arrived in Peshawar, and arranged for me to visit the camps where women refugees embroidered cloth supplied by the charity with fine Kandahari stitch-work. Back at Ockenden's head office in Peshawar, the cloth was made into tablecloths and baby clothes and marketed locally, thus providing the women with an income to support their families. I liked the idea of supporting the women by buying their work and over the next few years I organised small selling exhibitions of Afghan embroideries and carpets in my own home.

Two years later, Helena moved to the Danish Sewing Project (Dacaar), an income-generation programme working with Afghan women embroiderers, many of them widows, where she used her knowledge to design clothes for the expatriate community living in Peshawar. Her designs were based on the traditional hats and *chapans* worn by Afghans and combined Western and Afghan styles. Working closely with a group of Afghan women embroiderers who came each morning to the sewing centre from the refugee camps, Helena learnt the various embroidery stitches and began to incorporate them in her work. She was painstakingly meticulous about detail – a perfectionist. When she was working out a design, the colour combination of the silk yarn and every stitch had to be exactly right. If she wasn't satisfied, she would unpick her work and start again. Once she was satisfied with the design and colours, the Afghan women started the embroidery. Soon her unique and sophisticated clothes were the talk of Peshawar. Everyone wanted a hat or jacket designed by Helena incorporating traditional *tarshoumar* embroidery from eastern Afghanistan.

CHAPTER 4

Out of the Nomad's Tent and *The Living Daylights*
1986–1987

One day, outside the Peter Jones department store in Sloane Square, I bumped into Rufus Reade, who I had known since my days as a secretary in Edinburgh, where he ran a business called Out of the Nomad's Tent, arranging tours to Turkey and India and importing Anatolian kilims.

'Would you like to share a shop with me?' he asked suddenly. 'A friend of mine has just bought an old bakery near Waterloo Station. He's offered me the ground floor and basement, so I've come down from Edinburgh to take a look at it.'

While my selling exhibitions in Finlay Street had proved popular, they were not the easiest way to earn a living. I had been thinking for some time of opening a shop, but lacked the courage to take the financial plunge on my own. Rufus's offer that morning seemed heaven-sent.

Roupell Street, close to the South Bank Centre, consisted of a row of Georgian artisans' cottages that had survived the Blitz. The old bakery, with its lovely bow-fronted window, was opposite a busy pub. At lunchtime the regulars would stand on the pavement nursing their pints and watch me go in and out of the shop. On occasion they would wolf-whistle and say, ''Ere, luv – where's yer flying carpet, then?' Sometimes their comments were decidedly racist.

A few days before we were due to open, Rufus arrived with a lorry-load of stock from Edinburgh. We worked around the clock to get everything set up. My wooden furniture from Rajasthan and the Swat valley and Afghan nomadic jewellery and embroideries were displayed on the ground floor. Rufus's Turkish kilims were stacked in piles in what had been the coal hole. His friend Nick, the landlord, had arranged for the floor to be dug out an extra few feet so that customers could walk upright without banging their heads on the ceiling joists. The new floor was made of concrete.

Rufus hung his kilims around the walls of the coal hole, instantly transforming it into the interior of a Turkish nomad's tent. Since the publication in 1977 of *Undiscovered Kilim* by David Black and Clive Loveless, the first oriental carpet specialists to introduce collectors and interior decorators to

20th-century tribal rugs, the popularity of this humble weaving (traditionally used for wrapping around more valuable carpets during transit) had soared. Suddenly there was an insatiable appetite for covering floors, tables, chairs, sofas and stools in Turkish kilims.

Even on the morning of the private view, we were still far from organised. With our combined stock littered about the floor, the shop looked a complete mess. I was panicking that we would not be finished in time, but Rufus was far more laid back. As I struggled to put on something smart for the occasion in the limited space of the outdoor privy, surrounded by crates of wine glasses and unwashed tea mugs, Rufus was still hanging kilims on the wall wearing sandals and a tee-shirt, quite unperturbed as the first customers arrived.

The evening was a huge success. My sister Mary helped, and the two of us couldn't take the money or wrap the goods quickly enough. Towards the end of the evening, as the frantic pace subsided, I went down to see how Rufus was faring in the basement. I could see immediately that something was amiss. The air was thick with dust, but Rufus, surrounded by potential customers and in full selling mode, seemed oblivious. As he flung one kilim after another down on the floor, clouds of concrete dust billowed up. The next day we bought the largest can of floor sealant we could find. It did the trick, and we never experienced the problem again. Rufus returned to Edinburgh and I began my new life running the shop.

One morning, the old-fashioned bell on the back of the shop door jingled and Francesca entered. She had come to ask for a job as a shop assistant. Her father, she explained, was Peter Stiles, an orthopaedic surgeon at the Royal Surrey County Hospital in Guildford. Back in 1974 Peter had operated on the victims of the IRA pub bombings in Guildford. As a result of that experience, he had become part of the Guildford surgical team that volunteered their skills (and holidays) once a year in October to operate, free of charge, in the trauma hospitals in the North-West Frontier and Afghanistan. Francesca had heard much about Afghanistan from her father and had worked for a short time as a volunteer with the British NGO Afghanaid at their London office in Charing Cross Road. In Peshawar, Afghanaid's office provided assistance to refugees fleeing the conflict in Afghanistan and ran a programme to teach tailoring to disabled Afghans. Although I wasn't actively looking for an assistant, I realised I needed someone to mind the shop while I travelled several times a year to India and Pakistan to buy stock. Francesca, with her ethnic clothes, black curly waist-length hair and an array of silver rings on every finger, certainly looked the part.

It was my lucky day when Fran came through the door. I could not have found anyone better. During the two years that she worked for me, she proved to be a great help and support and a wonderful friend. She never once let me down and the customers loved her for her cheerful, helpful personality. I felt confident leaving the shop in her capable hands and it gave me the freedom to travel every few months to Peshawar.

Peshawar was a fascinating place. Like a magnet, it drew me back again and again. When I was there I felt completely at home, and I missed it with a fierce longing when I was back in London. Its name comes from the Sanskrit and means 'city of men', and it is the oldest city in Pakistan, dating back to several thousand years BC. It became the winter residence of the Buddhist Kushans and a centre of both Gandharan art and pilgrimage. Throughout its long history Peshawar has had many rulers – Afghan Ghazavids, Mughals, Sikhs and finally the British. All have recognised its strategic importance, lying as it does at the foot of the Khyber Pass. Peshawar is best described as the meeting place of the Subcontinent and Central Asia, and in the 19th century the British Commissioner Major-General Sir Herbert Edwardes wrote of the city as 'the Piccadilly of Central Asia'. The ancient narrow streets of Quissa Khawani, the Bazaar of the Storytellers, were crowded with refugees, rickshaws, tongas, handcarts and laden donkeys. In Kipling's day the bazaar would have been even more colourful, with Hindu merchants, Sikhs, sadhus, snake charmers, and women wearing brightly coloured saris, all mingling with wild frontier tribesmen. It was easy to lose one's way in the labyrinth of tiny, meandering streets. In the quiet cul-de-sacs, away from the noise and clamour of the bazaar, I would come across houses with wooden doors decorated with Hindu symbols – carved peacocks, elephants and lotus leaves – a reminder that the building had once been a Hindu home before the madness and massacres of 1947 forced the occupants to leave.

There was still a sizeable community of Sikhs living in Peshawar. Together with the Punjab and Kashmir, Peshawar had once formed part of the Sikh kingdom ruled by the charismatic one-eyed warrior Maharajah Ranjit Singh, a wily politician with 'a passion for beautiful women and boys, a taste for laudanum and addiction to alcohol in the form of his own lethal homemade cocktails'.[8] His drunken orgies at court shocked his 19th-century European visitors.

During Ramadan, when Muslim restaurants did not serve food, I would make my way to the Sikh gurdwara tucked away behind the fish market where vegetarian *thali* was served free of charge. Inside the cool stone temple, I would sit on the tiled floor eating chapatti and dhal surrounded by Sikh women wearing colourful shalwar kameez and listen to them chanting prayers.

It was not at all uncommon to see red and fair hair amongst the Afghan refugees and peoples of the frontier. Over the centuries, invasion and migration from east and west – Persians, Greeks, Mongolians, Central Asians, Indians, and British and Russian – had all contributed to the gene pool and left their mark on the local physiognomy. One morning I passed a Turkmen lad with a pale freckled face, eyes grey as a stormy sky and hair the colour of copper beech leaves. Their eyes were often of the most extraordinary colours, rarely seen in the West – violet, deep sapphire and light yellow-green, like the eyes of the Afghan girl in a red shawl whose photograph, taken by American photographer Steve McCurry, appeared on the front cover of *National Geographic* magazine.

The nomadic Kutchi women fascinated me. Their foreheads, chins and cheeks were tattooed with small dark-blue crosses, their legs encased in woven puttees and their black shoes decorated with shocking pink and acid-green woollen pompoms. You could hear them coming a mile off as they elbowed their way through the throng, announcing their presence in the bazaar with loud, argumentative voices. Accustomed to walking with their camels, sheep and goats for hundreds of miles on migration, enduring searing summer heat and bitter Afghan winters, these big-boned women were subservient to no one. With unveiled faces they would stride boldly through the bazaar looking men dead in the eye. From time to time they would stop outside a shop doorway and, in loud hectoring tones, demand alms. The shopkeepers quailed when they appeared, as they knew full well that the women would not leave their premises until they received a coin.

The bazaar was full of Pushtun tribesmen, Mujahideen fresh from fighting in Afghanistan, and it was common to see one or two strolling through the crowded streets holding hands. I found this public show of affection strange, particularly as the Qur'an forbids homosexuality; however, the French anthropologist Louis Dupree suggests that these public gestures of holding hands 'are usually simply manifestations of friendship'.[9] In Afghanistan, homosexuality carried the death penalty, which could take various forms: being stoned by a crowd, hanged, burnt or thrown head first from a tall building or minaret. The Taliban introduced a novel way of despatching their victims – toppling a wall of stones on them and crushing them to death. However, despite the religious teachings, there is a long-practised tradition in Afghanistan of men having sexual relationships with young *bacha bazi* or dancing boys, usually orphans or poor boys, who dress in women's clothing, wear make-up, and sing and dance at weddings. Vulnerable and powerless, the boys are exploited and sold to provide entertainment for wealthy men. Although child sexual abuse and prostitution carried the death penalty during the Taliban's rule, it was almost impossible to enforce the law as those who carried out the abuse were frequently powerful and well-armed warlords and commanders.

The Mujahideen wore enormous black, white and gold striped silk turbans. Vain and conscious of their sartorial appearance, they would sometimes tuck fresh flowers behind their ears. Periodically they would stop in the middle of the crowded busy bazaar, reach inside their tunics and pull out little round silver boxes. Opening the lid, they would take a pinch of olive-green *naswar*, a locally produced narcotic snuff made from tobacco. Using thumb and forefinger, they would carefully and daintily place it inside their bottom lip, where it would remain for hours, gradually seeping into the bloodstream. On the underside of the box was a mirror. Just like women applying make-up, the Mujahideen would gaze at their reflections, comb their beards and moustaches and apply *kohl* (antimony) around their eyes as though it were the most normal thing in the world.

There was one Mujahid in particular who I would frequently see in the Old City. One morning I came across him surrounded by a group of young Mujahideen. He had the most startling cat-green eyes rimmed with black *kohl*, a patrician aquiline nose and pale olive skin. Beneath an immaculately rolled Chitrali hat perched rakishly on the back of his head, he had tucked a rose behind his ear. Long, flowing black locks fell onto his shoulders. He sauntered casually through the crowded bazaar with his friends, stopping every now and then to take a pinch of *naswar* from his little silver box. Then he would turn the box over and admire his reflection in the mirror. Although I had seen him many times before in the bazaar, I felt afraid of him, but I can't for the life of me explain why.

In Peshawar I stayed with Helena Beattie, and we would explore the shops in the Old City together. We shared a great interest in and love of Central Asian embroideries. Without a doubt our favourite shop was run by the brothers Abdul and 'Hadji' Makoo. Abdul, always referred to as 'Muallem' (an honorific title meaning teacher), and 'Hadji' (meaning one who had undertaken the pilgrimage to Mecca) had a tiny, dusty shop on the top floor of Murad market, an ancient and dilapidated building set back from the main Ander Sher Bazaar. Not only did they have by far the best embroideries at reasonable prices, but both brothers had a great sense of humour. They were kind and funny, and Helena and I would spend many happy hours in their company. For the first time in many years, I was supremely happy as I sat cross-legged on the floor of the Makoos' shop, trawling through piles of fragments of old embroidery.

When I look back, I realise how immensely lucky we were to experience life in Peshawar before the Taliban and al-Qaeda took up residence. Despite the occasional bomb exploding in the Old City, we were free to walk wherever we wished in the narrow lanes and alleys. We felt relaxed sitting and conversing with Afghan men, laughing and exchanging light-hearted banter. I really loved Peshawar. Whenever I returned to Pakistan, I felt like a homing swallow, back where I belonged. I understood completely the sentiments of Gertrude Bell, who in May 1917 wrote from Baghdad to her family in Darlington:

I wonder what inheritance from Cumbrian farmers [her mother, Mary Staid, was descended from Cumbrian sheep-farmers] can have developed unexpectedly into so compelling an at-home-ness with the East. I have grown to love this land, its sights and its sounds. I never weary of the East just as I never feel it to be alien. I cannot feel exiled here. It is a second native country. If my family were not in England I should have no wish to return.[10]

Throughout the 1980s, thousands of refugees from all over Afghanistan poured daily across the border to Peshawar to escape the fighting. Afghanistan's population stood at 15 million before the Soviet Union invaded in 1979. By the mid-1980s, two million had been killed and some five million had made their way across the border to safety. They were settled in vast camps throughout Pakistan. Many of the refugees were widows or disabled. As a direct result of circumstances beyond their control, many poor and illiterate women now found themselves breadwinners for their families. While in their home villages in rural Afghanistan women would have enjoyed the freedom to leave their homes each day to tend their fields and collect water and firewood, in the refugee camps it was a different matter altogether. Surrounded by men from different villages and tribes, women were forced to observe a far greater degree of seclusion. Bereavement, trauma and purdah brought mental health problems. To give the women something to focus on and also to enable them to earn a living, various NGOs introduced carpet-weaving, an occupation ideally suited for women as it enabled them to support their families while remaining in the privacy of their homes. More important, it was an occupation permitted by the mullahs, who disapproved of women leaving their homes to go to work.

Many of the refugees employed in the NGO carpet-weaving programmes came from tribes where the activity was not part of their heritage. For the most part, the pieces produced in these programmes were of inferior quality compared to those woven by the Turkmen and Uzbeks, whose legendary skill in weaving was passed down from one generation to another. I looked at some of the NGO carpets with a view to selling them in London, but they were poorly woven, the designs crude and childlike, the wool brittle and the colours too bright and harsh for Western taste. Unfortunately, so many NGOs jumped on the bandwagon and started carpet-weaving programmes that their storerooms were filled from floor to ceiling with largely unsalable rugs. Helena and I were well aware of the problem and began to think about an alternative project to carpet-weaving that would still allow the widows to remain in their homes.

As I sat in the London premises of Out of the Nomad's Tent one morning, surrounded by purchases from a recent visit to the Peshawar bazaar, I was

James Bond 007 (Timothy Dalton) and Kara (Maryam D'Abo) wearing Afghan costume which I bought in the bazaars of Peshawar for the film 'The Living Daylights'.

ACAF project manager, Mohammed Ali Tarshi with his son.

Bob Darr looking at oriental carpet designs.
(Photo courtesy of R. Darr.)

Tents for Afghan refugees beside the Chitral river.

The summit of the Khyber Pass. The plain of Peshawar can be seen in the distance.

Waiting for the Afghan border to open at Torkham on the day of Ghaffar Khan's funeral, with interpreter Mirwais, and Scheherezade Faramarzi.

A painted Afghan lorry at the Kyber Pass.

Khudai Khidmatgars ('Servants of God') on their way to attend the funeral of Ghaffar Khan.

The Afghan army escorting the cortège of Ghaffur Khan.

Firing a Kalashnikov in Dera Ismail Khan village, where guns of every description are crafted by hand.

Falcons captured in Afghanistan were in high demand in Saudi Arabia for hunting. This one was about to depart for Jeddah.

Francesca Stiles, me, and Lucy Fielden at the Private view of the Decorative Arts of Central Asia exhibition, Zamana Gallery.

With Khanullah and Bismullah's children at their home on the day I fell ill with bacterial menigitis in 1988.

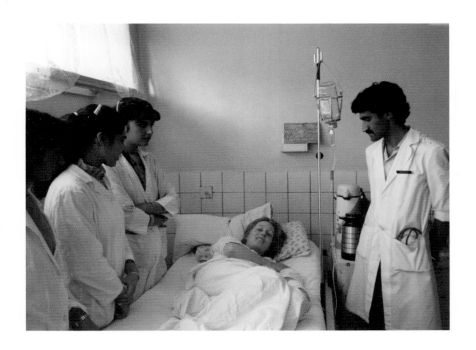

Above and right: In the intensive care ward at Jumhuriat Hospital, Kabul, very ill indeed.

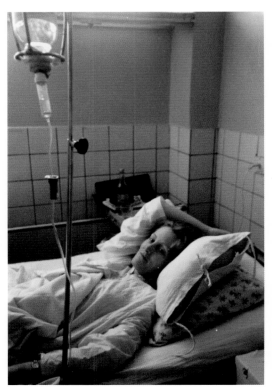

Invitation card to the exhibition at Joss Graham Gallery to raise money for the Jamhuriat Hospital,
showing textiles and jewellery from Afghanistan, Gardner porcelain and wood from the Swat valley.

Sometimes the Mujahideen would let me ride their horses before a Buzkashi match.

Friday's entertainment. Buzkashi match at Charsaddha refugee camp.

Jalil weaving on his 'pit' loom in his home in Pubbi Jalozai.

Gul Agha (in the red scarf) with children at the Pubbai Jalozai refugee camp.

*Ian McWilliam, Mohammad Gul (our chowkidar) and Mumtaz
make friends with a goat at the gates of 10 Canal Bank Road.*

An early morning ride with Fiona Gall.

Girls of the Kalash tribe in Chitral.

Jamilla, Tarshi's 18-year-old niece, assisting on the silk project in Peshwar.

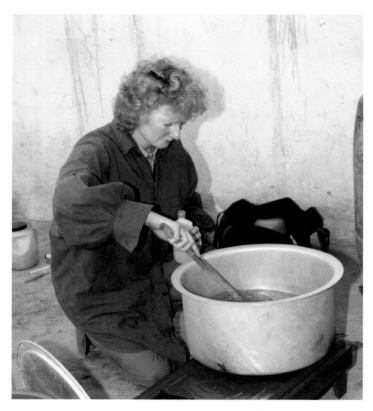

Jenny KilBride de-gumming silk at the ACAF office in Peshwar.

Dyed silk drying in the yard of the ACAF.

assailed by the uncomfortable thought that I was earning a living from other people's misfortune. The oriental carpets, textiles and jewellery I was selling were family heirlooms that the refugees had been forced to part with out of necessity and not from choice.

On a visit back to London from Peshawar, Helena told me about a family of silk-weavers living in a refugee camp south of Peshawar. She and I both knew about the ancient tradition of silk-weaving that had existed in Central Asia and Afghanistan. For well over a thousand years, silk had been traded between the two great empires of China and Rome, transported by merchants through the oasis towns along the Silk Road. We were particularly interested in *ikat*, an Indonesian word meaning 'to bind or tie', and used to describe the intricate and sophisticated form of resist-dyeing of yarn prior to weaving. This tying and binding of the yarn produces the extraordinary dramatic and blurred effect that is the most recognisable characteristic of *ikat* that is woven in countries as geographically diverse as Guatemala, Japan, India and Indonesia. However, the finest, most dramatic and exotic examples were those produced between 1800 and 1890 by the Turkmen weavers and Jewish dyers in the oasis towns of Khiva, Bukhara, Samarkand and the Ferghana valley, where it was referred to as *Abr*, meaning 'cloudy'.

Silk *ikat* was a luxury fabric, and its manufacture a closely guarded secret. It was worn by the powerful emirs of Central Asia and by wealthy merchants as a means of showing off their status within the community. The well-to-do often wore several coats one on top of the other. There were strict rules on the wearing of *ikat*, so those of a lower social standing wore clothing of a more inferior quality. The cloth, woven on narrow looms, was made into women's trousers and dresses, men's coats, curtains for yurts and covers for bridal beds. Scraps of *ikat* cloth were used as patchwork in household embroideries such as covers for the Qur'an, mirror bags and curtains to cover prayer niches. *Ikat chapans* (coats) and *khalat* (overcoats padded with cotton) were also given as prestigious gifts to honour a guest or as 'robes of honour' to reward achievements in battle.

In 1863, the Hungarian traveller and spy Arminius Vámbéry gave a vivid description of the Emir of Khiva paying Turkmen mercenaries in *ikat* robes for delivering the severed heads of his enemies. Disguised as a ragged dervish from 'Stamboul', Vámbéry entered Khiva and encountered a clerk (to whom he refers as an accountant) sorting four different kinds of brightly coloured silk coats, some with large flowers worked in gold thread. The clerk described the coats as four-head, twelve-head, twenty-head and forty-head coats. 'The most simple coats were a reward for having cut off four heads of enemies, and the most beautiful a recompense for forty heads.'[11] The following morning, he watched as a hundred horsemen arrived in the principal square of Khiva, covered in dust.

Each of them brought at least one prisoner with him, and among the number children and women also, bound either to the tail of the horse or to the pommel of the saddle; besides all which, he had buckled behind him a large sack, containing the heads of his enemies, the evidence of his heroic exploits. On coming up, he handed over the prisoners as presents to the Khan, or some other great personage, then loosened his sack, seized it by the two lower corners, as if he were about to empty potatoes, and there rolled the bearded or beardless heads before the accountant, who kicked them together with his feet until a large heap was composed, consisting of several hundreds. Each hero had a receipt given to him for the number of heads delivered, and a few days later came the day of payment. [12]

Helena and I made an appointment to visit the textile department of the Victoria and Albert Museum, which houses a fabulous collection of Central Asian *ikats* purchased new at the end of the 19th century and passed on to the museum via the India Office. The colours were as bright and vibrant as when they were first woven, but it appears that *ikat* was unappreciated by early travellers to the region, who found the designs quite outrageous and ostentatious; some even complained of the horrible colours. Vámbéry describes the Emir of Bohkhara's escort of high functionaries, distinguished by their snow-white turbans and wide silk garments, as 'more like the chorus of women in the opera of Nebuchadnessar than a troupe of Tartar warriors'.[13]

Since the 1920s a simple *ikat* design had been woven in Afghanistan, so Helena and I began to discuss the idea of setting up an income-generating *ikat* silk-weaving project in the camps.

Over the next two years, while I remained in London writing letters to aid organisations with the aim of raising funds, Helena set about carrying out research in Peshawar. One day she wrote saying that she had heard about a group of silk-weavers in a small village called Qurchangee in Jowzjan province in north-west Afghanistan. This group, who wove an unusual type of *ikat*, had featured in a documentary made by the French anthropologists Annie Zorz and Bernard Dupeigne in the 1960s. The film, said Helena, could be viewed in Paris and Bernard, now the curator of the Musée de l'Homme, would be able to tell us where we could view it.

On Helena's next leave, she came to stay at Finlay Street and we organised a trip to Paris to meet Bernard. Two journalist friends, Julian Gearing and Chris Hook, who had travelled many times with the Mujahideen, were planning to attend a UN conference on Afghanistan in Paris, so we arranged to travel together. Chris, a tall, handsome Aussie, offered to take Helena to Paris pillion on his motorbike. Very racy, I thought, and I was rather envious. Julian and I travelled by train.

Bernard greeted us in the foyer of the museum. He had arranged a special private viewing of the documentary for us at a small cinema down the road. As we left, he pressed a small pamphlet into my hands containing an article that he had written about the weavers of Qurchangee. It was illustrated with black-and-white photographs, one of which showed a small group of men dressed in striped *chapans*, white trousers, knee-length boots and turbans. Behind them it was just possible to glimpse their mud-brick homes with their beautiful domed roofs. The documentary told the story of the Qurchangee weavers, part of the exodus of a small group of Ulutepe Karaja Turkmen silk-weavers who during the 1930s had fled their farms in the rich alluvial plains around Samarkand to escape Stalinist repression and the famine brought about by the introduction of collective farming. They sought refuge in Faryab in Afghanistan, and were only able to regroup in villages insufficiently supplied with water. To support themselves and their families, they relied on women's carpet-weaving in addition to a little animal husbandry. Gradually the Turkmen moved west to Qurchangee and took up their old tradition of sericulture and silk-weaving, specialising in the production of head-shawls for women. During this time an Uzbek craftsman from Bukhara, Said Murad Urgunci, arrived at Qurchangee. There he taught some of his neighbours a technique they didn't know – the decoration of fabric by resist-dyeing the warps before weaving. During my travels in northern Afghanistan with Mary Burkett, it was quite normal to see men and women dressed in *ikat* clothing, particularly on Fridays as they congregated outside the mosques after prayers.

Bernard and Annie's documentary was fascinating, and we came away with the idea that, if we could locate the *ikat* weavers, then maybe they could pass on their knowledge and skill to a younger generation of Afghans.

A year later we received a letter from Bernard.

> ... I believe your project will be difficult to set up. The Turkmen refugees in Pakistan find they can make more money weaving carpets than weaving silk. Also I think you will have difficulty as women, but above all because of this – no one wants to abandon carpets for silk if one is not sure of earning as much. As for ikat, there remained extremely few craftsmen capable of making it in Afghanistan, and they haven't come to Pakistan. On the other hand Hadji Raouf, who used to make ikat in Afghanistan, is still living in Aqcha. He wrote to me asking if we would send money to help him. You might perhaps try to send him money through the bank and ask him to send you ikat.

I should have listened to Bernard's sound advice, but I was so intent on setting up a silk-weaving project that I couldn't accept I would not succeed.

Earlier in the year, Helena had been in touch with the NGO Intermediate

Technology in Rugby to ask if they knew of a silk-weaver and dyer who might come out to Peshawar to help us run the project.

'You should contact Jenny KilBride,' said director Martin Hardingham. 'She's an experienced silk-weaver and dyer with a silk-weaving and church vestment-making workshop near Brighton. She would be a good person to help you set up your project.'

I invited Jenny over for supper so that Helena and I could get to know her. During the meal she described her early life and upbringing, which seemed fascinating to us. Her family were part of a Roman Catholic arts-and-crafts community called the Guild of St Joseph and St Dominic, based in Ditchling, near Brighton. Founded at the end of the First World War by engraver and sculptor Eric Gill, the idea of the guild was based on the medieval notion of protection and promotion of artists' work and attracted wood-engravers, sculptors, printers, poets, painters, silversmiths and calligraphers who wished to share their Catholic faith in work and domestic life. Into this community of craftsmen, which included the painter and poet David Jones and printer Hilary Peplar, came Jenny's father Valentine KilBride, a silk-weaver and dyer, in 1924. He brought his looms and specialised in designing and producing ecclesiastical silk vestments. Jenny had inherited the workshop and her father's looms after his death in 1982. Virtually all her many siblings were silk-weavers.

Jenny mentioned that she was planning to visit Pakistan to see an old friend, now a Catholic priest working in Lahore. I told her about the silk available at the Peshawar sericulture centre, but as I was not a weaver myself I was uncertain of its quality. She said she would be more than happy to travel on to Peshawar and bring back some skeins of silk and then weave some samples in her workshop to assess its quality, and let us know if we could use it in our project. After she left, Helena and I agreed that, if we could raise the necessary money, Jenny would be the ideal person to help us set up the project.

One afternoon, Emma Porteous, the costume manager of Eon Productions at Pinewood Studios, rang to ask my advice. The company was making a new James Bond film, *The Living Daylights*, and they required authentic Afghan clothing for the Afghanistan sequences. I suggested that the simplest thing might be for me to travel out to Peshawar and buy the costumes myself. Emma thought this sounded an excellent idea.

'The producer will want to meet you, so I'll arrange for a car to bring you to Pinewood.'

The soft leather couch was comfortable and luxurious. I seemed to sink down in the cushions forever.

'Say, you're the girl who's going to Afghanistan to buy the Afghan costume?' Albert R. 'Cubby' Broccoli sat behind his desk drawing on a large Cuban cigar. A cloud of smoke billowed out and filled the space between us.

'Well, not Afghanistan exactly, but the North-West Frontier of Pakistan.'
He seemed a little confused. 'Not Afghanistan'?

'No. I can buy everything in the bazaar in the Old City of Peshawar.'

The production manager, Anthony Waye, handed Cubby a sheaf of papers.
He glanced through them, then pushed them towards me.

It was a list of clothing required for the film: shalwar kameez for 100
Mujahideen, 30 labourers and ten camel-drivers, clothes for 30 children,
and dresses for 70 women, as well as outfits for 'Bond', 'Kara' and various
assorted villains. I had never before bought such large quantities of clothing,
but I wasn't unduly worried. I felt confident that, with the help of my Afghan
contacts in the Peshawar bazaar, I would be able to buy everything in the time
required.

'OK,' said Cubby, leaning back in his chair and taking another drag on his
cigar. 'How much money are you gonna need?'

At that moment I wished I had an agent to negotiate on my behalf. I had
no idea how much I should ask for. Finally, we agreed on £1,100 for two weeks'
work, and a further £12,000 to cover the cost of the wardrobe. As filming
was due to start in Morocco, they needed everything by the second week of
August. It was already mid-July, so I would have to move quickly to get a visa
and air tickets. I made some suggestions to Tony Waye for additional clothing
such as Afghan *chapans*, waistcoats, Chitrali hats, *pattus*, embroidered caps and
Soviet belts, cap badges, badges of rank and other insignia.

'Emma says she wants the women's dresses to be second-hand. She doesn't
want them looking too new,' said Tony.

Word spread quickly through the studios that I was off on a buying mission.
As I was leaving, the props department waylaid me in the corridor.

'While you're out there, can you get these for us?'

A scrappy, hastily-typed list was thrust into my hand: 40 coloured horse
blankets, ten camel bridles and trappings, ten pairs of camel kneepads, six
wooden saddles for mules, a selection of coloured materials for bedding,
carpets and felts for luggage, rope panniers for the Red Cross parcels, wall
hangings, cushions, embroideries and rifle sling-covers.

'Oh, and while you're there, can you look for something diaphanous and
sexy for Kara? You know the sort of thing – see-through trousers and tops … '

I just laughed. They obviously had no idea how impossible it would be to
find anything diaphanous in a strictly Islamic society!

A few days later, the chauffeur from Pinewood arrived at Finlay Street with
£12,000 in cash in a brown envelope. I felt nervous carrying so much cash
on the number 74 bus as it wound its way through the streets of Fulham, and
clutched my handbag tightly on my lap.

'And where are you off to this time?' enquired Margaret, the cashier at Coutts bank in Knightsbridge, who knew all her customers by name. 'Somewhere exciting?'

She took the envelope and disappeared. Minutes later, the manager emerged. Whatever he thought about my wanting such a large amount of money converted into Thomas Cook traveller's cheques, he made no comment other than 'Would you like them in fifties or hundreds?' A few minutes later he reappeared holding a stack of traveller's cheques.

'These must all be signed before you can leave the building, but for your security, Miss Sandys – and I hope you don't mind – I am going to lock you in this little room.'

I bought my air ticket to Pakistan from Sajid, a Pakistani travel agent who ran a bucket shop in Piccadilly. I had used his agency many times in the past and he had never let me down, always finding the cheapest flights to India or Pakistan. He booked me on the overnight flight to Islamabad, which was perfect. Providing there were no delays during stopovers in the Middle East, I would arrive in time to catch the early-morning PIA flight to Peshawar. Then I would have a whole day ahead of me to start buying.

The monsoon rains had already arrived in the North-West Frontier, and the runway at Peshawar was like a sauna. Heavy rain fell from leaden skies, and the taxi and autorickshaw wallahs were wet and miserable as they touted for business in the airport car park. Wrapped in woollen *pattus*, grim-faced Afghan refugees sloshed through mud and puddles in oversized rubber galoshes. But I was happy to be back in a country I loved. For the next fortnight I would have to live with frizzy hair and damp clothes, but at least the rains had brought relief from the unrelenting summer heat.

Pausing only to check in and deposit my suitcase at Dean's Hotel, I made my way to Engineer Zabiullah's shop, situated down a side street in Saddar Bazaar. The shop was tiny and stocked just the usual textiles and jewellery that could be found in any Afghan shop in Peshawar. What made the shop special to me, however, was its proprietor. Gentle in manner and quietly spoken, Engineer Zabiullah was, like most Afghans, a victim of the war. In his homeland he had been a civil engineer, a well-educated man earning a reasonable salary and maintaining a good standard of living. Now a refugee, he was struggling to support his family by selling trinkets. He must have found his change in status humiliating, but never once in all the years that I knew him did he ever complain of his misfortune or lose his innate good manners and courtesy towards me.

His face beamed when I entered, and he greeted me as warmly as if I were a long-lost member of his own family. Before we could discuss business, he insisted on bringing tea and sugared almonds. For half an hour or so, we sat on the floor exchanging news – it would have been gross bad manners on my part to launch straight into business. Finally, I judged the moment right to explain about the James Bond film and the things I needed to purchase. Having only 14 days, I couldn't possibly buy everything on my own. So, I asked, could he shop around for me, in the next four to five days, for items that I required in bulk so that I could make a selection? It would save me an enormous amount of time and effort trawling through the bazaars in the rain when I had so much else to do. And I hoped to give Engineer Zabiullah some good business on which he could make a decent profit. Then I picked my way through puddles, dodging waterfalls cascading off the corrugated tin roofs, to the Makoo brothers in Murad market. The street was slippery with rotting refuse, the monsoon drain filled to overflowing with sour-smelling rubbish.

By the end of the day I had made good progress. Everyone had responded with enthusiasm, and I arranged to return in four or five days to make my final selection and discuss prices.

Having been on the go ever since leaving London, I decided to call it a day. At Dean's I had been given a small annexe at the back with a bathroom complete with a Victorian stone bath on claw-and-ball feet. Enjoying the luxury of a hot bath, I watched the geckos hang upside down from the ceiling using their sticky toes. From time to time their tongues would snap up an unfortunate fly. The annexe was large enough for me to store the goods before taking them to my shipping agent in the Old City, and had the added advantage that I could come and go with merchandise without the hotel staff observing my every move. It was also mango season and, for a small fee, the room boy brought me a bag of them. Unbelievably sweet and juicy, they could only be eaten leaning over a basin. I became completely addicted to them.

With so little time, everything had to be planned like a military exercise. Before leaving England, Emma Porteous had emphasised that the 70 women's dresses should look old and worn. 'I don't mind if they're used or in poor condition,' she had said. I harboured a romantic notion that I might be able to buy dresses direct from the Afghan women in the camp. I wanted them to benefit financially so they could buy themselves new clothes. The Tibetan managers of the Ockenden Venture offered to take me to a camp some distance from Peshawar. Their project manager would act as my interpreter.

The wet weather made the refugee camp appear even more bleak and depressing than normal. Children wearing thin cotton clothing sheltered from the rain by huddling together on string charpoys in open-fronted shops, their bare feet black with mud. The 4x4 bounced and slithered towards the small mud-walled dwellings. Sitting in the back seat, I gazed out of the window at this desolate scene and hoped the women would be pleased to part with their old dresses in exchange for money.

The women crowded round as the interpreter explained our visit. Their faces were tattooed with indigo, scarred by leishmaniasis (caused by the bite of the sandfly) and lined and weathered by hardship, and expressed undisguised suspicion. From the back of their mud hovel, they produced one ragged dress for which they wanted an exorbitant sum. It was then that I became aware of the awful reality of their situation. These women had arrived just a few weeks before from Logar and Paktia provinces, having fled their homes with just the clothes on their backs. They had no spare clothes to part with. I felt ashamed of my naivety.

Back in Peshawar I approached Grethe Laurensten, the manager of the Danish Sewing Project (Dacaar). She invited me to her office, but when I arrived she was in tears. Through her sobs I managed to grasp what had happened. That morning she had gone to collect the beautifully embroidered cloth and to pay the women for their work. As so often was the case when embroidery came in from the camps, it was dirty. The women had to fit in sewing work around their daily chores of cooking and looking after children, and it was often covered in ghee or flour. So it had to be washed. But the dye in the machine-made cloth was not fast and had bled into the embroidery.

'It's all ruined, and it is my fault. I cannot sell this now.' Tears coursed down her cheeks. 'My head office in Denmark will be angry with me for wasting so much money. They will sack me.'

'Don't worry, Grethe. I'll buy all this ruined embroidery, on condition your project can use it to make seventy dresses for me in ten days.'

She brightened instantly. 'Oh yes, we can do that!'

True to her word, Grethe produced the dresses on time. The payment for them more than covered the expense of the ruined cloth. As I still had to buy the Mujahideen costume, Grethe suggested I contact Afghanaid. So I met Bruce Wannell, who managed the Afghanaid office in University Town. He agreed that the tailors could sew 40 pairs of shalwar kameez in a week. 'But you'll need to select and buy the cloth first, and bring it here.'

In a side street just off Chowk Yadgar, shops sold cloth of a suitable camouflage hue such as the Mujahideen wore. I bought several bolts for the tailors, plus wool Chitrali hats in assorted colours, grey *pattus* and *keffiyeh*, the checked cotton headcloths introduced by Arab jihadists and adopted by the Mujahideen. Finally, I found a stall selling silk turbans in white, black and shades of grey to complete the Mujahideen outfits. Woven in the silk mills of Multan, they were over nine feet in length and utterly beautiful. I chose a black one for Bond.

The props department at Pinewood had asked me to find rope panniers for a scene in which Red Cross parcels filled with raw opium are transported on camels, but in all my visits to Peshawar I had never come across rope panniers and I was doubtful that I would find them. By a stroke of good fortune, however, on my last day in the town, I came across the perfect panniers in the jute bazaar.

My shopping almost complete, I returned to Engineer Zabiullah's shop in Saddar. There he had assembled piles of woven Baluchi camel headdresses decorated with pompoms, beads and tassels, and stacks of woven carpet covers for saddles. There were women's pleated 'shuttlecock' chadors, with the embroidered fitted headpiece and crocheted lattice grille, in shades of khaki, pale blue, royal blue and brown. A collection of beautiful striped silk *chapans* would be ideal for the diamond smugglers. To complete the outfits, I purchased waistcoats and a selection of the red tie-dyed scarves used by the Turkmen as cummerbunds around their *chapans*.

Tariq Sultan, my shipping agent, had an office in Chowk Yadgar, and in his dusty top-floor room I packed everything into aluminium trunks for transportation to England. The only thing I had failed to find in Peshawar was something diaphanous and sexy for Kara! In the end I bought a pale-blue shalwar kameez, the bodice intricately embroidered in white Kandahari stitch-work, which she wore in the film.

'Everyone is delighted,' wrote Anthony Waye on my return.

A year later, Eon Productions invited me to the private view of *The Living Daylights*. It was an emotional moment. The camels, their jute panniers loaded with Red Cross parcels, looked magnificent in their Baluchi headdresses and colourful trappings. The dresses sewn by the widows at the Danish Sewing Project from the ruined pieces of embroidery looked perfect on the women and children. James Bond, played by Timothy Dalton, galloped across the desert with the Mujahideen wearing the clothes sewn by the disabled Afghanaid tailors. The diamond smugglers wore the fabulous strippèd *chapans*. I thought of Engineer Zabiullah in his tiny shop in Saddar Bazaar, and of all my friends there who had given me so much help. Without them and the assistance of Afghanaid and Dacaar, I would never have been able to buy everything in just two weeks.

It was Helena who first introduced me to Anne Hurd in Peshawar, and I liked her immediately. When she stopped in London on her way back to the United States in July 1987 we discussed the silk project and I mentioned that Helena and I were looking for funding for Jenny KilBride. Anne thought this sounded like a project her organisation might support. She already ran The Mercy Fund, a US pro-Mujahideen charity in Peshawar, which she told me operated mobile basic-health units for women in the camps and tribal area. Together with her boyfriend Kurt Lohbeck, a cameraman and reporter for CBS News, they offered their home as a hostel to assist and brief newly arrived journalists. Helena stayed with them for a number of months when she first arrived in Peshawar.

Anne was tall, willowy and sophisticated, with something of the Southern belle about her. She was always elegantly dressed and never wore shalwar kameez, as many expats working in the camps did. Helena and I often wondered what she saw in Kurt, who dressed like a cowboy and seemed rather brash and opinionated.

On their next visit to London, Anne and Kurt invited me to breakfast in the Hyde Park Hotel to discuss the possibility of The Mercy Fund funding the silk-weaving project. The fund's Washington director wanted the organisation to get involved in income-generating projects for women and our silk project seemed ideal. While I liked Anne, I now had reservations about her organisation. Over the previous year, rumours had been circulating in University Town that The Mercy Fund (nicknamed 'The Murky Fund') was a front for the CIA and that no one in Peshawar had ever seen any of the basic-health units. It was said in some quarters that Kurt and Anne were biased in their unconditional support of the Mujahideen commander, Abdul Haq, who was a frequent visitor to their home, and believed he would make an ideal future president of Afghanistan. Intrigue, gossip, suspicion and jealousy were always swirling around in University Town, and it was almost impossible ever to get to the truth. I didn't want to believe the rumours, yet neither could I ignore a vague feeling of uneasiness. Warning bells were ringing.

It seemed to me, as I sat in the dining room of the Hyde Park Hotel eating scrambled egg on toast, that The Mercy Fund seemed to have an awful lot of money floating around and that maybe they were involved in something more than humanitarian aid. I left the hotel saying I would consider their kind offer and let them know.

I decided to consult Helena and wrote to her in Peshawar confiding my misgivings. For several years Helena, Jenny and I had worked hard to get the silk-weaving project off the ground – particularly Helena, who had contributed an enormous amount of time carrying out research in both Pakistan and England. Now that we were being offered funding, I suddenly felt anxious that we might lose control of the project. Helena agreed that we should politely decline Anne's offer, so I continued to search for funding. In Peshawar, an American friend, Nancy Jamieson, directed me to the offices of a small American NGO called Afghan Cultural Assistance Foundation. She thought the project manager, Mohammed Ali Tarshi, an Uzbek from an important family in the north of Afghanistan, might be able to help me find silk-weavers living in the camps.

The ACAF office was situated behind a row of oily auto-repair shops in the back streets of Shaheen Town. This was a largely residential area, almost entirely populated by Afghan refugees who were wealthy enough to pay rent and therefore escape living in the tented camps. By chance the American director, Robert Darr, had arrived that week from California and was staying at the office.

Bob Darr wasn't like any of the other Americans that I had met in Peshawar. For a start, he spoke fluent Persian and dressed in Afghan *pirhran-tombon*, quite unlike his compatriots who gossiped, rumour-mongered and drank beer from the bottle in the American Club bar. There was a quiet spirituality about Bob as he sat cross-legged on the floor, eating *qabuli pilau* with his right hand from a communal platter and conversing with ease in Dari with Mohammed Ali and his brothers, just like a member of the family. For a moment I wondered if he was a convert to Islam. Later, as I came to know him better, he confided that he had been studying Sufism, learning Arabic and reading the Qur'an for a number of years. He was on a spiritual journey, but had not yet made the decision to leave behind his own Catholic religion.

'We work with aid organisations sending medicines, vegetable seeds and humanitarian aid to Afghanistan,' he told me. 'We're currently involved in sending wheat to the centre and north of Afghanistan, which is experiencing a famine. We also support carpet-weavers in the refugee camps. The carpets are woven specifically for the American market, and the wool is dyed using natural dyes.'

Many NGOs had introduced carpet-weaving programmes in an attempt to provide work for refugees. The designs, drawn by an *ustad* on graph paper, guided the weaver in selecting the correct colour and exact number of knots to wrap around the warps, rather like painting a picture by numbers. The *ustad* often incorporated carpet motifs from Turkey, Iran, Afghanistan and Central Asia, producing a rug that bore little resemblance to the traditional Afghan ones. The weavers knew they would be paid a salary regardless of the quality of the work they produced, so carpets were often poorly woven, cockled and misshapen. Often 'dead' wool, taken after a sheep had been slaughtered, was used. It was cheaper to use this than the imported merino, but the wool was brittle and lacked lustre, resulting in the fibres breaking and shedding. So, much as I should have liked to, I never bought rugs from NGOs. I preferred the traditional and authentic designs of Afghan tribal rugs woven by the Turkmen and Uzbeks who brought their pieces direct to the bazaar in the Old City. The amount of money the weavers could earn depended on the quality of the carpets, so there was an incentive for them to produce high-quality workmanship. Many were exceedingly fine and beautifully woven. Neverthless, I asked to see the rugs being woven for ACAF, thinking they might be suitable to sell in Out of the Nomad's Tent.

Mohammed Ali unlocked a nearby storeroom. Carpets were piled high from floor to ceiling. As he pulled out a few to show me, I could see that the designs were reminiscent of Pakistani carpets and bore little resemblance to traditional Afghan or Persian designs. While the blue and green colours were attractive, the quality and design were not suitable for the London market or my British customers. I was intrigued, however, to know whether these carpets sold well in America.

'Oh, yes,' Bob assured me. 'They're particularly popular with interior decorators who don't want the traditional red Afghan rugs.'

These were early days in the production of vegetable-dyed carpets. By the beginning of the 1990s, in response to increasing demand from the Western market for carpets with muted colours to fit in with modern neutral colour schemes, weavers in Iran and Afghanistan began to change from dyeing wool with the popular synthetic dyes used since the mid-19th century to using vegetable dyes and mordants. With madder root, they could produce a soft red colour that was more pleasing to European taste than the harsh reds produced by the chemical dyes so popular in Afghan rugs. The various roots and plants were indigenous to Afghanistan and easily available, and carpet production blossomed. The vegetable-dyed wool rugs seen today in homes throughout the world are often referred to as *chobi*, from the Farsi meaning 'wood', a reference to the natural colours created by vegetable dyes, or 'Ziegler', the name of the design produced by Ziegler & Co, a German company based in Manchester, in 1883. Ziegler & Co commissioned leading designers and master weavers from Iran and Europe to create carpets for the European market with a softer palette. Today in Afghanistan the name continues to be used to describe the traditional Persian Sultanabad design woven by Afghans from hand-spun vegetable-dyed Ghazni wool.

I took the opportunity to discuss with Bob and Tarshi what help they could give me in locating silk-weavers in the camps. Tarshi felt sure he could find weavers amongst the Turkmen and Uzbek communities. He was knowledgeable about silk production as his own family had been involved in spinning and weaving silk in Afghanistan, and he agreed to make enquiries in the camps and keep me informed. At last I felt I was making progress and left the ACAF office with a sense of euphoria. I felt that ACAF was an organisation I could work with. This eventually proved to be the case, but it would be several years before the project got under way.

CHAPTER 5

Garam Chashma, Chitral
October 1987

It was early autumn and I was in Peshawar to buy Christmas stock for Out of the Nomad's Tent. Helena and I decided to take a short break during one of the frequent religious holidays and travel over the Lowari Pass to Chitral.

The small village of Garam Chashma lay two hours north-west of the town of Chitral. Located close to the Afghan border, its name means 'hot springs', and sulphurous water boils out of fissures in the earth's crust. In such a geologically volatile region, it was not unusual to feel the ground beneath your feet shake with small tremors each day.

We hitched a lift in the back of a Suzuki pick-up, and bounced and lurched up a dirt road that had been made by blasting out the granite rock face of the Lutkho River gorge. Far below us the ice-blue water of the turbulent river tumbled and foamed in a series of spectacular waterfalls and whirlpools. From time to time we had to duck to avoid overhanging ledges as the Suzuki hugged the rock face in which the marks of pneumatic drills were still visible. The road was so narrow that two vehicles could pass only with the greatest difficulty. When vehicles did meet, as was inevitable on this sole route in and out of Garam Chashma, passengers in the outside vehicle at the edge of the ravine were afforded a heart-stopping view of the swirling river below.

A vast mountain range covered with snow towered over the village (behind which lay Badakshan), blocking out sunlight so that the main street, lined with small wooden shops, chaikhanas and restaurants, remained icy with frozen slush and dank even at midday. Being so close to the Afghan border, the small bazaar was an important staging post for the Mujahideen, who would take time out from fighting the Russians to walk over the mountains to buy necessary supplies, weapons and packhorses in the bazaar.

Not a woman was to be seen as Helena and I made our way through the bazaar, ignoring hostile stares from the men, until we found ourselves at the far end of the village. On a flat piece of dusty ground the size of a football pitch, young men and boys were playing an energetic game of donkey polo. A crowd had gathered to watch, whooping and jeering as the boys tried to get their stubborn mounts to turn this way and that in pursuit of the ball. Some donkeys offered a quick uncomfortable trot, while others steadfastly refused to move at all.

We wandered further up the valley to where groups of Uzbek and Tajik Mujahideen were busy attending to their pack animals. Horses were being shod, and others were standing hobbled and clothed in heavy felt rugs made of sheep's wool to prevent them from growing thick winter coats. This was important because otherwise the horses, when loaded up with weapons and provisions, would sweat profusely as they picked their way through the rocks and boulders on the steep narrow trails and mountain passes leading into Afghanistan. At night, when temperatures dropped, a horse standing still with a thick wet coat would be liable to catch a chill. Excessive sweating also caused the loss of essential electrolytes – vital salts such as sodium, chloride and potassium – which could result in muscle stiffness, dehydration, colic and even death.

A vast, yellow full moon hung in the night sky as we made our way back to Hotel Innjigaan, built for tourists visiting the hot springs. The indoor swimming pool, normally full of hot sulphurous water, was drained and empty. It was now October, and the hotel was closed for the winter. Apart from a visiting journalist, we were the only guests. Winter was fast approaching, and we knew that snow would soon close the Lowari Pass, the only road in and out of the Chitral valley. Up in the mountains there had been a heavy snowfall overnight and even now it might not be possible for us to make the return journey by road. I suggested to Helena that I return to Chitral to book us both seats on a PIA flight back to Peshawar, leaving her to enjoy an extra day at Garam Chashma.

As we walked down the hotel drive to search for a 4x4 to take me down the valley, we stopped for a moment on the bridge that straddled the fast-flowing river. Fuelled by snow-melt from the peaks above Garam Chashma, the glacial water thundered over the boulders with a deafening roar. Our attention was drawn to a group of nomad women and children camped close to the water's edge. The women wore heavy, dark-purple ankle-length velvet dresses with wide sleeves covered in gold brocade and silver thread, their heads covered by similarly embellished heavy velvet dupattas. We had seen dresses like these in shops in Shinwari Plaza, but we had never actually come across Afghan women wearing them. We longed to get closer for a better look at their costume, but held back out of respect. Eventually we sat on a rock and surreptitiously observed them from afar. A woman filled a blackened kettle from the river to make tea. Small children sat in the sand while older ones searched for sticks to make a fire. A few of the women began to roll up bedding and pack away their belongings. The small group must have arrived from Afghanistan the day before and camped that night beside the river.

A white Suzuki pick-up truck was parked on the edge of the main road. An elderly Afghan man, wearing a snow-white turban, a waistcoat and a long plain *chapan* woven from camel hair, was helping the nomad women into the back. I hesitated, but he beckoned to me and invited me to sit with the women for the journey to Chitral. They were refugees from Afghanistan and had walked for 40 days through the mountain passes to escape the fighting. A month earlier, they told me, they had been attacked by Russian helicopter gunships as they struggled through snow-filled mountain passes. Their bright clothing and camel caravan had been easily visible, and they had proved an easy target for the Russian helicopter pilots. Of the 80 people who started the journey, more than half had been killed.

The elderly man tied my backpack on the flat tailgate of the Suzuki alongside a spare tyre and their bedding rolls, and indicated I should climb in and sit with the women. More men climbed aboard and seated themselves cross-legged on top of the bedding rolls and my backpack. Eventually we were all crammed together, men, women and children. I didn't mind being squashed up against the men as this was a family group and I just felt honoured that I had been accepted by them and included in the pick-up.

As the vehicle moved off, a fine white dust billowed up from the wheels and covered us. Hair turned white, eyes became bloodshot. The old man reached inside his waistcoat and pulled out a small dried apricot, a sliver of onion and a small piece of *qurut*, hard dried cheese made from fermented yoghurt, which he offered to me on the palm of his gnarled hand. Even in that moment of utter bleakness, as the family was leaving Afghanistan possibly forever and travelling into an unknown future, the Afghan tradition of offering hospitality to the guest was not forgotten. It was a humbling moment. As the road descended into the gorge and the snow-capped peaks above Garam Chashma gradually disappeared behind the horizon, the nomad women started to wail in distress at leaving their homeland.

The pick-up swung around the hairpin bends. Unaccustomed to the motion of the vehicle, one by one the children started to suffer from car sickness and vomited over the side. Soon the adults were affected too. The women held their heavy dupattas to their mouths and quietly retched while the men leant out over the tailgate and heaved out the contents of their stomachs into the swirling dust just as the wheels of the vehicle went over a rock in the road. The vomit soared up into the air, where it hung suspended for a second or two before falling back to earth, spattering my backpack in half-digested yellow dal. It was a miserable journey.

Eventually the Suzuki drew up beside the river on the outskirts of Chitral. Cold and stiff, we climbed out of the back, but the children were too shaken and traumatised; they just sat bewildered and unable to move. I lifted two little girls out of the 4x4 and sat them down beside the road. They weighed next to nothing and were undoubtedly malnourished; I could feel their bones through their thin, vomit-sodden flowered dresses. Forlorn and shaking uncontrollably, they crouched where I placed them, one of them urinating into the sand.

The moment had come for the refugees to pay for the journey. The driver, surveying the vomit in the back of his pick-up with an angry scowl, was further incensed by the streaks of yellow dal, which had now dried hard to the sides of his vehicle. He demanded 350 rupees from the elderly headman, which even to me seemed an excessive amount. I intervened.

'You're charging them too much. They're Afghan refugees and have lost everything. Let me pay for their journey.'

The driver pushed me away irritably, saying 'It's none of your business'.

I hung around on the periphery of the group, hoping my presence would persuade the driver to lower his demand. Eventually a price of 250 rupees (about £6) was agreed, and I left the group making their way slowly down the river bank to the shingle beach where they would camp for the night. War can bring out the best or the worst in people, and I could only feel anger towards the driver for taking advantage of the refugees' vulnerability. He was not unique – there were many at this time who took the opportunity to make money from people rendered powerless by events beyond their control.

In the comfort of the Tirich Mir hotel, I watched the glow of the refugees' campfires across the river. The flames flickered in the cold inky dark for about two hours and then went out.

Helena arrived later that evening, having been given a lift in a pick-up coming down from Garam Chashma. Early the next morning we went out into the bazaar and purchased parcels of *kishmish*, raisins mixed with dried nuts, tea and sugar, and made our way to the refugees still camped on the stone shingle where I had left them the night before. They were either too exhausted or too confused to acknowledge our gift, so we thrust the food into their hands and left. We could only hope that some aid organisation would come to their rescue and provide them with tents and food.

Two months later, on a dark December afternoon, I was back behind my desk in Out of the Nomad's Tent when the bell above the door jangled frenetically and a tall, elegant lady with an abundance of red hair entered the shop. Jane De'Athe, Artistic Director of the Zamana Gallery, had come to ask if I would be interested in staging an exhibition of textiles from Central Asia, the North-West Frontier and Afghanistan.

The Zamana Gallery is part of the (then) recently-built Ismaili Centre, a large grey marble building on Brompton Road opposite the Victoria and Albert

Museum. It specialised in exhibitions of Islamic art. Jane and I had met the previous year during a private view of *A Thousand and One Nights*, an exhibition of photographs of Sind taken by the renowned French photographers Roland and Sabrina Michaud. I had lent some cushions, embroidered by the Rabari tribe who lived in the Thar Desert in southern Pakistan, to give colour to the exhibition. I already knew all about the Michauds. One of my most treasured possessions is their book *Caravans to Tartary*, a stunning collection of photographs recording their travels in 1970 with Kirghiz nomads during their annual migration through the Wakhan valley in north-eastern Afghanistan. To finally meet them at the Zamana was a great privilege.

Jane's offer was a wonderful opportunity, and I felt extremely honoured to be asked to exhibit at such a prestigious location, but in reality I was very small fry compared to all the big names in the tough, competitive world of antique textiles and oriental carpets. I thought long and hard about Jane's offer, but decided that organising an exhibition of such a calibre on my own would be too much.

I knew from working with Joss Graham that he would be the ideal person to share the exhibition. Not only had he been in the oriental textile business a long time, but also he was particularly knowledgeable about embroideries and artefacts from Central Asia and Afghanistan. I sounded him out, and he agreed. *The Decorative Arts of Central Asia* would run for two months, from 11 May to 10 July 1988.

Needing to buy stock for the exhibition, I decided to fly back to Pakistan immediately after Christmas so that everything would arrive in time for the start of the exhibition. I would also be able to catch up with Helena and hopefully make some progress on the silk-weaving project. An old school friend, Lucy Fielden, was coming along for the adventure; she and I had known each other since we were 12 at Lawnside and I was looking forward to her companionship.

CHAPTER 6

Jalalabad, and Death in the Swat Valley
January 1988

The weather in Karachi was perfect, the clear deep-azure skies a welcome change from cold, grey England. Neither Lucy nor I had much money, so we booked into the Shalimar, a cheap hotel not far from Zainab market. We shared a room, with stained mattresses and sheets that looked as though they hadn't been washed in weeks. The pale-blue walls were splattered with red streaks, as if someone had been murdered; the previous occupants had obviously been chewing paan leaves and betel nut and had used the walls for target practice.

For a few days Lucy and I browsed happily through the covered bazaar that sold everything: carved onyx, dried fruit, cheap cotton clothes and antique copper and brass. I had come to visit Kishor Kumar Maheshwari, a Hindu merchant whose family originated from Jaipur in neighbouring Rajasthan. Kishor held a stock of beautiful embroideries from Sind, the Thar Desert and the Rann of Kutch. The cushions that had decorated the Michauds' exhibition at the Zamana had all been purchased from his shop. On previous visits, Kishor had promised to take me on a buying trip to the desert villages in Sind, but now was not the time as Lucy and I were in a hurry to reach Peshawar and planned to visit Quetta en route.

After eight hours travelling by bus through bleak, stony desert we arrived in Quetta, the provincial capital of Baluchistan. The name Quetta comes from the Pushto word *Kwatta*, meaning fort. Before 1947 the town was a popular station of the British Army. Set in a mountainous amphitheatre on a geological fault line, the city was all but destroyed in 1935 when an earthquake killed some 40,000 people.

The British NGO Health Unlimited offered us a room in their large house in Satellite Town, a residential area high on a hillside above the dust and pollution of Quetta with magnificent views of the dun-coloured mountains of Baluchistan. Automatic gunfire from the garden below filled the air for most of one afternoon as a family celebrated the birth of a boy. As Lucy and I sat on the veranda writing letters home, we watched the red tracer shooting up, arcing and descending to earth, and tried hard not to think of where the bullets might land. A year before in Peshawar, a Frenchman playing tennis at the American Club had narrowly missed death when a plummeting bullet gouged his cheek; it could so easily have come down through the top of his skull.

The next day we roamed up and down Zarghoon Road, the main high street, visiting carpet shops and buying kilims and woven saddle bags. The atmosphere in Quetta was tense and strained. Tired and thirsty, we went into a back-street chaikhana. The chaiwallahs were busy plying back and forth between the tables and a large 19th-century brass Russian samovar in the corner, where they filled colourful cracked porcelain teapots with boiling water for green tea. The teapots and small round teacups, known as Gardner (pronounced 'Gardeenair' by Afghans), were well over a hundred years old but still in use. In the 18th century an Englishman, Francis Gardner, founded a manufactory near Moscow that produced porcelain dinner services for Empress Catherine the Great. The porcelain was stamped on the base with the Russian imperial eagle above the Muscovite coat of arms of Saint George killing the dragon. With increased Russian expansion into Central Asia in the 1870s, the bazaars in the oasis towns along the Silk Road provided lucrative outlets for Russian merchandise. Mass-produced Gardner teabowls, teacups and teapots with oriental designs, sometimes with Arabic inscriptions painted in gold around the inner edge of the bowls, were transported thousands of miles across inhospitable desert to the various Khanates. Gardner porcelain became highly prized by nomads and merchants alike, and was passed down the generations. The pieces were much cherished as status symbols, so much so that, if one was cracked or damaged, it was carefully and meticulously repaired with metal rivets. When Uzbeks and Turkmen fled across the Amu Darya River to Afghanistan in the 1920s to escape a guerrilla uprising against Soviet repression, they brought their Gardner porcelain with them and now the cups and teapots could be found in chaikhanas the length and breadth of Afghanistan. As I sipped my tea from the ancient cup, I thought of the long journey it had made from Moscow across the steppes of Central Asia to its resting place in a chaikhana in a back street in Quetta. If it could speak, what tales it could tell!

The other occupants of the tea house were a collection of wild-looking hawk-nosed Mujahideen on rest and recuperation from fighting the Russians near Kandahar. They wore enormous black silk turbans and sported luxuriant black beards and moustaches, and scowled at us menacingly across the tables, their eyes rimmed with kohl. We didn't know it then, of course, but in the years ahead they would come to be called the Taliban.

Poring over a map of Pakistan one evening, we contemplated travelling to the North-West Frontier by bus via the Bolan Pass and on through the tribal territory of Waziristan. However, everyone in the Health Unlimited house said it was too dangerous for foreigners, particularly two women travelling without a male escort. In the end, we bought tickets on a PIA domestic flight, and flew high above barren desert scarred by flash floods, with sunlight glittering off white salt pans. Below us lay the harsh terrain and mountains of Waziristan, a wild, lawless area of Pakistan. An hour later we touched down in Peshawar.

Kurt Lohbeck and Anne Hurd offered us accommodation on the top floor of their comfortable house on Khushhal Khan Khattak Road in University Town, which they operated as a hostel for visiting journalists. Also resident was Steve Masty, who managed the American Club. I had met Steve many times over the years on my visits to Peshawar. A large man with a personality to match, Steve was an extraordinarily gifted and talented musician, singer, freelance journalist and author, who had once written speeches for Ronald Reagan and had a degree in Scottish literature. He kept us entertained in the evenings at the club playing the guitar and singing his own witty songs about the Afghan Mujahideen.

It wasn't long before I was introducing Lucy to the shops of Abdul 'Muallem' Makoo and Engineer Zabiullah. For the next few days we wandered through the bazaars in the Old City buying textiles, carpets and artefacts for the Zamana exhibition.

Despite snow on the mountains, I wanted to visit the Swat valley to buy carved wooden furniture for the Zamana exhibition from shops in the small towns of Mingora, Khwazakhela and Madyan. I knew Lucy would find the trip interesting, so we boarded the local bus bound for Mingora. On our first night in Swat we booked into a cheap hotel on the main street. As I was unpacking my rucksack, Lucy went to the bathroom for a shower and let out an ear-splitting yell – a man's face was peering down at her through the ventilation shaft! By the time I got to the outside landing, the culprit had fled, leaving behind the chair on which he had been standing. As we checked out of the hotel en route for Madyan, further up the Swat valley, we made a formal complaint. The manager just smirked.

The weather was bitterly cold. The mountains, covered in fresh snow, sparkled against the crystalline sky. The aroma of kebabs barbecuing on a charcoal brazier wafted on the piercingly crisp air and made our mouths water as we sloshed through mud and slush down the high street of Madyan.

The only heating in our hotel room was a single-bar electric heater that only functioned when the hotel's diesel-fuelled generator roared into life for a few hours each day. That evening we ate chappali kebabs in the local chaikhana, the grease sticking to the roofs of our mouths. With only the light of the moon illuminating the silent streets, we walked back from the restaurant in near-darkness, slipping and slithering in the slush. The generator was quiet, the electric heater dead. We settled down for the night in the ice-cold hotel room, fully clothed inside our sleeping bags.

For breakfast the next morning, the hotel manager brought us hot *paratha* – a kind of chapatti fried in ghee – a boiled egg and a cup of sweet milk tea. Fortified for the day ahead, we made our way on foot up the valley to the godown of Friends Corporation.

The warehouse – always referred to in Pakistan as a godown – was situated high up on the hillside behind the smart Madyan Tourist Hotel. Wooden furniture from the Swat valley was piled high, carved wooden chests, tables and chairs stacked on top of one another. In the dark and dank interior, Lucy and I sat on the mud floor sorting through carved wooden bowls that back in England I sold as fruit bowls. Each one had to be carefully inspected for repairs, cracks and damage by rats. The bowls were traditionally used for mixing flour and water to make bread, and some still retained a residue of caked-on dough, which the rats loved; their tooth-marks could be clearly detected around the edges, and their droppings were everywhere.

We found strings of carved wooden amulets into which had been inserted tiny scraps of folded paper with written prayers or astronomical calculations said to ward off evil. These amulets were tied around the necks of cows and goats to protect them from illness and disease. There were Qur'an stands and small carved wooden chests with sliding doors for storing clothing and belongings. Resting against the walls were huge, intricately carved columns used to support the roof beams of homes and mosques. Made from the single trunks of deodar pines, these columns decorated with carved Corinthian, Ionic and Doric scrolls resembled those found in ancient Greek temples, another reminder of Swat's Græco-Bactrian past. Finally, I bought two columns and a giant 19th-century carved wooden mosque door which would, I hoped, be the centrepiece of the Zamana exhibition. Its sill had been worn down by the feet of the many thousands who, over the years, had entered the mosque to pray.

Later, the owner of the hotel invited us for a lunch of freshly caught trout. Lucy and I sat in warm winter sunshine on the veranda, poised high above the raging waters of the Swat river, eating fried fish and chips and listening to the thunderous roar as the river made its way south down the valley.

Back in Peshawar, one crisp, cold morning as we stepped down from the Afghan bus outside the gates of Lady Reading Hospital close to the entrance of the covered bazaar, we learnt of the death of Abdul Ghaffar Khan from our friend, Susie Howman.

I'd first met Susie a year before at Hever Castle, near Penshurst in Kent, where I was selling Afghan carpets to raise money for Sandy Gall's Afghanistan Appeal (SGAA), a charity he founded in 1983. Susie arrived driving a tiny white van, but she had an ulterior motive: to ask Sandy for a job with his charity in Peshawar. After the sale, when Susie opened the door to her van I saw the interior was filthy, covered in feathers and bird droppings.

'What on earth have you been transporting in this?' I asked, recoiling from the stench.

'Pheasants,' she replied.

Her father, Keith Howman, was Director General of the World Pheasant Association, and he and his wife Jean reared endangered and exotic game birds at their home in Kingston upon Thames. The association had recently released pheasants into the Margalla Hills overlooking Islamabad, so Susie was keen to go and work on the North-West Frontier.

Her bold initiative at Hever Castle had paid off. She was now working as an administrative assistant for Sandy's charity, which operated a prosthetic workshop in the basement of the Lady Reading Hospital treating mine victims, amputees, and patients with polio, club foot and other disabilities.

'Bacha Khan died in the early hours of this morning in the Lady Reading Hospital,' she announced.

Bacha Khan, she explained, meant King of Chiefs, and was a nickname for Abdul Ghaffar Khan, a colleague of Mahatma Gandhi, who had been a thorn in the side of the British during the days of the Raj. He had campaigned tirelessly for a homeland for the Pushtuns, and spent 40 years of his life in jail or in exile.

Susie had heard all about him from the physiotherapists working for SGAA in the Lady Reading Hospital.

'He's so revered here that his body will lie in state for two days in Jinnah Park before being taken across the Khyber Pass into Afghanistan. He's going to be buried in Jalalabad, and foreigners will be issued with special visas to allow them to attend the funeral. I'm going to go. Why don't you and Lucy come, too?'

I said we'd give it some thought.

Lucy and I moved on through the crowded covered market of Ander Sher, with its shops selling gold jewellery for Muslim brides, past the entrances to Shinwari Plaza and Murad market, before crossing the busy Chowk Yadgar to the open-fronted booths of the money changers. Neither of us had any local currency left and we needed to change some traveller's cheques. The money changers, all fat and prosperous, sat crossed-legged on raised concrete platforms surrounded by black cash-boxes, counting wads of afghani and rupee notes in full view. They gave a good rate and transactions were carried out more quickly than in the bank.

There was never any privacy when it came to changing money as this part of Peshawar was always crowded, like London's Portobello Road market on a Saturday morning. The mere sight of a Western woman changing money attracted men and boys, and the spectacle of me fumbling to extract traveller's cheques hidden in my money belt under layers of clothing was too good an entertainment to miss. They would stand gawping and staring, watching my every move. However, on this particular day news of Bacha Khan's death had spread throughout Peshawar, and mourners wearing the distinctive pillar-box-red clothing of the Awami Party were pouring into Chowk Yadgar from narrow side streets. Many of the tribesmen were weeping openly.

Lucy and I joined the jostling crowd waving their party banners as they made their way to Jinnah Park to pay their respects to their beloved leader. Below the battlements of the Bala Hisar fort, we crossed the Grand Trunk Road intersection and entered the large municipal park, where on warm summer evenings it was usual to see youths playing cricket, parents strolling with their children and families picnicking on the grass. Now a chill wind blew down from the Khyber Pass, whipping up torn sheets of newspaper and black plastic bags that danced and swirled across the road and got caught in the scrubby thorn bushes. A few drops of rain fell, black clouds were rolling in from Afghanistan and a faint rumble of thunder in the distance heralded an approaching storm. The normal occupants of the park, the picnicking families and cricketing youths, had been replaced by thousands upon thousands of banner-waving Awami Party members. A wave of red spread across the park as far as the eye could see. Following the crowd, we soon found ourselves alongside the raised dais on which Ghaffar Khan's body lay in state in an open coffin.

A sudden flash of fork lightning was followed instantly by a deafening crack of thunder. Icy rain fell with the ferocity of a monsoon deluge, and within seconds Lucy and I were soaked. As we joined the mourners leaving the park in search of shelter, we couldn't help noticing that their hastily dyed clothing, now sodden, was leaking red dye. From their pillbox hats, rivulets of dye ran down their faces and dripped from their noses like blood from a head wound. It was difficult to ignore the impression that some terrible massacre had just taken place.

The American Club was always the best place to hear the latest news, and that evening the conversation around the bar was all about the forthcoming funeral. The journalists confirmed that there would be a four-day truce between the Mujahideen and the Afghan communist regime to allow the funeral cortège to cross the Durand Line at the border at Torkham so that Abdul Ghaffar Khan could be laid to rest in Jalalabad. Entry visas were being offered by the Afghan government to journalists and foreigners. Indeed, anyone could go as long as they obtained a visa from the Afghan consulate in University Town. I couldn't wait to go. To be present at such an historic event was an opportunity I was not prepared to miss. Susie, who had embraced life on the Frontier and was never one to turn down the offer of an adventure, was determined to go, too. She would travel with Whitney Azoy, an American freelance journalist and author; she wasn't sure how they would actually get to Jalalabad, but said they would find a way somehow, even if it meant hitching a lift with the mourners. Excitement was in the air and I took it for granted that Lucy would be up for the journey as well.

At breakfast the next morning I flicked through the *Frontier Post* and the *Times of Peshawar*. Both were dominated by news of Ghaffar Khan's death and gave vivid accounts of his life, how he championed the right of women to an education, built schools and madrassas, and encouraged the Pushtuns to turn away from the ancient culture of violence, vendettas and blood feuds that had dominated their way of life for centuries. He founded a political movement, the Khudai Khidmatgar, meaning Servants of God, based on Gandhi's notion of Satyagraha that opposed British rule in India through strikes, non-violent protests and mass civil disobedience. Inevitably this brought Ghaffar Khan into conflict with the British administration and he was repeatedly jailed. Known as the Gandhi of the Frontier, his ultimate goal was a united, independent, secular India and he became a respected member of the Indian National Congress Party fighting for freedom and independence.

Kurt Lohbeck and Steve Masty discussed the funeral and travel arrangements to Afghanistan. Kurt was intending to film the event for CBS News and offered Lucy and me a seat in their minibus. The funeral cortège was leaving at 7 am from Jinnah Park, so we would all leave at dawn, taking the road through the Khyber Pass to the border crossing at Torkham. The funeral was due to take place around 11 am, and Steve and Kurt estimated it would take us about three hours to travel the 90 miles to Jalalabad.

The Indian prime minister, Rajiv Gandhi, and his wife Sonia were flying in to Peshawar from New Delhi to pay their respects – the first time since 1947 that an Indian head of government had set foot on Pakistani soil. Lucy and I felt it was such an important event that we made our way again to Jinnah Park, pushing through the crowds to the open coffin just as the Gandhis arrived. Later that evening, on our way home to Khushhal Khan Khattak Road we stopped at the Afghan consulate to obtain our visas, and it was while Lucy and I were waiting in a queue for our passports to be stamped with an entry visa that we met Scheherezade Faramarzi, an Iranian journalist working for Associated Press.

'I have a spare seat in my car if you would like a lift to Jalalabad tomorrow,' she said. I thanked her, explaining that I would be going in Kurt and Steve's minibus.

'Well, if that doesn't work out, I'm staying at Dean's Hotel. Just give me a call.' And she wrote her room number on her business card.

Back at the house, we were met by Kurt at the front door.

'Steve and I have decided that you won't be travelling with us tomorrow,' he declared.

'But why not?' I asked, brandishing my passport. 'I have my visa for Afghanistan.'

'Because, Harriet, you are not a journalist or a war photographer. You're an oriental-carpet dealer. There may well be trouble at the funeral and we don't want to be responsible for you.'

'Fair enough, but no one need be responsible for me,' I replied hotly. 'I can take care of myself.'

'I've decided not to come with you,' Lucy then announced. She didn't feel well – flu, she thought. I respected her decision, but was sad that she wasn't coming. Despite this setback, I was determined to get to Jalalabad.

I telephoned Scheherezade. 'The Americans have decided I can't travel with them after all. Do you still have room in your car? It will only be me. Lucy's not coming.'

'Sure,' she replied. 'It will be great to have you with us. Gujar, the driver from Dean's Hotel, will be taking us with Mirwais, a young Pakistani student from Peshawar University, who is coming with us to act as my interpreter. Donatella Linari is coming, too; she works at the Italian tuberculosis hospital. But there's still room for you. Wait outside your house tomorrow at 5.30 am. We'll pick you up.'

I stepped out of the house an hour or so before dawn, and stood alone in the freezing dark beneath a vast clear night sky glittering with stars, hoping Scheherezade had not forgotten her promise of the night before. The muezzin had yet to call the *azan*, the early-morning call to prayer.

I waited on Khushhal Khan Khattak Road and listened to the familiar night sounds of Peshawar – a dog barking, a cockerel crowing and the firing of an AK-47 assault rifle. I watched the red and green tracer soar gracefully into the dark sky before falling back towards earth. A small pack of bickering, snarling feral dogs trotted by, far too intent on their mission to scavenge in the rubbish dump at the end of the street to pay much attention to me. I shivered, pulling my coat around me for warmth. Then I saw the welcome sight of headlights bobbing towards me as the car bumped across the potholes, and smiling faces at the window. In no time I was in the back seat, cosily sandwiched between Donatella and Scheherezade. Leaving University Town behind, Gujar carefully manoeuvred the car out into the busy Grand Trunk Road and turned north towards Jamrud Fort, which marks the entrance to the Khyber Pass leading to the Afghan border.

Gujar was lugubrious and unflappable, a veteran of chauffeuring journalists and war photographers around the Frontier. Before Partition in 1947, he would bring sahibs and memsahibs on sightseeing tours through the Khyber Pass.

As we climbed the hairpin bends to the summit, he pulled the car over for a moment so that we could look back and admire the view of the plain of Peshawar spread out below us, bathed in early-morning mist. Further on, he pointed out the regimental badges of British regiments carved into the hillside, and huge concrete anti-tank traps placed in the valley during the Second World War to prevent a possible incursion by the Germans. Descending round more bends, we passed the smugglers' bazaar at Landi Kotal.

We were early at the border crossing at Torkham, and there had been no sign of the funeral cortège on our journey through the Khyber. As we stood waiting for the iron gates into Afghanistan to open, the border guards insisted we have breakfast with them in their checkpoint up on the hillside. Soon we were sitting on string charpoys, warming cold hands on glasses of sweet milk tea and nibbling slices of bright-yellow sponge cake. Although it was dawn, the sun had yet to rise above the mountain peaks, so it was still bitterly cold. Even the soldiers of the Khyber Rifles, hardy men of the Frontier, had wrapped woollen scarves around their heads. At the foot of the hill, below the checkpoint, the Afghan-Pakistan border was a hive of activity. Suddenly we heard the sound of cheering, and rifle shots rang out.

'Quick! The funeral cortège has entered Afghanistan!' I said, catching a glimpse of the gun carriage bearing the body of Abdul Ghaffar Khan, just disappearing through the gates in a cloud of dust.

Abandoning our half-drunk glasses of tea, we raced out past bemused soldiers and down the hill to the roadside. An endless convoy of assorted vehicles – painted Afghan lorries, pick-ups, coaches and 1950s Chevrolets – was winding down from the Khyber Pass carrying mourners wearing the red berets and shirts of the Khudai Khidmatgars. There was a carnival atmosphere at the frontier, with mourners waving and cheering, vehicle horns blaring out the 'Colonel Bogey March', and red flags fluttering from windows and bonnets.

We urged Gujar to drive as fast as possible to catch up with the cortège. He put his foot down, and we shot through the gates at speed and joined the convoy. Through the open window I breathed in the cool, crisp, clean air of Afghanistan. My heart soared, and I felt euphoric. It was wonderful to be back.

The road to Jalalabad runs across a flat, semi-arid desert. That morning, away in the distance the colossal snow-capped peaks of the Hindu Kush towered above the dust haze, shimmering so brightly against the deep-blue cloudless sky that it hurt my eyes to look at them. Bombs placed in culverts had destroyed many bridges along the way, so we bounced and jolted across dried-out riverbeds. Just past Samarkhel, we spied some bored-looking Afghan conscripts lounging on the gun turrets of their Soviet-built tank parked by the road. Scheherezade, in journalist mode with notebook and pen in hand, instructed Gujar to turn off into the desert so that she could interview them.

The soldiers' faces brightened up no end when we asked if we could pose with them for a photograph. They seemed genuinely delighted to be visited by three foreign women in their lonely outpost, and invited us to sit on their tanks, saying that they were only sorry they couldn't offer us tea. Interviews concluded, we were off again, mingling with the assorted vehicles of the mourners.

The Afghan regime had sent soldiers and hundreds of Sikh men and boys to line the 30-mile stretch of road between Torkham and Jalalabad to welcome the 50,000 or so tribesmen attending the funeral. They stood for mile after mile, smiling and waving at the motorcade as it passed by. I was intrigued to know why there were so many Sikhs in Afghanistan, and asked Gujar.

'Many, many Sikh people living in Afghanistan,' he explained. 'Coming from Peshawar. Stay here in Afghanistan at Partition time. Not want to make journey to Punjab because many Hindu and Muslim people being killed at that time.'

The Soviet-backed Afghan regime was treating the whole funeral as a public-relations exercise. Every now and then there would be a break in the crowd to reveal a man dressed in a white doctor's coat seated at a small table beside the road, stethoscope around his neck, pretending to administer to a patient. The three of us could only laugh at the clumsy communist propaganda.

Gujar parked his taxi beneath tall pine trees alongside the vehicles of other mourners, many of whom had arrived in buses from Peshawar. We joined the funeral procession down an avenue lined with giant pines towards the burial site in Sheesham Bagh, the beautiful walled orchard given to Ghaffar Khan by the Afghan government in 1946. During his years in exile, Jalalabad had been his home and the orchard was to be his final resting place.

In the orchard, it crossed my mind that there was still no sign of Kurt or Steve. It was only after the bomb exploded that I saw them. We were anxiously running towards the gate in the wall, fearful for the safety of Gujar and Mirwais, who we had left sitting in the taxi an hour before, when I came face to face with Kurt as he came bursting in through the gate, swinging his television camera wildly from side to side in his endeavour to film the scene. My instant impression was that he didn't seem very au fait with operating the camera, and I marvelled that CBS News employed him.

'The funeral's finished. It's all over. You've missed everything,' I said, feeling a certain malicious satisfaction that I had made it to Jalalabad and witnessed the funeral in its entirety, whereas Kurt, who had refused to take me in his minibus, had missed it. In the car park, the windscreen of Kurt and Steve's minibus had been blown out and they had only missed by minutes becoming casualties themselves.

By the time Scheherezade filed her copy, the sun had begun to set. Curfew was not far off. For our safety the Afghan soldiers brought us to the Spinghar Hotel, now dormitory accommodation for Afghan soldiers. A young soldier brought cold, gritty rice and kidney beans, and set three plates down on an empty bed.

'I am sorry. This food is not nice. It is cold. It is soldier's food and kitchen is now closed for the night. If there was no war I would invite you to my home and my mother would cook very good Afghan meal for you,' he said apologetically.

Then he left us, locking the door behind him. In the morning, the door was unlocked and we emerged into the corridor crowded with shaven-headed Afghan soldiers preparing for duty. We joined a queue of them waiting to wash at a row of handbasins set into the wall. After living in Peshawar, I found it a strange experience to be washing alongside men who seemed so indifferent to our presence. Mirwais and Gujar approached us with broad smiles, none the worse after a night in a dormitory with the soldiers. What a relief to see them. Scheherezade had been particularly worried for the safety of 19-year-old Mirwais, having assured his mother that she would take care of him. By now, news of the bomb blast and casualties would have reached Peshawar and she must have been frantic with worry when he hadn't returned. The young soldier who had brought us food the previous evening escorted us out of the hotel and insisted on taking us to have breakfast at the local chaikhana before we departed for Peshawar.

'You cannot leave my country without me giving you a meal,' he said.

For the last 24 hours we had scarcely eaten anything, so we were ravenous and grateful for the fried eggs, tea and paratha. Then he guided us to the road leading out of town and bade us farewell. His honour had been satisfied, and he refused all offers of payment for the meal. Such is Afghan hospitality to the guest. With Gujar back behind the wheel, we headed out across the desert towards the Khyber Pass, carefully avoiding Russian T-32 tanks careering across the road from all directions.

Back at Khushhal Khan Khattak Road, I received a frosty reception. Lucy was pleased to see me, but the others thought I had been very irresponsible in staying overnight in Jalalabad, even though I explained that we'd had little option *but* to stay, the KHAD having placed us under house arrest for our own safety. I wasn't sure if their disapproval was genuine concern for my safety or had more to do with the fact that I had defied Kurt by making my own way to the funeral. He knew very well that I had witnessed the whole event, and was annoyed that he had missed it. At the American Club later that evening, Susie told me that she and Whitney Azoy had been given a lift in the minibus by Kurt, who had seen them trying to hitch a lift as they walked along the Grand Trunk Road. They had journeyed back to Peshawar with Kurt and Steve after the funeral, with a bitterly cold wind blowing through the smashed windscreen of the damaged minibus and a bunch of bananas bought for the journey splattered all over the interior.

March, and I was back home in Finlay Street, awaiting the shipment of wooden furniture from Swat and textiles purchased in Peshawar for the Zamana exhibition.

Bob wrote to me from California. There was a possibility, he said, that I could use the Afghan Cultural Assistance Foundation's no-objection certificate, which would enable the silk project to be run in conjunction with his carpet-weaving project. He suggested that some of the woven silk products could be sold in the US, but he also raised a number of concerns. He accepted that it might be necessary to have a European in charge of design and to manage certain aspects of the project, but the management should not be top-heavy with Europeans. It was essential that Afghan refugees should be the beneficiaries and paid fairly without a middleman, and if the project was to be managed by ACAF then any local management must be acceptable to Mohammed Ali Tarshi, his Uzbek project manager. Because ACAF was intending to move into the north of Afghanistan to work on various projects when the war came to an end, would the silk project be sufficiently mobile to be established in Afghanistan?

I wrote back answering Bob's queries and attaching a budget, which included living expenses and a salary for Jenny managing the project in Peshawar. I would raise the money in the UK through ARIN which, being a registered charity, would give the silk-weaving project more credibility. A month later Bob wrote again, offering me the use of the no-objection certificate that ACAF had obtained in 1986 to work in Pakistan, 'since ours are both simple craft projects'. Things were at last moving ahead and, as I still required textiles and wooden furniture for the Zamana exhibition, I needed to return to Peshawar and the Swat valley. In particular I had to sort out the shipment of a 19th-century Afghan sword that I had found in Murad market a year before, but which for some reason had not arrived. The blade, of damascened steel, was engraved with Kufic calligraphy, and I hoped to get it back to England in time for the exhibition.

The motorised auto rickshaw bringing me from the airport came to a halt outside a dark, narrow cul-de-sac leading off Peshawar's busy Saddar Bazaar. A broken neon sign dangled at a crazy angle from the eaves of the corner building with the words 'Khyber Hotel' and a red arrow pointing skywards towards a flight of stairs.

I squeezed out of the small rickshaw door, paid the bearded Afghan driver five rupees and, dragging my suitcase behind me, descended into the gloom of the cobbled cul-de-sac. Men crouched in the gutter urinating; others emerged tying the drawstrings of their baggy shalwar, their shifty eyes avoiding mine. An emaciated white cat, his fur grey with dirt, stalked across the doorway. I remembered him from previous visits to the Khyber and bent down to scratch his scarred and scabby head, but he darted away, eyes full of fear; dogs and cats living feral in the streets were more accustomed to abuse than affection. I gazed at him sadly as he perched on a sewer pipe several feet above my head.

A flight of worn brick stairs with a maroon painted handrail led to an upper floor with an inner courtyard. The rooms on the first floor were reserved for long-term residents – hippies, budget travellers and mystics who had made the Khyber Hotel their home. Their rooms were neatly decorated with Afghan embroideries and carpets, small fringed palms flowed from terracotta pots, bright orange nasturtiums twisted their way up pieces of string, and small gardens bloomed outside each grey door. Sometimes the doors to these rooms would be open while the occupants entertained visitors and from within wafted the exotic aroma of hashish and incense. Throughout the hotel an aura of peace and calm pervaded, a small oasis from the cacophony of noise, dust and bustle of the teeming bazaar, and a haven for the weary traveller.

Continuing up to the floor above, I stopped briefly to catch my breath and leaned over the balustrade to gaze beyond the washing that was drying on ropes stretched from wall to wall in the courtyard below. The manager approached me. His long face was dominated by a very large hooked nose, and his beard was of the goatee variety rather than the luxuriant bushy type favoured by the people of the region. On his shaven head perched a rather grubby white embroidered pillbox hat. Initially I was uncertain about him, and on my guard. However, despite his rascally appearance he turned out to be kind and helpful, later arranging for me to visit Dera Ismail Khan, a village in the tribal territories surrounded by fields of opium poppies where guns of every description are crafted by hand. Until I arrived in the North-West Frontier, I had always believed the saying that you could judge a person's character by their face. While this is no doubt true, on many occasions in the North-West Frontier I found that some of the more rascally- and villainous-looking characters turned out to be the most honest, charming and trustworthy.

In the manager's office I filled out the forms required to be completed by all residents on arrival – name, address, passport number, expiry date and date of issue, and next destination. These details would be handed on to the Pakistani police. A fan turned noiselessly overhead, the silence punctuated by the horns of the rickshaws in the street below and the snores of the cook sleeping on the charpoy in the corner, his greasy turban covering his face.

The Khyber Hotel, built during the days of the Raj, offered cheap accommodation and hot showers. The thought of relaxing under hot water after a 14-hour flight from London was high on my list of priorities. My tired, jet-lagged face peered back at me through a toothpaste-splattered mirror above the cracked communal washbasin on the landing. Placing my toothbrush gingerly on the glass shelf, I noticed small black droppings decorating the glass. Were they from mice? I examined them intently for a few seconds but, as house sparrows were flying to and fro from an overhead pipe to the edge of the mirror, I assumed they must be bird droppings. To the left of the basin was the shower room, about five feet square with just four hooks for hanging clothes. Thick water pipes ran around the wall at head height, making an ideal place for balancing shoes. The window ledge was just wide enough to balance my clean clothes. I watched in anticipation as water dripped through the rosette, then down it came in a deluge, spluttering and hissing. I pushed the window half-closed to prevent anyone watching from the buildings opposite. This had to be done carefully, so as not to send the clothes tumbling down onto the roof below. The roof acted as a refuse tip and incinerator for the Khyber Hotel, and heaps of orange skins, cardboard, paper, pieces of glass and wire lay smouldering in a half-burnt heap.

The weather in the early part of April in Pakistan was still cool and pleasant; the hot weather had yet to arrive. At night I needed a quilt for warmth, so I borrowed one from the hotel. It was not particularly warm but very heavy, filled with cotton fibre rather than feathers and covered with brightly coloured synthetic material with a floral motif. A detachable thin muslin sheet, stained and grey beyond belief, covered the quilt. I wondered how many sweaty bodies had slept under it and made a mental note to bring my own sleeping bag and lining sheet next time.

Not yet acclimatised to the time difference, I was woken at 5 am by the *azan*. A beam of sunlight streamed through the patterned coloured glass panes above the door, projecting the spectrum of the rainbow onto the green walls. Lying on the rope charpoy, I listened to the sounds floating up from the street below: car horns, cockerels crowing, the incessant barking of pi-dogs scavenging in packs amongst the refuse, and the *put-put-put* of the auto rickshaws. On the roof of the house opposite, boys were exercising their flock of domesticated white pigeons by keeping up a continuous whistling and twirling of giant flags to prevent them landing and re-entering the dovecots. In a tight group, sunlight glinting off their plumage, the pigeons soared, dived and changed direction like a shoal of sardines.

I made my way to the Old City and the Flying Coach bus station on the Grand Trunk Road. A young boy stood on the oil-stained forecourt, calling out the destinations of the minibuses plying between Peshawar and the Swat valley. 'Charsadda-Charsadda-Charsaddaaaah! Mardan-Mardan-Mardaaaan. Mingora-Mingora-Mingoraaaah!' He wore a dirty, torn shalwar kameez, and his pinched, dirt-encrusted, pockmarked face and filthy feet encased in broken plastic *chapli* indicated that he was very poor, possibly a refugee. Taking his responsibility seriously, he seemed old beyond his years as he worked tirelessly to guide passengers to the waiting minibuses. The more passengers he could find to fill the seats, the more quickly the minibus departed and the greater the revenue for his boss – and possibly for him, too.

Seeing me searching for the correct bus while trying to avoid stepping in pools of vehicle oil, he approached, enquiring, 'Charsadda-Mardan-Mingora?'

'Mingora,' I replied, holding out my ticket. Quick as lightning, he grasped my bag and threw it up onto the roof of the appropriate minibus, where men waiting with ropes lashed it down amongst suitcases, overnight bags, rucksacks and wooden boxes full of mangoes. Finally, a heavy tarpaulin was spread over the luggage to keep out the fine grey dust of the road.

The journey took us through the town of Mardan, where my grandfather, G.O. Sandys, had been stationed for a year while serving as an officer in the Royal Scots. He had hated his time on the Frontier. When we were children, he used to tell us stories about his life in Mardan.

'One day,' he told us, 'a man entered the cantonment carrying fruit in a wicker basket on his head, wrapped up in a white cloth to keep away the flies. My friend, a fellow officer, bought an apple from him and ate it, but by the evening he was dead. The white cloth, you see … ' – my grandfather would pause for a moment, watching our faces to gauge our reaction – '… had been used to wrap the body of someone who had died from cholera.'

The road to the Malakand Pass at the entrance to the Swat valley was a feat of engineering. One side had been cut out of the rock face, on which were painted in large lettering thought-provoking phrases such as 'Better to be late than *the* Late', or 'Speed thrills but kills' – not that the drivers took any notice. The minibus twisted and turned up the hairpin bends, overtaking on blind corners into the path of oncoming lorries transporting giant tree trunks felled in the pine forests of upper Swat and Kohistan down to Peshawar.

Pathans are well known for their courage. This characteristic, combined with the fact that many chewed *naswar*, a locally produced narcotic snuff made from tobacco, meant that most drove recklessly, without thought for the safety of their passengers. Despite large solid concrete blocks positioned every few yards to prevent vehicles from veering over the edge and down to the swirling muddy waters of the Peshawar River a thousand feet below, there were many moments throughout the journey when the wheels went too close to the edge for comfort. Sitting in the front seat of the minibus – the ladies' seat – required nerves of steel. If my face showed any fear the driver laughed manically, turned up the volume of the radio blasting out Pakistani pop music and put his foot on the accelerator. Then, taking both hands off the steering wheel, he unscrewed the lid of a little silver tin kept in a pocket in his waistcoat, took a pinch of dark green *naswar* and popped a wad behind his lower lip.

A magnificent magnolia tree with extraordinary palmate leaves grew in a lay-by, marking the site of a religious shrine. This was always a welcome sight to me, an indication that there were only a few more miles and a few more hairpin bends to negotiate before the road arrived at the summit of the Malakand Pass, called Churchill Picquet, where as a young officer Winston Churchill had fought in a skirmish against Pathan tribesmen. The road then dropped down into the beautiful scenic valleys of Swat.

A small donkey lay on the verge, its eyes glazed and its jaws opening and closing in agony exposing rows of teeth like a crocodile. It must have been hit by a vehicle, but no one had thought to put it out of its misery; instead children exacerbated the animal's pain as it lay dying. Giggling and laughing, they repeatedly kicked its body and pulled its tail and ears.

As we passed through the town of Saidu Sharif, where Alexander the Great fought a decisive battle against the Kushans in 329 BC on his way to invade India, there was a sudden screech of brakes and a sickening thump. The minibus skidded to a halt. A passenger wrenched open the sliding door and leapt out into the road, returning in just a few seconds with the unconscious body of a young boy in his arms. The child, no older than eight or nine, had run out into the road without looking and had sustained a head injury from which dark blood oozed and dripped. His limp body was gently positioned on the man's lap. As the minibus continued its journey, a small trickle of blood began to run backwards and forwards down the aisle, stopping, twisting and turning with the movement of the vehicle. Beside me, enveloped in a dark-blue embroidered chador with scalloped edges, a large local woman held her head in her hands and rocked her ample body from side to side. '*Bismillah ir-Rahman ir-Rahim,*' she whimpered in distress, and wiped her eyes with a corner of her chador. '*Bismillah ir-Rahman ir-Rahim.*'

Back in Peshawar, I went to my shipping agent's office to find out why the sword I had bought a year before for the Zamana exhibition was still lying in the office.

Tariq Sultan came from an old Peshwari family. He was charming, with old-fashioned courteous manners, and he had been shipping my goods to the UK for years. In all the years that I used his company, I never once offered him a bribe; he knew my strong views on the subject. Still, there were occasions when, I suspect, he tried it on. He would say to me, 'Customs are suspicious about you, Miss Harriet, because you are coming so many times here to Peshawar. They think that you are dealing in Gandhara pieces.'

'Well, you know I don't believe in buying Gandhara. You know I think it's wrong.'

'Oh yes, I am telling them, but still they are coming to my office.'

I could never tell if he was asking in a roundabout way for a backhander to bribe the customs officials. On this occasion he said, 'It is becoming difficult for me to ship the Swat wood for you. The Pakistani customs are saying this furniture is ethnographic and it is illegal to send it out of the country. But of course I will do my best for you, Miss Harriet.'

Then he took a sip of his milk tea and waited, knowing that I needed the chests and chairs for the Zamana exhibition.

I smiled sweetly. 'Thank you, Tariq Sultan. I'm sure you will do your best. I know you won't let me down.'

When I enquired about the Afghan sword, he explained that he hadn't been able to send it because it was 'ethnographic'. I needed to get a special permit signed by the office of the Minister of Ethnography before he could include it in my next consignment.

'You should go and see them. Maybe they are giving you permission,' he said, writing the address on a piece of paper.

Later that afternoon, I made my way to the minister's office on the Jamrud Road. I was directed to the garden at the rear of the building, where the minister was taking tea with guests, so I sat down on a seat in the shade and waited patiently. On the far side of the lawn, I noticed several Siberian falcons attached by jesses to a wooden rail. Their hoods were decorated with tiny bells that tinkled when they shook their heads. When I expressed an interest in the falcons, I was given a thick leather glove and allowed to hold one.

'Where are they from?' I asked the falconer.

'They have been captured in northern Afghanistan. They are waiting to go to Saudi Arabia. They are used there for hunting.'

The birds had been caught in nets as they migrated from eastern Russia to South Africa and then transported across the mountains to Peshawar for sale to the Saudi Arabian market. The revenue from the sale of these birds helped to finance the war against the Soviets.

At last the tea guests departed and the minister came over. He had seen me handling the falcon and was curious to know what I was doing in Peshawar. I explained that I had come to see him about obtaining a permit for the export of the sword and, after we had chatted together and I had drunk the obligatory three or four cups of sweet milk tea, he signed the required document. Whether he was expecting a small gratuity I can't be sure, but I never offered, and he never asked.

It wasn't only the sale of falcons that raised much-needed finance for the seven Mujahideen groups to purchase military hardware. Further finance came from the mining of semi-precious and precious stones such as emeralds and 'stone of the midnight sky', or lapis lazuli, from ancient mines in the Panjshir valley and Badakshan. The 6,000-year-old mine at Sar-i-Sang in the Hindu Kush provides the world's only source of high-grade lapis, much sought-after by jewellers worldwide. In Peshawar, the place to buy lapis was Namak Mundi, the old salt bazaar in the Old City. A London gemmologist visiting Peshawar to buy lapis to make chess pieces for the Sultan of Brunei took me to visit his supplier, who sold stones of the finest quality. In a small, dusty room filled with blue rocks, I learnt about the different qualities. First grade was deep blue with tiny flecks of iron pyrites (fool's gold); the lowest quality pale blue and streaked with white calcite.

Lapis has been prized since antiquity. The golden sarcophagus of Tutankhamun is richly inlaid with it, and small lapis beads have been found in Neolithic tombs. During the Mughal era, lapis was ground into the finest pigment and used by miniaturists. In Europe the most important Dutch and Renaissance artists referred to lapis as 'ultramarine', and used it to paint the robes of the Virgin Mary. Revenue from the export of lapis now helped Ahmad Shah Massoud's Jamiat-i-Islami group to purchase weaponry.

Throughout the rest of April, Joss Graham and I busily prepared for our exhibition at the Zamana Gallery, *The Decorative Arts of Central Asia*, which would open in May. My consignment of goods, bought in Peshawar and the Swat valley, arrived just in time for the opening. Tariq Sultan had come up trumps – when I unpacked the boxes, there was the sword!

Our invitation list for the private view consisted of members of the Afghan royal family and the Afghan diaspora living in London, textile dealers, and friends who supported the Afghan cause. We felt it would be diplomatic to invite the Afghan Chargé d'Affaires, Mr Sarwar, who was also the brother-in-law of President Najibullah.

In the same building were located the prayer hall and religious centre for the Ismaili community. For this reason, and because the majority of our guests were Muslim, alcohol was out of the question. So we decided to give the whole evening a truly Afghan flavour by serving *dogh*, a yoghurt, mint and cucumber drink traditionally served on hot summer days in Afghanistan. For background, I provided tapes of Afghan music that I had purchased from a Californian friend, Noor Mohammed Khan Afghani, an ex-hippie and musician who played the Afghan *rehbab*. We had met by chance at the Wagah-Attari border crossing some years before. Noor was a convert to Islam; he lived in Hashtnagri in the Old City of Peshawar and had his own recording studio there.

When Mr Sarwar accepted our invitation, I became anxious about the content of the Peshwari songs. Would they be about jihad, holy war against the infidel Russians?

'Don't worry, Harriet,' Noor assured me. 'They're traditional *ghuzzals* from the North-West Frontier.'

During the evening, Joss and I were introduced to Mr Sarwar.

'If you are interested in buying Afghan carpets, why not buy in Kabul? I can give you a visa,' he said. 'Come to my office at the embassy. Just telephone my secretary to arrange an appointment.'

Later that week, we went to Mr Sarwar's small office on the top floor of 31

Princes Gate, at the northern end of Exhibition Road, to fill out our visa forms.

'Miss Harriet,' said Mr Sarwar. 'I liked that Afghan music that was playing at the Zamana Gallery. Could you please get me a copy?'

A few days later, with Noor's *ghuzzals* copied onto a fresh set of cassettes, I drove by the Afghan Embassy. The main door was slightly ajar. As there was no parking space immediately outside, I stopped on a yellow line, jumped out and ran to the open door. Anxious not to incur a parking ticket or disturb the secretary by making her descend two flights of stairs, I placed the cassettes, wrapped in brown paper, on the bottom step of the stairs, thinking as I did so what a pleasant surprise it would be for Mr Sarwar. I heard no more.

A couple of years later I happened to be in Delhi. Mr Sarwar was now the Afghan Ambassador to India and, since I required a visa for Afghanistan, I decided to pay him a visit.

The rickshaw delivered me to the front gates of the imposing embassy, but when I announced that I had come to see the ambassador the chowkidar and embassy staff cast disapproving glances at my modest mode of conveyance, and were reluctant to allow me to enter. I had to wait in the entrance hall until a member of staff finally escorted me up a wide, red-carpeted staircase with gilded banisters and into a palatial high-ceilinged room decorated in plaster stucco from which hung huge glass chandeliers. Seated behind his desk at the far end of the room was Mr Sarwar, quite dwarfed by an enormous picture of his brother-in-law, President Najibullah. As I walked the length of the room, I was acutely conscious of my shabby attire – I had just arrived back in Delhi after a week in a tent at the Pushkar camel fair in Rajasthan. With typical Afghan graciousness, Mr Sarwar came out from behind his desk to shake my hand. He welcomed me as though I were the most important person to enter his office that morning.

'How very nice to see you, Miss Harriet. And how is Mr Joss?'

He indicated that I should take a seat, and ordered a tray of tea. While I sat there, the telephone on Mr Sarwar's desk rang incessantly, but he simply picked up the receiver and replaced it so that we could continue our conversation.

'Did you ever receive those tapes of Afghan music?' I asked.

He slowly replaced his teacup on the saucer before replying.

'Ahh. So it was *you* who left those tapes on our staircase. My secretary came downstairs and thought the parcel was a bomb. We called the London Fire Brigade, and the bomb disposal unit closed off all of Exhibition Road for two hours while they opened the parcel. Miss Harriet, you caused us *so* many problems!'

CHAPTER 7

Jamhuriat Hospital, Kabul, Afghanistan
July 1988

It was still dark as I stepped out through the gates of the YWCA into the steamy heat of Delhi at 5 am. The first pale pink and grey streaks of dawn were just beginning to appear and the sweet, cloying scent of frangipani and the aroma of wood smoke from cooking fires wafted in the early-morning air. A sweeper, bent double, the end of her sari pulled over her head, carefully and methodically brushed fallen leaves and flower petals from the pavement using a small palm-frond whisk.

I had arrived the day before from a tour of desert towns in Rajasthan buying stock for Out of the Nomad's Tent. Before leaving London, Joss and I had arranged to rendezvous in Delhi and fly to Kabul together. Now he was arriving on an early flight and I was on my way to meet him.

I didn't have long to wait before an auto rickshaw whirled to a stop in front of me.

"Allo, memsahib, where you go?' the driver asked in a tired, resigned voice.

His blue-checked *lunghi* wrapped around his thin waist and a frayed unbuttoned shirt revealed a near-emaciated body. His demeanour was typical of a poor low-caste Indian worn down by relentless poverty. It was as though the burdens of life were too great for him to bear; hardships and misfortunes had drained from him all enthusiasm and zest for life.

He balanced my suitcase precariously beside him while I squeezed into the back of the tuk-tuk. Just as we left the side streets and joined the main road leading to Indira Gandhi Airport, the front tyre of the rickshaw punctured. Drawing up on the hard shoulder, the driver turned the vehicle on its side and struggled to change the wheel, finally asking me for my assistance. Having no idea how to do such a thing, I was of little help. By now the sun had risen above the horizon, a blazing disc of gold sweeping away the delicate colours of early dawn. The road was crowded with traffic: lorries, buses filled with commuters, cars, rickshaws and hotel minibuses plying to and from the airport. Standing at the side of the road by an upturned rickshaw, I became an object of amusement. Drivers honked as they passed, leering lasciviously from their cabs, children screaming, 'What eez your nem?' from car windows. Eventually, after what seemed like eternity, the puncture was repaired, and we were on our way.

Despite the delay I arrived in good time at the airport and met Joss, who had arrived just a few minutes before. Together we boarded an Indian Airlines flight for the two-hour flight to Kabul. The aircraft circled once above Delhi, which was covered by a haze of pollution, before turning north. The neat patchwork of fields and tiny villages of the Punjab gradually gave way to arid desert, criss-crossed with *nullahs* (watercourses). Ahead lay the scrub-covered foothills of the Sulaiman mountain range, formed when the Indian and Asian plates collided some 80 million years ago. The iron-red, ochre-yellow and grey rock strata of the concertina-creased mountains are testament to the enormous tectonic pressure over millennia that forced the land to buckle upwards. Far below, I could see tiny ribbons of bright emerald green in the narrow grey canyons and gorges, evidence of agriculture and habitation.

The aircraft banked sharply to begin its tight corkscrew descent from 30,000 feet to Kabul's Bagram airport. The sparkling snow-capped peaks of the great Himalayan mountain range, like the teeth of a dinosaur, stretched away to the far horizon, merging into the dense ink-blue sky before disappearing over the rim of the earth. The aircraft spiralled down over the Sulaiman mountains. Laid out below, nestling in a dusty plain at the foot of the Paghman mountain range that surrounds the city, were the dun-coloured flat-roofed buildings of Afghanistan's capital.

During the summer months at this time, the Mujahideen were very active in the mountains and controlled all the passes leading to Kabul. They would fire rockets from the mountain peaks into the city, and *Stinger* missiles supplied by the Americans at incoming Russian military aircraft, on a daily basis. It was not unknown for civilian aircraft to be targeted – hence the corkscrew descent to avoid being hit.

Our aircraft landed at speed and braked sharply. As it taxied along the runway, helicopter gunships hovered overhead in groups of four. Others lined the tarmac runway in rows, their rotors turning in readiness to scramble. Huge iron-grey Soviet Antonov supply planes, with red stars on their tails, came in to land every five minutes, throwing out magnesium flares that left white trails in the azure sky as decoys against the Stingers. During our stay in Kabul, Joss and I would hear the constant drone of the Antonov engines as they brought in supplies day and night to a city under siege.

Most of the passengers disembarking at Kabul airport were the families of diplomats, children coming out to join their parents for the summer holidays, Afghans returning home after a visit to Delhi, and Indian businessmen. Those remaining on board were backpackers, mainly Aussies taking a cheap flight through a war zone en route to Europe. They gazed at us enviously as we made our way to the exit.

Customs and immigration was a fairly casual affair, conducted in a corrugated-iron hut. Our visas checked, we were soon outside in the searing heat of Kabul, striding out across the tarmac. A Russian tank stood guard at the airport gates. Young fair-haired conscripts, their faces red and peeling from the harsh Afghan sun, lounged beside the gun turret, wearing blue-and-white-striped tee shirts and cowboy-style canvas hats. Once outside the gates, a roguish taxi driver grabbed our bags and a small boy reached for mine.

'Baksheesh, baksheesh!' he demanded in a shrill voice, but neither Joss nor I had any local currency to give him.

The taxi's upholstery was torn, with stuffing protruding from the vinyl. Metal springs dug into our backsides from all angles and empty Pepsi bottles rolled around the floor. The road was in a deplorable state after years of shelling by the Mujahideen and wear and tear caused by the metal treads of Russian tanks, and the broken suspension guaranteed that we felt every pothole on the journey between airport and hotel.

The Kabul Hotel in the centre of the city was a huge concrete monstrosity of Eastern-bloc architecture. The interior was gloomy – the brown curtains were closed to keep out the summer heat. The walls and large pillars supporting the ceiling were painted nicotine brown and cream. Even the threadbare staircase carpet was brown, and there was dust everywhere. With no tourists passing through Kabul for years, no one seemed to make an effort to keep the hotel clean, tidy and decorated. There was an air of lethargy and despondency amongst the hotel staff, who appeared depressed and deeply weary after eight years of war. As we waited for the manager to locate the huge hotel register (which had not been used for years and couldn't be found), my eyes wandered to the tourist posters hanging above the reception desk. Dating from the 1960s–70s, the heyday of Afghan tourism, the posters showing Afghans playing the traditional sport of *buzkashi*, smiling Afghan children in traditional dress, the sacred blue lakes of Band-i-Amir and the giant stone statues of the Buddha at Bamiyan were now faded, the paper yellow, torn and fly-spotted. Yet, despite their dilapidated appearance, they served as a reminder of that once-happy, peaceful, prosperous time when tourism flourished in Afghanistan.

After our journey from Delhi we were hungry.

'Is there a menu?' we enquired of the morose elderly waiter who appeared, dressed in a stained black jacket and trousers, white shirt and maroon cummerbund.

'No, no menu. Just fixed meal,' he replied tiredly.

'Well, what can we eat?'

'Roast chicken, salad,' he replied.

This custom of only offering guests a set meal was not part of Afghan culture, but had been introduced by the Soviet regime. Dry, overcooked and very stringy, the chicken had obviously been running around the Kabul bazaar for many months, and was well beyond its sell-by date. Like the salty beans on the side of the plate, it had been prepared well in advance and reheated. A tired, gritty salad and pale, limp greasy chips accompanied it.

Afterwards we made our way through the dusty streets to Sarakh-i-Murgh, or Chicken Street. Infamous during the hippie era of the 1960s–70s for its cheap hotels and hashish, it was here that travellers would stay for weeks or months, even years, taking drugs until either their health or their money ran out. Although the hippies had long since departed, the merchants' shops had remained, but we were disappointed to find them shuttered and closed for the Muslim festival of Eid, which comes at the end of the holy month of Ramadan. We pressed our noses to the windows. Through the dust-encrusted panes we could see Afghan embroideries, Russian brass samovars, 19th-century Gardner porcelain teacups and teapots, antique Turkmen jewellery, Afghan carpets, kilims, woven tent bands, camel headdresses, copper pots, inlaid weaponry and musical instruments – in fact everything that we had hoped to find and more.

At the far end of Chicken Street we came to the flower market, where the smell of open drains was masked by buckets of sweet-scented blooms. From there it was only a short distance to the more up-market Shar-i-Nau, or New Town, where Afghan carpet-sellers advertised their wares by hanging embroideries and carpets from upstairs windows and balconies. This was the nerve centre of the Afghan carpet trade, where foreign buyers, humanitarian aid workers, diplomats and Russian soldiers would come to buy a souvenir of their visit. At a small roundabout, Afghan carpets were laid out in the middle of the road; buses, lorries, cars and horse-drawn vehicles drove over them for hours as they negotiated the roundabout, covering them with dust and grit. This was a widely used method of dulling the brightness of the harsh chemical dyes of newly woven carpets. The merchants would lay them out under the hot sun to help fade the light-fugitive dyes, a popular little ploy to age the carpet artificially and dupe some unsuspecting buyer. No doubt many a customer walked away with what they thought was a genuine antique Afghan carpet!

Before we left England, Alastair Hull, an importer of Afghan tribal rugs and artefacts with a business in East Anglia, had given us the name and address of a carpet merchant in Shar-i-Nau. Despite the war, Alastair had continued to make frequent buying trips to Afghanistan. He had started his business in 1968 and had made a name for himself as the largest importer of Afghan slipper socks, knitted in coloured wool by village women in Paghman province. Alastair knew more than anyone about where and from whom to buy in Kabul, and had generously given us various names and addresses.

With a few helpful directions from local Afghans, Joss and I finally arrived outside a large emporium. A maroon-painted board hung above the main entrance with 'Hamidullah Handicrafts' in both Farsi and English. Hamidullah owned the shop but his nephews, Khanullah and Bismullah, both in their twenties, managed it. The interior was dark and mysterious. A staircase led up to a large room stuffed from floor to ceiling with rugs and carpets from every corner of Central Asia, that exuded an interesting smell of camel, goat and sheep, stale sweat, dust, rancid butter and smoke, combined with the mothballs scattered around the shop to prevent insects devouring the valuable stock.

The sight of so many beautiful pieces thrown down in front of us by Khanullah and Bismullah conjured up romantic visions of families on migration across the mountains and steppes of Afghanistan. The very fabric of Afghan carpets told its own story. Each piece carried the aroma of the animal whose hair had been used in its weaving, and the intricate design gave clues to the tribe that had woven it.

Every so often the brothers would show us beautiful saddlebags of the Turkmen tribes, the Kirghiz, Ersari, Sarouk and Kazakh. These exquisitely woven bags would once have held grain, flour, cooking pots and small children, carried on camels and donkeys during migration. Piled along one wall was a stack of enormous Labijar kilims woven with bold colours and geometric designs. Lifting them off the stack for us required considerable physical strength from Khanullah and Bismullah. Clouds of dust billowed up from each freshly opened kilim, and motes danced in a beam of sunlight.

Kilims were traditionally used by the nomads to insulate the floors of their tents on cold winter nights, or were spread out around the campfires for the family to sit on, so protecting them from the stony desert ground. Smaller kilims were used as tablecloths known as *dastarkhans*. Then there were the dark-indigo, blue-black-aubergine-coloured Baluchi rugs and grain sacks called *bolesht*. Their limited colour palette reflected the harsh environment in which they were woven, there being few plants or roots available for extracting natural dyes in the deserts of southern Afghanistan.

After several hours, we had a considerable pile set aside. Everything had gone far better than we expected, and we seemed to have achieved a great deal in a comparatively short time. We all agreed that we would leave the final selection and bargaining of the pieces until the end of the week. Joss and I were now flagging. The heat was stifling, and I didn't feel particularly well. My whole body ached. Sensing our fatigue, Bismullah offered us tea, which we gratefully accepted.

In all Muslim countries hospitality is generous, but the Afghan variety surpasses most and can be almost overwhelming, with food being pressed upon the guest or visitor at every opportunity. Drinking tea plays an important role in Afghan society. Two battered bright-blue enamelled tin teapots with hinged lids and plates of *noql-e-badomi* (sugared almonds), pale-green sultanas, dried mulberries and toffees wrapped in silver paper were placed before us. In one teapot was the traditional green tea flavoured with cardamom, and in the other black tea, often jokingly referred to by refugees living in Peshawar as Russian tea or *chai Shuravi*.

Refreshed, we returned to the shop in Chicken Street, through whose dusty window we had peered the day before. A GAZ lorry with three young Soviet conscripts guarded the entrance to Chicken Street to prevent any Russians wandering in. It wasn't unusual for Russians to have their throats slit in Kabul's back streets, so Joss and I made sure to speak loudly in English wherever we walked.

The shop housed a wonderful collection of 19th-century embroideries and silk *chapans*, some of them lined with ermine. Although they were expensive, we ended up buying some. Walking through the streets I developed a nagging headache but dismissed it as being caused by the heat and glare of the sun reflecting off the stone walls. Back in my hotel room, I took two aspirins and fell fast asleep.

Next morning I woke feeling drugged. I should have realised that I had the beginnings of a fever, but instead I joined Joss for another day of shopping and haggling in the bazaar. First stop was Hamidullah's, before moving on to yet another contact of Alastair's called Noor Sher. We looked for Gardner porcelain but found very little. We did find a nice Kashgari teapot, but the shopkeeper wanted too much for it. As the day wore on, I felt increasingly unwell. Khanullah and Bismullah invited us to share a lunch of kebabs and boiled lamb in onion sauce, a traditional dish called *dopiaza*, but I had completely lost my appetite. They were also keen to show us their collection of *dhurries*, flat-woven cotton floor coverings, but I had now developed a powerful and agonising headache. I tried hard to be useful, but by late afternoon I admitted defeat and told Joss I was going back to the hotel. That night my temperature was 39.4° C.

The following day, a Friday and the Muslim holy day, I awoke feeling refreshed, full of energy and with no sign of a fever. Khanullah and Bismullah invited us both for lunch to meet their families. A few days earlier, Bismullah had confided that he had 11 children.

'Eleven!' I exclaimed.

He laughed. 'Yes, eleven.'

I couldn't work out if he was teasing me. Possibly half the children were his and the rest belonged to his brother, as their wives and families lived under the same roof. When we arrived at their home, Bismullah called out the children and lined them all up in ascending height to present them to us. There were indeed 11, the youngest a baby just three weeks old. I was amazed that they were so quiet, but Afghan children are taught to be well behaved and respectful when guests are present. Bismullah and Khanullah invited us to sit on a large kilim spread under a tree in the courtyard.

A small boy handed us a bar of soap and poured water from a copper ewer over a basin for us to wash our hands before the meal, as is the Muslim custom.

Dishes piled high on flat oval plates began to arrive from the kitchen, carried by Bismullah's daughters. With great concentration the little girls carefully placed the dishes in the centre of the kilim – *qabuli pilau*, yellow rice with carrots and raisins topped with boiled lamb, *boulanee*, leek-filled pastries, and *ashak* (my favourite), small parcels of pasta filled with leek and covered with a meat-and-yoghurt sauce, strongly resembling Italian ravioli; legend has it that Marco Polo brought the recipe back from Central Asia to Italy. To finish the meal we were served fresh fruit and *firni*, cold thick-set custard made from corn flour flavoured with cardamom and decorated with finely chopped pistachio nuts, a traditional Afghan dessert made for special occasions. Afghan food is delicious and, to honour the guest, always abundant. More and more food was pressed upon us, the brothers selecting the choicest pieces of meat from the platter of rice and placing them upon our plates.

Unfortunately, my usually healthy appetite had all but disappeared, and the headache had returned with a vengeance. 'Eat, eat,' they urged as still more food arrived from the kitchen. I struggled to do justice to the wonderful meal, not wishing to offend our hosts or their wives and daughters, who had spent all morning in the kitchen crouched over a hot stove. With the headache had come an extraordinary thirst. Despite consuming jug after jug of cold water throughout the meal, my thirst remained unquenched. I suspected that I had contracted a virus while travelling in India before meeting up with Joss. The pain was so severe that I said I had to return to the hotel, and we walked slowly back through the hot streets.

I lay down and took my temperature, which again registered 39.4° C. I hoped that after a good night's sleep the fever would be gone. But that night the pain intensified. My head felt as though it was going to burst, and there was such pressure behind my eyes that I thought they might pop out from their sockets.

Through a gap in the curtains, I watched a battle taking place between the Russians and the Mujahideen on the outskirts of the city. A searchlight swept the hillsides around Kabul. White light flickered in the night sky like an electrical storm. The dull *crump* and *thump* of the shelling carried on the night air. At dawn I woke to the sound of tanks rumbling past my bedroom window. In the street about 20 Soviet tanks were passing the Kabul Hotel. The metal tracks shook the whole fabric of the building. Conscripts lay on their backs fast asleep on top of the tanks, exhausted after a night of fighting, their arms and legs sprawled around the gun turrets.

I was too ill to join Joss for breakfast, so he set out to find a doctor. He returned a little later.

'I've spoken with a Doctor Farid Homayoun. He'll see you at nine o'clock this morning at the Jamhuriat Hospital. There's a taxi waiting to take us as soon as you're ready.'

The hospital was a large concrete building, set back from the road at the top end of Chicken Street. It was built in the 1970s as a gift to the Afghan people from the American and British governments.

Like all the hospitals in Kabul at this time, it was overcrowded with patients requiring attention; the overstretched staff strove to do their best with limited medical facilities. They worked in an atmosphere of near-constant fear and stress, exacerbated by the daily indiscriminate shelling of the city by the Mujahideen.

It says much for the dedication and care of the staff of the Jamhuriat that I survived, partly due to their swift diagnosis. Within an hour, my blood had been sent off to the laboratory for analysis. My head and chest were X-rayed Afghan-style – a novel experience, as the staff moved around me wearing enormous lead pinafores. Finally, I was put on an IV drip in a small side room, alongside a beautiful little baby girl lying in a cot who solemnly surveyed me with unblinking black almond-shaped eyes like two shards of obsidian. Two hours later, the blood tests had been analysed. I was taken upstairs to the intensive care unit and asked to lie down curled up with my knees touching my chest and my chin tucked right in so that my back was curved outwards.

Dr Govind Singh, a Sikh, and Dr Farid Homayoun explained that, in order to make a complete diagnosis, they needed to extract spinal fluid from between my lumbar vertebrae. Several doctors leant over me, speaking in Farsi while they felt for the correct area to place the needle. Earlier in the day Joss had registered our arrival in Kabul with the British Embassy and informed them of my illness. They agreed to send a French doctor from the embassy to attend, so that a second opinion could be formed. The several local anaesthetic injections in my back did nothing to disguise the pain of the especially thick needle being inserted into my spine. My mind worked overtime as I heard and felt the crunch of gristle as the needle penetrated between the vertebrae. I begged them to stop, but they continued putting the needle in, maybe six or seven times, until they managed to draw out the fluid. They showed Joss the vial filled with cloudy liquid. It was only later that the doctors confided to me that the needle was blunt and had been used many times before. In time of war, medical equipment was difficult to obtain in Afghanistan, and needles were used repeatedly.

Finally the doctors gave their diagnosis: 'Madam, you have bacterial meningitis'.

I did not then understand the seriousness of my illness, and assumed I would be discharged after a day or so.

'Madam, you must stay here in Jamhuriat ten or twelve days minimum. *Minimum*,' Dr Singh stressed.

Meningitis is an infection of the fluid in the spinal cord and around the brain. It causes inflammation and swelling of the membrane that covers the spinal cord, causing a severe headache and stiffness in the neck. Left untreated it can cause long-term complications including hearing loss, mental retardation, blindness, paralysis and seizures. In the worst case it can result in brain damage, coma and death. But if caught quickly it can be treated effectively with antibiotics. It was my great good fortune that Joss was with me and that Dr Singh had dealt with over a hundred cases of acute bacterial meningitis. From the flu-like symptoms, high temperature and severe headache he instantly recognised and diagnosed it.

Later that day, Joss received a letter from the Vice-Consul at the British Embassy. He brought it to the hospital for me to read.

Dear Mr Graham,

Following our meeting this morning when you registered I have had a discussion with our French doctor Giles Manuel who has now visited Miss Sandys at the Jamhuriat Hospital. Dr Manuel feels that Miss Sandys is well enough to travel and advises that she returns to Delhi as soon as possible because of the very poor nursing and hygiene standards in Kabul. He is particularly worried about the risk of infection from unsterilised needles. Given these factors, combined with the warning letter I gave you this morning advising all British and other nationals for whom the Embassy has Consular responsibility to leave Afghanistan as quickly as possible, I would advise you and Miss Sandys to obtain seats on the first available commercial flight to New Delhi. As agreed, I would be grateful for a quick telephone call at the Embassy confirming your final travel arrangements.

By this time, however, I was too ill to move. There was no alternative to staying in the intensive care ward. I was just relieved to be in a hospital, and was confident that I would be well looked after. Joss agreed to continue buying stock in the bazaar for both of us.

For days the pain was so intense, agonising and incessant, with no let-up or reprieve, that I couldn't eat, sleep or talk. Each heartbeat sent blood pumping through my veins and arteries and up into the inflamed lining of my skull. The inflammation created pressure that had no other way to escape than through my eye sockets. My eyes felt as if they were going to burst. I was exhausted by the pain, and death would have been a welcome release. I felt no fear of dying, so I prayed silently, 'Please, God, let me die. Take away this pain, please, *please*.' But the pain just continued, hour after hour, day after day.

Every four hours a nurse would inject Bulgarian penicillin into the vein in the crook of my arm. Sometimes, when she couldn't find the vein, she would hunt for one in my wrist or thumb or the back of my hand. She found veins where I didn't even know they existed. As she pressed the plunger and the acidic solution flowed, it burnt its way along my veins like lava. The nurse's nocturnal visits were the worst. She would wake me in the early hours and I came to dread the sight of her, knowing the pain that was to come and that I would not be able to prevent myself from crying out loud. Then children from the neighbouring women's ward, who were looking after their mothers, would appear at the door attracted by my screams, pushing and shoving to get the best view of the evening's entertainment. It was the hours before dawn when I felt most alone, worn out, miserable and sorry for myself. Hot tears of self-pity ran down my face and soaked into the pillows. Then I would hear my mother's voice in my head: 'Pull yourself together, Harriet. Stop crying, don't complain. Keep a stiff upper lip at all times.' I thought of the stoicism of the Afghans, and felt ashamed at my weakness.

Early each morning, on their way to their carpet shop, Bismullah and Khanullah would bring me food – a small earthenware bowl of fresh yoghurt, a white peach or a hard-boiled egg.

'My wife has cooked this for you,' Bismullah would say, pulling the egg, still warm, out of his waistcoat pocket. Or 'I am sorry, Miss Oriot, but there was no yoghurt in the bazaar this morning. The Russian soldiers have taken it all.' And he would hand over a bunch of grapes instead, or peel me a white peach.

In London Joss and I had both come to know a young Afghan refugee, Juma Bahran. His family were Hazara, and owned a grocery shop in Chicken Street. A few days before I fell ill we had called in at the shop and given the family news of their son. Now, in appreciation of our friendship with Juma, his brothers came to see me daily with little gifts of food – a packet of salt biscuits, a box of Laughing Cow cheese. After our departure from Afghanistan Juma told us that, in retribution for these little acts of kindness, KHAD had arrested one of his brothers and incarcerated him in the notorious Pul-i-Charkhi prison, where he was tortured. As the descendants of Genghis Khan's soldiers, Hazaras are traditionally looked down upon in Afghan society, and KHAD must have become suspicious and wondered why or how he knew us. Juma's brother was released only when one of his torturers recognised him as a friend.

An elderly man occupied the bed next to mine. His face had an unhealthy yellow tinge, the skin stretched like parchment across his skull. One morning he raised a thin blue-veined hand and waved feebly at the jug of water on the table beside his bed. I struggled out of bed, filled a glass with water and held it to his lips, but after taking only a few sips he fell back, exhausted. I was too innocent of death to realise he was dying.

Above my bed, a ceiling fan rotated noisily, stirring the hot, stale air. Unable to read or sleep, I lay watching a gecko hunt for flies on the ceiling. The large propeller-like blades of the fan began to swing from side to side, the points of the blades hitting the plaster ceiling with force. Concerned that the fan might come crashing down on top of me, I wondered what I should do. Should I get out of bed or stay where I was? As I continued to watch in fearful fascination, it slowly occurred to me that everything else in the ward, including my bed and the water in the jug on the bedside table, was shaking too. Kabul was experiencing an earth tremor, possibly the beginnings of an earthquake. I had to get out of the building. With no time to waste, I lifted the drip from the hook on the metal stand and, holding the bag aloft, walked out into the corridor.

Female patients from the ward next door were making their way in an agonisingly slow procession along the corridor towards the stairs that would lead them down to the safety of the courtyard. Their pale, unhealthy faces were contorted with pain, bodies stooped and twisted. Every step seemed to be like torture for them as they shuffled along the long corridor, leaning heavily on their daughters for support. Seriously ill, these Afghan women were, like me, desperate to escape the building, frightened that they might be entombed under tons of concrete. As soon as we reached the top stair, a young doctor, his white hospital coat flapping, came running up, two steps at a time, shouting and waving his arms.

'Go back. Go back to your beds. It's all over.'

And the women, like the march of the dammed, turned and slowly retraced their steps back to their ward.

Joss was able to visit me at any time of day. He collected empty Russian vodka bottles from the Kabul Hotel, filled them with boiled water from the kitchen and carried them clanking up the street to the hospital to make sure I had a cordon sanitaire around me. The doctors had told him that secondary infection was a real concern, so he washed everything I touched and kept a bar of soap in his shirt pocket to wash my hands after every contact with anything. One lunchtime he came to see me, having spent a busy morning in Chicken Street and Shar-i-Nau. He was carrying cheap plastic holdalls bulging with textiles. Eager to show me what he had bought, he turned the bags upside down and shook out the contents.

In a trice everything was in a heap in the small space between my bed and that of the dying man. Joss rummaged through the pile and with great enthusiasm held up a 19th-century silk velvet *ikat* robe lined with fox fur, which would have graced the shoulders of a nobleman living in the Emirate of Bukhara a hundred years earlier. Then he plucked from the pile a pair of fine leather knee-boots covered in stitch-work that would have been worn by women living in Samarkand and Bukhara in the mid-19th century. I could see in an instant that, with his vast knowledge of oriental textiles and his eye for quality and detail, Joss had found and purchased an excellent collection of exquisitely fine embroideries. Most were Turkmen, but others came from the Uzbek Lakhai, a tribe who migrated from Central Asia and settled in the towns in the north of Afghanistan shortly after the Russian conquest of Central Asia in 1875.

Amongst the embroideries he had bought were *segoshas*, V-shaped embroidered hangings used to cover and disguise bedding rolls stored during daytime around the walls of the dome-shaped felt yurts used on migration by the nomadic tribes of northern Afghanistan. The *segoshas* and other small items such as coat cuffs and facings, little money purses and small amulets with long intricate tassels, were covered in minute embroidery stitches of coloured silk. The triangular amulets were lovingly made by mothers for their offspring to protect them from illness and disease. Some of the tassels were finished with a tiny white or blue bead to guard the child against the evil eye and death. Child mortality in Afghanistan at that time was one of the highest in the world, with one child in five dying before its fifth birthday. The fabric to be embroidered was first folded over a triangular piece of paper or card inscribed with a special prayer or *sura* from the Qur'an. Once the prayer was safely folded, the fabric was heavily embroidered. Mothers would pin these amulets to their children's clothing, in particular boys, who in Afghan society were considered to be more fragile in early life and also more important than girls.

Soon the smell of mothballs, stale sweat from the used clothing and the dust of ages pervaded the ward. Joss was taking a risk and would be in for a sharp reprimand should we be discovered by the hospital staff. I glanced anxiously at the door, but fortunately no one came to disturb us and soon all the textiles were neatly packed away again. It was a bitter blow for me to be prevented from joining Joss in the bazaars. However, I was delighted at his success in finding such lovely textiles. My only concern was that he might have misinterpreted my silence as a lack of enthusiasm and appreciation for all his hard work. If the truth be known, I was worn out from the constant pain. Speaking was just too much of an effort.

That evening, Joss arrived carrying a mattress and pillow from the Kabul Hotel. He had bundled his bedding into a taxi and intended sleeping in the main corridor outside the intensive care ward. Days later, when I was well enough to ask him why he came, he said, 'I didn't think you were going to survive the night'.

About midnight there was a terrible commotion – the sound of running feet, shouts and fists banging on doors. Joss appeared in the ward dragging his bedding, which he arranged on the floor next to my bed.

'One of the doctors is being chased down the corridor by gunmen,' he reported. 'It's probably safer if I stay here.'

The next day we asked the staff about the hubbub. A patient, who had died earlier that day from cancer, had relatives in the KHAD. They had arrived at the hospital armed with pistols to take the doctor away for questioning, or worse. The doctor had fled down the corridor with the KHAD in hot pursuit, locking himself in a store cupboard. As far as we understood, he survived the ordeal and was soon back on his rounds.

During the doctor's daily rounds, every patient was visited and an up-to-date assessment made of his or her condition. Further treatment was a joint decision made by all the doctors, consulting together at the foot of the bed. The majority were young women in their mid-twenties who had grown up during the Soviet occupation. All were well educated, emancipated and very charming. No *chador* for them; in starched white coats, they were treated as equals alongside their male colleagues.

'Here in Kabul I am free,' said Dr Jamilla, a beautiful young woman with large green eyes. 'I could never wear a chador at work. It would interfere with my care of the patients,' she added, laughing.

For my benefit, my daily medical report was given in English. One morning the senior hospital consultants and female junior doctors congregated at the foot of my bed for a brief visit as part of their daily hospital round.

'Good morning, Miss Oriot. How are you today?'

I said I had a severe pain shooting up the right side of my skull. Dr Singh squeezed drops into my eyes to dilate the pupils and shone a torch. Returning half an hour later, he ripped the sticking plaster off the back of my hand and removed the butterfly needle.

'OK. Let's go.'

'Go where?' I asked, confused.

'To the Noor Eye Hospital,' he replied.

I got out of bed and walked shakily behind him out into the corridor, then down the stone staircase to the main hospital entrance. All I had on was a long Indian cotton nightshirt, which I hoped wasn't too transparent. The air outside hit me like the blast of heat from an opened oven door.

The Jamhuriat Hospital had no ambulances, so Dr Singh strode across the courtyard in search of a vehicle to take us across Kabul, leaving me resting against a pillar, the hot wind drying the sweat running down my spine. Visitors and patients stared at me, and I hoped they couldn't see through my nightshirt as I had nothing on underneath. After a few minutes he returned with a Soviet army 4x4, and motioned for me to climb into the back. As luck would have it, Joss arrived at that moment and joined me for the journey to the eye hospital.

The 4x4 had been parked for many hours in the hot sun, and the metal seats had long since lost their cushions – you could have fried an egg on them. The vehicle no longer had functioning suspension or hydraulics, so the driver had to pump the brake pedal frantically to stop it at intersections to avoid colliding with Soviet tanks. The journey was torture. Each time the 4x4 passed over a shallow crater in the road, Joss and I were jolted on the metal seats. The pain in my head was unbearable, so I grasped the overhead roll bars, pulling myself up so that I half-crouched, half-stood, my head bumping against the canvas roof.

The Noor Eye Hospital was linked to the Moorfields Eye Hospital in London and, considering all the problems Kabul was suffering at the time, my treatment was swift and excellent. My eyes tested, we returned to the Jamhuriat in the 4x4, this time with me sitting in the front seat with the driver.

One morning, the doctors gathered at the foot of my bed.

'We are sorry that we did not visit you yesterday,' they said, 'but a car bomb exploded in the vegetable bazaar. We were in the operating theatre all day carrying out emergency surgery.'

They conferred together in Farsi, then asked whether I wished to ask them any questions before they moved on.

How could I mention the pain caused by the injections of penicillin? In light of the horrendous injuries sustained by the Afghans in the wards on the floor above, my discomfort seemed insignificant. However, the doctors noted the œdema in my hands; my fingers were so swollen that they resembled uncooked Cumberland sausages. They conferred again and decided that from now on the penicillin would be put in the IV drip, rather than injected straight into the veins in my hands. This would give the penicillin crystals time to dissolve so they could drip into my bloodstream via a dextrose solution round the clock. They also decided that I was now well enough to be given a bath.

The female hospital orderly entrusted with this task appeared to be a cross between an Afghan prison wardress and an Aeroflot stewardess – very large, very formidable and severe in demeanour. With much gesturing, she indicated that I should follow her to the bathroom. Using a Russian pickle-can that she filled from an oil drum, she poured cold water over me. This pickle-can was the one that floated all day in the men's urinals on the far side of the room. Because of the severe water shortage in Afghanistan and the lack of electricity to pump the water up from the underground cistern, water was only available in the hospital for three hours a day; hence the men's urinals were kept constantly filled with water for flushing the latrines. She scrubbed me all over using a long-bristled brush, the kind used for washing floors or removing mud from a horse's thick winter coat. After I begged for mercy, she relented and I was allowed to continue my 'bath' unaided.

Later that evening, the dying man fell into a coma. Throughout the night I listened to his rattled breathing until finally, in the early hours of the morning, he took one last breath, his eyes turned up in his skull and his lips curled back. His family, who had gathered around his bed to be with him in his final moments, began to wail. His wife flung herself on his body, rocking him like a child in her arms in an outpouring of grief. Time and again she let him fall back heavily onto the bed, as though trying to force air back into his lungs and so bring him back to life. Eventually her children took her by the arm and, sobbing, she was gently led away.

For a few minutes all was quiet in the ward, until the flickering flames of candles and soft voices announced the arrival of two women holding strips of white cloth. They were the hospital orderlies whose duty it was to prepare the corpse for burial.

Omeda and Begum were poor, illiterate women from the mountainous Panjshir valley in eastern Afghanistan, responsible for performing the most menial tasks in the Jamhuriat Hospital such as cleaning the wards, emptying the bedpans and preparing the dead for burial. As patients slipped away from life, Omeda and Begum would draw near the beds and comfort them. Over the days, I had grown fond of these two kind, motherly souls. Every morning they would arrive with a broom, a mop and a pail of water. '*Salaam aleikum*, Oriot jan,' they would say shyly, before sloshing water under the bed and swirling the mop around. They wore blue hospital-regulation overalls over their colourful traditional Afghan dresses, their wrists were decorated with silver bracelets, and around their necks each woman wore several strands of coral and glass beads.

Now, outlined by the light of flickering candles, they were going about their work quietly and efficiently. I lay in bed, listening and watching as Omeda and Begum fussed around the dead man, chatting and crooning to him like a mother singing a lullaby to her child. First they wrapped a strip of cloth around his head, tying a knot under his jaw before rigor mortis set in, then moved on to tie his toes together. Omeda and Begum were no strangers to suffering and sadness. Poverty, war and the general harshness of the lives experienced by so many women living in Afghanistan at this time had given them great understanding and empathy, and their worn faces radiated warmth, kindness and serenity.

They handled the corpse with great dignity and gentleness. Finally, when they had finished their ministrations, they wrapped it in a white shroud and, when a male hospital orderly arrived with a trolley, the three of them carefully lifted the body from the bed and wheeled it away.

The remaining male patient in the bed across the room from me vomited frequently into a metal bucket on the floor. At 8.30 one morning, while Joss was visiting, he vomited one last time, lay back on the bed and died. Screaming women flung themselves on his body, tearing at his hair, until he too was lifted onto a stretcher and wheeled away.

By now I had been a patient in the Jamhuriat for eight days. Gradually the pain began to decrease, at first for a few seconds, then for a few minutes, until a whole hour would pass. On the tenth day, when I was discharged, Joss went to the bazaar and bought presents for the nurses and doctors. We thanked them profusely for all their care.

'Why are you giving us presents?' asked one nurse. 'It is our duty.'

Back at the Kabul Hotel, the waiter with the morose expression greeted me like a long-lost relative, beaming from ear to ear. Although I had lost two and a half stone (16kg) in weight, I had no appetite for the dry chicken, pallid chips and gritty salad presented at dinner that night. As I picked at the food, the kitchen door swung open and the waiter arrived, proudly holding aloft a plate on which two blancmanges wobbled, one shocking pink, one electric green.

'The cook has made this especially for madam,' he announced as he set them down in front of us.

Touched by this little act of kindness, I made an effort to eat the pink blancmange. It tasted scented and synthetic, the consistency so rubbery that the spoon bounced off it. Fortunately, Joss helped me out by eating both!

Getting a flight out of Afghanistan was problematic. My stay in the Jamhuriat meant we had missed our return flights, and I was not insured. In the bazaar Joss managed to get a call through to my sister who arranged for Cesarina, the travel agent in Eccleston Street adjacent to Joss's shop, to book us a new flight. Two days later we flew out of Afghanistan on an Ariana aircraft bound for New Delhi. The airport was a zoo, crowded with people desperate to get out of the country, and we had to push our way onto the flight. From the window of the departure lounge we watched plumes of sand ascending high into the air as mortars fired by Mujahideen landed in the sand dunes bordering the airport. Staff instructed us to run one by one as fast as possible across the airstrip to the waiting aircraft, its engines running in preparation for a hasty departure. Three weeks later, on 1 September, a massive shelling of Kabul airport by Mujahideen using surface-to-surface missiles blasted the runway, destroyed aircraft and detonated an ammunition dump and fuel store. Joss and I were lucky to get out when we did.

Out of the Nomad's Tent remained closed while I convalesced. I had planned an exhibition of Afghan artefacts at Martin & Frost, a department store in Edinburgh, to coincide with the city's festival, but I was too ill to travel. Mary (always a rock in a crisis) and Francesca packed up my stock, sent everything by lorry to Edinburgh, unloaded it at the other end, set up the exhibition and ran it until I was well enough to take over. A global recession was on the horizon, so Rufus and I reached a decision not to renew the lease on Out of the Nomad's Tent. In many ways, it was a relief. The shop was off the beaten track and required a lot of expensive advertising to tempt customers through the doors. To thank the doctors and medical staff in the Jamhuriat, Joss and I organised a Christmas exhibition in his shop in Eccleston Street and sent £10,000 raised from the sale of textiles we'd bought in Kabul. The situation in

Afghanistan had deteriorated since we'd left in August. The first phase of the Soviet withdrawal had taken place that month and the final withdrawal of all Soviet troops was scheduled for February 1989. The doctors at the Jamhuriat wrote with depressing news. There was an embargo on all airfreight going into Kabul from either Prague or Delhi and they were in despair at the situation – no medicine, no fuel, no food.

Beryl Beynon, a doctor with a medical practice in Beverley in Yorkshire, contacted us. She and her husband Peter ran a charity called Jacob's Well Appeal. They had experience in sending containers of medicines through the Soviet Union to Afghanistan and now asked if we could help them fill containers with medical equipment to send out to the eight Kabul hospitals. Through Francesca's father, Peter Stiles, hospitals in Surrey were contacted and asked if they would donate spare medicines and equipment. Boxes of medical supplies began arriving at Finlay Street and, through Jacob's Well Appeal, the medicines and equipment were soon on their way.

Without the daily responsibility of running Out of the Nomad's Tent, I was now free to go to Peshawar and concentrate on the silk-weaving project. Joss agreed to sell my remaining stock in his shop, so Francesca and I packed everything into boxes and loaded it into the back of a lorry for delivery to Eccleston Street.

In February 1989, seven months after my stay in the Jamhuriat Hospital, the Soviet army withdrew from Afghanistan. Armoured vehicles and troops retreated across the bridge spanning the Oxus river, and Kabul fell to the Mujahideen.

Chapter 8

Number 10 Canal Bank Road, Peshawar
February–May 1989

I wrote to Bob Darr in California, saying I aimed to be in Peshawar in early March and hoped to meet up with him at the ACAF office to discuss the silk-weaving project. The Galls had offered me a room in their house in University Town overlooking the Jamrud Road, and I was looking forward to seeing Sandy's daughters, Michaela and Fiona. Michaela was an artist, tall and Junoesque with deep red hair. She and her older sister Fiona, who worked for SGAA in Peshawar, shared a strong personality and a dry wit. Fiona suggested I join her at evening classes to learn Dari. The second-most widely spoken language in Afghanistan after Pushto, Dari derived from the official language of the Sassanian Empire ruled by Darius, King of Persia from 522 BC. Two young Afghan men taught us using a method that focused on enabling us to speak Dari almost immediately, rather than learning the alphabet and Arabic script. By the end of the first two-hour period, we were able to put together fairly basic sentences, and had begun to master the traditional Afghan greeting. The boys made the lessons imaginative and enjoyable, and within a few weeks we were translating some of Aesop's fables. Fiona, with her dry humour and wicked sense of fun, teased them mercilessly, so lessons were often punctuated by raucous laughter. They took the teasing in their stride.

I practised my new language on the rickshaw drivers and merchants in the bazaar. At first it was difficult to stop them speaking English but gradually, as the weeks passed, I became more confident and fluent; once I could give rickshaw drivers directions, I felt I was making real progress. And as soon as I had learnt to count up to a thousand, I started to negotiate prices for carpets and textiles with the merchants in Dari.

Bob arrived in Peshawar, and over lunch at ACAF in Shaheen Town we discussed the silk-weaving project at length. It was agreed that I could run the project alongside ACAF's existing carpet-weaving programme. This suited me perfectly. It meant that I could work within an established organisation that already had an office, a project manager and vehicles. In addition I would not require a no-objection certificate from the Pakistani government, which all humanitarian aid programmes required in order to work in the North-West Frontier. I could maintain my independence within ACAF and would only have to raise sufficient funds to cover the purchase of the raw materials (yarn, dyes and looms), fuel for the 4x4, weavers' salaries in the initial stages, and a small salary for myself. Bob made it clear that I would be wholly responsible for raising all the funds and for marketing the woven fabric. ACAF's contribution would be the use of the outside courtyard for dyeing the silk yarn, an office with a telephone and a vehicle. Mohammed Ali Tarshi would keep the accounts.

Bob mentioned that Tarshi had identified some Uzbek and Turkmen silk-weavers living in a refugee camp called Pubbi Jalozai, about 25 miles south of Peshawar.

'We're going out there this Friday,' he said. 'There's going to be a *buzkashi* match, so come with us and then we can go on and meet the weavers.'

Mohammad Ali Tarshi would drive us out to the camp and act as interpreter and negotiator. As we turned off the Grand Trunk Road and entered the camp, I drew my dupatta tight around my face as Tarshi inched the Toyota through the crowded Afghan bazaar. A white pick-up with the blue logo of a Western charity spoke of foreigners, infidels. People stared at us with undisguised hatred and spat at the wheels. Islamic fundamentalism was increasing its grip on the minds of the refugees.

Buzkashi means literally 'catch goat' or 'goat dragging' and is played by the Turkic-speaking peoples of Central Asia and northern Afghanistan on Fridays and feast days. It's a brutal game, possibly introduced as early as the sixth century AD by tribes migrating westwards into Central Asia and Persia from Mongolia. *Buzkashi* tests the limits of horsemanship and demands huge stamina of horse and rider. The Turkmen horse, an ancient breed closely related to the Akhal-Teke, was the preferred mount of eastern warriors some 2,500 years ago. Over the centuries their fame spread from China as far as Italy – the Chinese called them 'Celestial'. Today in Afghanistan, only wealthy landowners or great *Beys* can afford to own these horses, and vast amounts of money are spent on their breeding, training and diet. Training starts in earnest at the age of five and the young stallions are taught to assist the rider by rearing and using their chest, forelegs and powerful jaws in attacking an opponent's horse. In their book *Caravans to Tartary*, Roland and Sabrina Michaud give the following description of the game:

> The day before a game a goat is ritually slaughtered; its entrails are removed and it is then filled with sand, sewn up and soaked all night in cold water, to give it body and weight. The feet are cut off to make it harder to get a firm grip on an object which may weigh between sixty and eighty pounds. The following day the skin is taken to the chosen playing area and put in the centre of a circle marked out with

quicklime. The players, who vary from six riders to an unlimited number, gather round the circle and then at a signal from the leader of the boz-kashi they launch themselves at the headless goat. A goal is scored by grabbing hold of this 'ball' and galloping away with it, right round a pole that has been erected far away on the steppe, then carrying it all the way back again and throwing it into the circle ...[14]

A rutted track led from the camp to a flat and arid landscape – orange sand dotted with black stones, stunted acacia trees, thorn bushes and litter. After we had bounced and jolted for a further half-hour or so, crossing several dried-out river beds, Tarshi parked on the edge of a desolate, windswept desert. Below us a crowd of men and boys were sitting crouched in the sand. A plume of dust rose from beyond the mud dwellings and thorn trees, and a sound of drumming hooves and muffled cries heralded the imminent arrival of the horsemen. The ground trembled and a murmur of excitement rippled through the crowd. Suddenly the riders emerged through the dust, whips clenched in their teeth, the horses' flanks dark with sweat, tails and manes streaming in the wind, nostrils dilated, wild-eyed and whinnying. About 40 horsemen thundered straight towards the assembled crowd. One of the horsemen leant out of the saddle and reached down for the bloody goat carcass. He deftly positioned it across the pommel of his saddle and then, in a shower of pebbles, grit and swirling dust, galloped away, pursued by the rest of the horsemen.

Bob and I watched from the safety of the Toyota, but I was keen to get some close-up photographs, so I stepped down from the vehicle to join the crowd. I immediately realised I had made a big mistake. Traditionally women do not attend *buzkashi* matches, yet in the early 1980s the Afghans had welcomed foreigners with warmth and courtesy to their matches held each Friday at Charsadda, a camp about seven miles outside Peshawar, and had even allowed me to ride their stallions before the match. But things had changed over the last few years. The rise in fundamentalism and increase in religious fervour had turned men's minds against Westerners. I felt a sudden sharp pain between my shoulders, then another on my back. The boys were throwing stones. I made for the safety of the 4x4. Too late! In that instant, a single horseman detached from the group and thundered towards me at a flat-out gallop, holding the disembowelled goat with one hand, its back legs dragging in the dirt. Whip clenched between his teeth, the horseman (*chopendoz*) tried in vain to heave the heavy carcass across his saddle as the rest of the riders bore down upon him in hot pursuit. The crowd scattered in panic, falling over each other trying to escape being trampled. The teenage boys took full advantage of the mayhem. They deliberately knocked into me, groping and grabbing at me, laughing and confident that in the general confusion no one would notice. The *chopendoz* cursed and shouted, raining blows on his opponents' heads with his short-handled whip as they tried to wrestle the goat from him. The men's faces ran with blood as the leather thong cut through to the bone.

The ground trembled. Then, like the parting of the Red Sea, the horses tore past, their flanks dark and dripping with sweat. I glimpsed the bright-red lining of their flared nostrils and foaming mouths wrenched open by savage bits as their riders hauled on the reins in a vain attempt to control their speed. Their hooves showered me with grit and dust before the riders disappeared amongst the scrub. As I made my way back to the safety of the vehicle, the boys continued to throw stones.

The camp of the Turkmen weavers nestled in an arid tract of land in the shadow of the Kohat mountains. Behind high, biscuit-coloured mud walls lay quiet courtyards and the traditional domed roofed homes of the Turkmen. The sight of these beautiful roofs just visible above the high walls made me feel, for one brief moment, that I had been transported to northern Afghanistan.

The shady streets were peaceful after the unpleasant experience of the *buzkashi* match. A small stream ran along the edge of the dirt track; mulberry and eucalyptus saplings had been planted in it at regular intervals. This provided constant water to the trees' roots and, in exchange, the foliage gave shade from the harsh sun. A group of Turkmen women passed by, wearing red silk dresses and the traditional high hats draped with white scarves. Children gathered around the 4x4. The little girls wore dresses of bright green and pink floral-printed Russian cotton, their heads were shaved save for a single long lock of hair hanging down the back, and they wore beautiful embroidered caps. They competed to hold my hand as they led us through the dusty lanes.

Tarshi led the way through a small door in the mud wall, and we entered a large compound. Gul Agha, a small, thin Turkmen woman, her head covered with a red scarf, stepped out of the door of her domed house followed closely by her husband, Jalil. Surrounded by children and family members, they invited us to enter the cool interior of their home. There was no tension, only warm hospitality and acceptance such as used to exist in Afghanistan before the war, when foreigners were welcomed.

The house was very simple. The walls were made entirely from mud mixed with straw, the floor of smooth beaten earth. The domed roof was a marvel of craftsmanship, simple and beautiful, with flat baked mud bricks placed so as to form arches within the cupola, similar to a Byzantine basilica. The centre of the room was dominated by Jalil's 'pit' loom. From the heddles, silk warps stretched 20 feet across the room to the far wall, where they were wound around thick polished bamboo sticks and weighted with stones to create the tension. The 'pit' loom seat was made from the same mixture of mud and straw as the walls, and at the bottom of the pit were two pedals that alternated the heddles. An overhead string shot the shuttle back and forth with a resounding *clack* when pulled, giving rise to the name 'flying shuttle' loom.

While Bob and I drank green tea, Tarshi suggested to the family that they might be interested in weaving fabric in return for payment. The men of the family were all silk-weavers and, like Jalil, had taken jobs as labourers filling in potholes on the Grand Trunk Road near Lahore. They were away from their families for weeks at a time, working long hours in summer temperatures that often reached 40° C or more. The Turkmen came from cooler climes and were unaccustomed to the heat of the Punjab, so the chance to weave silk in their own homes, surrounded by their wives and children, was an offer none of them refused.

Before Bob departed for California, we agreed that ACAF would purchase a good supply of silk yarn from the sericulture centre in Peshawar. I suggested that I should be responsible for dyeing the yarn; I felt it was important to maintain some control over the colours used, particularly as the fabric was going to be sold in London and to the expatriate community in Pakistan. Seventeen-year-old Saleh Mohammed, brother of Tarshi's young wife Kowkee, would help me dye the yarn. Tarshi would then take the yarn to the weavers in the camp, and return a fortnight later to collect the woven fabric and pay the weavers for their work. This seemed an excellent arrangement and I agreed that I would take responsibility for marketing the woven silk fabric.

The Pakistan Forestry and Agricultural Department was a substantial building constructed during the days of the Raj, set back from the busy Grand Trunk Road in a wooded area behind Peshawar's polo ground. In one wing was a sericulture department.

The Chief Officer, Mr Mir Baz Khan, was busy signing papers and giving orders to his obsequious staff. I was shown in to his office and sat down at the far side of his large desk, waiting for him to finish his business. I had arrived that morning without an appointment in the hope of purchasing silk yarn for the Pubbi Jalozai weavers.

Time ticked by. I waited. Conditioned by years of working in a government institution, Mr MBK was pedantic in the extreme and very conscious of his status and authority. He was a large man of dark complexion, who wore a large white Chitrali hat. He seemed in no hurry to acknowledge my presence, but continued writing, and from time to time speaking on the telephone. I whiled away the time by reading – several times over – a large poster with illustrations showing the different stages of the life cycle of *Bombyx mori*, the silk moth. Behind his chair hung a map showing the villages in NWFP that participated in rearing silk cocoons, and high on the wall was a large black-and-white photograph of Mohammed Ali Jinnah, founder of modern Pakistan.

Finally, Mr MBK put down his pen.

'Madam, which country are you from? Germany?'

'No, England.'

'Ah, madam. So you are a Britisher. What is your business?'

'I'm working with Afghan silk-weavers and I have come to buy silk yarn for the project.'

'Why you working with these Afghans? Why you not work with Pakistani weavers?

'I am working with Afghans because they are refugees.'

'What is your salary for this work, madam?'

'I am paid a local salary.'

'*Only* local salary … ?' I detected a note of disdain in Mr Mir Baz Khan's voice. He leant back in his chair and pondered my request. Then he tried a different tack.

'Madam, where is your husband?'

'I don't have a husband.'

'No husband? Not married? No children? Why not? Why your father not find you good husband?'

I sighed and tried again. 'Please, Mr Mir Baz Khan – would it be possible to buy some silk?'

'Madam, you are in such hurry. First you must take tea.'

He barked an order in Hindko, the local dialect of Punjabi, and a minion arrived bearing a cup of sweet milk tea that he set down before me. Unfortunately I hated it, much preferring the green tea flavoured with cardamom served by Afghans in the bazaar. Out of courtesy I drank it, but inwardly I was seething at having my personal life cross-examined.

Warming to his theme, Mr MBK put down his teacup.

'Mrs Mir Baz Khan and I have found good husbands for all our daughters. All are married. All *very* happy. Girls should marry early. Then marriage is easy. They adjust. If leaving marriage too late then maybe some problem coming between husband and wife. Madam, take my advice. You should return to your country and ask your father to find you good husband.'

I tried hard not to show my irritation, and Kipling's 'Oh, East is East, and West is West, And never the twain shall meet' came to mind. During the years I worked in Peshawar on the silk project, I would sit countless times at Mr MBK's desk, and each time, somehow or other, he would manoeuvre the conversation round to the subject of husbands and marriage. While I fumed silently at his inability to take me seriously, what he found most difficult to understand was the fact that my father allowed me to travel alone without a chaperone.

It soon became apparent to Mr MBK that I knew next to nothing about how silk yarn was produced, so he took it upon himself to educate me. We set off together on a conducted tour of the sericulture centre.

The leaves of the mulberry tree form the staple diet of the silkworm, so around the back of Mr Mir Baz Khan's office in the grounds of the Forestry and Agricultural Department were nurseries full of mulberry saplings. Mr MBK guided me between the rows of saplings where gardeners were busy coppicing the small trees to provide rooting stock. The long thin branches were stacked in piles on the ground and the gardeners were carefully cutting each branch into six-inch segments and binding the sticks into bundles.

A hardy tree that can survive harsh climates and a variety of soils, the mulberry was ideally suited for growing in the Frontier district, where many villages clung to precipitous mountain slopes and fields were often terraced. The small bundles of mulberry cuttings were destined for these remote villages, where the production of silk was a cottage industry providing an important source of income for poor rural families.

'These twigs will go to the villages. Soon they will grow into mulberry trees. Then women, girls feeding leaves to silkworm, and ...' He broke open a cocoon and extracted the brown pupa, holding it out on the palm of his hand. 'This very good food for chickens. They like very much. So you see, madam, sericulture very important for rural areas.'

The reeling of silk from cocoons was taking place in the outbuildings. Cocoons were thrown into cauldrons of boiling water to dissolve the sericin, a natural gum secreted by the silkworm as it spins silk to create a cocoon around itself. The young man in charge of the reeling process combed the surface of the water, gathering up from the cocoons handfuls of silk filaments that he attached to a hexagonal wheel above his head. As he turned the handle to reel the silk onto the wheel, the cocoons bobbed and jumped as though they had suddenly come alive in the boiling water.

When eventually enough silk had been wound on to the wheel to form a skein, the wheel was detached and the silk left to dry before being removed from the wheel.

In the storeroom I selected skeins of different deniers for the project, a thicker one for the warps and a slightly thinner one for the wefts. I packed the silk into the Toyota and drove straight to the ACAF office. Saleh and I were keen to start dyeing the silk as soon as possible, so within minutes water was bubbling in a large aluminium cooking pot over a gas burner in the backyard.

Silk fibre in its natural state contains a heavy coating of sericin, and this gives silk a harsh feel. As I handled the skeins they looked and felt more like horsehair. To reveal the lustrous quality of silk it first has to be de-gummed, but neither Saleh nor I realised this. In our enthusiasm we plunged the skeins straight into a dye-bath, but they became entangled with each other and it took several frustrating hours to untangle them. Although the yarn had taken the dye, in certain places where there was a particularly heavy concentration of sericin the yarn remained white. To our dismay, as soon as the weavers used our yarn, the undyed areas cropped up time and again in the woven silk fabric as little white dashes, making it impossible to sell. Furthermore, the finished woven silk felt stiff to the touch. There was no lustre and it rustled like taffeta.

In the 19th century, *ikat* silk woven in the oasis towns contained a high proportion of sericin. In Khiva, the Hungarian traveller Vámbéry observed,

> The oriental ... is fond of the Tchakhtchukh or rustling tone of dress. It was always an object of great delight to me to see the seller parading up and down a few paces in the new Tchapan to ascertain whether it gave out the orthodox tone. [15]

However, our silk was being woven into scarves and marketed to expatriates who expected it to drape softly around their shoulders, not to rustle!

In those early days it was trial and error, a case of the blind leading the blind. If we de-gummed the yarn too much, the fibres broke during the threading-up of the loom and during weaving. Our lack of knowledge was frustrating but, little by little, through research – particularly by Saleh, who took it upon himself to learn from the weavers in the Old City – we learnt that we should de-gum the yarn prior to dyeing by boiling it in soapy water.

Jamilla, Tarshi's 18-year-old niece, became my assistant. Pretty and intelligent, with a strong personality, she had had the courage to say 'no' to an early marriage. She accepted with alacrity the opportunity to help me in dyeing the silk, which gave her a chance to get out of the house and earn some money. We worked together day after day, mixing the dyes and experimenting with colours. Together we weighed the dye on the scales and carefully measured out salt to set it. Cheap, coarse yellow soap normally used for washing clothes and readily available from the bazaar in Shaheen Town was grated into shavings using a cheese grater. Added to the boiling water, it dissolved the sericin as we had hoped. Jamilla spoke no English, so I had no alternative but to struggle by with my limited Dari. Gradually as the weeks passed, my knowledge of Dari improved, helped by attending the evening classes and working daily with Jamilla. She taught me the names of all the different colours that we produced, and the words for all the equipment.

I had been staying with the Galls for a number of weeks, but now my room was required for two volunteers arriving from England to work with SGAA. The boys appeared one morning in March in an old British ambulance that they had driven overland from the UK. The ambulance had been purchased by SGAA for use in Peshawar and, although no one realised it at the time, it would be put to use across the border in Afghanistan almost as soon as it arrived.

It was the incessant sound of sirens blaring day and night, as ambulances wound their way down around the hairpin bends of the Khyber Pass bringing wounded to the Peshawar trauma hospitals, that first alerted us to the fact that some huge offensive was taking place just across the border. Gradually news began to filter through. With the Soviet withdrawal from Afghanistan earlier in the month, the Mujahideen wanted to prove to the world that they were not just a guerrilla force fighting in the mountains, but were also competent at capturing towns and cities. Their ultimate goal was Kabul but, protected by mountains, the capital proved a more formidable obstacle than the less-easily defended royal winter capital of Jalalabad in the flat desert plain. Gulbuddin Hekmatyar's Hesb-i-Islami, the most fundamentalist of the seven Mujahideen groups fighting against the Soviet occupation, had captured the small town of Samarkhel a few miles from Jalalabad where, just a year before, Scheherezade, Donatella and I had posed with the Afghan conscripts beside their tank. Now Hesb-i-Islami were poised to capture the airport and city of Jalalabad.

That evening I joined friends at the American Club. We sat outdoors on the first-floor veranda under a clear night sky enjoying the cool evening air, sipping Budweiser and eating pizza. Above the beat of the jukebox we could hear the wail of the ambulance sirens. Just before closing time, some Swiss doctors in white coats entered the bar asking for donations of blood. A number of operations were being carried out in the ICRC (International Committee of the Red Cross) hospital, and supplies of blood were running low.

'There has been a big battle around Jalalabad. We have received a lot of casualties, so we are starting to operate at five am tomorrow,' they explained.

The SGAA ambulance left immediately for the front line. I went the next morning to donate blood.

The battle raged throughout March. During the day I watched fighter jets piloted by the Afghan air force scorch across the sky, leaving vapour trails above the Khyber Pass, and at times I could clearly hear the sound of bombing. It seemed for a while that the Mujahideen were winning the battle, but after Hekmatyar's men shot dead captured Afghan government troops in cold blood, the tide turned against them. In all, 15,000–20,000 died during the battle and the trauma hospitals in Peshawar were overflowing with wounded. A journalist friend aged so much after witnessing the scenes of bloodshed and carnage around Jalalabad that I hardly recognised him.

One afternoon, while browsing in the small handicraft shops tucked away down a side street in Saddar Bazaar, I met Peter Jouvenal, the freelance cameraman I had first met at Joss Graham's shop. He was negotiating to buy a collection of Soviet cap badges, leather army belts with brass buckles displaying the hammer and sickle, and other bits and pieces of Soviet military regalia. Russian conscripts, ill-treated by their officers, poorly paid and poorly fed, frequently sold items of clothing and even their weapons in exchange for money to buy food. Eventually these items found their way into the Afghan handicraft shops in Peshawar. The leather belts were popular in the UK, and I sold dozens of them in Out of the Nomad's Tent.

'I'm about to go off on a long assignment inside Afghanistan,' Peter told me. 'Providing you pay the rent each month, you're welcome to use my room during my absence. The house is on the canal bank in University Town, quite close to the tribal area. Most expatriates don't like to live on that side of the canal. They consider it too unsafe.'

Number 10 Canal Bank Road was a modern, brick-built house overlooking a wide canal that channelled snow-melt from the Safed mountains through University Town to the Old City. Peter, together with others, had set up the agency Frontline Television News, supplying TV companies with photographs and film footage of the Afghan war. Like Peter, the cameramen were freelance, and most were ex-army; their military knowledge proved useful. The house was also the BBC office in the North-West Frontier, and home to various freelance journalists. Like all the houses along the canal bank, Number 10 was surrounded by a high security wall built of cement blocks topped with three strands of barbed wire. This was because houses built on that side of the canal were only a short distance from Khyber Agency, a tribal territory where Pakistan government writ and law did not exist. Most expatriates considered it a 'no-go area' and preferred to live on the opposite side of the canal, which was deemed safer. Inserted into the security wall was a large corrugated-iron metal door with a bullet hole in the centre that acted as a peephole. Through this tiny aperture, our chowkidar, Mohammed Gul, could see whether visitors to the house were friend or foe before opening a small door in the main gate and allowing them into the compound.

Already living in the house were two freelance journalists: John Jennings, a tall red-haired ex-US Marine from Tucson, Arizona, and Ian McWilliam, a Scot who had lived most of his life in Canada. Ian had taught for a while at a boys' school in England and at Peshawar's Edwardes College before becoming a stringer for *The Daily Telegraph*. John was breaking into journalism and writing for Pakistani publications. When BBC correspondent Lyse Doucet recommended him to Reuters, he was hired as a local stringer. His knowledge of weapons and tactics gained from his days in the Marines, as well as being a qualified emergency medical technician, were useful skills for his forays inside Afghanistan with the Mujahideen. He had a knack for languages and learnt to speak Dari quickly. From time to time Rory Peck, a freelance cameraman who often worked with Peter on assignments, would spend a few days at Number 10. An eccentric Anglo-Irishman, old Etonian and ex-Grenadier Guardsman with a wild disposition, he would arrive from London, fill the fridge with smoked salmon, pâté and cheese from Fortnum & Mason, and then disappear inside Afghanistan with his camera for weeks at a time.

Finally, there was Hamed Elmi, a young Afghan journalist employed by the BBC's Pushto and Farsi departments. The front room overlooking the courtyard was his office, where he came each afternoon to interview the Mujahideen. The commanders would arrive in small groups at our metal gates wearing enormous black turbans, *pattus* slung over their shoulders. Sometimes I would glimpse them being formally greeted by Hamed or Mohammed Gul on the terrace, amongst terracotta flower pots overflowing with geraniums and orange marigolds. For the most part they were powerful men, well over six feet in height, with jet-black beards and eyes rimmed with *kohl*. They epitomised the appearance and bearing of fierce warriors.

As a result of these meetings we were often the first to hear the latest information from the front line before it was relayed to Bush House in London. Hamed always made sure that the purdah curtain was drawn across the room so that he and the Mujahideen were seated on one side of the flimsy cloth and I and the boys were on the other. At first, I found it very strange to be hidden from view behind a curtain, but the longer I lived in Peshawar the more I came to appreciate Afghan culture. It simply would not have been acceptable for the Mujahideen to see me unveiled in my home or living unmarried in the same house with men to whom I was not related. They would have found it deeply shocking and it would not have reflected well upon the reputation of the BBC, which was held in high regard throughout Pakistan. The curtain preserved my privacy and modesty and had only been hung across the room to protect me from the lascivious gaze of these battle-hardened Islamic fundamentalists.

It was often remarked in Peshawar that expatriates fell into the following categories: Mercenaries, Missionaries, Misfits and Mavericks. In his book *Frontline: The True Story of the British Mavericks Who Changed the Face of War Reporting*, David Loyn describes of the kind of men who passed through the portals of Number 10:

> The city was full of glamorous, fit young men going into danger and coming out with their pockets full of cash. There were parties, but none as large or loud as Rory's parties, and there was gossip in this city where the last thing you came across was a fact, but there was no gossip as good as that heard in No 10 Canal Bank Road. Amid the journalists, aid workers, diplomats, spies and soldiers, they stood out: freelance adventurers, drawn to something deep in all of us, the same thing that draws people to fast cars, sky diving, Russian roulette and cocaine – the desire to explore the border between life and death.[16]

The interior of Number 10 was spartan. The bookshelves along one wall of the sitting room were empty save for pieces of shrapnel, a row of shell casings in various sizes, live bullets from a Soviet 'Dushka' heavy machine gun, and a Gideons Bible. Outside on the veranda were metal trunks filled with Peter's Soviet militaria, ready for shipment to the UK. Inside, the house was covered in a thick film of dust that blew in constantly from the dirt road. On my first day I set about cleaning the sitting room with the help of the chowkidars, Wadood and Mohammed Gul. The men heaved the large, filthy Labijar kilim out into the courtyard, where they took it in turns to beat it hard with Rory's cricket bat, releasing clouds of choking dust. Parveen – a poor woman from the bazaar who came daily to clean the house and wash clothes – appeared, dragging the garden hosepipe behind her. She turned on the tap and water flowed across the sitting-room floor. Then the four of us worked in a line, sweeping muddy water from one end of the room to the other with yard brooms before finally pushing it out through the front door.

I slept badly during my first night in Peter's room. There was a constant scratching sound from inside the clothes cupboard. In the morning, I found a large quantity of army rations – packaged Meals Ready to Eat – that Peter would take with him in Afghanistan. They had been eaten by mice. The bottom of the cupboard was full of droppings and the mice had made nests in his army socks. In the bathroom, a cockroach lived under the rim of the lavatory bowl. Every time I went to sit down, it would announce its presence by waving its feathery antennae. Although the water dislodged it when I flushed the loo, a few seconds later it would reappear, bobbing around in the swirling water. It would then calmly climb back up the porcelain bowl to its original hiding place.

There were a huge number of mosques in University Town, practically one at the end of each street. There was a small one just behind Number 10. At dawn, the *azan* was always preceded by the muezzin blowing down the microphone to test whether the speakers were working properly. Then he would twiddle a few knobs on the microphone, which nearly always resulted in an ear-splitting screech like a band testing its electronic equipment before a gig. Clearing his throat and taking a deep breath, the muezzin would begin the call to prayer – '*Allahu-Akbar. Allahu-Akbar…*'.

Dogs barked, babies cried, cockerels crowed and donkeys brayed.

The call to prayer from the myriad of small mosques spread out across University Town was never synchronised. As soon as the evocative high-pitched tenor of the muezzin finished in one mosque another would begin, so that the call to prayer could last as long as ten minutes. It reminded me of the grandfather clocks at Graythwaite. My father would wind them up each week and adjust them so that they all chimed the hour at slightly different times.

Soon after the *azan*, the sun would rise above the horizon, an orange disc in a cloudless, deep-blue sky. Each new day would begin with familiar sounds. *Clack! Thwap! Clack!* – the banging of the mesh screen door as Mohammed Gul and Wadood entered the house to fill the kettle from the kitchen sink to make early-morning tea for Ian, and the opening and closing of the fridge door in the kitchen as they placed inside Russian vodka bottles filled with boiled water from the kettle to be consumed ice-cold later in the day – Peshawar's water was unfit to drink direct from the taps.

From my bed I could hear the voices of Afghan children driving buffaloes, goats and fat-tailed sheep along the canal bank and the chowkidars speaking quietly in Dari as they moved around Number 10, and the soft *swish-swish-swish* as Wadood swept the dust from the veranda below my window with a hand-held whisk, followed by the sound of water gurgling out of the hosepipe as he watered the nasturtiums, marigolds, zinnias and cosmos in their terracotta pots.

Each morning around 7 am there would be a knocking on our metal gate, then the scraping sound of the giant bolt being slid back, followed by the traditional Afghan greeting, '*Salaam aleikum. Chitor asti?*' as Mohammad Gul welcomed the arrival of Ian and John's *munshi*. Lessons were held outside my bedroom window on a small raised terrace surrounded by roses and shaded by a beautiful bottlebrush tree. Here, Ian and Mirwais, reclining on carpet cushions made from Baluchi saddlebags, would converse in Pushto. As I listened to them, I thought of my mother's great-great-grandfather, John Tulloch Nash, the son of General Joseph Nash. Born in India in 1831, he entered the Indian Civil Service and was sent to Bhundersoo in the state of Bhurtpore (now Bharatpur) in Rajasthan. On leaving Bhundersoo, he wrote to his mother, Dina Margaretha, 'I served for two long years without ever seeing a white face, or speaking a word of my native tongue'.

Ian and John were linguists. John spoke exceptionally fluent Farsi, Ian spoke Pushto, and both were able to read Arabic script, something I never mastered. I would often join John for breakfast in the dining room behind the purdah curtain, but Ian always preferred to eat breakfast alone in his room. Each morning, Mohammad Gul would bring us a pot of tea and fresh Afghan naan from the bakery at the end of our road. This unleavened bread, large and flat with small slits cut into the dough, was baked in a traditional tandoor oven set into the ground. It was delicious when eaten hot and smeared with butter, but became tough and chewy when cold. Left for a couple of days, the bread became rock-hard like the notorious ship's biscuit. Sometimes, when I was shopping for textiles in the bazaar, Afghans would invite me to share their meal. If it happened to be a 'meatless' day, I would watch them tearing up pieces of stale naan and dropping them into a large bowl of broth. As the naan absorbed the liquid, it would swell and expand, becoming a savoury bread-and-butter pudding that the Afghans called *sherwa*. They would then scoop up the soft mush with their hands and pop it in their mouths with great proficiency. I, on the other hand, struggled with the slippery naan, which more often than not fell with a *plop* into my lap.

Like me, Fiona Gall was a keen rider.

'Why don't you come over to our house early tomorrow morning before the sun rises and ride the Médecins Sans Frontières horses?' she suggested one day.

As the following day was Friday, the Muslim holy day, all shops and offices would be closed. I accepted her offer with enthusiasm.

It was just a short walk from Number 10 to the house of the French doctors in Park Lane, always referred to as 'the White House'. Before dawn, before even the first call of the muezzin, I walked through silent, deserted streets. In March, the air was still pleasantly cool. Tethered at the bottom of the garden in Park Lane were half a dozen stallions used by the doctors to transport medical supplies over the high mountain passes to clinics based deep inside Afghanistan. An Afghan *syce* (groom) had already saddled two horses, so they were ready and waiting for us. My saddle was a traditional wooden Afghan one with a high pommel. A small dark-red, hand-woven carpet of Turkmen design fitted over the pommel and wooden seat area. The stirrup leathers were of one length and impossible to alter; the stirrup irons, being heavy and solid, would prove to be most uncomfortable during the ride and bruised my ankles. As dawn broke, Fiona and I rode out from the doctors' compound, through the quiet, dusty streets and across the railway line that led to the Khyber Pass. Then we crossed the canal that divided University Town from the Tribal Agencies and soon reached farmland.

The stallions were lean and fit. Despite their slight build and poor conformation, they were accustomed to hard, heavy work as both pack and riding animals on the long arduous journeys into Afghanistan. Journalists would tell me that, on their forays with the Mujahideen, they would often find the high mountain passes littered with the carcasses of horses shot by Russian helicopter gunships, or that had broken their legs negotiating scree and boulders or fallen off the narrow mountain paths into ravines through sheer exhaustion.

Once out into open farmland, we let the horses have their heads. They galloped like the wind past smoking brick kilns and, being sure-footed, made light of the rutted tracks that ran between fields of alfalfa and sugar cane. Jumping irrigation ditches, we would scorch through mud villages at breakneck speed, scattering chickens and donkeys. Mangy mongrels darted out from houses straining at their chains, barking and snapping at the horses, while barefoot children ran alongside throwing stones at us, screaming and shouting.

On, on we galloped until we were right amongst the opium poppy fields, acres of beautiful pink, white and purple striped petals and large green seed pods. In the shadow of the Safed mountain range, we stopped to give the horses a rest. To the north of us lay a huge wall of snow-capped peaks – Afghanistan.

The stallions had well-formed crested necks and mouths of iron. We could only stop them with the greatest difficulty. Because they had not been castrated, they could on occasion be extremely aggressive. That day, as Fiona and I rode side by side laughing, chatting and enjoying the cool morning air, our horses came too close together. With no warning, ears pinned back flat against their skulls, the stallions lunged at each other, emitting ear-splitting screams. Fiona's stallion opened its jaws wide like a crocodile, showing an impressive range of teeth that closed with a resounding 'snap' on the crest of my horse, narrowly missing my hand. For what seemed like eternity but was probably only a few seconds, the horses smashed their heads together, each endeavouring to gain a hold on the other's jugular. Rearing up, they lashed out with their front hooves as Fiona and I tried in vain to pull them apart. Stallions will fight to the death, and to be in close proximity to such aggression was an experience I would not be in a hurry to repeat! Before too long, calm was restored and the horses continued as though nothing had happened.

We turned for home, edging our horses around orchards and wheat fields past tribal elders surveying their crops and small children who ran after us shouting, 'Angrez, Angrez!', the Urdu for 'English'. Two young men up to their waists in water in the *nullah* were washing their grey horse, preparing it for a day's work harnessed to a tonga. It would spend the hours between dawn and dusk earning its owners a living by ferrying people across town.

These exhilarating rides gave us a sense of freedom, an escape from the daily tension of living in a strict Islamic society surrounded by poverty, human suffering and the occasional car bomb. It was wonderful to be able to ride the spirited Afghan horses, to gallop and feel the wind in our hair, to abandon the dupatta and shapeless clothing we all wore and to be ourselves, if only for a short while.

April was always a glorious month in Peshawar. For about six weeks before the hot weather arrived, the days were warm and pleasant like an English summer. The roses in the garden began to flower profusely, having been watered well by the heavy winter rain. Jasmine, orange blossom, flame trees, bottlebrush, jacaranda and hibiscus soon followed. As the flower buds burst into bloom, the upper canopy of the trees became a riot of colour that lasted for several weeks. Amongst the jungle of lush green grass at the base of the trees grew geraniums, marigolds, sweet peas and nasturtiums. From my bedroom window I would watch a hoopoe – the messenger of God – searching for grubs in the grass. Pale lavender jacaranda petals carpeted the grass in our small garden before the intense summer heat arrived with a vengeance in May, sucking out the moisture and turning everything brown.

Peshawar was spared the enervating, hot and desiccating winds that blow across the plains of northern India because of cool air flowing from the Hindu Kush. Nevertheless, the thermometer frequently climbed to nearly 40° C in May and early June. John Tulloch Nash, a volunteer with the Bengal Yeomanry Cavalry during the Indian Mutiny in 1857, described the 'blazing hot winds', the 'insufferable heat' and the 'flaming furnace' endured by the volunteers as they rode along the Grand Trunk Road, criss-crossing the states of Upper India to track down the sepoy mutineers involved in the massacre of women and children at Cawnpore. At Oudh he wrote, 'We could not retain our feet in the burning stirrups, and the ground was heated to such a degree, as not to be borne by the naked foot'.[17] By day, the brick walls of Number 10 absorbed the heat; by nightfall the house was like an oven, and even the inside walls were hot to the touch. Ceiling fans provided some relief and the bedrooms had primitive air conditioners, boxes set into the walls that were nicknamed 'wall bangers' because of the noise they made. The boxes spewed out cold air that smelt unpleasant and gave me respiratory problems. The heat made it impossible to sleep until I solved the problem by soaking a bedsheet in cold water and wrapping myself in it. Although I had to repeat the procedure several times in the night, it worked very well.

John Tulloch Nash describes an innovative method of bringing some relief from the heat. Beneath their tents, when pitching camp after a long day in the saddle, a large deep hole was dug in which the men sat, and in this 'living tomb' they read, smoked, told 'mirthful' stories, sang songs and wrote their journals, and 'so contrived to while away the weary and fiery hours, as pleasantly as rabbits are wont to do in their appropriate warrens'.[18]

At Dari class, the missionaries told me about a special pre-dawn Easter Sunday service at St John's Cathedral. Dating from the days of the Raj, the Anglican cathedral was built in the Gothic style in 1852 as the church for the military garrison and cantonment. That Easter Sunday morning, the cathedral's interior was decked with coloured streamers and fairy lights. The largely Pakistani congregation sang hymns in Urdu. Just before sunrise, the pastor invited us to step out into the garden. We stood in the dew-soaked grass and watched as the deep orange sun rose up from behind the roofs of the cantonment. Then the voice of the pastor rang out – 'Alleluia. Christ is Risen!' – and the congregation chorused, 'Alleluia. He is Risen indeed!' Perhaps it was because I was far away from my own home and country that I found the simple service so moving.

One afternoon, in the garden of the American Club, I gave a short talk on oriental carpets to a small group of expats. During their time in Peshawar many had bought carpets in the bazaar, but they did not have a great deal of knowledge about what to look for when buying. I spoke about the importance of carpet-weaving in nomadic communities, the meaning of the various designs and how to tell whether the wool had been dyed using chemical or vegetable dyes. I finished by telling them about the ancient tradition of silk-weaving in Afghanistan, the *ikat* weavers of Qurchangee and ACAF's plans to start a silk-weaving income-generating project in Pubbi Jalozai camp.

Just as I was leaving, Michael Keating introduced himself, and explained that he was working for Operation Salaam, a UN project to encourage Afghan refugees to return to their homeland after the withdrawal of Soviet troops. His boss, Prince Sadruddin Aga Khan, an international civil servant and UNESCO's special representative and coordinator of Operation Salaam, would be arriving in Peshawar a few days later. UNESCO had allocated money for the restoration of archaeological sites and the heritage of Afghanistan. Michael thought the silk-weaving project would be of great interest to Prince Sadruddin as it fulfilled UNESCO's criterion of revitalising an ancient skill in danger of dying out altogether as a result of the war.

'Could I bring him out to the camp and show him your project?' he asked.

A few days later, with Tarshi leading the way in the Toyota, Michael and the Prince followed us in convoy down the Grand Trunk Road to Pubbi Jalozai. Born in France, Prince Sadruddin was the son of the Aga Khan III, spiritual leader of the Shia Ismaili sect, and a Parisienne mother. Educated in Switzerland and at Harvard, the Prince was cultured and westernised, and spoke several languages. In Gul Agha's small compound, Turkmen children crowded round, wide-eyed and curious, staring at the dapper Prince in his immaculately tailored grey suit while I explained about the *ikat* weavers in Jowzjan province and the importance of sericulture in Afghanistan and how it had been destroyed by ten years of war.

He listened with interest, then asked, 'Would you be prepared to go to Afghanistan to set up an *ikat* weaving and dyeing programme for UNESCO in Mazar-i-Sharif?' For a moment I hesitated. Everything was happening so fast. What if the weavers were no longer living in Qurchangee? Would I be able to find them? Were they even still alive? I suddenly felt very insecure. Up until then it had all been rather a fantasy. Now it was reality. I took a deep breath. It was now or never.

'Yes, I'd be happy to go to Afghanistan,' I replied.

'Good,' said the Prince. 'Then you must prepare a proposal for a pilot project. Michael will explain all the details.'

Each week Tarshi drove me to Pubbi Jalozai to visit the weavers. He had purchased a traditional hand loom from weavers in Afghan Colony, a residential area in the south of Peshawar, and transported it to the camp. Now he wanted me to see the loom assembled and operating. During the visit, Gul Agha asked me if she and her family could give me lunch on my next visit.

'They would like to cook a chicken for you,' said Tarshi, who was acting as interpreter as I did not understand the Turkic language. Knowing that the family was desperately poor, the last thing I wanted was for them to buy and kill a chicken just for me. I knew they could not afford the expense, so I made some excuse.

On the return journey to Peshawar, Tarshi said, 'You know, Harriet, Jalil, Gul Agha and all their family are upset with you. They think you do not want to eat with them because they are so poor.'

'But Tarshi, I don't want them to spend money buying a chicken for me. They're very expensive.'

'You don't understand, Harriet,' he replied. 'You will offend them if you continue to refuse their hospitality. You should eat a meal with them.'

I was embarrassed that my misunderstanding of the Afghan culture, where people will give their guest the best possible food even if other members of the family have to go without, had unintentionally caused offence. And so, on my next visit to Pubbi Jalozai, I accepted a meal.

The Qur'an teaches hospitality and to honour the guest, whether invited or not. The guest should be honoured even if the whole family, including the children, stay hungry. As soon as Gul Agha and her daughters placed the dishes on the *dastarkhan*, it became apparent that the tiny chicken in the metal *karai* was intended only for me and Tarshi. The family would not be joining us. As I chewed on the scrawny legs of the fried chicken, children, their faces encrusted with dirt, peered in through the open door and windows of Gul Agha's house to watch me eat. Numerous pairs of hungry eyes watched my every mouthful. Chicken was a luxury; Tarshi later told me that the family might eat chicken once a month if they were lucky.

During my travels around Pakistan I frequently experienced extreme kindness from complete strangers. One day I decided to travel south to India, but my visa had expired. After waiting many hours in the visa office of the Indian Embassy in Islamabad, the clerk announced the office was now closed for the weekend. Impatient by nature and not wanting to wait two more days in Islamabad, I decided to push on to Lahore, thinking (wrongly, as it turned out) that I might get a visa there. The sun was setting as the flying coach pulled in to Lahore's bus station. As I stepped out into the busy terminus, I regretted my hasty decision to embark on a journey with no prior planning. I had left my guidebook behind in Peshawar and, as I did not know Lahore well, I had absolutely no idea where I might stay the night. I hailed an autorickshaw. The driver was fat and his teeth were stained red from chewing betel nut. As I sat in the back seat, I noted that his body was covered in thick black hair which, damp with sweat, curled through the holes of his string vest. Soon the lights of Lahore petered out, and as we bumped along the unlit road I realised what a fool I had been. I should have stayed with friends in Islamabad, but my impatience to reach India had now placed me in a situation where my safety was at risk. Finally, we came to a stop outside a small hotel. The interior was typical of low-budget hotels in Pakistan. The walls were painted pale blue and the room lit with a single fluorescent tube that gave a harsh bright light. Behind the reception desk the manager picked his teeth with a toothpick and, while he and the driver conversed in Urdu, he gazed at me lasciviously. I knew I could not stay the night in such a seedy place so, taking control of the situation, I announced that the hotel was quite unsuitable, ordered the driver to take me to the bazaar and paid him off.

Amongst the bright lights of Anarkali, the narrow streets were crowded with families shopping after a day's work, and the air full of the smell of cooking kebabs, frying gulabis, cheap hair oil and spices. While the men deliberately jostled into me, there were at least women and children present, so I felt safe. I searched both sides of the street for a hotel, but after 20 minutes of walking I had come to the end of the bazaar. On my right was a municipal park with swings and benches. It was now well after 10 pm and I was weary and afraid. As a last resort I could always curl up on a bench, I thought, as I began to look for the entrance.

As I passed a huge marble archway leading to an office complex, a soft voice spoke from the shadows.

'Where you go, memsahib?'

An elderly chowkidar stepped out into the light, dressed in iron-grey shalwar kameez and black beret, the uniform of a government employee.

'I've been looking for a hotel, but I can't find anywhere to stay,' I blurted, his question and kind tone of his voice making tears well up in my eyes.

'But you can stay here, memsahib. Come.'

He beckoned me to follow him. For a few seconds I hesitated. Was I about to jump out of the frying pan into the fire? But what was the alternative – a night on a park bench? I decided to trust him and followed him under the arch.

'You may have my room,' said the chowkidar, showing me a typical night-watchman's room with a string charpoy and an upturned tin box that served as a small table. 'I sleep other place. Tomorrow I bring you breakfast.'

Then, having made sure I had everything I needed, he disappeared. I unrolled my sleeping bag on the charpoy, thanked God for sending me a guardian angel, and was soon sound asleep.

In the morning I awoke to the sound of cocks crowing and the roar of traffic as Lahore began a new day. There was a knock at the door and the chowkidar entered carrying on a tray a glass of sweet milk tea, a fried egg and a *paratha*. As I departed I thanked him profusely for his kindness to me and offered him some rupees to cover the cost of my breakfast.

'No! No, memsahib!' he said, taking a step back, and I knew in an instant that I had insulted him. 'I *not* take money!'

As he walked with me out to the road to hail a rickshaw, I asked, 'Why did you invite me to stay here?'

'Last night when I saw you walking in the street, I thought – she reminds me of my daughter.'

His words made me think about my own culture. Would we in Britain, seeing a stranger in the street, take them in, feed them and then set them on their way without expecting any reward other than the pleasure of having helped another human being? Furthermore, this experience, like so many others during my travels, served only to increase my faith that, in all the dangers and difficult moments, someone was guiding and watching over me.

Mike McGovern, a tough Irish-American engineer, shared my interest in oriental carpets. During his time working for USAID he had collected some fine and interesting pieces that he was keen to show me. While I was looking at his carpets, proudly arranged on the floor of his home, I told him about my project with the silk-weavers and Prince Sadruddin's visit to Pubbi Jalozai.

'The Prince has asked me to put together a project proposal for UN funding, Mike, so I need to find myself a job here in Peshawar if I'm ever going to get this project up and running. I can't stay here much longer without earning some money.'

'Well, you can come and work in my office. I'm leading a group of newly qualified Afghan engineers on a USAID-funded project called the Short Term Assistance for Rehabilitation Team, or START for short. The aim of the project is to look at the feasibility and financial cost of rebuilding roads, bridges, irrigation systems, power cables and electricity generators destroyed by the Russians during years of war.'

He went on to explain that START was part of Prince Sadruddin Agha Khan's Operation Salaam to restore war-torn Afghanistan so that it was a country fit for returning refugees.

'Afghan engineers are sent covertly inside Afghanistan to assess the damage, and come back with photographs and reports. The reports need to be typed up and the English corrected. That's something you could do. I've also just employed two young Afghan women in the START office as secretaries, so you might like to help them operate the computers.'

Years before, Elizabeth Winter had thrown me a lifeline by inviting me to join the committee of ARIN; now Mike, by offering me employment when I most needed it, was doing the same. I would be earning a local salary, about 400 rupees (approximately £10) a week, but I was grateful. It would mean I could continue paying the rent at Canal Bank Road and ultimately stay longer in Pakistan to get the silk project up and running properly.

I started work at Mike's office in the middle of April, during the holy month of Ramadan. Each morning, just after dawn, I walked the short distance along the canal bank to the START office. The working day began at 7 am and finished at midday to allow those fasting from sunrise to sunset to go home and rest during the heat of the day. I loved the early mornings. The air was cool, and I could just see the mountains of Afghanistan rising through the haze of pollution and dust that hung perpetually over Peshawar.

The secretaries, Najiba and Marina, were both in their early twenties. Marina, with porcelain skin and short, fashionably-cut dark hair, came from a well-to-do Peshwari family. As we got to know each other, she gradually began to tell me a little about her life. She was married while in her teens to a relative, and had gone to live with her husband in one of the tribal areas close to the Afghan border. Society was conservative in the tribal areas and her husband forbade her to work. Well educated and sophisticated, Marina was isolated, bored and lonely, living so far from her family. To compound matters, her husband became violent. Eventually, after several beatings, Marina escaped and took refuge with her parents back in Peshawar. Initially they returned her to her husband but at last, seeing how unhappy she was, they relented and accepted her back. At 21 she was divorced and unlikely ever to remarry. I was amazed at her courage in leaving her husband, but most of all I was impressed by her great determination to have a career and make something of her life.

Najiba was a refugee from Afghanistan. Her warm, kind, affectionate nature and ready laugh belied the sadness she felt at having to leave her homeland. Back in London a few months later, I sent her a birthday card to which I received a reply.

Dear nice Harriet, Thank you very much for your beautiful card. I am so happy that you remember my birthday. I think of you every day and miss you very much. Our office moved on 17th July to Abdara road. After you left everything in START going sad for us. Marina works in the mornings and I work afternoons. We can't see each other. When you come I'll tell you all story but now I don't like take your time and I am very sorry I couldn't reply you soon. I hope very much to see you soon. With all best wishes to you and your family, Najiba.

During Ramadan, the Afghan staff in the office fasted from 5 am to 7 pm. I decided to fast too. One evening, the Tarshis invited me to their home for *iftar*, the breaking of the fast. Tarshi's wife, Kowkee, and her mother and mother-in-law had prepared special meat dishes and laid them out on the *dastarkhan* in the main room with bowls of fruit, yoghurt, salad, dates, dried apricots and several different types of chutney. I felt honoured to be included. On the day of Eid, the family again invited me to spend the day with them and share in their happiness and joy at the ending of Ramadan. '*Eid Mubarak*' was on everyone's lips, gifts were exchanged, and all the children had been given new clothes, which they wore with pride.

Throughout the hot summer I worked hard at preparing the project proposal for UNESCO but, with no previous experience and no one to share the responsibility, I struggled. How could I know in advance, without actually being in Afghanistan, the costs of personnel, transportation, supplies and equipment? How many weavers would be employed on the project? What salary would they expect? What would be the cost of dyes, mordants, looms, spinning wheels, silk yarn and cocoons? Then there were operating expenses – telephone, fax, telex, electricity and rent – not to mention transportation, airfreight, rental of trucks, diesel for Toyota Land Cruisers and money for their maintenance. Then there were other miscellaneous expenses – salaries for a project manager, typist, bookkeeper, and design and marketing consultant, airfares – the list went on and on. Preparing the budget for UNESCO was a challenge. It tied my brain into knots, but by June I had completed the proposal and delivered it to the UN offices in Islamabad.

What concerned me most was that I had only the word of the family in Pubbi Jalozai that the *ikat* silk-weavers in Afghanistan were still alive. Tarshi told me that a Turkmen, Khodai Nazar, would be travelling shortly to Aqcha. If I prepared questions that I wanted answered, Tarshi would translate them into the Turkic language, and ask Khodai Nazar to seek out the silk-weavers and get answers during his time in Aqcha. I had met Khodai Nazar in Pubbi Jalozai and, although he looked a bit of a rascal, I knew it was my only opportunity to get real and concrete information. His departure was imminent, so the three of us met at the ACAF office to go carefully over the questions I had prepared. The journey from Peshawar to Jowzjan province and back to Peshawar, crossing war-torn Afghanistan, would take him many months, he said, and would be dangerous because he was of fighting age; if he encountered government soldiers, they might think he was Mujahideen.

'Listen to this,' said John one morning at breakfast, and proceeded to read aloud from *The Times of Peshawar*.

Two persons were blown to bits along with their Vespa scooter near the gate of the laboratories adjacent to the University of Peshawar yesterday, when one of the two bombs being carried in the scooter exploded. The incident took place around 11.45am while Arbab Zahir, leader of the Puktoon Students Federation, and another person believed to be an Afghan national were carrying the two one-and-a-half kg locally manufactured time bombs towards Spin Jumaat Chowk. Both men were killed instantly when one of the devices exploded. Arbab Zahir was identified by his face and some upper parts of the body which were littered over a large area.

On visiting the main Palosi-Spin Jumaat Road where the blast took place, these reporters saw splashes of blood all over the place. Pieces of human bodies were spread over an area of 100 yards, while mashed limbs were hanging from nearby trees. Only three legs of the victims of the blast were found from the site and a 25-feet part of the boundary wall of Peshawar University was also splattered with human blood.[19]

Peshawar at this time was seething with drug smugglers and arms traffickers, and was full of spies and informers. Gossip and intrigue were rife. KHAD was very active in Peshawar, so assassinations were a frequent occurrence and car bombs regularly exploded in the Old City and on buses. Fortunately it was less common for bombs to go off in the residential area of University Town. However, for those of us who ventured into the labyrinthine streets of the bazaar, there was always a slight feeling of unease. Most of us ignored the possibility of being caught up in a bomb blast and being injured or worse because, human nature being as it is, you never think it's going to happen to you.

A new parade of Afghan handicraft shops had recently opened on Jail Bridge, beside Hotel Galaxy. Parking the Toyota in the newly constructed parking lot, I went in to investigate what they stocked. There wasn't much to buy but, not wanting to disappoint the new proprietors, I purchased some small textiles from the Hazara shopkeepers before driving on to another part of the bazaar. Half an hour later, when I passed the shops again on my way home to Canal Bank Road, the windows had been blown out, and rubble and glass littered the road. A car containing a bomb had parked in the space that I had occupied only a little while earlier. The bomb destroyed many of the new shops, killing the occupants. I had been drinking tea with them only an hour before.

Almost worse than the fear of being caught up in a bomb blast was the daily verbal and physical abuse experienced by many expatriate women in the streets of Peshawar. So we were encouraged to adopt local dress and cover our heads when shopping in the Old City. This didn't worry me at all. I was accustomed to it; during the early 1970s it had been the fashion for girls doing the Season or working in London to wear a scarf when walking in the streets. The most coveted were silk Hermès scarves, worn with the knot tied *on* the chin, not under it. The level of threat was displayed on the noticeboard in the American Club, and American citizens were often banned altogether from venturing into the bazaar. Most organisations looked after their staff, ensuring they travelled in vehicles with a driver. Attacks against westerners appeared to increase towards the middle and latter part of the 1980s. Video-cassette recorders became available in Pakistan for the first time and found their way to the refugee camps. Afghans living in Germany sent pornographic videos to their relatives, which poisoned the minds of a largely illiterate population and worsened the negative view of Western women. At the same time, Arab Wahhabi jihadists, largely from North Africa and Saudi Arabia, arrived to fight alongside the Afghan Mujahideen, bringing with them their own strict form of Islam. As the attacks became more frequent, some NGOs received death threats.

One morning, as Helena Beattie and I were walking through Ander Sher, she stopped suddenly and erupted like a firecracker, shouting furiously in Dari at a man who had thrust his hand between her legs as he passed by. Helena was not going to let him get away with it. He slunk away, looking furtive.

'You have to publicly shame them,' she said. 'How dare they do that? Can you imagine if a Western man did that to *their* women? He'd be shot!'

Apparently, she had called him the most intimate part of a female donkey, which, according to the Afghan girls in the sewing project, was *the* worst insult to hurl at a man.

As a woman working alone in Peshawar, I was especially vulnerable. Before ACAF offered me the use of their Toyota pick-up in the spring of 1990, I had to walk everywhere and use local buses, rickshaws and tongas. A woman without a male escort was considered to have loose morals, so Tarshi would send his four-year-old nephew to chaperone me through the back streets of Shaheen Town to guard my virtue. I learnt never to sit next to the driver on an Afghan bus, as he would take every opportunity to touch my thighs as he changed gear. In the bazaar, men would whisper obscene remarks, or hawk and spit. One afternoon, as I was riding in the back of a tonga, another one came up fast behind us, carrying a group of teenage boys. As it drew level there was a sudden flash, followed by a resounding *thwack*. Looking down at the seat, I saw a large split in the faded green vinyl and white kapok stuffing oozing out. The boys were consumed with mirth as one of them brandished a bamboo metal-tipped cane used by teachers to keep order in class. It had missed my thigh by only an inch. On another occasion, an Afghan lorry driver deliberately swerved so that his wheels caught a large puddle. A wall of muddy water engulfed me, leaving me dripping wet and humiliated.

Shinwari Plaza, a modern edifice built within the ancient Ander Sher bazaar to replace the old Murad market (no longer able to cater for the increasing numbers of Afghans wanting premises to sell handicrafts), was close to Chowk Yadgar and named after one of the North-West Frontier tribes that inhabit the mountainous region along the Afghan border. During the winter months, when the sun set around 4pm, the call to prayer would echo through Shinwari Plaza from the beautiful Mahabat Khan mosque, built in 1630 during the reign of the Mughal emperor Shah Jahan. The entrance to the mosque was just off Ander Sher Bazaar, so the traders would shut up shop, draw down heavy metal security shutters and disappear to say their prayers before going home.

The quickest and cheapest way for me to travel home to University Town was by the bus that stopped at the top of Ander Sher. Shaped like a silver cigar case, the bus would emerge from the gloom and dust, announcing its arrival with an ear-splitting toot of its musical horn. Coloured light bulbs decorated the bus and flashed in time to the music like a Somerset carnival float. The bus was always packed with refugees returning to the camps. I would make my way to the front to sit with the sisterhood, ignoring hostile glances from the men. The men's eyes spoke volumes. *Kaffir. Infidel* – I could *feel* their disapproval as 30 pairs of eyes bored into my back. The Afghan women, veiled in their pleated *chadors*, shifted up to make room for me. As more and more women joined the bus on the half-hour journey home, we were soon all squashed together like sardines in a tin. There was an overwhelming aroma of wood smoke and unwashed bodies. Slowly and quietly, the questions would begin.

'*Germania? Francia?*'

'*Nay. Man as Inglistan astum.*' No, I am from England.

'*Ahh, Inglistan.*'

Like Chinese whispers, the information was passed from woman to woman, speaking quietly through their crocheted visors.

'*Shadi? Aulod dori?*' Are you married? Do you have children?

'*Nay. Aulod na dorum,* I would reply, and this new nugget of information would wend its way around the group. *She doesn't have children!* Afghans have a saying: 'A house with children is a bazaar. A house without children is a *mazar* (grave).' In such a conservative society a woman's status, prestige and, to a certain extent, her power within the home, increase according to the number of children she produces. Sons are particularly important, and every woman hopes to give birth to many sons who will eventually till the fields, support their parents in old age and fight jihad. I could sense their pity and consternation.

Then it was my turn to ask the questions. Which part of Afghanistan did they come from? How long had they been living in Peshawar? How many children did they have?

I loved these conversations. The women accepted me unconditionally, and always made me feel welcome and comfortable.

'Brake *shor!* Brake *shor!*' the adolescent ticket collector would scream out in a mixture of English and Pushto, while standing on the running board, to indicate the next stop to the driver and passengers. Then, with a screech of brakes, the bus would come to an abrupt halt, and I would jump down at Spin Jumaat chowk. At that time of the evening, around 5 pm, with Afghans and Pakistanis returning home from work, there was never a tonga or rickshaw available, so I would start the 20-minute walk to Number 10 in the dark. To give myself courage I would hold a stone in the palm of each hand until I reached the gates. Sometimes I carried a bamboo cane; the moonlight glinting on the metal tip was enough to make the groups of youths think twice about approaching me, or worse.

Inevitably the daily abuse took its toll. Not only did my stomach knot with fear each time I left the sanctuary of Number 10, but I began to feel dirty and violated. No amount of scrubbing with a nail brush under the shower seemed to make me feel clean.

Surrounding the marble-flagged courtyard of Shinwari Plaza were shops selling antique Afghan embroideries, 19th-century Turkmen jewellery, strands of semi-precious stones, and *zere zamin* – the Persian word for 'under the ground' (in other words, archaeological antiquities). Art smuggling was big business in Peshawar and the North-West Frontier. Many archaeological sites had been exposed by Soviet bombing, and there was much looting from Neolithic, Gandharan and Hellenistic sites. Many pilfered artefacts ended up in auction rooms in New York and London. In one auction house in London, I had seen a beautiful stone Gandhara Buddha, possibly from the Swat valley, with the marks of a pneumatic drill bit running down the back of the statue, indicating that it had been deliberately removed from the rock face. I would frequently be offered small clay Buddhist statues, or tiny animals crafted from gold, carved cornelian seals depicting the head of Alexander the Great, bronze and silver coins, stone beads, pottery shards and bone combs taken from tombs by grave-robbers. I felt it was immoral to buy any antiquity, and when the merchants offered them to me I always refused.

The trade in *zere zamin* was controlled by the Peshawar mafia, who also had links with the heroin trade. They acted as middlemen between the warlords who stored the priceless antiquities in fortified compounds in the tribal areas and the foreign antiques dealers who came to Peshawar to buy on behalf of private clients. My path crossed one day with just such a dealer, a Persian who had a business in the West End of London. We met at a buffet lunch in the Pearl Continental Hotel and soon discovered we had mutual friends in the art world.

He was occupying a suite of rooms on the top floor and invited me to see what he had bought that morning in the bazaar.

'Here, hold this,' he said, placing a tiny solid gold sculpture of an ibex in the palm of my hand. 'It is more than two thousand years old.'

I held it up to the light. It was delicate and beautifully crafted, and I could only feel a sense of sadness at the loss to Afghanistan of its cultural heritage. Suddenly there was a knock at the door, and four or five Afghan men, who I knew by sight and most by name, came in. These were the big boys, who dealt in the most expensive textiles and *zere zamin*. They acknowledged me with a curt nod and I was asked to wait next door. Behind the closed door I could hear the murmur of voices as a deal was transacted.

I had first met Kiran Velagapoudi when she was working as an assistant to Joss Graham. She had been brought up in southern India, where her father owned sugar-cane mills, and her mother was German. In early 1989 I encouraged her to travel with me to Pakistan, where she found a job at the Danish Sewing Project (Dacaar) in University Town. With our shared interest in textiles, we loved exploring the shops of Shinwari Plaza, and soon became well known to all the shopkeepers.

It was impossible for us to walk under the giant portico and enter the marble-flagged courtyard unobserved. A low balcony ran around three sides, over which the shopkeepers hung kilims and carpets, *ikats* and Afghan dresses. By the time Kiran and I had climbed the wide staircase leading to the first, second and third floors, each filled with yet more shops selling handicrafts, word would have circulated and the shopkeepers would be primed for our arrival.

'Ah, Kiran bibi, you move through the bazaar like a horse.'

The Afghan carpet merchant, sitting cross-legged in his shop, gazed admiringly at Kiran who, with her pale olive skin, almond-shaped eyes, regal bearing and fluent Urdu, was much admired by all the Afghans who met her. To Afghan men the Turkmen horse, native to the steppes of Central Asia, is considered more important even than a woman. So comparing a woman to a horse is therefore considered the greatest of compliments. She received many a marriage proposal.

'Why don't you marry me, Kiran bibi?' the merchant continued, a twinkle in his eye, knowing full well what the reply would be.

'Now, Mohammad, you know that's quite impossible,' she replied in a scolding school-marm tone. 'As you know, I am a Hindu.'

'Ah, noooo problem, Kiran bibi. You become Muslim!' replied the carpet merchant, relishing the opportunity to be mildly flirtatious with Kiran.

These conversations were always light-hearted and reflected the good relationship we had developed with the merchants over many months of frequent visits to the bazaar.

One afternoon, as we were sitting drinking green tea with one of the shopkeepers, a plate of toffees before us, the conversation turned, as it often did, to religion. To illustrate a point, Kiran took four (now empty) Chinese porcelain teacups from the tray and turned them upside down. She placed three in a row, and one separately so that it formed the apex of a triangle.

'Look,' she said, pointing to the first cup, 'this is me, and I am Hindu. This second cup is Harriet, and she is Christian.' Pointing to the third, she said, 'And this is you, Ahmed. You are Muslim. The cup at the top of the triangle is God.' Then she shuffled the three cups around until they ended up all touching the single cup. 'You see, we all believe in the same God. It's just that we take different routes to find Him.'

Some months earlier, Kiran had engaged the services of a tailor called Qayum, who she had discovered working as an assistant to Ahmed Sultani, one of the wealthiest antiques dealers in Shinwari Plaza. On first acquaintance, Qayum had all the appearance of a rogue; an unfortunate cast in one eye made him look shifty and far from trustworthy. He had scars on his face from leishmaniasis, which was common in Afghanistan, where poor sanitation assisted the spread of the disease. But how wrong first impressions can be – Qayum proved to be quite the nicest, most charming and most trustworthy of all the Afghans we ever dealt with in the Old City. He invited us to his home on numerous occasions, for clothes fittings or a meal, and introduced us to his wife and children.

Kiran and I would wander through the market in search of suitable and unusual fabric for Qayum to sew into shalwar kameez for us. I would simply hand him the material, but Kiran, with her natural flair for design, had very decided views on how she wanted her outfits to look. A few days later she would appear wearing a magnificent creation, designed by her and cut and sewn by Qayum, all without the use of a pattern. Ultimately he became a good friend, sewing beautiful shalwar kameez for both of us.

Over the years I learnt through experience, and often the hard way, who to trust and who not when conducting business in the Old City. On my first few forays to the bazaar in the early 1980s I was naive and far too trusting. I was at a disadvantage being a woman and, as I had not yet mastered the art of negotiating Afghan-style, the merchants ran rings around me. In a shop up a side street in Ander Sher I discovered a beautiful green silk Turkmen *chapan* with fine embroidery around the collars and cuffs, so perfect and intricate that it was difficult to believe it had been sewn by human hand. The coat was lined with printed chintz exported from Russia to Central Asia sometime around 1880. I desperately wanted to buy it, and spent all afternoon haggling. Finally, a mutually acceptable price was reached but, not having sufficient cash, I left a deposit, promising to return the following day to pay the balance. When I went to hand over the balance the merchant announced, 'This is not enough,' and quoted a price significantly higher than we had agreed.

'But we agreed a price yesterday.'

'Ah, yes. That is your mistake, Madam. That was yesterday, but now it is today and price is different!'

Negotiating and striking a deal was a game to the Afghans. It was all about power and out-manœuvring your opponent. I had been unwise enough to allow the merchant to see just how much I really wanted the *chapan*. By not paying the full amount on the first day I had left myself wide open to being exploited. I paid the difference and left with the *chapan* tucked under my arm, vowing never to return to that particular shop.

A year later the same merchant recognised me in Ander Sher.

'Why you never visit my shop, Madam? Come, I show you some very beautiful textiles.'

'You know very well why I don't visit your shop. You cheated me when I bought the green *chapan*.'

'Ah, Madam,' he replied, in a tone used to mollify a fractious child. 'I thought you were tourist. Now I see you are serious businesswoman.'

'Then that was your mistake,' I replied, turning abruptly on my heel. In all the years I spent in Peshawar, I never did return to his shop.

Happily, that kind of incident was very rare. For the most part I was treated with great warmth, kindness and respect. Sometimes the merchants would say, 'Oh, Oriot jan, you are like my sister,' or 'Oriot jan, you are family,' which I always took to be the greatest compliment. The Dari word *'jan'* tacked onto the end of my name means 'Miss' and is also a term of affection used for good friends.

Many Afghans that I encountered during my time in Peshawar shared the British sense of humour. Once they saw the funny side of a joke, there was no controlling their laughter.

Sadaart Market was a modern, five-storey concrete block in the storytellers' bazaar near Jail Bridge. Built originally as a hotel, the bedrooms had been taken over by Turkmen refugees and turned into shops from which they sold kilims, carpets and saddlebags woven in the camps. Mohammed Qul Andkhoi, who lived in Afghan Colony, had a shop on the first floor. Late one Thursday evening I paid him a visit, to drink tea and to look at some of his carpets.

From somewhere above my head came *Baaa, baaa, baaa* … Noting my surprise, Mohammed Qul said, 'Tomorrow Juma, Oriot jan,' and drew his finger across his throat. Then he reached for a bamboo ladder hidden behind a stack of carpets and positioned it under a trapdoor in the ceiling.

'Come,' he said, indicating that I should follow him as he shimmied up the bamboo ladder. We emerged through the trapdoor onto the flat roof of the hotel. Tethered in the corner, munching away on a pile of alfalfa and enjoying the last rays of the setting sun, was a large fat-tailed sheep, its thick fleece dyed bright pink. How Mohammed Qul had managed to carry it up the ladder to the roof was a mystery – it was the size of a small donkey. I stroked its head affectionately.

'You can't kill it, Mohammed Qul. It's far too beautiful.'

'No, no, Oriot jan. Tomorrow Juma [Friday and a day of rest]! My wife, my children eating sheep.'

He found it hugely funny that I should care so much about the animal. Back downstairs, the pantomime continued, me acting the horrified foreigner and Mohammed Qul winding me up by drawing his finger across his throat and going into ever more lurid detail of how he was going to despatch the sheep. By now he was laughing so much that he could scarcely stand upright. He clutched his sides, tears streaming down his face. For months this would remain a joke between us. I only had to step through the door of his shop and cast my eyes towards the trapdoor in the ceiling for him to start laughing uncontrollably.

Mohammed Qul repeatedly invited me to come and stay a night at his home to meet his family.

'Oriot jan. Please. You come, stay with my family for Juma. My wife, my daughters, they want meet you. They cooking for you *qabuli pilau*. You like Afghan food?'

I made polite excuses until finally I couldn't think of any more reasons not to go, and I agreed. He so desperately wanted me to stay in his home that I decided it was churlish to deny him the pleasure he would gain by introducing me to his family. Mohammed Qul beamed with happiness.

'OK, Oriot jan. Roze-char shambey [Thursday], you come here my shop closing time. Then we go my house'.

And so, on Thursday at around 5 pm, as the merchants closed up their shops for the weekend, we set out together for his home. His was a simple family, not wealthy or well-to-do, but they welcomed me with great warmth and hospitality. His wife and daughters must have been cooking for hours, as dish after dish of delicious Afghan food was placed before me. That night I slept in a room with the women of the family and the only moment of awkwardness was when they all got up to pray at dawn and I stayed behind in bed.

Most of my business was conducted with Turkmen and Uzbeks. Because their own women were held in high regard for their carpet-weaving skills, I found them easier to deal with than the conservative Pathans, whose women lived a life of strict purdah behind the high mud walls of their fortresses. The Pathans, from Pakistan's tribal area and south-east Afghanistan, seemed barely able to conceal their contempt when I entered their shops, alone and un-chaperoned, and I avoided doing business with them. The exception was a young blue-eyed Afridi from Khyber Agency called Abdul Wahab, who sold wonderful silver earrings from a tiny booth at the entrance to Murad Market.

In his book *British and Indian Army Campaigns on the North-West Frontier of India 1849–1908*, Captain H. L. Nevill describes the Afridi character:

> Ruthless, cowardly robbery, cold-blooded, treacherous murder are to an Afridi the salt of life. Brought up from his earliest childhood amid scenes of appalling treachery and merciless revenge, nothing can change him; as he has lived a shameless, cruel savage, so he dies.[20]

Right from the start, my relationship with Abdul Wahab was difficult, but he did have quite the best jewellery, so I persevered. Initially I didn't like him. He had a volatile and tempestuous disposition and it didn't take much for him to erupt into histrionics. When this happened, there was nothing I could do but sit back and wait until he had finished ranting and raging about his pet subject – politics and the current situation in Afghanistan. He was particularly suspicious and untrusting when it came to money. During bargaining he became so agitated that his voice would rise several octaves until he was incoherent and his broken English so garbled as to be quite unintelligible. It took many visits over several years before I could establish a relationship of trust.

On one occasion, as I handed him some duty-free gifts for his wife and children, he placed them to one side and said, 'And you have brought nothing for me?' I was momentarily nonplussed, having always understood that it would not be culturally correct for me to bring gifts for a man. Even looking a man in the eye could give the wrong impression and, as dealing with Abdul Wahab was always like walking on eggshells, I had to be extremely careful not even to laugh too loudly and always to behave modestly in his presence.

'Well, what would you like me to bring you from England?'

'I would like … ' he said, running his fingers over his cheeks and through his beard, ' … some perfume to put here.'

By this I understood he wanted some aftershave. It just so happened that my flatmate in Finlay Street, Mark Hutchinson, worked for Procter & Gamble. Back in London, Mark presented me with a large bag of free samples that included bottles of Old Spice aftershave, which I passed on to Abdul Wahab during my next visit. He took it without a word of thanks and placed it out of sight under his *pattu*. I knew he was pleased, even though he could not bring himself to say so.

'How many children do you have?' I asked him once. He mentioned only boys' names.

'What? No daughters?'

'No, no. No daughters.'

'Not even one?' I persisted.

He hesitated, then said rather grudgingly, 'I have one daughter.'

'Oh, how nice. And what is her name?'

'Ariana.'

'That's a beautiful name. Why didn't you tell me you had a daughter?'

'Because daughters not important.'

I knew only too well from my own family experience that boys were considered more important than girls. My grandfather was an only son, having lost his identical twin brother in the First World War. Both my father and my brother were only sons. When I was 12, and just in case I was in any doubt as to why boys were so important, Myles explained it. We were sliding around on frozen flood water, when he suddenly said, 'Our parents wanted a boy to run the estate and carry on the family name, but they got Mary. Then they got me, which was what they wanted. But they wanted another boy and got you.' The feeling that I was not the boy my parents really wanted had remained with me all my life. Abdul Wahab's words touched a nerve. Words spilled out of my mouth before I could control myself.

'But that's not true! Daughters are *very* important. Just as important as boys!'

In that instant I knew I could be in deep trouble for challenging his conservative, patriarchal culture. I waited for the fireworks; instead he looked me straight in the eye for several moments, as though weighing up whether or not to trust me. Then, glancing behind him to check that no one was waiting by the door to his booth, he leant forward and said in a quiet voice something that surprised me.

'I say I do not have a daughter because I do not want to love her. One day she will marry and go to another man. She will leave my house and I will lose her. For this reason I do not want to love her.'

From that moment, I knew I had crossed a boundary in our relationship. I was honoured that he had felt able to confide his true feelings, and our relationship improved. I would often stop by his shop for lunch and he would send a boy to bring the most delicious spicy chicken in tomato sauce, which he knew I particularly liked, cooked in a *karai*, a cast-iron metal dish with handles. During these moments I always made a point of asking about his family, and Ariana in particular.

The Anglo-Indian soldier Colonel Sir Robert Warburton, who was born in a Ghilzai fort in 1842 to an Afghan mother, describes his own experiences of the Afridis in *Eighteen Years in the Khyber*.

The Afridi lad from his earliest childhood is taught by circumstances of his existence and life to distrust all mankind, and very often his near relations, heirs to his small plot of land by right of inheritance, are his deadliest enemies. Distrust of all mankind and readiness to strike the first blow for the safety of his own life have therefore become the maxims of the Afridi. If you can overcome this mistrust, and be kind in words to him, he will repay you by great devotion, and he will put up with any punishment you like to give him except abuse. It took me years to get through this thick crust of mistrust, but what was the after result? For upwards of fifteen years I went about unarmed amongst these people. My camp, wherever it happened to be pitched, was always guarded and protected by them.[21]

It was Abdul Wahab who told me about the prostitutes. Close by the fort on the Grand Trunk Road, a complex of hostels was home to a large number of Afghan men.

'The women come by bus from Lahore on Fridays,' he said.

Prostitution is illegal in Pakistan, but in the old walled city of Lahore there is a red-light district known as the Heera Mandi, or Diamond Market. During the Mughal era, courtesans performed traditional songs and dances for the entertainment of the elite. During the Raj, these dancers were seen as prostitutes, and brothels were set up in Heera Mandi for British soldiers. The girls that perform today in the Heera Mandi fall into two categories. There are those who sing and dance because it is a family tradition passed down through the generations, and those who resort to prostitution because they have no other way of supporting themselves or their families. These prostitutes call themselves 'dancing girls', which comes under the banner of performing arts and is perfectly legal in Pakistan.

Kiran and I once spent a night in the heart of the Heera Mandi, sleeping on charpoys in the courtyard of a miniature Mughal fort where once the dancing girls would have come to entertain the local ruler. The fort belonged to a very handsome young Pakistani with the deepest blue eyes (an Afridi, of course), a friend of both Kiran and the cricketer Imran Khan. He kindly chauffeured us around in his open Cadillac, showing us the sights of Lahore before escorting us through the crowded narrow streets of Heera Mandi, past the dancing girls and open stalls selling kebabs and fried chickpeas. Tiger skins carpeted the stone floor of his fort and the whitewashed walls were adorned with snow leopard skins and 17th- and 18th-century weapons used by Sikh warriors. There were shields covered with buffalo hide, spears, arrows, battleaxes, tulwar swords with curved blades, and vicious katar daggers, which, we were told, were traditionally hidden up sleeves or in the folds of garments.

Kiran and I tried to ignore the high-pitched whine and bite of the mosquitoes as we lay on charpoys gazing up at the stars. The smell of the spicy food cooking in the bazaar wafted in over the high walls of the fort. For a while we listened to the clamour of the bazaar and the jingle of bells tied to the legs of the dancing girls as they stamped their feet in time to the music of tabla and accordion, before we finally drifted off to sleep.

What Abdul Wahab said next shocked me.

'Also Afghan women are coming from the camps to visit the men. These very poor women. Husbands are *shaheed* [martyred] by the *Shuravi* [Soviets].'

The war in Afghanistan had destroyed these women's lives. Left widowed and unable to support their families, they had had to resort to the most desperate of measures simply to survive.

During the months I lived at Number 10, the chowkidar Mohammed Gul was a true friend to all of us. He was always cheerful and good-natured, and had a terrific sense of humour. When he laughed his whole body shook. He accepted our idiosyncrasies and eccentric behaviour because, for all our faults, we were part of his 'family'. Day and night, he looked after and watched over us like a mother hen.

'I'm going to the American Club,' I said to him one evening. I always told him where I was going, an ingrained habit left over from my childhood.

'Take my bee-cee-clette, Oriot,' he said.

Mohammed Gul's black bicycle was of Chinese manufacture, very solid, with huge wheels and substantial handlebars. One revolution of the pedals propelled the rider along at a spanking pace, so much so that one day Mohammed Gul arrived with large white bandages round the calf of his leg and his hand. He had lost control of his bee-cee-clette while cycling down Canal Bank Road, and had ended up in the greasy, murky waters of the canal. We laughed and laughed as he described how his turban and cap filled with water and floated away. Now he was offering me the use of the bicycle so that I could reach the American Club in a few minutes rather than walk alone through the streets late at night.

One summer, Peter Jouvenal brought him to London to stay for a while in his house in Wimbledon, and I joined them at Tootsies restaurant in Covent Garden. The waitresses wore very short black Lycra mini-skirts, and I wondered how Mohammed Gul, who had never been out of Afghanistan and Pakistan in his life, would cope. As I caught him looking at the waitresses' legs, he dissolved into giggles.

I awoke one morning to the sound of voices in the yard. Curious to see who was visiting us at such an early hour, I pushed open the mesh fly-screen door and stepped out onto the veranda. Near the metal gate stood a tall, Robinson Crusoe-like figure with long, unkempt hair, his red beard matted with dust. He was dressed like a Mujahid in iron-grey shalwar kameez and leather chappals, a *keffiyeh* draped loosely around his neck. For a moment I wondered if he was a Nuristani, the fair-haired people from the north-east of Afghanistan, but as I watched him talking in Dari with Mohammed Gul and Wadood it was clear from their body language that they knew each other well. Mohammed Gul was laughing and giggling, as he did when he was pleased to see someone. The visitor turned towards me, alerted by the 'clack' of the screen door, and in that second I recognised Rory, just back from six weeks of filming the Mujahideen in action inside Afghanistan.

He looked tired, gaunt and dirty and had lost a lot of weight. His feet were caked with dirt and yellow, overgrown toenails protruded from his chappals like an eagle's talons. After living with the Mujahideen for weeks on a diet of black tea, stale naan, rice and dhal, he must have been really looking forward to tucking into his supply of Stilton and smoked salmon from Fortnum's. I didn't know how to break the news to him that we had eaten it all a few weeks previously because it was going rotten in the fridge. When I told him, he made no comment and just made his way up the outside staircase to his small turret overlooking the canal. Years later, when I read David Loyn's book *Frontline*, I discovered Rory had mentioned that the one thing that really annoyed and upset him was coming back to Number 10 and finding the contents of his Fortnum's hamper had been eaten. It just wasn't 'done,' he said.[22] I felt very guilty.

Nothing was seen of Rory for two days until suddenly he reappeared, clean-shaven in tee shirt and shorts. 'I want to have a party,' he announced.

Rory's wild parties were infamous in Peshawar. He asked if I would like to come with him on his motorbike to help buy the booze from Kharkhanai, the smugglers' bazaar just a few miles up the Jamrud Road at the entrance to the Khyber Pass. You could buy just about anything in Kharkhanai – clothes, fridges, televisions, word processors and air conditioners. The goods were imported through Pakistan to Afghanistan, then smuggled back through the mountains of the Tribal Areas, so avoiding the need to pay duty. It was common knowledge amongst the expat community that it was possible to buy vodka and caviar looted from Soviet bases by the Mujahideen.

Rory's motorbike was a cross-country scrambler, with mudguards painted bright yellow and sky blue. Revving the engine, he released the clutch and we roared off, scattering the goats grazing along the canal bank. Passers-by looked askance at us as we sped by at speed – a Western woman seated on the back of such a bike? *Aahh, haram!*

At Spin Jamaat Chowk we turned left, heading north to Jamrud Fort. Built by the Sikh ruler Ranjit Singh, this marked the border between the North-West Frontier Province and Khyber Agency. On the smooth tarmac road, Rory took off at a terrifying speed. He found danger exhilarating; fear was not an emotion that he seemed to experience, and he had little respect for those who did. Knowing this, it was more than my pride was worth to ask him to slow down. I held on for dear life, and prayed. Coming up fast behind Afghan buses belching out clouds of black sulphurous exhaust, we roared past at full throttle, narrowly missing pedestrians, camels, cyclists, bullock carts, oncoming horse-drawn tongas and auto rickshaws until we swept into the entrance of the smugglers' bazaar.

Rory wasted no time in purchasing bottles of vodka and cans of Beluga caviar, which he placed in a rucksack on my back. The shops in the bazaar were notorious for openly selling opium and cannabis, the latter in neat blocks with colourful wrappers. The shopkeepers demonstrated how they rolled the cannabis between sheets of plastic to make it wafer-thin and easier to smuggle. Back on the motorbike, we returned at speed down the Jamrud Road, only stopping to buy two huge green watermelons from the fruit vendors at Spin Jamaat. 'For the fruit punch,' he explained. I clutched both melons under my arms, hoping I could maintain my balance and not fall off the back of the bike.

Back at Number 10, Rory gave me the task of removing the black seeds from the pink flesh of the melons. This was easier said than done, as watermelons have a huge number of seeds. Into the pink syrupy mush he poured neat vodka and bottles of rum. We ordered food from a local Afghan restaurant, which was delivered by rickshaw. Rory despatched Mohammed Gul to the tandoor bakery at the end of our lane, and minutes later he cycled back into the yard with a mountain of fresh naan wrapped in a cloth to keep it warm.

The party went with a swing and continued into the small hours. At some point just before dawn, I woke to the sound of shattering glass. Rory was standing alone in the sitting room. He had lined all up the empty honey and peanut butter jars he could find and was hitting them hard with his cricket bat so they sailed into the air and smashed on the beam that divided the room. Wadood and Mohammed Gul, crouched at the far end of the room, were patiently sweeping up the glass fragments.

The entertainment continued into the morning. Rory organised a game of musical chairs beneath the bottle brush trees. Each time the music stopped, he soaked the loser with the garden hosepipe. This caused great amusement to Wadood and Mohammed Gul as the wet clothes of the participants became transparent.

In October, orthopaedic surgeon Peter Stiles of the Guildford surgical team arrived, bringing with him his daughter Francesca, and Simon Jones. Simon ran a small removals company in Fulham and had helped me move my stock to Joss's shop when Out of the Nomad's Tent closed. Accompanying Peter was a former SAS officer, Rupert Chetwynd, who organised the surgical team who volunteered their annual holidays each October/November and travelled at their own expense to treat wounded Mujahideen in the North-West Frontier. Peter and Rupert were en route to Afghanistan on a fact-finding mission for Sandy Gall's charity, and while they were away I would take Francesca and Simon to Swat, Chitral and the Kalash valleys. I was really delighted to see them all; there is always something special about meeting good friends in far-flung places. Staying in adjacent rooms in Dean's Hotel were the author Idries Shah and his journalist daughter Saira. I had worked with Idries' sister, Amina Shah, on various Afghan fundraising events in London, so I went along the corridor to say hello. With them was the author Doris Lessing, who they had brought with them so that she could see at first hand the situation in the Afghan refugee camps. As a result of this visit, she went on to write *The Wind Blows Away Our Words*.

From Chitral, Fran, Simon and I took a passenger 4x4 to the Rumbur valley, one of three valleys inhabited by the Kalash, a pagan people whose origins are shrouded in mystery. With their European features, fair skin and green or hazel eyes, the Kalash claim they are the descendants of soldiers of Alexander the Great's army – possibly Kurds. Others say that they were pushed out of eastern Afghanistan from Nuristan sometime in the tenth century by Islamic armies from the west. I had visited the Kalash valleys before with Helena, but it always came as something of a shock – or should I say a refreshing change? – to see unveiled women walking and chatting openly with men in the streets. The women wore black dresses, yokes and sleeves colourfully embroidered in red and yellow thread, and dark-brown woven goat's-hair headdresses with a long, heavy flap falling down the back almost to the waist, covered in cowrie shells. Their necklaces were formed from many strands of red and white beads. As they passed us in the road, they smiled and called out a welcome, '*Ishpata, Baba, Ishpata, Byia,*' which sounded to us uncommonly like 'Sparta'.

Lying on a charpoy on the veranda of a Kalash-run hotel, I could feel the vibration of constant small tremors, like an underground train passing beneath buildings in London, as strata shifted deep within the earth's crust. A full moon hung over the valley. A festival was taking place that night and the Kalash invited us to join them on the dance ground high up the mountainside behind the hotel, accessible only by climbing a steep and rocky goat track. We could hear drumming and chanting as we made our way in the moonlight. On the dance ground, made from packed beaten earth, girls in all their finery and wearing magnificent headdresses had already formed a long line, their arms around one another's waists. They called for us to join them. Facing the girls was an equally long line of boys. As each line began to turn in a circle, those positioned in the middle had the advantage that they could remain largely stationary while those out on each limb had to run at a fearsome speed to avoid getting left behind or falling over, which caused a great deal of laughter and merriment. The two lines completed their circle, and the boys and girls ran full tilt at each other, stopping just short of colliding. It rather reminded me of a Highland reel. The memory of dancing that night with the Kalash in the mountains will always remain with me. It was a great privilege.

Simon and Fran returned to England, but I stayed on in Peshawar as Jenny KilBride was coming out for a couple of weeks over Christmas as a volunteer to work on the silk-weaving project. We were still experiencing problems with the de-gumming of the silk yarn, so her knowledge of silk-weaving and dyeing would be invaluable.

CHAPTER 9

Women must not swing their hips!
Peshawar, December 1989–June 1990

I first met Juliet Crawley in 1986 at the Bamboo Bar, an expatriate watering hole where alcohol was served in the evenings at round bamboo tables under a starlit sky. She was with Dominique Vergos, a tall, handsome Frenchman, who in a previous life had worked as a fashion photographer for *Vogue* in Paris until he gave it all up to work for the CIA, gathering intelligence in Afghanistan. He and Juliet met when she arrived in Peshawar that year to work for the British charity Afghanaid. They made a striking couple – Juliet reserved and stylish, Dominique tall, mysterious and very attractive. They married in 1987.

On the evening of Christmas Day 1988, while Juliet was inside the house looking after her baby, Fynn, Dominique was shot dead at the gates of their home. Their Afghan chowkidar at the time was arrested by the Pakistani police. Accounts differ as to what exactly happened, and numerous versions of his death circulated in University Town. One suggested that he was killed late at night when he went outside to feed the dog, another that he had had an altercation with the chowkidar after returning home following an evening at the American Club and in the ensuing struggle the Kalashnikov had accidentally gone off, killing him. Juliet never believed the night watchman was responsible. Because Dominique had worked as a spy against the Russians in Afghanistan using photography as a cover, Juliet suspected the involvement of KHAD. In fact, Dominique had received a warning from the French Embassy only a few weeks earlier that his life was in danger. Juliet never did discover who was responsible and his death remained unsolved.

Juliet was straight out of the mould of those gallant Victorian ladies who faced tremendous hardship in far-flung reaches of the British Empire, and she coped with the tragic turn of events with extraordinary courage and emotional self-control and a stiff upper lip. But behind her carapace of reserve was a warm and generous personality. Like many of us living in Peshawar at that time, she had come to the city because she wanted to help others. After Dominique's death she made the decision to stay on, bringing up Fynn with the help of Natalie, Dominique's daughter from his first marriage.

As I approached Juliet's house in early December 1989 to discuss her generous offer to use her home as a venue for Christmas lunch (it was the anniversary of Dominique's death and Juliet was planning to be away over Christmas), I came across a group of Afghan refugee children playing in the dirt outside her gate. Four little boys, hessian sacks laid out on the ground for gathering dried leaves and firewood, were crouched on their haunches chattering to a tiny, fair-haired boy who, like them, was playing in the dirt.

'Hello, Fynn,' I said, recognising Juliet's two-year-old son.

A pair of beautiful green eyes fringed with dark lashes gazed back at me, solemn and uncomprehending. Realising he probably didn't understand much English, I tried Dari.

'*Chitoristi* [how are you], Fynn?'

I was immediately rewarded with a shy smile. Seeing me talking to the child, Juliet's Afghan chowkidar emerged through the gate. An imposing figure with a bushy black beard, Chitrali hat and Kalashnikov, he gently picked Fynn up off the ground, cradling him in the crook of his arm. His fierce, craggy face melted into tenderness and he spoke softly to Fynn in Dari as he carried him around. Fynn looked utterly at home in the chowkidar's arms and it was obvious that this was a special relationship. Just like children born during the Raj, Fynn was looked after by servants, an ayah, gardener, cook and chowkidar, while Juliet was out at work. So it was little wonder that he understood Pushtu, Dari and Urdu far better than English.

I decided to bake a traditional Christmas cake. Almonds, walnuts, raisins, sultanas and spices were available in the dried fruit market in Saddar Bazaar behind Green's Hotel, and from the grocery shops around Spin Jamaat I bought flour, eggs and butter. Attaullah Jan, a charismatic retired Pakistani army major who ran the popular Honey Bakery in the Mall, lent me a metal cake tin and supplied ready-made marzipan to cover the cake.

Returning home through the gloom and smog of a winter's evening on an Afghan bus with the cake tin on my lap, I noticed outside St John's Cathedral a banner advertising a Nativity play organised by local missionaries and Christian NGOs. It would take the form of an open-air son et lumière, with expatriates acting out the Christmas story. There would be real camels, sheep and a donkey. For the benefit of the locals, the play would be translated into Pushto, Urdu and Farsi. This was an event not to be missed, and Ian McWilliam and I decided to go.

At St John's, a handwritten sign in English, Dari and Pushtu requested that 'all weapons … be left at the church gate'. There was already quite an assortment of AK-47s leaning against the wall. Inside, the neat rows of plastic chairs in the forecourt of the church were already filling up, not with the audience of expatriates and Pakistani Christians I had expected, but with bearded, turbaned

Afghans and Frontier tribesmen. I was confused. Throughout the 1980s there had been a steady increase in radicalisation of the Afghan population by Sunni Wahhabis. The ideology of Wahhabism, similar to Deobandism, had infiltrated mosques, madrassas and refugee camps throughout Pakistan. When students trained in Pakistani madrassas became the Taliban and entered Afghanistan after the Soviet withdrawal (*Talib* is the Arabic and Pushto word for student), Saudi Wahhabis, with their message of violent jihad, encouraged the Talibs to abandon their non-violence. I had often encountered groups of Wahhabis in Kissa Quwani bazaar, easily identifiable by their North African and Middle Eastern features and baggy trousers that finished just below the knee rather than at the ankle.

Muslims view the Christian belief that Jesus is the Son of God as heresy, as the Qur'an clearly states that Allah did not beget a son. One of the most frequent insults hurled at foreigners in the streets of Peshawar was '*kaffir*', meaning infidel or unbeliever, because of the Christian belief in the Trinity, which Muslims consider to be a denial of the oneness of God. Yet I also knew that Christians, like Jews, are considered 'People of the Book'. If Christians were thought to be infidels and unbelievers, why, I pondered, had these tribesmen come to see a Nativity play? My knowledge of Islam at that time was limited, though I did know that Jesus is revered as a great prophet and servant of God. Sadly, my observations of the treatment of women and the personal physical and verbal abuse that I had received in the streets had not encouraged me to study or find out more about Islam.

The play began. Candlelight flickered through the stained glass of St John's, and a collective 'ooh' and 'aah' floated up from the audience as a spotlight illuminated the Angel Gabriel descending on a rope to bring the Good News to Mary. A large gold star attached to a pulley jerked and bobbed past the window as 'Mary' arrived out of the darkness under a starry sky, riding on a donkey led by 'Joseph'. Shepherds guarded a small flock of Afghan fat-tailed sheep. The Three Wise Men, one of them an African member of the UN staff, rode in on Bactrian camels, magnificently attired and bearing gold, frankincense and myrrh. The Frontier tribesmen were thoroughly enjoying it. Plucking up courage, I turned to the large, bearded Pathan seated on my left, and in my ignorance I asked, 'Excuse me, but do you understand the story?'

'Of course,' he retorted, as if I should know better than to ask such a silly question. 'It is the story of the birth of the prophet Isu, Son of Maryam. It is written in the Holy Qur'an.'

Jenny KilBride was coming to Peshawar for Christmas, but unfortunately there was no room at the inn – Number 10 was full. John and Ian had returned from their travels and, although Rory had departed for Romania to cover the imminent downfall of the dictator Nicolae Ceausescu, John had let Rory's vacant room to Deanna Hodgin, an American journalist. Deanna had initially stayed at Kurt Lohbeck's house, but after he made unwelcome advances she gratefully accepted the opportunity to stay with us. She was a great addition to Number 10; it wasn't until she arrived that I realised just how much I had missed having female company, girly chats and gossip.

Deanna told me that her grandmother was Amish but had left the community to marry her grandfather. She had been brought up understanding Amish traditions; clothes were required to be plain, with no adornment or embellishment to draw attention to the wearer, and fastened by means of buttons rather than hooks and eyes. But there was nothing plain or demure about Deanna. She had great courage, coupled with an outrageous sense of humour and zest for fun. She had just returned to Peshawar from travelling alone inside Afghanistan with a Hazara Mujahideen group, and her stories and anecdotes of her experiences kept me in hysterical laughter for days. Years later she wrote to me:

> I was smuggled into Afghanistan. Bandits held us up at Teri Mangal but we negotiated a bribe and moved on to Logar province where we were bombed pretty heavily for a couple of days. Then we walked all day for a couple of days and a night to Paghman, right past a Soviet radio post. I followed the muj for two months, finally being smuggled into Kabul while it was still under Soviet occupation. That was scary. I had to keep moving all the time.

An Australian friend, who lived in a small lane behind Number 10, offered Jenny a room for the next two weeks. One of his housemates was returning to spend Christmas with her family, so her room would be vacant. On an overcast, cold, wet day, with a keen wind blowing down from the Safed Koh, I set out with clean sheets and pillowcases to make up the bed for Jenny. I slipped and slithered through the mud trying to avoid the puddles, wrapping my black, embroidered wool Kashmiri *phiran* tight around me to keep out the wind. Something caught my eye in the verge on the top of the canal bank. Curled up in a tight ball, shivering in the bitter wind, was a tiny white puppy with black ears and a distinctive black patch over one eye, half-buried amongst the litter and detritus that always swirled around the canal bank. It gazed at me with eyes the colour of labradorite. It could not have been more than six weeks old. By now the rain was turning to sleet, and the sheets were beginning to get wet, so I hurried on. If the puppy was still there when I returned, then it was coming home with me, I decided.

With Jenny's room prepared, I retraced my steps. Sure enough, the puppy was still there. It was undoubtedly a pi-dog, the name given to the ownerless half-wild mongrels that are common around Asian villages. The term 'pi' came originally from the Hindu word *pahi*, meaning 'outsider'. Although feral, pi-dogs make excellent guard dogs and are easy to domesticate. Most expatriates living in University Town had one as a guard dog and most Pakistani families did too. Only male dogs were used, bitches being considered too much of a nuisance because of the risk of them becoming pregnant. Picking the puppy up, I saw it was a bitch. Her tiny body fitted into the palm of my hand. The fact that she was so close to the canal led me to think that someone had tried to drown her. I tucked her inside my Kashmiri *phiran* for warmth and took her back to Number 10, and that is how Mumtaz came into our lives.

I wondered about the boys' reaction, but they greeted her arrival with equilibrium. They expressed no great enthusiasm or objection to her living at Canal Bank Road. So she stayed, sleeping in a small cardboard box near the kitchen stove, and became part of our family.

To keep myself busy until Jenny's arrival, I worked throughout the early part of December as a volunteer with an Afghan reconstruction NGO. I knew many of the engineers from my days working for Mike McGovern at START. The Afghan engineers had moved on and set up their own NGO in a building on the Grand Trunk Road. My task was to edit and correct the English of the engineers' reports on the state of canals, dams, roads, irrigation channels and water pumps in Kunar, Paktika, Paktya, Logar and Herat provinces after ten years of bombardment by the Russians. Next to my office was the map-drawing room, where blueprints of the surveyed sites were prepared by architects. Large photographs illustrating the damage to villages, roads and culverts were displayed on the walls. My office was on the fifth floor of Hadji Gul Plaza, with stunning views of the Kohat mountains, Swat and the Khyber Pass, now covered with a sprinkling of snow. I felt particularly privileged to be working with an entirely Afghan team. I was the only foreigner in the office, and a woman, but the engineers treated me with great kindness and courtesy, sending a car for me to Number 10 each morning. We all ate lunch together, and shared much laughter.

Two days before Christmas, Ahmed Shah, one of the young engineers in the office, drove me to Khan Road Runners, the bus depot on the GT Road, to meet Jenny. There was no sign of her. I checked all the bus companies just in case she was in a 'Ladies Only' waiting room, but there was no sign of her there, either. Realising she must have been delayed on the way from Islamabad, Ahmed generously left me his car keys, explained how the engine could be de-activated by pressing a button under the steering wheel to prevent anyone driving off in it, and disappeared back to the office in a rickshaw.

As soon as he had gone, men came crowding around the car, cupping their hands around their eyes, and pressing their noses to the window, gawping and leering. Fortunately the vehicle had been fitted with special darkened 'purdah' windows, which prevented them seeing inside. Eventually Jenny's bus arrived. She had brought silk dyes with her from England, a gift from Ciba-Geigy, and we had much to talk about. As we motored back to University Town we talked non-stop, making plans for the days ahead.

Jenny came to Number 10 for dinner one evening. Deanna contributed a bottle of Jack Daniel's whiskey, and had us doubled up with laughter. During her recent journey with the Mujahideen, she told us, her knickers had gone missing in the wash. When she mentioned that the dhobi had not returned them, the Mujahideen commander bought her seven pairs, each embroidered with brightly coloured mis-spelt days of the week. She brought them out to show us. We used the knickers as table napkins, and thereafter, for some reason for which I have no explanation, they languished for days on the top shelf beside the Dushka shells and the Gideons Bible.

On Christmas Eve, Ian suggested that Deanna, Jenny, John and I might like to come with him to the midnight service at All Saints' Church, in the heart of the Old City.

As we stepped out of the rickshaw, we thought at first we had arrived at a mosque. A full moon cast light on a beautiful white plastered building with a fluted, onion-shaped dome topped by a golden cross. When it was built in 1883, on land purchased by the Church Missionary Society to commence missionary work amongst the Afghans in Peshawar, it was decided that the church 'should be oriental in aspect, cruciform in shape, with a dome in the centre, minarets flanking the front and each transept.'[23] Rather than facing south-west to Mecca like a mosque, All Saints' pointed towards the Holy City of Jerusalem. Behind the carved Kashmiri rood screen, marble plaques on the wall commemorated the young missionaries who came to Peshawar full of optimism and religious zeal, and lost their lives on the Frontier. Many died from disease soon after arrival. One, Annie Forde Norman, 'arrived Peshawar Mar 1883. Called home on Ascension Day 22 May 1884. Aged 26.'[24] A few were murdered for proselytising, but saddest of all were the memorials to children. A typical one read, 'In beloved memory of Alice died 22nd Nov 1866 aged 22 days and Minnie died 15 Feb 1868 aged 2yrs and 7mths. Children of Thomas and Eliza Hughes.'[25]

The simple white interior was lit with thousands of candles, and thronged with worshippers, poor Pakistani Christians from the Old City dressed in colourful shalwar kameez, their heads covered with white dupattas. As the service was not due to begin for a while, Ian led us up to the minaret beside the dome, which was in fact the church belfry. Two magnificent 19th-century cast-iron bells, with the date and name of the English foundry that had made them embossed on their rims, hung on wooden wheels. By now the main body of the church was crowded and it was difficult to find a seat in the Victorian wooden pews. The Christmas hymns, Bible readings and sermon were all conducted in Urdu and, as we were celebrating communion in a Muslim country, the wine in the chalice was lemon sherbet. None of us understood a word, but it didn't matter – there was such a wonderful atmosphere inside the little church. The simplicity of the service, the devotion of the Pakistani worshippers, and the fact that we were all far away from our own homes and families at Christmas, made it a memorable and emotional evening. I felt homesick as I thought of my own family gathered together celebrating the midnight service in the church overlooking the village of Hawkshead. It seemed a world away from where I was that evening. When the bells rang out at midnight, we stepped out into the cold night air and wished each other Happy Christmas; the clear, inky black sky above us was studded with stars.

Mrs Masjid, a Pakistani Christian working at the International Rescue Committee, had kindly kept in her deep freeze four turkeys that I had bought earlier that month. Early on Christmas Day I collected them by horse-drawn tonga, nursing them on my lap as it clip-clopped through the streets of University Town. It was something of a logistical problem to cook four turkeys and have them ready for lunch all at the same time; however, friends kindly offered the use of their ovens, and when they were cooked I transported all the turkeys – again by horse-drawn tonga – to Juliet's house.

Everyone arrived bearing dishes of food. There were about 20 of us, all from different nationalities, backgrounds and religions, but life in Peshawar and shared experiences had created a close bond between us. As I sat cross-legged on the floor, eating roast turkey, surrounded by good friends and sharing lots of laughter, I felt there was something very special about that particular Christmas Day. Deanna had suggested we should have a lucky dip to which everyone contributed one wrapped gift. She put them all inside a Baluch donkey bag, and at the end of the meal the bag was handed round so each person received a Christmas present.

During the meal there was a sudden commotion in Juliet's garden. Her two Afghan Buzkashi stallions, tethered alongside a Bactrian camel under a tree, had without warning begun to fight, rearing up and lashing out at each other with their front hooves. In the ensuing commotion all three animals broke loose, and galloped out onto the streets with the horses' *syce* giving chase. I went to help him round them up, and before long we had them tethered again in the garden.

Juliet kept a small rhesus monkey in the house as a pet for Fynn. Steve LeVine, an American journalist, decided the monkey smelt and needed a bath, so he gave it a shampoo in Fynn's blue plastic baby bath. A week later, the monkey was eaten by Juliet's guard dog.

On Boxing Day, Jenny and I took some Christmas cake to the nuns at St Michael's Catholic Church in the Mall. Sister Monica, from the Republic of Ireland, had spent 50 years of her life in the North-West Frontier working with the poor. Now she helped run a Catholic school in the precincts of the church.

'Look,' said Sister Monica, pointing out of the window to where children in pale blue uniforms and white *dupattas* were playing tag and hopscotch in the school yard. 'We have children here from all religions – Sikh, Muslim and Christian – playing happily together. We make no distinction. We say to the parents: "if you want your children to come to this school then they must be prepared to mix with children from other religions". And the parents send them here because they know they will receive a good education.'

When we told her about the silk project, she said in her soft, lilting Irish brogue, 'Och, look at all you young things. You come out here and face all kinds of dangers to work with refugees.'

'But Sister Monica,' I replied. 'We've done nothing compared to you! You've spent fifty years of your life working here.'

'Aah, to be sure,' she said modestly, 'it's nothing.'

For the next two weeks Jenny and I spent most days at the ACAF office in Shaheen Town working with Jamilla and Saleh. We experimented with the new acid dyes that Jenny had brought from England and struggled to find the best way to de-gum the silk skeins. It was a fine balancing act to remove the sericin to reveal the lustre of the yarn, yet retain enough of it to keep the thread strong for threading the looms. These were happy days, but they passed all too quickly. Jenny returned home at the beginning of January 1990, and I stayed on in Peshawar.

In the same month, the Swedish Committee for Afghanistan (SCA) donated US$16,300 to the silk project. At last I was beginning to see the fruition of five years' hard work. My life in Peshawar had settled into a comfortable routine of Dari classes in the evenings followed by supper at the American Club. The silk project was going well, and I was travelling 60 miles to Pubbi Jalozai every week to visit the weavers who were producing beautiful shawls based on the traditional red-and-yellow silk shawls worn by Turkmen women. I dyed the skeins with Saleh and Jamilla, but left it to the weavers to decide which colours to use, with the result that there were some fairly innovative combinations. The shawls were sold through Save the Children USA (STC) in its shops in Islamabad, Lahore and Karachi. In mid-January UNESCO invited me to Islamabad to sign a contract for $50,000 and I travelled there to discuss the budget. This was followed by a fax from the head of Arts and Cultural Life at UNESCO headquarters in Paris, Idrasen Vencatachellum, with guidance as to how the money was to be spent.

Mr Mir Baz Khan gave me several addresses of silk-weavers in Lahore and Multan. The weather was still cool and, as I needed to do further research on the de-gumming of silk, it seemed the ideal moment to travel south to the Punjab and Sind. In addition, STC had invited me to take a stall at the Lahore Cattle and Horse Show later in the year, so my visit to Lahore would give me an opportunity to meet their representative. From Lahore I planned to travel on to Karachi to visit interior decorators and women's magazines in order to promote the silk the Pubbi Jalozai weavers were producing. A few days before, Saleh had asked me to get him some more dyes, as the Ciba-Geigy dyes Jenny had brought were almost finished. If the silk-weaving project was to be sustainable, I had to find a company based in Pakistan that could supply Saleh. After much research I came across Sandoz Pharmaceuticals in Karachi.

To set out on long journeys from Peshawar required me to overcome my fears and dig deep to find courage. I dreaded the 1,000-mile journey, knowing I would encounter problems travelling alone. However, one night at the end of January I boarded the night train to Lahore. But when I arrived the following morning, the whole city was in the grip of riots. Crowds of students were demonstrating their opposition to Indian rule in Kashmir by marching through the streets, shouting slogans and waving banners. Clouds of black smoke billowed up from burning tyres, and rocks and stones littered the streets. A man stopped and offered to read my palm. On no account, he said, should you continue your journey to Karachi. I should have taken his advice, but I didn't believe in palm reading, and boarded the first available train for the 24-hour journey through the Sind desert.

Shortly after we left Lahore, three Pakistani men entered the 'Ladies Reserved' carriage. By the time we reached Multan I had had enough of their smoking and loud conversation punctuated with endless 'Yeah, man'. Despite repeated polite requests, they refused to leave the carriage. When the train halted, I explained the problem to the station police. They leapt aboard and set about the boys with bamboo lathis, hitting them hard about the head, shoulders and backs before kicking them out. I hadn't expected quite such violence; however, the police were not going to allow such flagrant disregard of the rules. For a while peace returned to the Ladies Reserved carriage as the train trundled its way south across the dusty plains of Sind.

Then the boys exacted their revenge. They ousted a poor woman from the third-class compartment, taking her seat. She entered our carriage swathed in a black abaya, dragging behind her two small, filthy children with matted hair. The boy and girl sucked and chewed on stems of sugar cane and spat out the fibrous pith. They picked their noses and stared at me. Their mother blew her nose on her fingers and wiped them on her abaya. After an hour or so, the little girl squatted to pee in the middle of the floor, and the yellow stream of urine zigzagged its way towards my feet and my backpack stored under the seat.

I arrived in Karachi to find a city under curfew. Supporters of the Muttahida

Qaumi Movement (MQM) political party were rioting in the streets. Founded in 1984 to protect the rights of the Muhajirs (Urdu-speaking Muslims who migrated to Pakistan at the time of Partition in 1947), the MQM were up in arms because they felt aggrieved that Muhajirs were being marginalised, with the best jobs and university places going to indigenous Sindhis. Sixty-six people had been killed that morning in running battles with the police. Tear gas and gunfire made it too dangerous to venture out and, because of the curfew, all shops and offices remained closed. Police vehicles mounted with machine guns patrolled the streets. For four days I remained confined to a hotel lobby unable to move about the city, or to visit Kishor in Zainab market or the interior decorators. I abandoned any hope of visiting Sandoz Pharmaceuticals and had no alternative but to catch a flight back to Peshawar. The palm reader was right. The whole journey had been a complete failure – I had achieved nothing!

On my return, Michael Keating handed me a fax from UNOCA in Islamabad, the UN office coordinating Operation Salaam. The *ikat* silk-weaving project had been approved by UNESCO in Paris, and they now required me to undertake a thorough survey to assess the needs of weavers in the village of Qurchangee. I was to procure all the necessary dyes, silk and equipment in Afghanistan, organise a workshop in *ikat*-dyeing for women as well as men, evaluate the training programme and produce promotional materials about *ikat* weaving. I felt daunted, yet elated that the project proposal had been accepted after all the years of work. Most of all, I was excited by the prospect of travelling to Afghanistan.

Bob Darr arrived in Peshawar in March and we travelled to Islamabad to sign the agreement between ACAF and UNOCA. He too had been offered a job with UNOCA to travel inside Afghanistan, on a UN-sponsored programme to help distribute food to Mujahideen areas in the northern and central areas of the country. During a journey with Tarshi in Afghanistan the previous year, he had seen signs of famine in the northern areas. Ten years of war had destroyed villages and farmland and left farmers unable to buy pesticides. As a result, locusts had bred unchecked and swept across the country like a Biblical plague, devouring everything.

The communist regime held power in the towns and cities where the wheat was stored; consequently, the rural population in areas controlled by the Mujahideen were experiencing the worst effects of the famine. Bob had been approached by UNOCA because of his knowledge of the area, his ability to speak Persian and the fact that he was not worried about travelling in a war zone. He would be required to liaise with government officials to obtain the release of the wheat. This famine relief programme was part of Operation Salaam to encourage the return of Afghan refugees to their homeland after 11 years in exile, and Bob was planning to leave Peshawar shortly. As he would be travelling to an area close to Qurchangee, I asked him to try and find out what he could about the *ikat* weavers.

Out at Charsadda, a retired Pakistani army major had set up a riding school complete with a mud-walled manège. To earn a little extra money, I offered to give riding lessons to expatriates on Fridays and soon I had 15–20 students. These lessons earned me £25 to add to my salary of £300 a month. My favourite students were two Norwegian children, Jorg and his sister Elsa, aged about eight and ten with white-blond hair and freckles. They were rewarding to teach because they learnt quickly. Within a few weeks they had mastered rising trot, trotting without stirrups and canter, so I decided they were ready to go out hacking in farmland in the tribal area. They were utterly fearless, and when we reached the *nullahs* they would cling to the pommel of the saddle as the horses slithered on their haunches down the near-vertical mud banks and into the water, which was often so deep it covered the children's legs. I was always worried they might slip off backwards when the horses scrambled up the far bank, but they clung on like limpets. Mumtaz, my pi-dog, would come with us on these outings, trotting contentedly behind the horses, but when we reached villages she would disappear, to rejoin us on the far side. She was intelligent enough to know that, if she accompanied us through the village, the people would have stoned her.

In the evenings, when the heat of the sun diminished, I would take Mumtaz out to the alfalfa fields behind Number 10 to exercise. As soon as we reached the field, she was off like an arrow from a bow, running in a wide arc and jumping the irrigation ditches, a tiny white blur in the distance. Perhaps she was descended from Indian hunting dogs, the lurchers used by the nomadic gypsies of the subcontinent to hunt a wide variety of quarry. She was extraordinarily loyal and biddable; it only needed one blast on the whistle and she would race straight back. Mumtaz was a free spirit and considered it beneath her dignity to be walked on a lead – she would demonstrate her disapproval by sitting down in the dirt road and flatly refusing to move.

John Jennings invited me to lunch at the American Club, so I decided to walk there, taking Mumtaz on the lead. During the week I always dressed in shalwar kameez, but this was a Friday and the streets of University Town were deserted. Because I was lunching at the club, I wore a denim shirt and US Army-issue disruptive camouflage trousers (with large pockets useful for carrying money) and covered my head with a scarf. We set out and crossed the little footbridge below the house.

At nearly every intersection along the canal bank were small, three-sided concrete incinerators for household rubbish. Once a week the refuse was set alight, sending acrid clouds of evil-smelling smoke drifting across the canal. Pi-dogs loved these tips and would scavenge in search of a tasty morsel, but they were a nuisance as they dragged out used sanitary towels, babies' nappies, and bloody bandages and dressings from the nearby hospital, scattering them along the road. This day a pack of dogs were snarling and bickering amongst the foul-smelling refuse. Mumtaz trotted past, ignoring them, as though to say, 'I could have been like you, but I've moved up in the world'. One dog broke away from the pack and set off at speed down the unpaved road, a pus-encrusted bandage streaming out behind. The rest of the pack followed in hot pursuit.

We turned down a road that ran past a beautiful little white mosque. Its large, double-fronted doors and windows had just been freshly painted bottle-green, the colour of Islam. For months, from the laying of the foundation stone, I had watched its construction. It was right next to a hospital treating wounded Mujahideen, and during the week I would often see patients sitting in their wheelchairs in the mosque's forecourt enjoying the sunshine. It was only as I drew near and heard the murmur of voices through the open windows that I realised the mosque was now open for worship. Friday prayers were in progress. I quickened my pace, hoping to get past without being noticed, but, just as I drew level with the entrance, the doors swung open, and the faithful spilled out into the forecourt. Some were pushing patients in wheelchairs; others were on crutches. I saw a large Mujahid detach himself from the crowd, and within a few strides he reached me. Towering above me and barring my way, he bent down, his thick black beard just inches from my face.

'This is bad! *VERY BAD!*' he said in a low, menacing voice in English, and then strode off. Shaken, my heart pounding, I wondered what I had done that was so *VERY BAD*.

I was unaware that a religious ruling, or *fatwa*, had just been issued by the mullahs from all the seven Mujahideen parties stating that:

> women must not wear perfume, decorative clothes or tight outfits. Veils must cover the body at all times and clothes must not be made of material that is soft or rustles. Women must not wear noisy bangles, masculine clothes or Western fashions, or walk in the middle of the street, swing their hips, talk, laugh or joke with strangers or foreigners.[26]

Although I had covered my head with a scarf, I was alone that morning without a chaperone, with a DOG on the lead close to a mosque, *and* wearing men's trousers, something I had done many times before. The Mujahid who accosted me must have just heard the *fatwa* during Friday prayers. I began to walk on, but Mumtaz had other ideas. She sat down on the unpaved road and refused to move. The harder I pulled on the lead, the harder she struggled, biting at the lead and wriggling like a fish on a hook.

'Come on, Mumtaz,' I hissed. There wasn't a moment to lose; the

Mujahideen were already coming out through the picket gate and into the road. There was no alternative but to drag her along behind me, and I hated myself for doing it. After a few minutes, she gave up the fight and trotted meekly beside me until we reached the club.

On Good Friday I volunteered to help hide chocolate eggs provided by the US Consulate General in the grounds of the International School for the children's Easter egg hunt. Sandy Gall's artist daughter, Michaela, was busy painting a life-size crucifixion for the Catholic church. Father Len, the Austrian priest, told her she had been sent by God to paint it in time for Holy Week. There were only a few days to go, and Michaela was working against time to finish the painting so that it could hang above the altar during the Easter services. At last it was completed. Abstract in style, it gave only a hint of a loincloth around the body of Christ. Father Len surveyed the finished work.

'Michaela! This is Pakistan. You cannot paint Our Lord naked on the cross! You must put some clothes on him otherwise the women will start to fantasise.'

On Easter Sunday morning, I attended Mass with the Galls. Michaela's painting hung above the altar, looking magnificent, with Christ now decently clothed.

After Easter I decided to travel to Lahore before the hot weather set in. At the Galls' house I had recently met Doctor Khan, a partially-disabled and retired Pakistani. He invited Michaela and me to visit him in Lahore so that he could take us to the small town of Changa Manga, about 20 miles outside Lahore, where silk was being produced. Tarshi's mother and mother-in-law wanted me to buy some cocoons so that they could hand spin the silk fibre to use in their weaving. I hoped my visit would provide an opportunity to meet Punjabi silk-weavers, and find out what they used to de-gum silk. I also wanted to see if I could purchase some flying shuttle looms.

The Khyber Mail bound for Lahore, Multan and Karachi departed from the railway station in the Cantonment at 10 pm. After a good meal at the American Club, friends drove us down to the station. Days earlier I had reserved seats and a sleeping berth in a Ladies Only compartment. This was one of the advantages of being a woman in Pakistan – when travelling by train or bus you had the right to ask for a seat or berth just for women and by law it had to be granted to you. No man could sit with you without permission. For two Western women travelling by overnight train it made sense to get a compartment where there would only be other women present. As a result of my reservation, an entire carriage was waiting for us. We had our own private accommodation consisting of two bunk beds, a washbasin and our own loo – a separate little room with a hole in the floor through which you could look down onto the rails. While it was good to have our own private 'arrangement', the aroma of urine was so strong that we had to hold our breath while squatting over the hole. It was difficult to balance, since the whole carriage rocked from side to side as the train hurtled at speed through the Pakistani countryside. Large toffee-coloured cockroaches emerged and scuttled around the edge of the compartment, waving their antennae. I had a phobia about cockroaches, but Michaela was quite undaunted. She proceeded to squash them one by one with her loafers as they emerged into our sleeping berth while I sat, in Michaela's words, 'like a daughter of the Raj' with my feet tucked up under me on the bunk bed.

From time to time through the night, the Khyber Mail stopped at various stations. Small boys on the platforms hawking sweet milk tea and roasted chickpeas shouted through the bars of the train windows, '*Chai-chai-chai. Channa-channa-channaaaah*'. Then, with a sudden jolt, the giant wheels of the steam train began to turn and we were off once more, rattling through the night towards Lahore. Michaela and I wrapped ourselves in our sleeping bags and settled down.

At dawn, I raised the blinds and sat watching the sun rise over the neatly ploughed fields of the Punjab. Bullocks were being milked in courtyards, and on the roofs mothers were combing, oiling and braiding their children's hair in preparation for school. Young girls were drawing water from the pump and carrying it home in brass chatties gracefully balanced on their heads.

Gradually the Khyber Mail entered the outskirts of Lahore and began to stop frequently to pick up commuters travelling to work. Outside our compartment the corridors were filling up with passengers. Soon they were banging and rattling on our door, shouting in Urdu to open up, but we were entitled to a Ladies Only carriage, and I was not about to give up our privileged accommodation. Besides, Michaela was still asleep on the top bunk. For a while I ignored the demands until, suddenly, the sliding door of our compartment was wrenched open a crack, straining the flimsy staple-and-hook lock to breaking point. An eye was pressed up against the small aperture and a man's voice demanded in English, 'Madam. Madam. Open up! We want to sit in here.'

'No, I'm sorry,' I replied. 'This is Ladies Only compartment. No men allowed.'

'Madam,' the man's voice continued. 'There is man in there. Open up!'

'No, there is no man in here. Go away!'

'But, Madam, *I know* there is man in there,' the commuter insisted. 'I can see his shoes!'

Looking around our compartment I saw, positioned on the floor, Michaela's size-nine loafers.

'Michaela, you'll have to show your face. They think your shoes belong to a man.'

Michaela sat up and shook out her mane of flaming red hair.

'Ah, Madam. I am sorry. Now I am seeing it is lady!'

For a short while we enjoyed some peace and quiet, but then the train stopped at the next station to allow yet more commuters to board, and it started all over again.

'Madam. Open the door! It is sitting time.'

'This is a Ladies Only compartment.'

'No problem, Madam. I have wife and children here.'

Eventually we relented, opened the door and welcomed a Pakistani family into our compartment to sit on our bunk beds. Charming as they were, we soon regretted our decision as the family began to ask the usual questions to which all foreigners are subjected: Which country are you from? What is your good name? What are your qualifications? Are you married? How old are you? Where is your husband? Michaela and I were distinctly relieved when the Khyber Mail finally pulled into Lahore.

The roads leading to Dr Khan's home were lined with jacaranda trees in bloom. A thick layer of pale lilac petals carpeted the pavements for mile after mile. Dr Khan lived in a small house in a quiet residential area, and he seemed to know just about anyone who was anyone in Lahore. It was entirely due to him and his network of contacts that the silk project finally began to take shape. Without his philanthropic assistance during those few days, it would have taken me a great deal longer to get things off the ground. The following day, he drove Michaela and me in his dilapidated car with a hole in the floor to villages where the women and girls reared silk cocoons and the men wove silk.

The villages were close to the National Park of Changa Manga, a vast forested area planted with mulberry trees by the British during the days of the Raj to provide hardwood for polo sticks, tennis racquets and hockey sticks. After Partition in 1947 India retained the industrial areas in the Punjab, and Pakistan ended up with Changa Manga. The mulberry trees that grew there were ideal for sericulture, and a cottage industry of rearing silk cocoons was soon established in the surrounding villages. With Dr Khan acting as interpreter, we were invited into several homes. The work was entirely carried out by women and children, who went several times a day into the forest to pick mulberry leaves to feed the voracious appetite of the silkworms. When the tiny grey eggs hatched, the minuscule worms were placed on chopped leaves laid out on bamboo shelves. By the end of the month they had grown into large white grubs and were preparing themselves for the final stage, the spinning of the cocoon. Drowsily they waved their heads from side to side, secreting a filament of silk coated with sericin that they wrapped around their fat bodies. This natural gum glued the fibres together and created the hard shell of the cocoon. Imprisoned inside, the worm metamorphosed into a brown pupa, finally emerging as a silk moth to start the cycle all over again.

By chance, an auction of cocoons was taking place in Changa Manga that afternoon. As we drove into the town square it looked as though snow had fallen on the flat roofs of the houses as tons of white silk cocoons had been spread out under the hot sun in preparation for the auction.

'Why are the cocoons on the roofs?' I asked

'The heat from the sun kills the pupa inside, otherwise it will eat a hole in the cocoon and emerge as a moth,' Dr Khan explained. 'If the silk filaments are broken, the spinner can't reel the silk off the cocoon.'

We were shown the best-quality silk and I bought a large hessian sack filled with cocoons for the Tarshis. We also purchased three unwanted 'flying shuttle' hand looms from local weavers who were changing over to the preferred and more modern mechanised Jacquard looms. Dr Khan took charge of the negotiations, arranged for the cocoons and looms to be transported by train to Peshawar, and helped me to locate silk-weavers living in Changa Manga. I needed to stay longer to talk with the weavers and learn the methods they used in preparation of the silk yarn, but Michaela had to return on the night train to Peshawar. She drove back to Lahore with Dr Khan who, she later told me, had taken her to the Shalimar Gardens and massaged her feet.

A family of silk-weavers invited me to stay the night in their house. Potters, weavers, spinners and dyers come fairly low down on the social scale in Pakistani society and this family was no exception. They were very poor, and the women illiterate. In the courtyard the women were crouched down, washing clothes in buckets of soapy water. Others were peeling vegetables for the evening meal. As soon as they saw me, the children came running. '*Angrez! Angrez!*' they shrieked, crowding round and staring, chewing sticks of sugar cane and spitting out the fibre. Flies crawled over their filthy faces, matted hair and snotty noses. One by one the women joined the children, prodding and poking me with their fingers, picking up handfuls of my hair and stroking my arms while discussing me amongst themselves as though I were some being from another planet. It wasn't every day that a foreigner walked in off the street and entered their home, and I honestly think they had never seen a foreigner so close at hand; they were just amazed at the colour of my hair and skin. The inspection seemed to go on forever. Neighbours were invited in, and more and more children emerged from doorways leading off the courtyard to stare at me.

It had been a long day, and I was tired and my patience sorely tested at being treated like some rare animal in a zoo. It was a relief when the men returned from the bazaar and, with a few sharp commands, sent the women and children packing. After a meal of chapattis, rice and dhal served in the courtyard, the three young men of the family showed me to my room containing a vast double bed covered with a gaudy satin quilt. It was quite obviously the honeymoon suite. Alone at last and able to relax, I undressed and climbed into bed having locked the door. Just as I was dropping off to sleep, there was a sudden crash, the lock hasp flew off, the door burst open and the three young men of the house walked in, one of them holding an enormous television in his arms. He placed it on a table at the end of the bed.

'Madam. You like blue movie?'

'No, thank you!'

'OK. You like to see my sister's wedding video?'

My heart sank. Video cameras too had only just arrived in Pakistan and were considered a great status symbol. Every family, even the poorest, wanted a film made of a family wedding. The only problem with wedding videos was that usually the cameraman was not very skilled. They were invariably out of focus, repetitive, incredibly boring and dubbed with soundtracks from Hindi movies. As I was in the rather vulnerable position of being in bed with few clothes on, I was not in a position to argue. There was little I could do but nod enthusiastically at the idea of the wedding video.

They plugged in the television and, after much twiddling of knobs, the video began. For two hours the boys sat on the end of my bed giving an incessant running commentary as they excitedly pointed to the out-of-focus guests. As the camera zoomed in and out, the picture shaking and wobbling, they cried, 'OK, OK, this is my uncle, this is my auntie. Look, look! This is my cousin's sister.' Then they would rewind a particular part of the video until they were sure I had seen the person in question.

It was a relief to get back to Dr Khan's house. He took me to the offices of *Dawn*, a widely read newspaper, to be interviewed, and then he suggested we might go to a 'key party' that evening.

'What's a key party?' I asked, intrigued to know more and hoping it wasn't what I suspected.

'Everyone throws their car key into a bowl, then you select a key and go home with that person for sex.'

I was surprised to learn that this kind of thing went on in Pakistan. When Dr Khan showed me pictures of himself at a nudist camp in Germany, I decided I had outstayed my welcome. The next day I caught the train back to Peshawar.

Outside the gates of Number 10, I heard the familiar *flap-flap-flap* of Mohammad Gul's chappals as he ran across the terrace to pull back the bolt and open the gates.

''Allo, Oriot,' he said, grinning as he took my bag and carried it indoors.

It was good to be home. John, alerted by the sound of the rickshaw, came out through the mosquito screen door and ran down the steps.

'Harriet. Don't be too upset – something happened to Mumtaz while you were in Lahore. Someone's kicked her badly. I took her to Vétérinaires sans Frontières yesterday and they checked her out. Her kidneys are OK and there's no internal damage, but her stomach and chest are really bruised.'

Mumtaz appeared around the corner, moving stiffly and slowly. As she rolled over onto her back, wagging her tail in greeting, I could see her stomach was a rainbow of green, black, red and purple. It was obvious from the extensive bruising that she had received a vicious beating. But who had done it? John could throw no light on the event. It had happened while he was out and he had found her like that on his return. The chowkidars didn't seem to know either, or, if they did, they weren't saying. I couldn't believe it had been either of them, as they were fond of her too. During cold nights Mumtaz slept beside Mohammed Gul on his charpoy under his pattu. Possibly she had gone out when the gates were open and had bounded up to someone in her normal friendly way. There were labourers working outside our gates on enlarging the canal and breaking rocks into gravel for resurfacing the road. Or perhaps she had approached some of the Mujahideen when they came to be interviewed by Hamed. In Islam, the 'wet' parts of a dog are considered unclean. Since she arrived at Number 10 Mumtaz had only experienced kindness. The beating, however, changed everything. While she continued to be sweet-natured, affectionate and loyal to us, from that day she became aggressive to strangers, and all the instincts of a wild dog that had remained largely hidden began to surface. When I walked in the streets, she became my bodyguard, snarling at anyone who came too close. Her favourite treat was to accompany me in the Toyota pick-up, standing on the passenger seat, paws on the dashboard, watching the world go by as we motored down the Grand Trunk Road. Afghans riding in the back of pick-ups from the refugee camps stared at us stony-faced.

'Khodai Nazar has returned,' Tarshi announced one day, and he handed me the replies to the questions I had given to Khodai Nazar months earlier on the eve of his departure for Afghanistan. The war had severely disrupted agriculture, silk- and rug-weaving in Qurchangee, and as a result about 40 families had left the village. However, of the 1,200 families left behind, a thousand or so were still engaged in weaving silk turbans and shawls that were sold in the towns of Aqcha, Kunduz and Mazar-i-Sharif. The weavers had ceased to weave *ikat* after the start of the war in 1979; it was just too expensive to produce. However, to my relief Khodai Nazar mentioned that two people with knowledge of *ikat* weaving still lived in Qurchangee – Sub Khan and Khedr Agha, both in their mid-70s.

The flying shuttle looms and silk cocoons purchased in Changa Manga eventually arrived on the Zulfikar Ali Bhutto Express from Lahore. Tarshi's sister invited me to her house so she could demonstrate how she prepared the cocoons for hand spinning by burying them in wet wood ash to dissolve the sericin. After several hours she removed the cocoons and rinsed them under a tap. The cocoons had collapsed into a soggy mass revealing the brown pupae, which she picked out and threw to the chickens. A few days later I watched Tarshi's mother and mother-in-law tease out the now-dried silk, and spin it using a drop spindle. The family set up one of the looms in their garden and, on my next visit to ACAF, Saleh pulled back a hessian sack covering the doorway into the garden and proudly showed me the loom threaded up with silk yarn. Unknown to me, this exceptional young man, who had lost his education to war, had quietly learnt how to weave by visiting and talking to Pakistani weavers in the Old City. His initiative and self-motivation proved to me that he was genuinely interested in the craft, and over the next few weeks I watched as he improved. He began incorporating the hand-spun silk yarn as wefts when weaving shawls. This was thicker and more uneven than the hand-reeled silk, giving the finished article a more interesting, distinctive traditional look and set the scarves apart from those produced in India or Thailand. Saleh had a natural talent for placing unusual colours together, colours that I would not necessarily have chosen, but his scarves were always innovative and soon they were selling well to expatriates. When he proudly showed me his first batch I was amazed at their quality and beauty. I felt something else in that moment, too, that is difficult to explain; a sense that all the hard work, danger and self-sacrifice over the years had been worthwhile. What better reward is there in life than to be a facilitator, to teach and pass on ideas and knowledge so that others might become inspired and motivated? It is not always the case. So often, and despite all our best efforts, 'seed' falls on stony ground.

Chapter 10

Under attack
Peshawar, November 1990–February 1991

More than six months had passed, and I was about to return to Peshawar from London. During the summer and autumn of 1990 I had been searching for someone with knowledge of silk-weaving and dyeing to come out and work on the silk-weaving project. Polly Cowe, a young graduate from the Inchbald School of Design, was recommended to me. She had been taught the intricacies of *ikat* weaving and was enthusiastic and keen to come to Peshawar. I explained that I had sufficient funds to pay for her travel, salary and living expenses, but there was just one small problem. I had anticipated that we might fly together from London to Peshawar, but Polly was currently living with her boyfriend in Germany and to buy a ticket for her to fly from Frankfurt to Heathrow was going to be an added expense.

I explained the situation to Sajid at Apex Travel in Piccadilly, the owner of the bucket shop that I had used many times over the years.

'OK, so this is what you do,' Sajid said. 'You buy two tickets with Lufthansa which goes London to Karachi with a stopover in Frankfurt. You send one of the tickets to your friend in Germany. She will be able to board the plane in Frankfurt and then you can travel on together.'

What would happen if the check-in staff at Frankfurt said she should have started her journey in London? It all sounded a bit shady and risky and I said so, but Sajid brushed away my concerns: 'There will be no problem'.

Polly's stricken face in the arrivals hall at Frankfurt Airport was the first indication that something was very wrong.

'They won't allow me to board. They say the ticket isn't valid. Even though I've explained that I'm working for a charity, they say I have to buy a new ticket.'

No amount of cajoling would get the Lufthansa check-in staff to change their minds. There was nothing for it. I would have to fly on to Karachi alone. Polly's boyfriend offered to pay for a new ticket at full price, double what I had paid Sajid in London, and Polly would follow on the next available flight a few days later.

Sirikit Reuchlin and her Dutch husband Maarten, First Secretary at the Consulate of the Netherlands, had invited us both to stay at their home in a smart residential area of Karachi. Despite her Thai name, Sirikit was Austrian. Tall, beautiful and elegant, she was a true diplomat's wife, effortlessly organising parties and hosting guests with charm and efficiency. Austrian friends in London had put us in touch and I often stayed with her and Maarten en route for Peshawar or London. Over the years, the Reuchlins had offered me warm and generous hospitality. Their wonderful, comfortable home, with its high ceilings, air-conditioned rooms and marble floors, was always so welcome after a long flight or months spent in Peshawar. When I described my life and work in the North-West Frontier I think Sirikit thought I was quite eccentric. It always amused me to read a handwritten label on a bottle on the glass shelf above the basin in the guest bathroom: 'Boiled water for brushing your teeth'.

Polly finally arrived at Karachi and I went to meet her in the Reuchlins' chauffeur-driven air-conditioned limousine. We stayed with the Reuchlins for a few days as we had a number of things to do in Karachi – buying dyes from Sandoz Pharmaceuticals for Saleh and canvassing interior decorators to see if they would consider buying the silk woven in Pubbi Jalozai – before departing for the North-West Frontier.

A few days later we bade farewell to the Reuchlins and set out for Peshawar. As I needed to draw out money from the project's account at Grindlays Bank to pay Polly, I asked Tarshi if I could use one of the ACAF vehicles.

'I cannot let you have the use of the 4x4. We only have one, as UNHCR asked for the return of the other when Bob closed down the office.'

This was sobering news. Although I was used to moving around town by local transport, I felt responsible for Polly's safety. At Grindlays, more bad news awaited.

'The ACAF account has been closed. There is no money in the account,' said the clerk at the till.

'What do you mean, "no money in the account"? This can't be right. I'm a signatory. I haven't closed the account.' Fear sent my heart racing. 'Please can you print out all the bank statements between July and December? I want to see when the account was closed.'

While we waited at the desk, I wondered what was going through Polly's mind. First I had messed up on her flight, and now there was no money to pay her.

I pored over the statements. 'Here is the month where bank account has been closed,' said the clerk, helpfully pointing with his finger.

'But where has the money gone? Who has drawn it out?'

'A Mr Mohammad Ali Tarshi. The money has gone into a new account – Cultural Assistance Foundation for Afghans.'

I was completely stunned, my mind whirring with thoughts and emotions.

Both Bob and Tarshi had indeed mentioned that ACAF's office was closing down in the summer, but neither of them had said anything about closing the silk-weaving project account at Grindlays. Earlier, when I spoke with Tarshi on the phone from London, he had reassured me that he would continue to run the silk-weaving project. We were both joint signatories to the account, but during my absence he had set up another humanitarian aid organisation with a similar name, removed the money that I had raised and put it into his new account without consulting or warning me in advance. If I had known what the next few weeks had in store, I would never have brought Polly out to Pakistan and exposed her to such a situation.

'It seems you have a case of fraud,' Sultan Aziz, manager of Save the Children USA in Islamabad, told us.

Over the previous year STC had been buying the silk scarves produced by the Pubbi Jalozai weavers and selling them through their various outlets in Islamabad, Karachi and the Middle East. Now Sultan Aziz confirmed my worst fears – he had been invoiced for the scarves by the new organisation set up by Tarshi, and had settled the account in good faith.

I have always hated confrontation, but when I thought of Helena, Jenny, Polly and all those who had helped and supported me over the years I knew I had to grasp the nettle and pay a visit to Shaheen Town.

The first thing I noticed as I made my way through the oily streets was a new sign – 'Cultural Assistance Foundation for Afghans' – at the entrance to the ACAF office. I entered the small courtyard, dreading what I knew was going to be an awkward and uncomfortable meeting with Tarshi.

Tarshi confirmed that he had indeed set up a new project and was now collaborating with Deborah Sciattino, an American who was now married to Kurt Lohbeck. I had met Deborah a number of times as she lived close by in Shaheen Town, and during my absence in England she had become friendly with the Tarshi family. It was ironic that, although I had turned down Kurt and Anne's offer to work with The Mercy Fund all those years ago, now through Deborah and Kurt my project had in effect been stolen from me. I had lost all control. I sat nursing a cup of green tea and feeling a sense of anger and disbelief. Worse was to come. Tarshi confirmed the rumours currently circulating in University Town (and which friends had warned me about on my arrival in Peshawar) that UNHCR funds allocated to ACAF for the rug-weaving project in the refugee camps had been embezzled by Bob. It was said that he had sold the carpets in California and kept the money. I was shaken by these allegations and found it hard to believe them.

During his many visits to Peshawar over the years, Bob always stayed at the ACAF office, which was also the Tarshis' home. Such was their close working relationship, mutual trust and respect that he was treated almost as a member of their family. I wondered how Tarshi could now be so disloyal to Bob by siding with those who believed that Bob had embezzled the funds, but I shouldn't really have been surprised. Throughout their turbulent and bloody history, Afghans have learnt to be consummate survivors, constantly changing sides and allegiances to serve their own interests. It was happening all the time between the various warlords inside Afghanistan. To be fair, Tarshi had a large extended family to provide for, and with the closure of the ACAF office he had had to do the best for himself and them.

More worrying and dangerous was the allegation circulating in Peshawar that Bob was a Marxist. On his return from Afghanistan with Tarshi, Bob had given talks in Peshawar to NGOs and UN agencies, explaining that much of the massive aid coming through Pakistan did not reach those most in need. He advocated the distribution of food inside Afghanistan and put forward the idea that NGOs should work with both the communist government and the Mujahideen in distributing famine relief. Needless to say, there were some in the expatriate community – particularly a small clique in the American Club that included Kurt Lohbeck – who did not share Bob's views. They saw the Afghan Mujahideen as the 'good guys' fighting to protect their country and heritage from a communist superpower and former Cold War enemy. Consequently they were unhappy about anyone liaising with the communist regime in Afghanistan. Others voiced objections against the UN, saying that it was too soon to expect the Afghans to return to their country because the infrastructure had yet to be put in place. Bob, however, felt it was important to deliver food to areas most afflicted by famine, regardless of who was in power, and because of this he was called a Marxist.

News travelled fast in Peshawar. Hearing that I had arrived in University Town, the staff at UNHCR wasted no time in summoning me to a meeting at their office. They wanted an explanation as to what had happened to their money.

'But the rug-weaving project is nothing to do with me,' I explained. 'I know nothing about that side of ACAF. I am simply running the silk-weaving project under the umbrella of ACAF with separate funding that I have raised myself.'

Shortly after this meeting I received a letter from Anders Fänge, Director of the Swedish Committee for Afghanistan, asking me to refund the $16,300 that SCA had donated to help me get the project up and running.

'Most of the money has already been spent on raw materials, looms, dyes, silk and weavers' salaries. If you want all the money back I shall have to pay out of my own pocket,' I told Anders. 'But what I can do is pay you back what is left in the account.'

Within days, I managed to collect the remainder of the money from Tarshi and return it to the SCA, an act that did not endear me to either Tarshi or Deborah. Perhaps because of this, events took a turn for the worse.

Because of my association with ACAF, it was assumed that I had something to do with the disappearance of UNHCR's money – a case of guilt by association. With Bob on the other side of the world in Sausalito, I was taking the full brunt of the whole unpleasantness. People who I had considered friends avoided speaking to me and crossed the road when they saw me. Invitations to social events dried up. At the American Consulate General, my subscription for membership of the club was declined. Steve Masty was behind the desk in the office at the time, and I was sure he would help.

'Steve, why won't they renew my membership?'

'Because, Harriet, you are not an American citizen.'

I knew this wasn't the true reason, as people of many other nationalities had membership cards. While there was much that I disliked about the club, especially the ridiculing and lampooning of Afghan culture, it was somewhere to go in the evenings, and a chance to meet friends and have a good meal. It was also a safe place to take Polly.

'Don't worry,' John Jennings said kindly when I told him what had happened. 'I can always sign you both in using my membership.' Throughout this difficult time, he stood by me and remained a good and loyal friend.

I kept Bob informed about what was going on in Peshawar, but he could throw no light on the situation and seemed as puzzled and confused about the rumours and allegations as I was. He confirmed that he had closed down the office in Peshawar because ACAF was producing more rugs than he could sell in the US. The global recession – which had prompted Rufus and me to close Out of the Nomad's Tent at the end of 1988 – played a part, but I also felt that the rug designs, colours and quality, about which I had had such misgivings, were partly to blame. Bob confirmed this, in his book *The Spy of the Heart*: 'About twenty percent of these weavings were stained or crooked. We had never been able to produce the quality that the European market demanded.'[27]

As each day passed it became more and more obvious that I was being ostracised by the expatriate community. I felt I was being deliberately targeted by someone, but was at a loss to know who or why. I was a young woman on my own without support or help, and therefore vulnerable and an easy target. It was the first time in my life I had ever been in such a situation. What I minded most was the slur on my name and reputation, but I was quite powerless to do anything about it.

One evening, feeling particularly low and anguished, I brought down the Gideons Bible from the top shelf where it languished amongst the Dushka shells, dusted it off and began to read through the Psalms until I reached Psalm 109.

> For wicked and deceitful men have opened their mouths against me; they have spoken against me with lying tongues. With words of hatred they surround me; they attack me without cause. They repay me evil for good and hatred for my friendship.

After reading the Psalm, like Christian in *The Pilgrim's Progress*, I felt eased of my burden.

Also circulating in Peshawar at this time was an article in the *Columbia Journalism Review* that was causing quite a stir amongst the expatriate community. Late in 1989, just around the time that Jenny KilBride arrived to help me in Peshawar, Mary Williams Walsh, south-east Asia correspondent for *The Wall Street Journal*, was on the point of revealing some irregularities in the Mercy Fund's fundraising activities and exposing their false claims about their work in Afghanistan. Just as well, I thought, that Helena and I turned down the fund's offer to work with it all those years before!

As a correspondent reporting from Afghanistan, Mary Williams Walsh had witnessed the brutality and carnage of the battle for Samarkhel and the infighting between the Mujahideen groups. She was one of the few American journalists who had the courage to question the US's unconditional support for the Mujahideen, and was about to expose the false propaganda and 'faked and distorted coverage of the war in Afghanistan by CBS News which boasts about its thorough and outstanding coverage of the war.'[28]

Mary Williams Walsh had become intrigued by the apparent political and media role of the Mercy Fund's operation in the North-West Frontier, 'which', she told her editors, 'is particularly effective because the Mercy Fund's director's boy friend [*sic*] is CBS's local correspondent for the Afghan war. He has been able to portray the war in his own way, with all the credibility of the CBS behind him.'[29] Because she questioned Kurt's reliability as a cameraman and CBS reporter on the war in Afghanistan, her membership of the American Club had, like mine, been suspended.

Journalists frequently stayed at Anne Hurd and Kurt Lohbeck's hostel in University Town; over the years, Helena, Lucy and I had all been guests there. Kurt would steer the journalists towards whomever he thought they should meet when it came to reporting on the war. On several occasions while staying at the Mercy Fund hostel I met the charismatic Mujahideen commander Abdul Haq, but I was always politely asked by Anne and Kurt to leave the room. Now, according to Mary Williams Walsh, it appeared that Kurt had selected Abdul Haq to promote as the next leader of Afghanistan, and to this end he was acting as his publicist. Some of the pieces of the jigsaw puzzle began to fit together. It became clear to me why I had been asked to leave the room during Abdul Haq's visits and why I had not been allowed to travel in Kurt's minibus to Jalalabad for Ghaffar Khan's funeral – I believe he did not want me to witness his extraordinary awkwardness in operating a video camera. However, I was still confused as to why I should be ostracised. There must, I thought, be a deeper reason, but so much gossip and intrigue swirled around Peshawar at this time that it was impossible to get to the truth. It would be many years before I learnt that I was simply a scapegoat because of my association with ACAF. Certain members of the American Club were incensed that Bob had just returned from working with the communist regime inside Afghanistan on a UN programme delivering wheat to famine-stricken areas. With Bob back in California, I was an easy target and focus for their anger.

Polly decided to return to celebrate Christmas with her boyfriend in Germany, and who could blame her? Such was her character that she managed to remain cheerful and supportive throughout the whole sorry saga. She made the most of her visit and enjoyed Peshawar, particularly our expeditions to the carpet shops. I was sorry to see her go.

War was looming in Iraq. The coalition invasion seemed imminent but no one quite knew when it was going to take place. All foreigners living in Peshawar were summoned for a briefing by the American Consulate General on evacuation procedures should war break out. After the briefing, the Americans hastily packed up their belongings and began to leave Pakistan. The rest of us were advised to lie low in the event of an anti-Western backlash. John Jennings had opted to stay, but had set himself up to ship everyone's belongings in case they had to get out of the country fast. I spent the last few days sorting out my affairs, finalising last-minute business in the bazaar and briefing Tariq Sultan on shipping my goods.

Rory Peck flew in to Peshawar on a Monday and proposed to Juliet, and Father Len married them the following day in the Catholic church. It would be the last time I would see Rory – in October 1993 he was tragically killed in Moscow, caught in the crossfire during fighting between ex-communists and the forces of President Yeltsin for control of the Ostankino TV station. But now, shortly after their wedding, Juliet sent Fynn with Peter Jouvenal, his godfather, to England for safety before departing with Rory to cover the war in Baghdad. And I was on my way to Kabul.

'If you go to Afghanistan,' said Tarshi, 'it will be very dangerous for you to return to Peshawar. Your safety cannot be guaranteed.'

But after all that had happened over the previous month, I didn't care anymore. I'd given eight years of my life to working with Afghan refugees in Pakistan. I was ready to take the risk.

PART III
Afghanistan

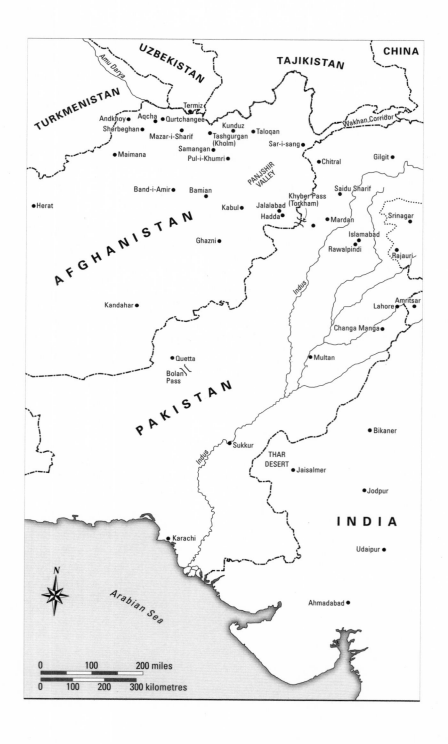

Chapter 11

Kabul and Mazar-i-Sharif – a reconnaissance
January 1991

On my first evening in Kabul, I sat alone in my bedroom in the annexe behind the German Club, attempting to read a novel by torchlight. Outside, snow was falling over the city. As I watched the flakes float softly to earth through the half-drawn curtains, I felt a deep sense of loneliness. I'd flown in from Islamabad earlier in the day on the small, six-seater Operation Salaam Red Cross aircraft. Two years had passed since I was last in Kabul with Joss, and I was looking forward to seeing Bismullah, Hamidullah and Khanullah in Shahr-i-Nau over the next two weeks.

A paraffin *bukhari* spluttered and gurgled away in the corner of the room, filling the air with fumes. The stove was next to useless and did little to alleviate the bitter cold. I huddled in my down sleeping bag and tried to write my diary. Away in the distance I heard a diesel generator roar into life. For a short while the electricity came on, but the voltage was only enough to provide a weak and intermittent eerie orange glow.

The dining room was no less sepulchral, and it soon became apparent that I was the only resident in the German Club. Waiters hovered around in the orange gloom observing my every movement, attentive to my every need. The snow had ceased to fall by the time I made my way back through the garden to my room. There was no light pollution from the city to dull the brilliance of the stars, and I marvelled at the beauty of the constellations. An enormous full moon hung above the Bala Hisar fort, so bright that my figure cast a shadow on the glittering snow. In the distance a dog barked, and red and green tracer bullets rose gracefully towards the heavens, followed a second later by the sound of automatic gunfire. Somewhere, on the far side of the city, a family was celebrating the birth of a boy.

Mr Salman Abu Ali, a Jordanian Palestinian and head of UNESCO in Kabul, was small in stature and impeccably dressed. He was fully aware of his important status.

'I am a close friend of His Majesty King Hussein of Jordan,' he informed me as soon as I sat down in his office.

I might have been imagining it, but I had the distinct impression that he considered my arrival in Kabul a disruption to his otherwise ordered lifestyle. First, I was a woman; second, I was British; and third, I didn't speak French, which was the language in which, after Arabic, he preferred to converse. My proposal to organise an *ikat* weaving training programme in Afghanistan had finally been accepted, and funding allocated by UNESCO in Paris. But now, as I sat in Mr Abu Ali's office, I was suddenly consumed with anxiety. The project's whole viability hinged upon whether or not I would be able to find the *ikat* weavers that Bernard Dupeigne and Annie Zorz had filmed in 1973 in Jowzjan. From Khodai Nazar's report I knew that two of the weavers were still alive, but I still had doubts as to whether the project would ever come to fruition. I explained to Abu Ali that it was my intention to travel to Qurchangee to find the *ikat* weavers.

'Before travelling to Jowzjan province, it is essential for you to get security clearance for the northern areas of Afghanistan from John Cleland, UN Head of Security,' he said.

Later that afternoon in John Cleland's office, he and I pored over detailed maps and finally located Qurchangee, a tiny village not far from Aqcha in the far north-west of the country. We discussed the risks of travelling there from Mazar-i-Sharif.

'There's currently some fighting between the militia and the Mujahideen around Balkh, and it wouldn't be safe for you to make the journey to Jowzjan province,' he announced. I felt hugely disappointed.

At the end of each day, I walked back through Kabul's unlit streets to the German Club. Because I was not employed as a member of the UN, I was not entitled to the use of a UN vehicle. Mr Abu Ali would leave the office with his car and driver, and I was left to make my own way home. I wasn't unduly concerned about walking alone in Kabul – it was, after all, what I had been doing for eight years in Peshawar – but one evening, as snow fell, I was followed.

The streets were all but deserted when I heard footsteps. I glanced over my shoulder and saw a man behind me. I tried to remain calm and ignore the feelings of fear; I quickened my step. The footsteps quickened too. By now the snow was falling heavily in great thick flakes. I was just one street away from the turning to the German Club but, unable to control my fear any longer, I began to run. The man behind me began to run too and, just as I saw the night watchman at the gates of the club, an Afghan overtook and stopped me. While it appeared he was simply curious and wanted to know what I was doing in Kabul and why I was walking alone in a snowstorm, the experience left me feeling shaken. He might have been a member of KHAD. When I finally got back to Islamabad, I reported the incident to Bruce Cahill at UNOCA and told him that if I was expected to work in Afghanistan then I should be given proper security.

'You're quite right, Harriet,' he said, with kindness and concern. 'I'll contact the office in Paris straightaway and suggest they make you a consultant; that way you'll have the use of a UN car and driver.' And without further ado he signed a document. A few weeks later, I received my pale-blue UN identity card.

Anthony Spalton, a friend from Peshawar now working in Kabul, invited me to join him for a drink at the UN Staff House, Kabul's equivalent of the American Club. On the way there he mentioned that a close friend of Deborah and Kurt Lohbeck was in town, staying at the club. Tarshi's parting words came back to haunt me – *If you go to Afghanistan, it will be very dangerous for you to return to Peshawar. Your safety cannot be guaranteed.* I couldn't take the risk that news of my presence in Kabul would filter back via the Lohbecks to the Tarshi family.

'I don't feel too happy about bumping into this guy in the club,' I said, and tried to explain to Anthony all that had happened in Peshawar and that my life could be at risk should word get about Peshawar that I had visited Afghanistan. So Anthony swung the 4x4 round in a wide U-turn, and we ended up drinking beer in the gloomy ballroom of the German Club.

Mr Abu Ali arranged for me to meet a Kabuli carpet merchant, a kind of Mr Fixit with whom UNESCO had worked successfully the previous year on the carpet-weaving and vegetable dye programme in Mazar-i-Sharif. An hour later, a small man with a disconcerting squint stepped into the office, dressed in a grey pinstripe suit, overcoat and grey karakul lambskin hat. Mohammad Ewaz Badghissi, an Ersari Beshir Turkmen from the village of Murachaq in Soviet-controlled Badghis, was one of Afghanistan's most famous master weavers of carpets. The two men greeted each other warmly. Mr Badghissi listened with interest to the proposed project and suggested I visit his home the following day to meet his family.

The president of the Afghan Exporters Guild, Mr Ziauddin Zia, was a close friend of Ewaz Badghissi and he took me to the Badghissis' house, hidden away down a small side street not far from Shahr-i-Nau. In the walled courtyard, all aspects of oriental carpet production were on display. Skeins of freshly dyed wool dripped from ropes stretched across the yard, drying in the warm winter sunshine. Bairan, Ewaz Badghissi's wife, was dyeing wool using madder root in a vat constructed from a mixture of mud and straw, over a wood fire. Dressed in a traditional purple silk Turkmen dress with fine embroidered cuffs and yoke, she stirred the simmering wool with a wooden paddle, periodically lifting the skeins up out of the dye bath to check the depth of colour. She was always called Hadji Bibi, *Hadji* because she had undertaken the Haj to Mecca, and *Bibi* meaning 'venerable lady', matron or grandmother.

Wahida, the Badghissis' daughter, was well educated and spoke perfect

English; she was also an accomplished carpet-weaver. Her father proudly showed me her work, unrolling carpet after carpet that his daughter had hand-knotted. All the yarn, both silk and wool, had been dyed in the outer courtyard by Wahida and her mother using only vegetable dyes. She showed me the 'cartoons' that she had designed, drawn and coloured herself. These intricate designs, drawn on graph paper with each tiny square representing a wool knot, provided the weaver with an exact guide from which to work. Wahida took me to a room reserved for guests, and placed before me a tray of toffees, sugared almonds and raisins and a pot of green tea flavoured with cardamom. In a corner her sister sat rocking backwards and forwards silently, traumatised, said Wahida, by the daily shelling of Kabul.

The room was dark, so it was some moments before I noticed an elderly grey-bearded man wearing a large white turban sitting cross-legged on the floor opposite me. His face was familiar. I pulled out of my bag the pamphlet Bernard Dupeigne had given me in Paris and had a quick look at the grainy black-and-white photograph. I was certain it was the same person.

'Excuse me,' I asked in Farsi, 'but are you Hadji Abdul Raouf?'

'Yes,' he replied.

I showed him the photograph of himself taken many years before by Annie Zorz, and he appeared fascinated. Pointing to a picture of a group of *ikat* weavers, he began naming each one. I was eager to ask how many of them were still alive, knowing that most of them were probably well into their seventies; Hadji assured me that they were all quite well and still living in Qurchangee. I asked if they would be prepared to travel from their village to Mazar-i-Sharif to train students in the art of *ikat* weaving, and he said that they would.

After many hours of discussion, a decision was made that the workshop would be set up in Mazar-i-Sharif in mid-April, after the end of Ramadan. The snow would have melted by then and the roads would be passable. The training project would last for six weeks; starting in April, it would be completed before the hot weather arrived in June. Hadji suggested that the students should come from a variety of villages and towns, such as Andkhoy, Qurchangee, Aqcha and Herat. Because Mazar was held by government militia and the students would be coming into the city from Mujahideen-held areas, only men over the age of 40 – who were considered beyond fighting age – would participate as students. Women would be included, too.

It was obvious that I must leave Kabul as soon as possible to meet with Mazar's governor, Mr Ansaree, to brief him on all the details of the forthcoming silk project so that he could help me find a good location. Hadji Abdul Raouf outlined what he and the weavers required in the way of site, location and facilities. There should be a lockable storeroom, a dyeing area with a concrete floor, drainage and a good water supply. We agreed to meet again on my return

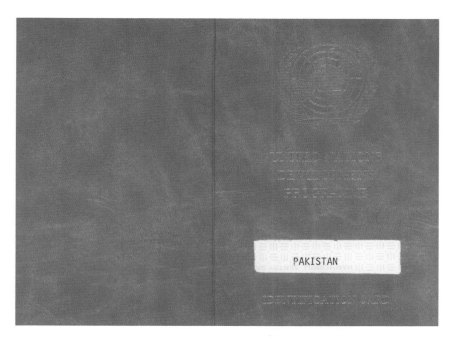

My pale blue UNESCO identity card.

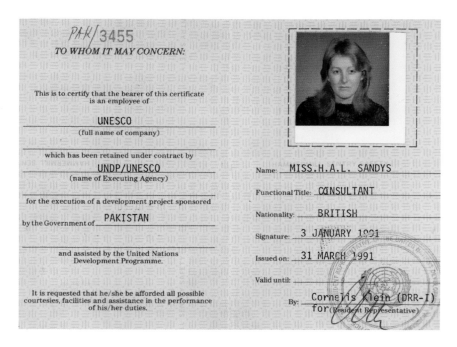

My UNESCO identity card.

Mausoleum and shrine of Hazrat Ali, fourth Caliph of the Prophet, at Mazar-i-Sharif.

Above: Swiss pilots hammering out a dent in the wing of the UN plane after it clipped frozen snow while coming in to land at Kabul.

Below: Supplies being unloaded at Kabul airport from a UN plane once used by Jackie Onassis for shopping trips to Paris.

Silk weaver, Pir Nazar from Qurchangee, de-gumming silk on the UNESCO ikat *project.*

Weaver from Qurchangee participating on the UNESCO ikat *project, Mazar-i-Sharif.*

Qurchangee weavers set up the ikat *project in the assembly hall of the Sultan Razia Girl's school, Marzar-i-Sharif. (Hadji Bibi Badghissi in purple.)*

A typical ikat *design (using chemical dyes) still woven in northern Afghanistan. (Photo courtesy of R. Darr.)*

Weaving ikat *on the UNESCO project.*

A weaver dying ikat.

Weavers from the UNESCO ikat project – Mr Ziauddin Zia, Mrs Ghafour and Hadji Abdul Raouf in the centre.

Dried grass and purple echinops hide the remains of Kurdish villages destroyed by Saddam Hussein's forces during al-Anfal.

Nararine Rasheed, director of the Kurdish Women's Union striding out across the hillside at Chamchamal.

Above: Peshmerga at Chamchamal. Next page: Women Peshmerga at a checkpost on the way to Chamchamal.

from Mazar-i-Sharif, this time with Mr Abu Ali, to discuss and plan the next stages of the project.

That afternoon, discussing in the Badghissis' home the setting-up of the silk project in April, all my doubts and anxiety melted away. I knew with certainty that the *ikat* silk project would now become reality. I remember thinking what an extraordinary coincidence it had been to find Hadji Abdul Raouf in Kabul. After all the years of research, planning, setbacks and difficulties, I couldn't quite believe I was finally in the same room with him. It seemed like Divine intervention, but of course there was a logical explanation. With heavy fighting in Jowzjan province, Hadji had moved his wife and family to the relative safety of Kabul, and was living next door to the Badghissis. His grandchildren were working for the family, weaving carpets in their backyard. It truly *was* a coincidence that one of the weavers who I had been working with in Pubbi Jalozai camp for two years was his son, Arif, without my realising it.

In the tiny UN plane bound for Mazar-i-Sharif, we climbed to an altitude of 25,000 feet above the frozen snow-covered Hindu Kush. I looked down at the jagged black rocks sticking out of the snow and wondered how families survived in remote valleys cut off from the outside world in such a bitter winter.

Halfway to Mazar, the Danish pilots removed their headphones and flicked on the radio switch.

'We think you might want to hear this.'

It was the BBC World Service, reporting that Operation Desert Storm had begun. Missiles aimed at Israel positioned on the outskirts of Baghdad had been destroyed, along with a nuclear power plant and a chemical-weapons arsenal. Now the centre of Baghdad was being bombed.

There was silence in the cabin as we all digested the news. We had all known that war was coming. The build-up of coalition troops on the Kuwait–Iraq border had been going on for months; nevertheless, it was difficult not to feel apprehensive.

Our aircraft lost altitude and the pilots prepared for the descent and touchdown at Mazar-i-Sharif. But as the plane began its approach, it suddenly dived to within 3,000 feet, cleared the runway, banked sharply right and pulled steeply up into the sky. According to the Danes – who, it seemed, were quite used to this sort of thing – a bombing mission was in progress. For the previous 12 years, Mazar had been an important strategic base for the Soviet army, which used the airport for air strikes against the Mujahideen. Although the Soviets had withdrawn from Afghanistan two years earlier, Mazar airport was still being used to launch bombing raids against the Mujahideen, by the Afghan army.

The runway was filled with MiG fighter planes, lined up waiting to be refuelled; others were landing and taking off, so it would not have been safe for us to land. Circling the airport, we made a second attempt and landed safely.

Near a UN vehicle parked on the runway that had come to collect us, we stood drinking tea and eating high-energy biscuits destined originally for Afghan refugees but that had somehow found their way into the airport canteen. The noise was deafening. Camouflaged Soviet helicopters coming in to land passed a few hundred feet above our heads. MiGs roared down the runway and taxied to a halt, engines running, while Afghan soldiers scurried around seeing to the refuelling and rearming of the aircraft. From nearby hangars, tractors with trailers rapidly brought fresh bombs to the aircraft. The bombs were so large and heavy that it required two men to lift them out of the trailer and load them into pods under the wings of the MiGs. The whole operation took only a few minutes. Then the chocks were pulled away from the wheels, the engines pushed to full throttle, and the MiGs roared off down the runway and up into the clear blue sky. Minutes later, we heard the distant thud of bombing.

The name 'Mazar-i-Sharif' means 'city of the Noble Shrine'. The centre is dominated by a magnificent beautiful blue mosque, the shrine and mausoleum of Hazrat Ali, fourth Caliph of the Prophet.

It was 14 years since I had last been in the city and now the Mujahideen, militia and government soldiers lived in a wary co-existence, for all Afghans respect the Blue Mosque as one of the most sacred sites in Afghanistan. For this reason Mazar-i-Sharif had remained unscathed. Now, as we drove towards the city, tanks and armoured vehicles were everywhere. Near the Blue Mosque, flocks of white doves flew high above the brilliant turquoise domes, weaving and turning in unison, the sunshine glinting on their wings.

The UN staff house was situated about a mile from the Blue Mosque, down a wide, tree-lined avenue. Square and squat, it stood back from the road with a small yard in the front and a large and beautiful rose garden at the rear. The house was not large, just a sitting room, hall, kitchen and spare bedroom on the ground floor and three bedrooms upstairs with a bathroom and communal sink on the landing. No one stayed very long as it had no bar facilities and was therefore considered a hardship posting. Most UN personnel came to Mazar for the day, returning in the evening to Kabul where there was a more exciting social life.

On the afternoon of the second day there was a knock at my door. Mr Ghafour, deputy mayor of Mazar-i-Sharif, would be arriving in half an hour to meet me, the manager announced. If President Najibullah was known as 'the bloody ox', then Engineer Mir Abdul Ghafour had earned the nickname 'the butcher of Mazar'. He arrived on time, a short, overweight man in an ill-fitting grey suit, the material stretched to breaking point across his ample form. I was struck by his reptilian appearance and the fact that he wore a black leather glove on his left hand. One side of his face was scarred by horrific burns, and an ear had literally melted into a grotesque shape. He had received these injuries, I was told, when he was trapped inside a burning tank during an altercation with the Mujahideen. His less-than-savoury reputation had preceded him. As I offered him tea, I felt nervous and ill at ease; however, in the months ahead I would meet him many times and, on each occasion, he was always unfailingly courteous and hospitable.

That evening I sat with two other guests, Anika from Scandinavia and Rob, an Australian working for the UN Food and Agricultural Organization (FAO), listening as the BBC World Service reported that there had been more than a thousand coalition bombing raids over Baghdad. My thoughts turned to my family at home. I hadn't told them I was visiting Afghanistan. With the outbreak of war looming in the Middle East, I knew it would cause them worry. Now that war had been declared, I was sure they would be wondering why I had not telephoned them from Number 10 to tell them why I wasn't returning to England immediately. All the other foreigners had made their evacuation plans and were leaving Pakistan on the first available flight. I now felt guilty for being where I was at such a time.

During the years of living in Peshawar I would often hear Afghans boast of their love of fighting or *'Jang'*, as they called it. 'It is in our blood,' they would say. At weekends, religious holidays and national festivals, bird and animal fights were a source of entertainment throughout Afghanistan. Dogfighting, partridge- and quail-fighting, cockfighting, ram-fighting and camel-fighting are all part of Afghan culture. Then there is the Afghan national sport of *buzkashi*, not to mention flying kites with strings encrusted with powdered glass, egg-fighting and competitive board games like chess and backgammon.

During breakfast one Friday morning, Rob invited Anika and me to a dogfight near a flour silo a mile or so from the staff house. The dogs used in these fights are known as Alabai, a type of sheepdog found from the Caspian Sea to China. They are descended from one of the most ancient breeds in the world, and were once used to hunt lions, tigers and wolves. Often referred to as the Turkmen wolfhound, the Alabai is distantly related to the Tibetan and Mongolian mastiffs and closely resembles the St Bernard. Over centuries the peoples of Central Asia have selectively bred the dogs for their aggressive temperament and exceptional stamina, using them to protect people and dwellings and also to guard grazing sheep and cows from attacks by steppe wolves. The dogs possess great muscular force, powerful thighs, sloping muscular shoulders and a strong, broad chest. I had seen similar dogs when travelling up the Karakorum Highway in northern Pakistan, their necks encased in iron collars with savage four-inch spikes and their ears deliberately cropped short to protect them from the jaws of wolves. No dogs are killed during the fights – the animals being far too valuable to their owners – but large sums of money change hands in the form of bets. The Taliban later banned these fights as un-Islamic. They introduced an alternative form of Friday entertainment – public floggings, hangings and executions that took various forms such as stoning women to death and crushing homosexuals under the tracks of tanks.

We arrived at a piece of desolate waste ground covered in litter and surrounded by dilapidated houses. The pungent aroma, which was difficult to ignore as we walked around searching for the *saag jaanghi* match, suggested that the ground was also used as a convenient latrine. We waited an hour but there was no sign of an impending match. Rob must have been given the wrong information regarding location; however, as Anika and I wanted to visit the shrine of Hazrat Ali, we asked him to drop us at the Blue Mosque.

Two small boys attached themselves to us as we circumnavigated the mausoleum. '*Paisa, paisa, baksheesh, baksheesh,*' they whined, plucking at our clothes. To escape their incessant pestering, we ducked inside the mosque and sought sanctuary in its peaceful and beautiful interior. Centuries before, Genghis Khan destroyed the building, believing that a great treasure was buried beneath its pillars, but the shrine was rebuilt in 1481 during the Safavid period and it is revered by both sects of Islam.

The interior of the mosque was decorated with ochre and midnight-blue tiles. Some of the walls and *mihrabs* were painted with garlands, leaves and flowers. Worshippers touched the internal structure of the mosque with quiet, devout reverence. Their fingers caressed the walls, door sills and jambs and carefully traced around the ornate ceramic tiles.

A small group of boys seated on a superbly woven carpet held copies of the Qur'an and rocked backwards and forwards as they learnt the religious texts by heart. At the centre of the mosque, Anika and I came across a huge cauldron made of bronze latticework and covered with tiny scraps of coloured cloth and an extraordinary array of different-sized padlocks clipped to the lattice. Here was the tomb of Hazrat Ali. Women in pale-blue and olive-green pleated *chadors* crowded around the metal cauldron, touching it with great reverence, bowing before the shrine and kissing the metalwork through their crocheted visors. It was difficult not to be affected by the sense of spirituality and sheer beauty of the Blue Mosque, or touched by the religious devotion of the worshippers as they whispered fervent prayers before the shrine. Emerging into the bright sunlight, we walked out across the great paved courtyard. White pigeons strutted around our feet and fluttered about our heads. According to Nancy Hatch Dupree, locals believe that 'should a grey pigeon join the flock, it will become totally white in just forty days, so holy is the site'.[30] Small family groups gathered on the vast paved forecourt were feeding pigeons with corn bought from nearby vendors, in the belief that it would bring them good fortune.

I had completed all I could for the time being and was ready to return to Kabul, but suddenly the weather turned sour. Black clouds rolled in and hung over the city, and rain fell for days on end, turning the streets of Mazar into quagmires. '*Ziod geel bud*' (there's a lot of mud), laughed an Afghan as he watched me carefully picking my way around water-filled potholes, trying to keep my balance as I slipped and slithered. Day after day Anika and I visited the UNOCA office. 'Is the UN plane coming in today?' we would ask the radio operator, only to be told that poor weather conditions made it impossible for the aeroplane to leave Kabul. Finally, after several days, the weather cleared. A UN vehicle took us out to the airport. We passed *chador*-clad women waiting in line by the side of the road to fill plastic jerrycans with diesel, and Bactrian camels loaded with firewood wended their way sedately past tanks, armoured vehicles and Afghan buses belching out black exhaust.

Mazar airport was dilapidated, and wreckage from destroyed aircraft and the rusting remains of burnt-out tanks littered the fringes of the runways. The air traffic control tower informed us that the UN plane would be arriving shortly. Young Afghan conscripts, wearing coarse grey woollen uniforms and French gendarme-style pillbox hats perched at a rakish angle on shaven heads, stared at us curiously as we stood on the windswept tarmac scanning the sky to the south for the first sight of the tiny UN plane. It suddenly appeared from behind a black cloud, a silver speck growing larger until it passed overhead, circled the airport once and came in to land. The aircraft carried essential goods for the various UN offices in Mazar. As the pilots stood drinking tea on the runway, a damp, cold wind began to blow. They looked to the south, pointing out the gathering fog. Within minutes it swirled in, enveloping everything and blocking out the sun.

'We must leave quickly,' said the Danish pilots. 'Get aboard now.'

As the aircraft took off, I could see only the tower of the flour silo above the dense white blanket that now covered the earth from the Russian border to the Hindu Kush.

Back in Kabul, I contacted John Fisk, Chief Technical Adviser of the International Labour Organization, and asked if he had a room in his house that I could rent during the rest of my stay in Kabul. I felt too isolated staying alone at the German Club. John kindly collected me in his white UN 4x4 and I soon felt quite at home in his comfortable house. To my surprise, the other spare room was occupied by Mr Abu Ali who, I felt, did not fully approve of me being there.

For three days and nights snow fell relentlessly. Over the city fell the magical stillness and silence that only occurs after a heavy snowfall. The snow deadened Kabul's normal clatter; no car horns sounded in the streets, no incoming rockets screamed overhead. With no buses running, Kabuli residents – women carrying umbrellas and wearing scarves, jackets and boots, and men in heavy overcoats and karakul hats – struggled heroically through the yard-deep snow to reach their places of work. On the third day, a large tree fell across the road outside our house, its boughs no longer able to bear the weight of snow. A few brave office workers continued to. stagger through the snow, carefully making their way around the tree en route to the Ministry of the Interior. With the roads blocked and telephone lines dead, Mr Abu Ali, observing the wintery scene outside, announced, 'The UNESCO office is closed today'.

At a loose end, I walked through the falling snow to spend the day with the Badghissi family. Kabul resembled an alpine ski resort; the houses looked like Swiss chalets with several feet of snow piled up on the roofs. Giant crystal stalactites hung from the gutters and eaves, their deadly sharp spikes a danger to those walking beneath. As the icicles melted in the sunshine they broke off, breaking into a thousand tinkling shards on the pavement. Above my head I could hear voices. A couple of young boys were balanced precariously on the corrugated tin roofs, armed with long-handled wooden shovels that they were using to push huge amounts of snow towards the eaves. It fell off into the street like an avalanche.

At the Badghissis' house I was shown into a large inner room with many windows, like a conservatory. It was a hive of activity. All of Ewaz's extended family – children, grandchildren, and war orphans given a home by Hadji Bibi – appeared to be involved in various stages of carpet production. Little girls and boys squatted low on the floor over their horizontal looms, feet flat on the ground, in that comfortable position so easily assumed by their race and yet so difficult for many westerners. Side by side, they chattered animatedly like flocks of swallows gathering on telephone lines before migrating to hotter climes, their nimble fingers a blur as they knotted coloured wool around the warps. In homes where rug-weaving is a tradition, Turkmen girls and boys learn to weave from the age of four and, by the time she marries, a girl is expected to have woven rugs and carpets for her new home. The more skilled the girl is at weaving, the higher the dowry price paid by her husband's family. In the past, when Turkmen tribes migrated with their herds across the steppes of Central Asia, their whole survival depended upon their livestock. The loss of sheep, goats and camels in a harsh winter could spell disaster. In such circumstances, the men of the tribe would take the carpets woven by their wives and daughters to sell in the oasis towns along the Silk Road, so providing essential finance to see them through a bleak period.

In one corner sat three elderly Turkmen women wearing beautiful silk dresses with intricately embroidered yokes. One rocked a tiny baby in a cradle and another stirred the midday meal simmering in a large cauldron on top of a wood-burning stove, while a third busied herself unwinding wool from a skein and rolling it into a ball. Like spokes supporting a wheel, each member of the Badghissi family from the youngest to the oldest had his or her own important responsibility that together contributed to the family's survival.

During the next few days, with the office still closed due to heavy snow, I spent an afternoon with Khanullah and Bismullah and their family. It was the first time I had been back to their home since Joss and I had had lunch in their garden two years before – the day on which I had begun to fall ill with meningitis. There had been a few additions since I was last in Kabul, and the children now numbered 14. Bismullah and Khanullah's wives and some of the children were all seated in a circle on a mattress in the main room with their legs under a low table. A huge quilt had been spread over the table, large enough to cover all the family up to their waists; over this was spread an oriental carpet that served as the tablecloth. Beneath the table was a *sandali*, a metal brazier filled with burning charcoal embers. This was the traditional way Afghans kept warm during the cold winter months in homes with no other form of heating. I had seen 19th-century *sandalis* for sale in the antiques shops in Chicken Street, but this was the first time that I had ever seen one in use. The family invited me to join them under the quilt to keep warm. All of us – men, women and children – spent an exceedingly happy afternoon tucked up together, leaning against carpet-covered cushions, talking, eating raisins, cake, toffees and *noql-e-badomi* and drinking copious amounts of green tea. It was an opportunity for me to thank the wives in person for all the times they had prepared hard-boiled eggs for me during my stay in the Jamhuriat hospital. They were glad to see me well again.

I was struck, that afternoon, by how quiet and well behaved the children were, something I witnessed time and again in Afghanistan. In Afghan culture, children are brought up to respect their parents, relatives and elder siblings and to be respectful and well-mannered in the presence of guests. During the many times I was a guest in Afghan homes, I never once heard children bickering, shouting, misbehaving or being rude to their parents. Undoubtedly tantrums did take place, but only behind closed doors and never in front of guests.

It was now time for me to leave Kabul and return to Pakistan. At the airport, the OSGAP (Office of the Secretary-General in Afghanistan and Pakistan) aeroplane arriving from Islamabad clipped its left wing on a high bank of frozen snow piled there by the snowploughs as it came in to land. The young Afghan conscripts who had come to see what was going on found it very amusing to watch the Swiss pilots climb out on the wings and attempt to hammer out the twisted metal plate with heavy iron mallets. Eventually the wing was repaired, the food and computers for the UN commissary unloaded, and we were cleared for take-off for the flight to Islamabad. The plane had once been the personal property of Jackie Onassis, who used it for shopping trips to Paris. The interior was open plan, with a semi-circular leather sofa and a walnut veneer table in the centre. I sat back on the sofa, enjoying the novelty of the plane's unusual decor, but even more I enjoyed the alcoholic drinks and canapés served by the Swiss stewardess once we were airborne.

I stayed the night in Islamabad with the BBC's foreign correspondent, Lyse Doucet. One could never be bored in Lyse's company. She has a great sense of humour and an infectious laugh, and is a highly amusing raconteuse. When it came to Afghan-Pakistani politics, local rumour and gossip, Lyse's ear was always very close to the ground. With her knowledge and wealth of experience of both working in Pakistan and travelling inside Afghanistan with Mujahideen groups, she was fascinating to listen to. Once we started laughing it was difficult to stop. During the early hours of the morning just before *Fajr* prayers, a tremendous earth tremor shook the house. The jolts only lasted a minute, but were severe enough to send us both racing downstairs and out into the compound in our nightclothes. In the short time it took us to get out of the house, more than 170 people died in Chitral, Nuristan and the Swat valleys. Many more died or were made homeless in the snow-filled valleys in the mountainous north-east province of Badakshan, the epicentre of the earthquake. But because the area was held by the Mujahideen, the Afghan government was unable to reach the area to offer assistance.

Ghafur was waiting for me at Peshawar airport. It was comforting to see his familiar face. I knew I would be safe as he drove me through a city wound tight with tension. I thought of the many times he had looked after me over the years, driving me here and there. He had waited patiently outside shops while I bought costumes for the James Bond film, and we had made the journey together through the Khyber Pass to Jalalabad in 1988 for the funeral of Ghaffar Khan. These shared experiences had created a bond between us and we greeted each other with warmth and affection as old friends do. He was, as always, totally unperturbed by the current tense situation in Peshawar. In his long life he had seen it all before. As a young man he had experienced the upheaval and killings at the time of Partition, and in his opinion nothing could ever be as bad as that again.

University Town seemed eerily quiet, with none of the customary white UN or NGO vehicles in the streets. All the expatriates had evacuated. Because Number 10 Canal Bank Road was beyond the canal and uncomfortably close to the tribal area, John had wisely relocated to a safer location on the other side of the canal, bringing Wadood, Mohammed Gul and Mumtaz with him. It was typical of John's altruistic and brave disposition that he had decided to remain behind in Peshawar so that the Frontline Television News and BBC offices could remain open. I was concerned about Mumtaz and toyed with the idea of bringing her home but, after much thought, I came to the sad conclusion that six months' quarantine followed by a life in London would not be for her. John agreed, and said he would be happy to take her on and look after her. When he was offered a stringer post with Associated Press in Kabul late in 1991 to cover the fall of the Taliban, he took Mumtaz with him. There she endured the shelling of the city by the Northern Alliance as they took control of the city. Eventually John took her back to the USA to live a quiet life at his parents' home in Virginia.

Ghafur drove up to the gates of the house, and honked the horn. As I stepped out I could hear the familiar *slap-slap-slap* of Mohammed Gul's chappals as he ran across the concrete yard to open the gate. 'It's Harriet!' I called out, and the bolt slid back and the gate flew open. Mohammed Gul, armed with a Kalashnikov, stood there grinning from ear to ear. Mumtaz bounded out from the garden, tail wagging, to give me an ecstatic welcome. Alerted by all the commotion, John appeared from inside the house, also with Kalashnikov in hand. It was good to be home.

I still had unfinished business to complete with the carpet and textile merchants in Khyber bazaar and Shinwari Plaza before returning to London, and I could think of no one better to drive me into the Old City than Ghafur. He arrived the next morning to collect me. The night before, I had found a large black embroidered dupatta that must have belonged to the previous occupant. It covered my shalwar kameez and reached nearly to the ground. With any luck, in the back of Ghafur's taxi I might be mistaken for a local woman. On our way to the Khyber bazaar, we passed a group of convicts shuffling in single file over Jail Bridge, thick heavy metal chains linking their handcuffed hands to their shackled feet and them to each other as they were walked to the Court House nearby. It was indeed a medieval sight.

Just before my departure for Kabul, I had set aside an assortment of small kilims and prayer rugs in Mohammed Qul Andkhoi's shop, promising him that I would make a final selection on my return to Peshawar.

'I'm leaving tomorrow for Karachi, then taking a plane to UK. All the foreigners have left Peshawar,' I said.

'All?' he asked.

'Yes, everyone has gone'.

Mohammed Qul looked crestfallen as he realised the lack of foreigners in Peshawar would adversely affect his business.

'OK, Miss Oriot. You buy more carpets and I give you cheap price,' he said, realising this might be his last opportunity of making a sale for some months.

As we sat negotiating prices, I heard shouting from the bazaar below. Through the dirt-encrusted window I could see a huge crowd, waving placards and banners, marching towards Sadaart Market, chanting, 'Death to USA. Death to UK. Death to Zionists. *Zindabad* Pakistan. *Zindabad* Saddam!'

'I'm sorry, Mohammed Qul. I have to go. Please take these rugs to Tariq Sultan in Chowk Yadgar. I will send you the money from England.'

'But what about these rugs here?' he said, pointing to his huge stock of rugs, carpets and kilims piled up to the ceiling, dismayed that I was leaving his shop without buying my normal quota. He began frantically throwing rugs down in front of me, sending up clouds of dust and a strong smell of mothballs. 'Madam Oriot, you not see these yet. Good price. Cheap price. *Very* good carpet. Or this kilim – what about *this* kilim?

'I am very sorry, Mohammed Qul. They're beautiful kilims, but I must go *now*. It's not safe for me to stay here in the bazaar. *Ba ma nekhoda.*'

Pulling the black dupatta over my head, I hurried down the stairs, passing Turkmen refugees slowly climbing up bent double under the weight of rugs woven in the refugee camps. They had brought the rugs to Sadaart Market in the hope of selling them to the shopkeepers.

Maarten Reuchlin used his diplomatic pass to meet me as I entered the arrivals hall at Karachi airport, and ushered me quickly through a side door to his air-conditioned car with its diplomatic number plates.

'Sirikit and Philip were evacuated to Holland two weeks ago,' he told me, adding, 'I'm afraid you won't be able to go into Karachi. It's just too dangerous. You will have to stay in the house for the next few days until it's time to catch your return flight.'

I was disappointed. I had three days before my connecting flight, and had hoped to spend the time buying Sindhi embroideries from Kishor in Zainab market, but Maarten was adamant – there would be no shopping expeditions to the bazaar.

Once home in London, I received a letter from Bernard Dupeigne.

Dear Harriet,

I was delighted to have some news of my dear friend Hadji Raouf. I suppose he is very proud to have been chosen to be a teaching artist of the UN!

Your work will be very useful for the future of artistic craftsmanship in Afghanistan. Congratulations!

CHAPTER 12

The *ikat* silk-weavers of Jowzjan
Spring 1991

The 20-hour flight on Ariana Afghan airlines to Kabul, with stopovers in Prague, Moscow and Tashkent, had been cold and uncomfortable. There had been no safety leaflets in the aircraft cabin, no demonstrations from the cabin crew of what to do in an emergency, no soap, towels or running water in the loos and, worst of all, no blankets. I froze for hours. The same meal was served twice, and the only choice was between 'Muslim' and 'vegetarian'. Vegetarian was simply Muslim minus the chicken – the stewardesses in the galleys just picked out the chicken with their fingers. But it was glorious to be back in Afghanistan.

The herbaceous borders around the tarmac at Kabul airport were filled with brightly coloured cosmos. In my three-month absence, spring had arrived. Buds and flowers were bursting out on all the trees, and white apple blossom, yellow forsythia and purple lilac brought a welcome gaiety to a city the colour of dust. There was still a thick covering of snow on the mountains surrounding Kabul, making the air cool and pleasant like a spring day in England, yet in another month the temperature would soar above 38° C. In the streets, young boys were selling bunches of bright-red tulips, which the Afghan soldiers stuck in the barrels of their Kalashnikovs.

When I arrived at the UN staffhouse I was given a warm and overwhelming welcome by people of many different nationalities, no doubt pleased to see a new face. The guest house, built in the 1920s during the reign of King Amanullah, was all dark polished wood ceilings and panelling. Grapevines and roses cascaded over a pergola in the large garden at the back. The roses had taken a beating during the heavy snowfalls in January; one afternoon I watched the Afghan gardener trying with loving care but without success to tie up the long, thorny stems.

In the bar that evening, as Griff the Czech launched into a moving Cossack love song accompanied by Jacek the Pole on an out-of-tune piano with missing keys, I met Edward Hornyold-Strickland. We had known each other since we were children, having grown up together in the Lake District. Although I knew he was coming out to Kabul to work for the HALO Trust (Hazardous Area Life-support Organization), a demining outfit, it was still a welcome surprise. I had met HALO's founder, Lieutenant-Colonel Colin Mitchell (affectionately known as Mad Mitch, the name given to him by his soldiers following his success in leading his Argyll and Sutherland Highlanders to retake a terrorist area of Aden in 1967), several times in London. He and his wife Sue would often invite me to drinks in their flat in Dolphin Square. Colin was teetotal, and on my first visit he poured me such a powerful G&T that when I left I could hardly find my way to the lift!

Edward would be leaving shortly for Pul-i-Khumri to take up the job of equipping and running the HALO office there, and we made plans to meet when I arrived in Mazar-i-Sharif. I told him I was hoping to get permission for his first cousin, Adrian Quine, to come out to Mazar to make a radio programme about the silk-weaving project for the BBC World Service. Adrian and I had met years before at Sizergh Castle, Edward's family home near Kendal. He possessed great entrepreneurial spirit, and had for some years been a successful freelance broadcaster and reporter for the BBC World Service and Radio 4, producing some excellent and unusual programmes for the BBC. I had suggested to Idrasen Vencatachellum, my boss at UNESCO in Paris, that Adrian might be just the person to make a radio programme about the project. He, Edward and I were close friends and it was going to be fun being together in Mazar.

Edward took me for lunch at a restaurant and kebab stall in a small park in the centre of Shar-i-Nau, full of Afghan families, mothers with babies, small children in pushchairs, and older children playing and running about. We ordered tikka kebabs – cubes of lamb and fat flavoured with spices, threaded onto large metal skewers and grilled over charcoal. A small boy approached us. He had bare feet and his clothes were ragged and dirty. He was carrying a shoe-cleaning box with polish and brushes, and pointed at our shoes indicating that he should clean them for us, but as we were both wearing canvas desert boots we shook our heads. Dejected, he turned away. I was conscious throughout the meal that he was observing us, but when he caught me looking at him he either pretended to be very interested in the leaves at his feet or disappeared behind a tree. The kebabs were delicious but tough, and a few pieces resisted all efforts to be chewed so they could be swallowed. After they had been well masticated, I discreetly removed them and left the gristle on the side of my plate, together with the cubes of strong-smelling mutton fat that I didn't wish to eat. We paid the bill and stood up to leave. The little boy saw his chance. He grabbed the chewed morsels and fat off my plate, thrusting them into his mouth. Here, in this idyllic setting beneath the pine trees amongst middle-class families, an Afghan child was starving. His action shocked me and brought home to me the extreme poverty of the people of Afghanistan, exacerbated by years of war.

I handed him the rest of our uneaten naan bread, which he hastily stuffed inside his shirt to take back to his family. A member of the restaurant staff shouted at him furiously, and he ran off.

Outside Kabul, the town of Khost in Logar province had fallen to the Mujahideen just two weeks before. Now Herat, in the west of the country, was under attack and about to fall any day. Kabul, on the other hand, was quiet except for the helicopter gunships clattering overhead at tree level and the occasional Antonov supply plane that made the windows of the UN staff house rattle. At night I could hear sporadic bursts of gunfire, but there were no incoming rockets during the day. Not yet, anyway – it was the calm before the storm. Throughout the winter months, the Mujahideen had been stockpiling rockets in the mountains ready for the spring offensive. Now they were preparing to launch them on the residents of Kabul to mark a very special anniversary.

No one warned me that 27 April was the anniversary of the Great Saur (April) Revolution. On that day in 1978 the People's Democratic Party of Afghanistan (PDA) overthrew the regime of Mohammed Daoud, who was killed the next day along with most of his family. The PDA was ideologically close to and dependent upon the Soviet Union. A year and a half later, during Christmas 1979, the Soviet army entered Afghanistan and so began the war between the Soviet-backed Afghan government on the one side and the Mujahideen on the other.

With Mr Abu Ali away in Paris, his two secretaries, Torpicai and Anisa, and I had the office to ourselves. As in all the UN offices, the window panes had been strengthened by strips of white adhesive tape to prevent the glass shattering in the event of a blast. One morning, as I was typing up a report, a rocket landed close by. Before my brain even had time to register, I was crouching under the heavy wooden desk. Torpicai and Anisa looked on in amusement. They had become so inured to the rockets that they hardly paused in their conversation. I felt rather foolish as I crawled out, and decided to take a leaf out of their book from then on.

With Mr Abu Ali's car and driver at my disposal, I asked to be dropped off at the Ministry of Foreign Affairs. I needed to send a telex to the Afghan Embassy in London requesting that Adrian be granted a visa to enter Afghanistan. As I crossed the open park in front of the grey concrete ministry, an incoming rocket screamed overhead. I did not hear it coming until it was right above me. It landed in a residential area half a mile away with a terrific explosion that shook the ground. I stopped for a moment, heart pounding, but in the park there was no cover except for a few neat rows of rose trees in a border. Rockets began to come in one after the other as the Mujahideen launched an attack to mark the 13th anniversary of the Saur Revolution but, as no one else in the park seemed to be taking cover, and remembering Anisa and Torpicai's sangfroid, I just continued walking, trying to look unconcerned like everyone else. By the end of the day, more than 40 rockets had landed on Kabul.

One evening in the UN staff house I met Jihad, a good-looking young Lebanese Muslim. I was intrigued by his name, and asked him about it. He explained that he had grown up during Lebanon's civil war in the 1970s and that it was not uncommon to give children born in conflict such a name; his home had overlooked the Green Line in Beirut. Now he was working as a volunteer agronomist with the FAO in Kabul, propagating plants and fruit trees.

It occurred to me, as we chatted, that there was much overlap between our two projects. High-altitude bombing by the Russians had destroyed many of the *kariz*, an ancient irrigation system used for centuries to transport snow-melt from the mountains for miles across the desert to villages through underground tunnels. All over Afghanistan, pomegranate, apricot, apple and mulberry trees had withered and died from lack of water. Without mulberry trees to provide leaves for the silkworms, there would be no sericulture in Afghanistan. I asked Jihad, as he showed me his greenhouses one afternoon, if he would be kind enough to propagate some woad seeds that I had brought from England and I hoped would have developed enough by April to transport to Mazar-i-Sharif.

A few days later I was summoned by Jihad's boss, Mr Hari Dewan, head of the FAO in Kabul, and reprimanded for giving the seeds to Jihad.

'You should have asked Mr Abu Ali first to talk to me about these seeds and then I would have spoken with Jihad. It is not your business to speak to him directly about this.' Chastened, I left the office. Later Jihad pressed the envelope of woad seeds into my hand.

'I am sorry,' he said.

'It's not a problem, Jihad,' I replied. 'I'll plant them when I reach Mazar-i-Sharif.'

This was my first experience of the hierarchical chain of command within the UN that so stifled the initiative of some of its more junior employees.

For the first few days in Mazar I had little to do until the arrival of Hadji Abdul Raouf, Mr Ziauddin Zia and the Badghissi family, who were flying up from Kabul later in the week. My bedroom in the UN staff house had a huge sheet-glass window overlooking a roof stacked with brown rusting oil drums where a small flock of white doves perched and fluttered. The males strutted, cooed and puffed up their chests in an effort to impress the females, chasing them around the oil drums. Suddenly, almost as though at some magic signal, the birds would launch themselves into the sky, wheeling and circling for several minutes before fluttering back down. From time to time a dove, confused by the reflection of the sky in the glass, would overshoot the roof and crash into my window. The noise sounded just like a rocket landing. Having only just arrived from Kabul, my nerves were on edge. I cursed the doves!

When, a week later, the Badghissis, Ziauddin Zia and Hadji Abdul Raouf arrived, the search began for a suitable site for the silk-weaving project. We drove through wet, muddy streets and stopped outside a high mud wall with two massive wooden doors opening into a large courtyard. Walking through the doors was like stepping back a hundred years. Here at last I had my first glimpse of the old and familiar Afghanistan, far removed from the rusting Russian helicopter gunships, lorries, empty petrol drums and paraphernalia of war that littered the outskirts of Mazar. This was the Afghanistan that I thought had been destroyed forever. A group of Bactrian camels sat couched in the mud of the caravanserai chewing the cud while Turkmen nomads, dressed in traditional cotton padded striped chapans tied at the waist with cord, loaded precious firewood and Afghan carpets into kilim panniers hanging either side of the camels' two humps. On wooden balconies above the courtyard, women wearing tall headdresses draped with red-and-yellow striped silk shawls were busy hand-spinning wool for carpets.

Beneath the walls, in shadows cast by the turrets of the caravanserai, two elderly men sat cross-legged on a *chapakat*, a raised square wooden platform covered with carpets. They were dressed in bright green-and-purple striped silk chapans with red-and-white tie-dyed cummerbunds around their waists. Their white trousers were tucked in to black leather knee boots, and they wore enormous snow-white turbans. During his travels through the steppes of Central Asia in 1863, Vámbéry describes these turbans as 'having a length of 7 ells' (nearly nine yards), which 'represents the pall that every pious Mussulman must bear on his head as a continual memento of death'.[31] The men chatted quietly, exchanging news and gossip, and sipped green tea from small round Gardner teacups, a large porcelain teapot on the carpet between them. Children soon crowded around me, excited at seeing a foreigner in their midst. The little girls wore dresses made from Russian cotton, printed with bold floral designs, and embroidered hats decorated with triangular amulets. Like the children in Pubbi Jalozai camp, their heads had been shaved save for a single long lock of hair.

During April and May rain and fierce gales swept through Afghanistan, bringing severe flooding and misery to a country already devastated by war. The Turkmen shopkeepers in the old bazaar were a valuable source of information as they exchanged news with farmers coming into town from outlying areas. They told us that floods had swept away half the small town of

Aqcha in a single night. At this point the whole UNESCO project hung in the balance. I worried that the weavers from Qurchangee would have to negotiate flood-water, government checkpoints, and mud roads blocked by landslides during their journey from their village in Mujahideen-held territory.

After ten anxious days of waiting, Hadji Abdul Raouf's son Mohammed Saleh, Abdul Subkhan, Abdul Karim, Pir Nazaar, and Tulak and Khudai Qul arrived from Qurchangee. Together with other weavers from Balkh, Faryab, Jowzjan, Kabul, Herat, Badghis, Parwan and Samanga, they began to organise the workshop in the assembly hall of the Sultan Razia Girls' School.

The hall was an ideal location, being large with a high ceiling, and cool and well ventilated. More importantly, the weavers, looms and silk were protected from the elements. A small stone lean-to was requisitioned and was soon operating as a kitchen producing a midday meal for the weavers. In the grounds of the school, the weavers immediately set to work to dig a hole in the ground to build the *aujakh* (a huge dye vat for the de-gumming and dyeing of the silk yarn). The hole and walls were lined with a mixture of mud and straw. An enormous circular cast-iron dish purchased from the bazaar rested on the walls, leaving a cavity beneath for firewood to heat water for dyeing the yarn.

The school, however, was dilapidated. The pupils sat at individual wooden desks facing a single blackboard. The floors were made from packed earth. During gales the broken catches on the classroom windows caused them to swing back and forth; shards of glass from the panes littered the ground around the school. The classrooms must have been unbearably cold and draughty for the girls during the winter months. For the first two weeks, until the novelty of having me at their school wore off, the girls would ask if I was married and comment that I didn't wear enough make-up or nail varnish. Every morning as I arrived, they tossed out of the upstairs windows roses that landed at my feet.

For several days Hadji Abdul Raouf had been preparing a 200-foot skein of silk in preparation for *ikat* dyeing. He tethered the skein so that it ran almost the entire length of the school corridor and then proceeded to walk up and down, closely inspecting it for broken threads. These he repaired by rubbing between finger and thumb. After de-gumming the skein, he took it out into the field and strung it between two trees to dry. The next morning when we all arrived for work, we were dismayed to discover a group of girls playing volleyball in the field using Hadji Abdul Raouf's precious silk skeins as a net! The school employed three toothless hags to keep the girls in order and they now advanced menacingly, swishing thin branches and swiping at them, until the girls scattered, shrieking and squealing.

I received an invitation from the teaching staff to join them for a mid-morning tea break in the school's staff room. The women seemed to spend much of their time drinking tea, gossiping and applying make-up. The headmistress was a formidable lady with coiffured hair, heavy eye shadow and beautifully manicured red-lacquered nails.

Adrian arrived from Kabul and appeared one morning at the gates of the Sultan Razia to interview the weavers for the BBC World Service. He was casually dressed in a short-sleeved shirt, with no tie. In government-held cities, Afghan men wore Western-style jackets and trousers and took great pride in appearing properly dressed for work. I tried to explain as tactfully as possible to Adrian that he would need to put on a long-sleeved shirt and a tie. 'This is a girls' school, Adrian, and you are representing the BBC.' Luckily we were old friends, so he accepted my comments with good humour. An hour later he returned looking very smart!

The project would never have been such a success without the help of the Badghissi family. Wahida became my interpreter and close companion. She and her mother, Hadji Bibi, taught me the age-old methods of vegetable dyeing and de-gumming silk used for centuries by the Turkmen. A strong alkali solution was prepared by leaving a grey, clinker-like substance called *ashkar* to dissolve overnight in a bucket of water. *Ashkar* was produced by burning the rhizome roots and branches of a plant that the Turkmen call *choghan*, which grows abundantly in the sandy loam and salt deserts of northern Afghanistan and Central Asia. They showed me the curiously shaped root stock, which, they explained, grew deep beneath the soil so enabling the plant to survive the extremes of temperature and climate. Later, the Royal Botanic Gardens at Kew could not identify the root stock, but it may be *Leontice leontopetalum*. When the silk was simmered in the *ashkar* liquid, the sericin dissolved from the fibres. Wahida told me that girls used *ashkar* for cleaning silver jewellery and for washing their hair. She and her mother also helped me set up a small natural dye workshop using madder root, pomegranate peel, walnut husks, almond bark, straw and the petals of *delphinium zalil*, a wild yellow larkspur called by the Turkmen *isparak* that grows wild in the rolling downs of Badghis. In the 19th century, the bright-yellow flowers were collected chiefly for export to Persia and India for dyeing silk. The weavers boiled the petals in the *aujakh* for several hours and then strained the flowers through a sieve. The substantive dye, mustard yellow in colour, required no mordant. It could be mixed with other dyestuffs to produce a varied range of colours – with indigo to produce green, with madder to produce orange.

The project was forging ahead. My days were filled and busy – there was so much to do. Everything in the workshop had to be made from scratch – the looms, the heddles, the *aujakh* – and every afternoon I taught vegetable dyeing to the schoolgirls.

By contrast, the evenings in the UN staffhouse were long and dull. There was only one other resident, a Swiss UN worker called Peter. He was very secretive about his work and I could never discover exactly what he did. One evening, he asked if I would like to join him as his guest at a dinner in the south of the city. On the way there, he explained that it was a gathering of all the military commanders and Soviet advisers of the northern provinces. As I had just spent nearly eight years living and working in Peshawar with the Mujahideen, the thought of socialising with the other side made me feel a little uneasy, but as we were just turning in to the car park it was too late to do anything about it

The concrete Soviet-style building was some kind of conference centre. The room was full of uniformed Afghan military personnel – this was very clearly an important gathering and a men-only evening. I tried to lose myself behind the great square concrete pillars down each side of the enormously long room as Peter was whisked off to be introduced. The dining tables, placed end to end to form one continuous seating arrangement, were spread with white cloths, and flower arrangements, vodka glasses and bottles of brandy and vodka were placed at intervals down the centre. Communist or Mujahideen, the Afghans are unfailingly courteous and soon I was escorted to my seat by two officers sporting an abundance of gold braid and decorations.

The speeches and toasts began even before the first course was set before us, and it was obvious that the officers on either side of me had already consumed a considerable amount of alcohol. The one on my left reached for the bottle and filled my glass with plum brandy, clinked his glass with mine, roared '*Zdarovye!*' and downed the contents in one gulp. Peter, sitting opposite me, appeared to be coping admirably. He was obviously an experienced hand at this, so I watched him closely to see what I should do. As far as I could tell, I was expected to toast the person opposite me, those to my left and right, and clink glasses with just about anybody whose eye caught mine. And in all cases knock back the glass in one gulp. Furthermore, apparently anyone could get up and propose a toast at any moment. As soon as someone stood up, the rest of us would lay down our knives and forks, push back our chairs, stand up, fill our glasses, clink glasses, shout *Zdarovye!* and gulp back the brandy. We toasted President Brezhnev, Mrs Thatcher, President Najibullah, Stalin, and anyone else who came to mind (I suggested Winston Churchill, and that seemed to go down well), and we raised our glasses to England, Switzerland, Moscow and Afghanistan. My friends on either side became increasingly drunk. Their eyes were bloodshot, their speech slurred. Towards the end of the meal, the officer on my left, suddenly and without warning, keeled over, his head landing in my lap. I looked across the table to Peter for help, but realised there would be none as Peter was in the same inebriated state. All I could do was try to push the Afghan officer back into an upright position, but he was a big man and he only fell back down again.

At last, the moment came for us to leave. What a relief! Even military top brass had to obey the nightly curfew. Not one man could stand upright without swaying on his feet, and that included Peter. The young Afghan conscripts manning the checkpoints were tense and jittery at that time of night, but we passed through without incident. Fortunately, the roads were empty, which was just as well as the 4x4 careered from one side to the other on our way home to the UN staff house.

I decided to ask Wahida if she knew of a family that I could live with as a paying guest, and she said she would ask her father. Living with an Afghan family would not only provide company, but also give me an opportunity to practice my Dari and really feel part of Afghan society.

Within a day or so she said her parents had found me a family, and after work she took me to their house so I could meet them. The house was situated in the old vegetable market and cleverly concealed by a massive caravanserai-style door. One of the children swung the door open and led us to a large inner courtyard with a fountain. Here lived the extended family of a wealthy retired carpet merchant, who I shall refer to as Hadji Baba (not his real name). There were babies, children, grandchildren, aunts, cousins, daughters-in-law and sons-in-law, all living together under the same roof, and from the moment I arrived I was treated as the 23rd member of the family.

I spent just over five wonderful and happy weeks in that house, and I now realise how incredibly privileged I was, as a Western woman, to be accepted to live with this special family. They treated me as one of their own and included me in all family gatherings and social events. During those five weeks, I spoke no English. Although the boys could speak a few words because they went to school, the girls were illiterate and spoke only Dari.

After the torrential rain and floods of April, summer arrived with a vengeance in May. By early June the daytime temperature in Mazar regularly exceeded 40° C. At night it was so hot indoors that it became difficult to sleep, especially for the unmarried women, children and babies, who all slept together in one large room on the ground floor. The girls thought it very strange that I was happy sleeping alone in the guest room, and would often invite me to sleep in the female dormitory. For a number of reasons I wasn't too keen on the idea, and politely declined their kind offer.

One day a number of metal bed frames appeared on the flat roof, and I saw the family arranging them in lines and covering the springs with mattresses and quilts.

'We are going to sleep tonight on the roof, Oriot jan. Why don't you join us?'

I loved the idea of sleeping out under the moon and stars and taking advantage of the cool night air, so after the evening meal I joined the girls on the third-storey roof, which offered stunning views across the rooftops of Mazar and a bird's-eye view of the courtyard below. It was a wonderful vantage point, from which the girls could watch unobserved through the balustrade the comings and goings of the menfolk.

Maryam (not her real name), Hadji Baba's daughter by his second marriage, and I lay on the metal beds and covered ourselves with quilts against the vicious bites of the mosquitoes. Above us clouds tinged pink and orange by the setting sun scudded across the heavens.

'Why are you not married?' she asked.

Usually my stock answer to this question, which I was constantly asked in Afghanistan and Pakistan, was that my father had failed to find me a suitable husband. As Maryam's own husband had been chosen for her by her father, this was something she would have understood. Most women in Afghanistan were married by the age of 20 so the fact that I was still unmarried in my thirties was a constant source of interest and concern to all the family. Marriage and bearing children, especially sons, gave a woman status within the home. 'Would you like us to find you a husband?' the older women often volunteered. One of Maryam's aunts had even offered me her son in marriage.

I thought for a moment about how to explain to Maryam that in my culture girls were expected to choose their own husbands, to fall in love first and then get married. Along the way I hadn't been particularly successful at finding Mr Right; instead I'd picked a few bad apples, which had left me wary of relationships. Many times I had wished for the old days, when fathers selected husbands for their daughters – then at least I would have been saved a lot of heartache. But there was also a part of me that enjoyed freedom, independence and ploughing my own furrow.

I didn't know how to explain that I had made some mistakes in my life and that now, even in my culture, I was considered 'on the shelf'. My limited knowledge of Dari did not allow me to explain in any great detail that I had 'missed the boat' when it came to getting married.

'When I was your age, Maryam, I fell in love with someone that I could not marry. My family would not have approved,' was all I could say, rather lamely.

Maryam gave a long wistful sigh. 'Ah,' she said. 'Like Romeo and Juliet.'

'How do you know about Romeo and Juliet?' I asked, astonished that she knew anything at all about Shakespeare.

'I once saw the film on television,' she replied.

The family owned a black-and-white set that was switched on in the evenings as background entertainment. The films were nearly all Hindi, transmitted from India. The poor reception resulted in a lot of flickering white lines and static crackling, making the films difficult to watch, but the girls loved the songs and raunchy dance routines. Shakespeare was popular in India and many of his plays had been turned into films.

Just then, we heard the main door opening and closing. Peering through the balustrade we saw Maryam's husband, Hussein (not his real name), enter the courtyard having just returning from work.

'Hide me,' she whispered, climbing onto my bed and crawling under the quilt.

Soon we could hear her sisters shouting for her and searching the rooms. I was giggling, thinking Maryam was playing a game, but she was serious. She definitely did not want to be found. Gradually the voices grew louder as the sisters climbed the last staircase to the roof terrace.

'Have you seen Maryam?' they demanded in unison.

I was in a dilemma. What should I do? I didn't want to betray her by giving away her hiding place; on the other hand, I was a guest in her father's house. To hide his daughter from her husband would be unforgiveable behaviour on my part, and a betrayal of their hospitality. Probably the expression on my face gave the game away, because she was immediately discovered.

'Maryam! Your husband is waiting for you. It is your duty to go to him,' the sisters cried, dragging the quilt off her.

I never fully understood why Maryam was so deeply unhappy in the early years of her marriage. My Dari wasn't fluent enough to understand all the nuances but, from what I could understand, she had taken a massive overdose of Valium on her wedding day and it had taken her two months to recover. 'Even now,' she told me, 'I have to take half a Valium each night before I can sleep.' It seemed to me at the time that her deep unhappiness stemmed from the fact that her father had married her off to a man 20 years her senior because he owed him money. In Afghanistan daughters are the possessions of their fathers, who decide and control their future. Maryam was the payment of the debt. She was highly intelligent and, had her circumstances been different and her father allowed her to receive an education, there's no telling what she might have achieved. Perhaps the reality of her marriage had put an end to her romantic hopes and desires of a different life and brought about her depression. Opportunity and choice had been denied her, and there was little she could do about her situation. Unlike me, who could flit away on an aeroplane, make decisions and have some control over my life, for Maryam the only escape was through Valium. I longed to tell her that once I too had suffered from deep depression and understood her misery better than she would ever know.

My illness had arrived out of nowhere like a tsunami. It was triggered by loss, starting as a mild anxiety and developing into full-blown depression with all the ghastly, debilitating side effects of panic attacks, claustrophobia and agoraphobia. It sapped my mental and physical energy and left me unable to function properly. Throughout it all I felt like a fly caught in a spider's web – the harder I struggled, the more tightly the depression entwined and enveloped me. It stole from me all the years when I should have been going to parties, meeting people and having fun. The stigma attached to mental illness was such that I felt too ashamed to share my troubled state of mind with family and friends. I believed I would be told, 'Pull yourself together – get on with it!' So I kept my anguish to myself and coped in silence.

In observing Maryam, I saw so many similarities, particularly in the way people reacted to her illness. There seemed little sympathy for her within her family and I was taken aback by their attitude. As a Muslim woman she was expected to accept her fate without complaint. My heart went out to her, but there was little I could do to help. I longed to say that, one day, life would get better, and she would emerge from the abyss into the sunlight.

Late one afternoon when I returned to the house after a long hot day working with the weavers, I found the girls putting on their pleated lilac chadors in the courtyard.

'Oriot, we are going to the bazaar to eat ice cream. Please come with us. But,' they added, 'you will have to wear one of these.'

I had always wanted to try on an Afghan chador, sometimes referred to as a 'shuttlecock', as I was curious to know how it felt to walk through the streets wearing one. Without hesitation I asked them to help me to put it on. Two of them pulled the tight-fitting headpiece with the crocheted visor over my head, explaining that the tighter I pulled the visor across my face, the easier it would be to see through the lattice. After a few tweaks of the pleats so that the cloth fell naturally, they stood back to admire their handiwork.

'*Ah, besyar khub. Maqbul!* (Ah, very good. Beautiful!) Now you look like an Afghan woman,' they laughed.

'But how do I walk in it without falling over'? I asked, barely able to get the words out as I was laughing so much. There seemed to be acres of cloth.

'Put your arms out like this, Oriot.'

Farida, who had married at 16 and already had six children at 25, demonstrated, holding her arms out wide.

'You take a corner of the cloth like this in each hand and then fold your arms back across your body.'

At last, when they were satisfied I had acquired the knack of holding the body of the cloth correctly across my chest so that I wouldn't trip up, we sallied forth into the vegetable market.

As we walked together through the narrow sandy lanes that twisted between the stalls in the vegetable market – where, I am sure, no UN personnel had ever ventured – I felt enormously privileged to be part of this family outing. Holding the hand of Farida's little boy, I felt entirely accepted by the girls as part of the gang. I was surprised how easy it was to see where I was going and just how protected I felt by wearing a chador; however, I really had to concentrate on keeping my footing on the uneven ground. In the West the chador is viewed as a sign of the oppression of women, but I could see that it gave the girls great protection from unwelcome stares. More importantly, the wearing of the chador gave them freedom to leave the house when they wished to shop in the market without being chaperoned by a husband or brother. Seeing the world through the crocheted visor was rather like looking out of a window through net curtains. I could see people clearly, but they could not see me. At one point a UN colleague passed by a few feet away. I laughed inwardly. If only he had known who it was.

Afghan men can tell everything about a woman, even when she is shrouded in yards of cloth. From her voice and the way she moves, they can tell her age and background. Are her nails manicured and varnished or broken and dirty? Is she is wearing high-heeled shoes or cheap plastic chappals? On one occasion, Wahida and I ventured out in chadors to buy okra for the evening meal from a stall in the vegetable market. I stood back while she chatted to the shopkeeper. After a minute or two he enquired, 'Who is your friend? Why doesn't she say anything?' then added, 'She has very pale hands and feet!'

Emerging from the narrow lanes into the main thoroughfare of Mazar-i-Sharif, we wended our way to the ice-cream parlour. It was packed with customers. Men and women were sitting together at tables and there appeared to be no segregation as is so often the case in Afghan restaurants, where there is usually a 'family' room. Male waiters hurried between the tables bearing trays of ice cream from the kitchen. The girls selected a table and threw back the folds of their chadors so that their faces were framed by the material. I followed suit and immediately a loud exclamation filled the room.

'Ooh, look – it is Oriot!' exclaimed Hadji Abdul Raouf, who was sitting in the corner with his wife Aapa and some of the weavers from the project. We all had a good laugh together.

I was amazed to see that many of the women were openly breast-feeding their babies, even though the waiters carrying plates of ice cream to the tables were totally strange men. This was my first introduction to the paradox in Islam that allows women to show their breasts while feeding their babies yet decrees that they must veil their faces in front of strangers.

Chapter 13

Folly on the Andarab River, a concert and a wedding

One morning, Edward Hornyold-Strickland pulled up outside the UN staff house driving a white Russian GAZ lorry. He had come to Mazar to buy fuel for the HALO vehicles, and suggested I might like to ride back with him and spend a few days at the HALO office in Pul-i-Khumri. It was Friday, all the offices had closed for the weekend, and I was in need of a break from the silk project, so was delighted at the opportunity to go to Pul-i-Khumri, the town where I had bought the camel saddlebag with Mary Burkett all those years before.

As we drove south-east from Mazar we passed through the most beautiful landscapes. Lime-green grass covered gently rolling mountains that rose above flat plains filled with orchards of mulberry, almond, apple and peach. Small bright-red wild tulips (L. *Tulipa linifolia*) grew amongst the grass, like poppies in the fields of Flanders. On the outskirts of Tashkurgan (also known as Khulm) the pomegranate trees were in flower, the brilliant orange blooms and dark-green leaves a stark contrast to the fields of yellow wheat. We passed through the narrow Tashkurgan gorge, a dark, forbidding craggy defile. Its steep rock face, blackened by burning fuel, showed it had once been a perfect ambush location. The propeller blades of a burnt-out Soviet helicopter stuck up like gravestones at the foot of the cliff. Once we had passed through the gorge, the countryside became a veritable graveyard of rusting petrol tankers, lorries and Soviet military vehicles, testament to fierce fighting.

At breakfast, Edward introduced me to the rest of the HALO demining group. Mathew Middlemiss and David Hewitson, both ex-army, were training local Afghans to detect and detonate Soviet mines. Kate Straub, an American nurse employed by HALO, was working in the Pul-i-Khumri hospital. Soon the subject of the day's entertainment came up.

'Let's go inner-tubing!' they all choroused.

This turned out to mean floating down the Andarab River holding onto the inflated inner tubes of tyres from Russian GAZ trucks. Everyone had been inner-tubing the previous Friday and they were keen to go again and to introduce me to the experience. All morning was spent in the bazaar in the company of Ahmed Shah, a handsome Afghan friend of Kate's, buying inner tubes from various auto-repair shops. Once they had been inflated by the mechanics, the black rubber tubes, which resembled giant doughnuts, were loaded into the back of a Toyota pick-up. The rest of us piled into a yellow taxi and drove ten miles south towards Kabul. The boys instructed the driver to stop alongside the river by a weir, where the fast-flowing water boiled and foamed. They agreed that this was the most convenient spot to launch our inner tubes into the river.

'Here's some rope. Tie one end to your trouser belt and the other end around the tube. Then if you fall off it won't float away down the river,' instructed Matthew. I did as I was told.

David was first to enter the river, and chose to go through the small weir, but the power of the water knocked him off the tube, which remained caught in the turbulence, going round and round like clothes in a tumble dryer. Ahmed Shah stripped down to a pair of indecently skimpy black Y-fronts. I simply did not know where to look. Traditionally Afghans are notoriously modest and Victorian about showing bare flesh, the men even swimming fully clothed. Noticing my discomfiture, he seemed to delight in prancing up and down in front of me with a cigarette hanging from his mouth, before he and Kate jumped into the river with a resounding *whoop* of glee.

Kate's giggles and laughter carried on the air as she and Ahmed Shah, sharing an inner tube, disappeared down the far side of the river. David and Matthew were already out of sight, having floated around a bend. Now only Edward remained in the shallows.

'Quick – get on, or you'll be left behind!' he shouted.

I hesitated for a moment, gazing across the wide, fast-flowing river, its surface patterned with eddies and whirlpools caused by strong undercurrents, and knew in that instant that I was about to do something unbelievably stupid. I had never been a strong swimmer, and a childhood memory of being sucked under by an Atlantic roller while swimming off a beach in northern Spain had left me with a fear of drowning. I thought of my parents' endlessly repeated mantra: *Never ever go on water without a life jacket.*

But peer pressure can motivate people to do things against their better judgement. I waded into the river, pushing the inner tube ahead of me. The higher summer temperatures had melted the snow in the mountains of the Panjshir, and the Andarab was in full spate. I fell forward onto the inner tube, and kicked and doggy-paddled into the middle of the river. The water was surprisingly warm, but I could feel the drag of the powerful current around my legs as I made my way towards the first set of rapids. Within seconds the waves grabbed and tossed the tube violently. I shot between rocks and crashed through a wall of white foaming water, which left me drenched and gasping for air. I hung on for dear life, crying, praying and babbling with fear. As we came around the bend of the river, I could see the others, bobbing like seals far ahead. If I got into difficulties none of them would be able to help. For an hour or so I floated alone on the river through the Afghan countryside. At one point an Afghan took a pot shot at us from the bank. Later we all agreed that we had heard the crack of the bullet.

The Andarab was wide at this point, about a hundred yards across, with occasional sandbanks that supported a thick growth of reeds. Ahead was a wall of white water, another stretch of rapids. Exhausted and scared of capsizing, I paddled furiously towards the sandbanks to rest. Reaching the reeds and feeling sand under my feet, I stood up, but the sand caved in under my weight and I fell back into the water spluttering. Now I came to appreciate the piece of rope given to me by Matthew as I hauled in the tube and struggled to jump back on. I had been in the river now for about two hours and was cold and tired; my teeth chattered like castanets.

I came across Edward, half-hidden in a clump of tall reeds. He too had stopped to rest. Never had I felt so relieved to see anyone. 'Don't leave me behind, Edward – *please*,' I implored.

I grasped hold of his legs and for a while we floated down the river together. The trick was to hit the rapids head on, but our combined weight hampered Edward's ability to steer, causing us to hit the waves side-on, sending both us both perilously close to sharp rocks where our tubes were in danger of being punctured. We separated just as David swept past us far out to our left and capsized in choppy water. We knew we must be close to the hydroelectric dam, as villagers working in their fields gesticulated and shouted frantically from the riverbank to warn us of the danger.

'Edward, we must get out *now*, before we get sucked into the turbines.'

We rested amongst reeds on a sandbank. Only a deep and fast-flowing channel of water now separated us from the riverbank. A farmer shouted to us to paddle across the channel, but each time I tried, the water flowed so fast and strongly between the sandbank and the shore that it swept the inner tube further downstream. I was exhausted after so long in the cold water and no longer had the strength to paddle through the strong current. The farmer stripped off his clothes and waded into the river, up to his neck in water. Grasping hold of the inner tube from behind, he pushed it ahead of him across the channel, so bringing me safely to the shore. An old man came down to the water's edge, held out his wooden crutch for me to hold on to and pulled me up the river bank. And so ended our folly on the Andarab River.

Back in Mazar-i-Sharif, posters were plastered on walls throughout the city advertising the imminent arrival of a troupe of state folkloric dancers and musicians from Dushanbe, the capital of Tajikistan. They were going to perform at Balkh University.

'And Ripe Plum is coming to sing too! She's Tajikistan's most famous female singer,' said Wahida.

Anyone of any importance in Mazar-i-Sharif society was attending the concert that evening, including Mr Ziauddin Zia and the mayor of Mazar-i-Sharif and his wife, Mr and Mrs Ghafour. Wahida was going with her parents and invited me to join her.

The architecture of the concert hall was Soviet in style, and the signs were written in Cyrillic. Heavy red velvet curtains hung across the stage. The crowd in the auditorium was made up almost entirely of Afghan and Soviet officers in uniform, with their wives and children. I sat between Mr and Mrs Ghafour in the front row, feeling extremely privileged but also ill at ease amongst so many members of the KHAD.

The dance troupe gave an exhilarating performance, singing folk songs of the steppes, playing traditional musical instruments and wearing costume of the many different ethnic groups of Central Asia. The crowd went wild, and children ran riot, paying not the slightest regard to the young soldiers who tried to keep them in order. Then it was Ripe Plum's turn to take the stage, to rapturous applause. A voluptuous lady of a certain age, she wore her auburn hair piled high on her head, and a great deal of make-up. She sang a repertoire of romantic songs in Dari and the Turkic language that tugged at the audience's heartstrings and sent them into raptures. No amount of stick-waving by the soldiers could prevent small children clambering onto the stage to press hand-written notes into Ripe Plum's hand, requests from their parents for her to sing a special song. Ripe Plum kissed the children and then, at the insistence of the crowd, sang more and more songs until finally, exhausted, she graciously brought the evening to a close. The audience showered her with gifts. Bunches of roses and carnations and pieces of jewellery flew overhead and landed at her feet. There followed endless formal speeches of thanks from the dignitaries of Mazar before the heavy velvet curtains closed for the last time, and the crowd dispersed.

There was great excitement in Hadji Baba's family – Maryam's younger brother was getting married in a few days' time. The silk-weaving project had come to an end, Mr Abu Ali had visited from Kabul and presented the school with a financial donation to pay a glazier to replace glass in the classroom windows, and the weavers had returned to their village in Jowzjan. It was time for me to leave Afghanistan, but the girls implored me to stay on for the wedding.

'You *must* stay, Oriot jan.'

'But I have no dress to wear.'

'No problem. Maryam will make one for you.'

Maryam was making all the clothes for the family. For days the girls had been visiting the fabric shops in Mazar, that stocked bolts of gaudy material imported from China. The girls liked lots of glitz and bling, and Maryam was busy on the sewing machine, morning, noon and night creating their outfits. As it turned out, she didn't have time to make me a dress, so she lent me one instead, a knee-length dress of royal-blue swirls with plenty of gold and silver thread. I loved it. It fitted me perfectly, and the colours went well with my hair.

'Tomorrow we go to beauty salon,' the girls announced as we reclined together on cushions on the *chapakat* in the courtyard. Leila, Farida's seven-year-old daughter, busied herself playing with my hair, combing and braiding it.

'You come too, Oriot jan. Have Afghan make-up.'

Early the next morning we assembled by the main door waiting for a taxi to arrive and take us to the salon. I was surprised that none of the girls donned chadors. As soon as the taxi pulled up in the street outside, they leapt inside without so much as a dupatta covering their clothes. I was completely confused. Would I ever understand this culture?

The aunts were already seated with their hair in rollers under beehive metal hair dryers. The salon walls were decorated with large posters of Swiss alpine scenes, deer drinking from crystalline pools, snow-capped mountains, thick conifer forests and red geraniums cascading from wooden chalet verandas. I sat and gazed up at them while my hair was washed, set in large rollers and sprayed with vast quantities of Russian lacquer. When I emerged sometime later from under the beehive dryer, and the rollers were removed, the lacquer had set my hair rock hard. I was rather hoping the hairdresser would brush it out, but she had other ideas. Reaching for a container of glitter, she proceeded to sprinkle it all over my hair. I looked a perfect fright. Medusa came to mind as my long red locks corkscrewed out of my skull like snakes.

I began to apply my make-up in front of the mirror, just a little foundation, eye shadow, mascara and lipstick, but the girls were horrified.

'No, Oriot jan! You *must* have Afghan make-up.'

The salon beautician, a giant of a woman, bore down on me. Grasping my jaw in her powerful hand and turning my face to the light, she painted in my eyebrows with strong strokes of a black pencil. Then, selecting a bright electric-blue eye shadow, she applied a thick coat across my eyelids as far as my eyebrows.

'Oh well,' I thought, resigned. 'I suppose it will match my dress.'

But my heart sank as I surveyed myself in the mirror. I looked like a circus clown and voiced my concern.

The girls crowded round me admiring the beautician's work and reassuring me.

'Ahh. You look *maqbul*, Oriot jan. *Bisur maqbul!* [beautiful, very beautiful!],' they cooed in unison.

I had my doubts, but there was no time to get back to the house to remove the make-up and wash out the lacquer and glitter. We went off to the wedding venue straight from the salon.

The ceremony took place on the first floor of a hotel on the road to the UN staff house. I had passed it many times and had visited it with Hadji Abdul Raouf as a possible location for the silk-weaving project. A band was playing in the corner and men and women were already dancing, not together but in separate groups. As soon as we entered the room, Leila bounded up to me.

'Ooh, Oriot jan! What have they done to you? You look so ugly!'

Her words did nothing to boost my confidence, but at least someone had the courage to tell me the truth! The girls were soon out on the dancefloor, gyrating their hips and twirling their arms above their heads to the beat of the music in a most sexy and seductive way. They gestured for me to join them, and all I could think of was how shocked the Mujahideen would be to see us at that moment.

During the wedding ceremony, the bride trembled so uncontrollably that she had to be supported in case she collapsed. No doubt she was nervous about the wedding night to come. She could not have been more than 17, but at least the groom was about her own age and they looked a well-matched couple. I hoped their marriage would be a happy one.

With the ceremony completed, everyone raced down the stairs to the street, where three coaches were lined up to take us on a tour of the city. Now the fun began.

'Quick, Oriot jan,' said the girls, laughing, and pushed me up the steps of a coach. 'We will all go in this one.'

And they surged onto the coach to bag the best seats, namely the ones by the windows. Soon we were off in convoy, travelling towards the city centre. Once the three coaches reached the concourse they accelerated and began to race each other on the main road that encircled the Blue Mosque. As one coach tried to overtake the other, the girls hung out of the widows screaming with excitement, urging their driver to go faster. The coaches roared more than three times around the mosque concourse at breakneck speed, each vying to be in front, the girls leaning out of the windows, and not a head covering in sight. It all seemed so surreal that I had difficulty believing I was really in Afghanistan.

Back at the house that evening, I was summoned to the bedroom of the young married couple. They sat one on each side of the bed, looking terrified. The elder sisters stood around giving them ribald advice. Then with a clap of her hands, Maryam called, 'Right, it's time to leave them. Everyone out of the room.' We traipsed out to leave the young couple to get on with it. In the morning there was a knock on my bedroom door. 'Come and see the sheet, Oriot.' The newly married couple's bed sheet was being held aloft by the mother and mother-in-law and paraded around the house for all the family to inspect and see that the bride had indeed been a virgin on her wedding night.

In Kabul, I worked for a final week in the offices of Kabul Radio and Television, editing the film footage of the Jowzjan silk-weavers. My contract with UNESCO was completed, and I flew back to London.

Over the next decade Mazar did not escape the war completely. In 2001, exactly ten years after my departure, the Taliban took control of the city. The Sultan Razia Girls' School became their headquarters and the girls were turned out. Eventually the Americans dropped a bomb on the school, partially destroying the building, but 300–400 foreign fighters continued to fight the Northern Alliance from the ruins. The Sultan Razia was rebuilt by the Americans, and in December 2002 it opened again to the girls of Mazar-i-Sharif.

PART IV
Iraqi Kurdistan

Chapter 14
A Land of Widows
July 1991 and August 1992

During the flight home from Kabul, the stewardess handed me an English newspaper. A name seemed to leap off the page at me. Three Western journalists had gone missing in March 1991 while attempting to trek from southern Turkey into Iraq in order to cover the Gulf War. Two bodies had recently been discovered in a remote valley, and one of them was named as Charlie Maxwell. But the Charlie I knew was no journalist – he was a barrister – and, anyway, why would he be travelling in northern Iraq? It seemed so out of character that I couldn't be sure that it was the same Charlie. Back in London, I made some enquiries. A good friend, Amanda Pelham Burn, confirmed my fears.

Charlie had volunteered to travel with his brother-in-law, the war photographer Nick della Casa, and his wife Rosanna. Nick hoped to interview the Kurdish leader Masoud Barzani, and Charlie, who had only a limited number of days off from his chambers in London, would bring back the interview and film for the BBC, leaving Nick and Rosanna behind in Iraq to continue reporting on the refugee story.

'No one really knows what really happened,' said Amanda. 'They've found Nick and Charlie's bodies, but Rosanna is still missing. It seems their guide might have murdered them.'

Charlie was not a close friend; nevertheless, the news came as a shock. Tall and well built, a former officer in the Black Watch, Charlie was a familiar face at drinks parties and Scottish balls, where he would spin me off my feet dancing reels. Amanda, who knew him rather better, was a close friend of his wife Alex, Nick's sister.

'Poor Alex has lost her brother, her husband and her sister-in-law,' Amanda went on. 'Rosanna's mother, Marigold Curling, is a doctor at St Bartholomew's. She's raising money for a hospital in memory of her daughter. It's going to be built close to the area where she went missing and called the Rosanna Hospital.'

Since Parthian times, the Kurds have inhabited the mountainous area where they live today. They are an ancient people with their own language and folklore but without a recognised country of their own, their population divided between Turkey, Iran, Iraq and Syria. Throughout history, the Kurds have constantly striven for independence, for a homeland of their own where they can be free to practice their own language and customs. Wilfred Thesiger, travelling through the region in 1949, wrote, 'their unquenchable craving for independence has led them time and again to revolt against alien rulers'.[32] After the successful removal of Iraqi soldiers from Kuwait by coalition forces at the end of the first Gulf War, the Kurds were encouraged by President Bush to rise up against Saddam Hussein. However, this brought terrible repercussions. As the uprising began, it became clear to the Kurds that the Americans were not going to help them, and that they were on their own. After a previous uprising against the Ba'athist regime in 1983, the Kurdish population of northern Iraq endured years of brutal treatment at the hands of Saddam, culminating in the al-Anfal military campaign. Al-Anfal means literally 'spoils of war', a reference to a story in the Qur'an glorifying the plundering of an enemy's land to justify the genocide. The campaign included the systematic destruction of some 2,000 towns and villages including mosques, schools, farms and power stations bordering Iran, with the aim of creating a cordon sanitaire. Human Rights Watch/Yale University Press's book *Iraq's Crime of Genocide: The Anfal Campaign against the Kurds* states:

> The principal purpose of Al Anfal was to exterminate all adult males of military service age captured in rural Iraqi Kurdistan. … Hundreds of women and young children perished too … Executions by firing squad, mass deportation, ground offensives and aerial bombardments, culminating in the bombing of Halabja in 1988 using chemical nerve agent gas, earned Ali Hassan al-Majid the nickname 'Chemical Ali'.[33]

The Kurds were now only too aware of what lay in store for them should their uprising fail. In the spring of 1991, four million Kurdish men, women and children began a mass exodus, fleeing across the mountains to seek sanctuary in Turkey.

Like everyone else in the UK at that time, I watched the daily news footage of exhausted Kurdish families struggling through snow, driving rain and thick mud as they made their way over mountain passes. Hundreds died, to lie in unmarked graves at the edge of roads alongside rusting trucks and cars abandoned when they ran out of fuel.

I was about to stage an exhibition in Finlay Street of Afghan embroideries collected in Peshawar, and as I usually donated a percentage to charity I mentioned to Amanda that I would like to give some money to the Rosanna Appeal.

'Then I'll bring Marigold along. I think you'd be interested to meet her.'

And so it was that I met Dr Marigold Curling. She shared with me her plans for the hospital and told me about the plight of the Kurds in Iraqi Kurdistan during the first Gulf War.

'The hospital is being built at Kanamarsi, an area selected by Kurdish leaders as being of special need,' she said. 'There are fifty Muslim and twenty-eight Christian villages, and the hospital is going to be built by a Kurdish non-governmental and non-political organisation called Kurdistan Reconstruction Organisation. The KRO was started in May 1991 and its main task is reconstructing the villages and agricultural systems destroyed by Saddam Hussein during the mid-1980s so that the population can return from refugee camps in Turkey.'

I told Marigold a little bit about my own work in Peshawar and Mazar-i-Sharif with the silk-weavers, and mentioned that I had known Charlie.

'I'd like to give some of the money raised from this exhibition to your hospital and to help the Kurds in some way, but don't really know what I can do.'

'I suggest you come to our next KRO meeting in north London and I'll introduce you to some members of the Kurdish community,' said Marigold.

A week later, on a baking hot July day, we met around a table in an ugly post-war concrete building on Caledonian Road in north London. As I talked with the Kurds about my work with the silk-weavers and the UNESCO programme in Mazar-i-Sharif, they in turn told me about the long tradition of carpet-weaving in their homeland. I had repaired many a Kurdish rug and donkey saddlebag in my time, and I loved the designs and colours of the vibrant tribal weavings. Some 30 million Kurds live in the vast geographical and largely mountainous area encompassing southern Turkey, Syria, Armenia, Azerbaijan, northern Iraq and Iran, all areas famous for weaving. At a subsequent meeting to discuss the Rosanna Hospital, one of the Kurds presented me with a beautiful illustrated book of Kurdish rugs and weavings.

'There are so many widows in Iraqi Kurdistan from the al-Anfal years, and more recently from the Gulf War,' they told me. 'If you want to set up a carpet-weaving workshop near Erbil or Sulaimaniya, KRO has the infrastructure and people on the ground to help you.'

Since returning from Afghanistan I had found it difficult to readjust to London life. I missed the close-knit community that was Peshawar, and working with the Afghans who over the years had given me far more in the way of warmth, kindness, hospitality and friendship than I had ever been able to give them. I missed too the light, colour and noise of Pakistan, the excitement, adventure and danger. Now, as I looked out at grey skies, grey pavements and grey people, I felt withdrawal symptoms that only another adventure would cure. During the years I had been abroad, friends had moved on and got married, and now had families. Most had moved out of London and were living in the country. What we had once shared – school, social life, the glue that had kept us together as friends – had, over the years, loosened. My more conventional friends could not relate to my experiences and I realised I had become a square peg in a round hole. I no longer fitted in. After so long living in an Islamic society, I felt deeply uncomfortable seeing people kissing openly in the streets and girls wearing indecently short skirts and crop tops. At parties, as I listened to snatches of conversation – the cost of school fees, the latest holiday, problems with the au pair, failed delivery of a new washing machine – I felt as though I had been beamed down to an alien planet from the flight deck of the starship *Enterprise*. My friends' lives seemed so materialistic, their concerns so trivial.

At the time I didn't realise I was experiencing culture shock in reverse. The months of living in a fundamentalist Islamic society, of having to cope and deal with everything on my own without back-up or working as part of a team, had inevitably taken their toll. The daily stress of walking alone in the streets facing physical and verbal abuse, and all the difficulties, dangers, problems and anxieties with ACAF, suddenly gave way one day to unstoppable tears. I couldn't pinpoint exactly what was causing the deluge. I wasn't conscious of being unhappy about anything in particular, but the tears just kept coming for days on end, like the bursting of a dam.

Now the idea of travelling to Kurdistan to see if it was feasible to set up a carpet-weaving and vegetable dye programme for Kurdish widows seemed very attractive, and I started to formulate a plan. My years in Pakistan and Afghanistan had made me an adrenalin junkie. Being on the move again I would, in a sense, be feeding my habit, and deep down I knew it, but I couldn't help myself.

With the aid of the KRO, I planned to travel to northern Iraq and carry out a feasibility project, the aim of which would be to identify plants from which vegetable dyes could be obtained, and to locate weavers and a local Kurdish organisation that could help set up and manage the project.

One afternoon I went to see David Black and his business partner Clive Loveless at their Holland Park Gallery. They were specialists in antique textiles, kilims, oriental carpets and Indian dhurries. I had known them both since my rug-repairing days and had often attended their exhibitions. For a number of years, David and Clive had been particularly active in promoting a project in Turkey producing contemporary rugs and carpets containing only natural plant dyes and hand-spun yarn.

For a century, Turkish carpet-weaving had been in decline. Weavers had all but lost the knowledge of natural dyes, and carpets were being woven using poor-quality machine-spun and chemically-dyed wool. But things were about to change. In the 1970s Dr Harald Böhmer, a teacher at the German school in Istanbul, developed an interest in rugs while wandering through the bazaars. He set up a laboratory in his home to chemically analyse the dyes used in old rugs and began recreating the formulae to reproduce the colours used a century before. He then started teaching villagers from Ayvacık and Yuntdag, on the Aegean coast south of the Dardanelles, how to dye wool using madder and indigo.

I was particularly interested in meeting Dr Böhmer before reaching Iraq. I wanted to find out from him what plants were used in his project for dyeing the wool and to share with him the idea of setting up a similar programme in Iraq. I felt confident he would give me an honest opinion as to whether it was feasible.

'I'm sure the Böhmers will have you to stay in Istanbul,' said David, handing me one of his cards with their address and telephone number.

Julian Gearing, then working for *The Middle East* magazine as a photographer and freelance journalist, had just arrived back in London from a visit to Bangkok. Over the years we had met frequently at various Afghanistan-related events in London and he now asked if he could travel with me to Kurdistan. He wanted to conduct interviews with Masoud Barzani and Jalal Talabani, joint chairmen of the Iraqi Kurdistan Front (IKF). Normally I preferred to travel alone, to be a free agent, so I wasn't at all sure about having company on the journey. In the event Julian turned out to be the best travelling companion anyone could wish for. He was good company and there were times in Kurdistan when I was extremely glad he was with me.

To prepare for our journey, Julian suggested we buy detailed maps of eastern Turkey and northern Iraq. Stanfords, the map and travel bookshop near Covent Garden in the West End, had the best selection of maps covering every corner of the globe and we found exactly what we were looking for. Now, as I began to pack my rucksack, I began to feel excited but also nervous at the same time. There was one more thing I knew I had to do – tell my parents where I was going. I wasn't looking forward to this, as I knew what their reaction would be. Finally, I plucked up courage and dialled their number, but when the moment came to tell them, I decided not to make any mention of travelling to Iraqi Kurdistan.

'I'm off to Istanbul to buy carpets for my business. I'll be away for a few weeks,' I said, and left it at that.

Despite never having met either of us, the Böhmers kindly offered to have Julian and me to stay. As I needed time on my own to talk to Harald Böhmer, we agreed that I should travel ahead and that we would rendezvous a few days later in Istanbul. It was naive and perhaps foolhardy for us to travel to Iraq at such a time, with little prior planning and no real back-up, but Julian was a veteran when it came to covering events in conflict zones so I felt confident. I had never been afraid to take risks in life. In fact, if I'm truly honest, I enjoyed the danger – it seemed to me that, if you always stand on the edge of a swimming pool too fearful to jump in, then you never learn to swim. Looking back on my adventures, I know that if I had pondered too long and hard on all the dangers and difficulties I *might* have encountered, I would never have stepped out of the front door of Finlay Street. Most likely I would have remained a secretary, sitting behind a desk in an office typing letters and regretting missed opportunities.

The Böhmers lived in Bebek, a beautiful residential area of Istanbul, just a short ferry ride from the city centre. On a tour of the city, Dr Böhmer took me to Marmara University, where the Faculty of Fine Arts had appointed him chief adviser to the natural dye research project Doğal Boya Araştırma ve Geliştirme Projesi, or DOBAG for short. In the ancient covered Grand Bazaar, we wandered through the labyrinthine passages looking at susanis, *ikat*s and the beautiful embroideries of Central Asia.

'Apart from madder and indigo, what other dyes did you use in the DOBAG carpets?' I asked.

'We used oak gall, acorn shells, buckthorn, wild camomile and weld, all plants you should find in northern Iraq,' he replied.

The crowded narrow streets around the back of the covered bazaar were a melting pot of humanity, reflecting the upheaval taking place at that time in the Balkans and newly independent former Soviet 'stans'. Women from the former Yugoslavia with peroxide hair were selling Balkan kilims for American dollars. Their strident voices could be heard everywhere as they bickered and bargained for cheap jeans and tee shirts to take back and sell in their war-torn homeland. Uzbek and Turkmen women, with mouths full of gold teeth and wearing bright woollen headscarves, sat huddled on street corners selling embroidered Central Asian *chapans*, caviar and bottles of Russian 'champagne'.

I met up successfully with Julian in a carpet shop owned by relatives of a Turkmen friend of mine, Omar Masom, who had a shop adjacent to Joss Graham in Belgravia. Together we planned the next step of our journey. Before leaving London, the KRO had given me instructions and the telephone number for its office in Ankara.

'When you arrive in Istanbul, telephone the KRO office in Ankara and give them your flight details. They will arrange a driver to meet you at Batman and drive you to the Iraqi border. Here you will pay him. Don't discuss with anyone in Istanbul where you are going.'

From Julian's hotel in the centre of Istanbul we telephoned the KRO offices in Ankara and London to finalise the arrangements.

From the port at Eminönü we caught the ferry to Bebek, and stood on the deck in brilliant sunshine admiring the domes and fluted minarets dominating Istanbul's skyline as the boat surged through the choppy waters of the Bosphorus. Bebek, with its popular cafe-bistro-bars and boutiques, was once the ideal location for Ottoman aristocrats, who built wooden summer houses with lattice verandas and palaces with ornate white stucco facades. A few beautiful 19th-century buildings still remained along the waterfront. That night we ate dinner with the Böhmers on their veranda overlooking the Bosphorus. Because we were leaving the next day before dawn, we turned in for an early night. The journey was going to be a long one. At 4 am Mrs Böhmer made us tea and breakfast, quite convinced we would get nothing to eat on the plane. This kind, unselfish act set us up for the day ahead. We stepped out of the Böhmers' home with our rucksacks on our backs just as the first pale fingers of dawn appeared in the night sky.

At Batman Airport, fighter aircraft were circling overhead before landing, an indication that eastern Anatolia had long been a troubled area. The Kurdish PKK, a separatist movement that craved independence from Turkey, was considered a terrorist organisation by the government, which since the days of the Ottoman Empire had brutally suppressed them, denied them their identity, and prohibited the use of their language and songs. As a result of this oppression, periodic acts of violence between the Turkish government and the PKK and had been going on for years, resulting in arrests and imprisonments, massacres and the forced deportation of Kurds from eastern Turkey.[34] Our driver was waiting for us at a nearby hotel, and soon we were speeding south through parched farmland towards the Iraqi border. The wheat had just been harvested, and the dry yellow stubble fields were a stark contrast to the emerald-green irrigated pastures that lay at the foot of limestone escarpments pitted with caves. The road we were taking to the border was marked 'unsealed' on our map – in other words, a dirt road. Clouds of fine dust engulfed us each time we passed a lorry. Ruins of destroyed mosques, towers and bridges caused by fighting between the government and the PKK littered the countryside; Turkish tanks and APCs were parked at major intersections.

Three hours later we arrived at Dernakh, the border crossing between Turkey and Iraq. With exit visas stamped in our passports, we shouldered our packs and set out to walk across the bridge that spans a tributary of the Tigris known locally as Nahr al Khabur – the Khabur river. Heat radiated off the wide tarmac road bridge, and pools of sticky oil from the huge number of trucks bringing aid into northern Iraq caused us to slip and slither. Halfway across the bridge, I stopped for a moment to rest. My backpack weighed heavily and my back ached. I was hot, tired and very thirsty. After the arid landscape of eastern Turkey, it was a pleasure to enjoy the sight of the fast-flowing ice-green and blue waters of the Khabur. As the river thundered between rocks in a narrow limestone gorge on its way to join the Tigris, a fine mist hung suspended in the air and cooled my face.

A handsome young man wearing the uniform of the Kurdish Peshmerga, consisting of grey baggy trousers, a short, tight-fitting jacket over a white shirt, and a black-and-white checked *keffiyeh* wrapped around his head, approached and held out a glass of cold water. An automatic weapon was slung over his shoulder and a bandolier of bullets across his chest. With a warm handshake and a beaming smile, he pointed behind him to the town of Zakho on the hillside overlooking the river. A sign stood at the end of the bridge, written in English in large capital letters: 'WELCOME TO KURDISTAN'. As we stepped off the bridge and entered the dusty, bustling town of Zakho, officials from the KRO office were waiting for us. From now on, they said, we were their guests and they would arrange our programme and onward travel. We'd made it!

Zakho was the headquarters of the Military Co-ordination Centre established by the coalition forces before they left the No-Fly Zone in northern Iraq. It was composed of army officers from the United States, Britain, France, Holland, Italy and Turkey. Their task was to monitor Iraqi compliance with the terms of the agreement to maintain peace within the Security Zone. It was also the main entry point into Iraqi Kurdistan for supplies of aid and for UN agencies and NGOs.

The KRO took us to stay overnight at one of their hostels specifically for visiting journalists and humanitarian aid workers. The next morning dawned bright and clear. By the time we had finished breakfast we could already feel the heat of the sun. At the KRO office Julian and I were given a travel guide prepared by the public relations office to help foreign visitors find their way around Peshmerga-controlled areas. This gave us basic information that we would need during our stay such as travel distances, main roads, accommodation, healthcare, travel costs and exchange rates. Most importantly for Julian, the guide gave the location of the various Kurdish political parties that made up the IKF. We discussed the aims of our visit and our proposed programme. The KRO decided to take us to the next large town, Dohuk, and we were soon speeding south through countryside dotted with small Byzantine churches with simple wrought-iron crosses on their flat roofs.

Situated between the Tigris and the Euphrates, Iraqi Kurdistan contains an ethnic mix of tribes and religions – Aramaic-speaking Jews, Assyrians (also referred to as Chaldeans and Syriacs), Zoroastrians, Turkmen, Arabs, Christians and Sunni and Shia Muslims, as well as followers of John the Baptist – all living alongside one another in harmony and tolerance. The strangest group of all are the Yazidis, descendants of the ancient Sumerians. Theirs is a strange and secretive religion. The Yazidis worship the Peacock Angel, Melek Taus, who refused to bow down before Adam despite God's command to do so and was cast down into hell. Yazidis have been persecuted for centuries as

'Devil worshippers' by followers of monotheistic religions in the region who equate the Peacock Angel with Satan.

On our way to Dohuk we stopped for lunch with a Kurdish family who lived high up a hillside, not far from where Charlie, Nick and Rosanna had disappeared in March the previous year. The women were dressed in colourful baggy trousers with scarves tied around their heads, and appeared completely at ease with us as they set out dishes of food on the ground and offered us glasses of sweet black tea. They chatted confidently and did not attempt to cover their faces in front of Julian. Looking up at the clear blue skies above us, it was impossible not to notice the coalition air patrols being conducted regularly over the area north of the 36th parallel. F-16 jet fighter aircraft screamed overhead before flying low up the valleys below the steep-sided mountains. However, it was not only the coalition forces that had aircraft in the skies of northern Iraq. Suddenly, aircraft appeared around the side of the mountain coming straight towards us, and flew low overhead with a deafening roar. Minutes later we heard the distinct sound of bombs being dropped in the next valley. We were just a few miles from the Turkish border. Julian remarked that it was likely that the aircraft came from Turkey and were targeting the PKK, who were operating their guerrilla campaign against the Turkish government from the relative safety of the Iraqi mountains. It was a bit too close for comfort for me.

From our vantage point we looked down on the rugged and inhospitable terrain, the precipitous sides of the mountains covered in scrub and stunted oak. Over millennia, snow-melt during winter and early spring had gouged out sharp V-shaped valleys in the friable yellow sandy soil and shale as the water roared down on its way to the Tigris. When Nick, Rosanna and Charlie had passed through this area, the valleys were filled with snow. Rosanna wrote in her diary:

> It's frightening and dangerous and I'm worried about how I'll get out ... The Kurds not only walk fast but wear galoshes – & they seem to be able to keep them on in deep snow & mud with only shirt and jacket ... Up, up and literally *over* the mountains.[35]

In Dohuk, the Kurds suggested we might like to see the reconstruction of three villages – Yakmal, Gund Kosa and Khabur – being built by the KRO for widows, the majority of whom were Christian. Between 1986 and 1989, command of an operation to exterminate the Kurds in the northern areas was given to Ali Hassan al-Majid, Saddam's cousin from his hometown of Tikrit. During the Iran-Iraq war, the Iraqi Kurds allied themselves with the Iranians, so Saddam had deliberately deforested the area and levelled the villages so there would be no sanctuary for Iranian Kurds coming across the border and aiding their Iraqi brothers.

In the KRO office in Dohuk, I discovered that the lithium battery in my SLR camera was dead. My camera was essential, and I was furious with myself for forgetting to pack a spare battery before leaving England. When I was working on the silk project in Peshawar, I experienced many setbacks. At times the obstacles seemed almost insurmountable and there were days when nothing ever seemed to go right, when everything seemed to go against me. But, as so often happens in bleak moments, suddenly something good occurs when you least expect it. This was one of those moments. A young man was despatched to search the bazaar for a lithium battery, and returned in an hour with exactly the right make, brand new in its original packaging. Dohuk was a fairly small town, there was no tourism in Iraqi Kurdistan, the country was surrounded by hostile neighbours, its economy was shattered due to international sanctions, and the whole area starved of aid. I never expected that this kind of battery could be found, but I had underestimated the Kurds and their country. With grateful thanks, and my wallet lighter by $20, I now had a working camera!

On the outskirts of Dohuk, Mustafa, our driver, pointed out a sinister-looking building by the roadside – the military barracks where Baghdad's intelligence network, the Mukhabarat, imprisoned and tortured Kurds.

'This is where the men and teenage boys were brought from the villages by military truck,' he told us. 'They just disappeared, and were never seen again.'

According to Human Rights Watch Middle East, the standard pattern was that, as soon as the trucks rolled to a stop in the courtyard of the detention centres, men and women were segregated.

> Men and teenage boys considered to be of an age to use a weapon were herded together. Roughly speaking, this meant males of between fifteen and fifty, but there was no rigorous check of identity documents, and strict chronological age seems to have been less of a criterion than size and appearance. [36]

After a few days of imprisonment and torture in these camps, those accused of being insurgents were taken away in trucks and executed en masse.

In the three villages, engineers were hard at work building houses and schools and digging channels for water pipes. The buildings were constructed from dressed limestone blocks. The widows invited us to drink tea with them. They told us that in 1988, at the height of the al-Anfal, of the 36 families in their village of Gund Kosa, 31 men had been taken away. All males considered to be of fighting age were targeted, and the women had never seen their husbands and sons again.

By the edge of the Khabur river we spent time with a group of Armenian

Christians, who had fled from a Kurdish separatist revolt in Turkey in the 1930s and settled in the area. Their village, like all the others, had been bulldozed by Saddam Hussein during the al-Anfal years.

'The Iraqi army came one day. They surrounded our village and took us all away in military trucks. They gave our sheep, goats and possessions to the Iraqi army. At the military detention centre in Dohuk they separated us into two groups – men in one group, women and girls in the other. Boys as young as fifteen were put with the men. We never saw our men again. Later, bulldozers came and flattened all the buildings. They even concreted over the spring to prevent us from returning.'

As we listened to their tragic personal stories, told with such courage, dignity and humour, I experienced for the first time the extraordinary ability of the Kurdish women to laugh and joke at their misfortune. It would not be the last.

For the next few days we visited more reconstruction sites, and one day we ate lunch, sitting on the grass beside a brook, with a group of Peshmerga who had made a small shelter from the sun using the branches of chinar trees. During a lunch of chickpea soup and rice, their Kalashnikovs and grenades hung from the branches above us.

During our return journey to Dohuk, Mustafa pointed out some of Saddam's many ostentatious palaces that dotted the countryside and hilltops and formed part of a large complex stretching throughout Kurdistan. One was perched like an eagle's nest on a mountain peak, no doubt so that he and his family could take advantage of the pure, cool air during summer. Just below it, a massive cave had been gouged out of the rock for the storage of military weapons. However, the Mother of all Palaces lay a few miles from Dohuk. The white sandstone Ashara palace, with its green tiled roof and interior decorated with green, black and pink marble from Italy, stood beside a large artificial lake that Saddam had intended to fill with freshwater fish. The palace had been looted by the Kurds; the fine white stucco ceiling, designed like the awning of a Bedouin tent, was pockmarked with bullet holes and scrawled with obscene graffiti. The Japanese ornamental tea gardens, with small bridges, waterfalls and water bubbling out of stone grottos, had now become a tourist attraction. Kurdish families sat beside a cascading waterfall, sipping Pepsi and relaxing in the evening sun while their children splashed and played in the artificial lake.

Over the next few days we drove for many hours through the mountains. The asphalt roads had been reduced to deep, wide corrugated channels by a combination of heavy trucks, tanks, armoured vehicles and hot sun. The road infrastructure was a 'work in progress' and we bumped along graded grit roads, our wheels throwing up clouds of dust as fine as talcum powder that turned our hair white and our faces grey. Positioned on road verges close to small towns and villages were large concrete edifices with portraits depicting Saddam Hussein in various poses and guises – in Ba'ath Party uniform and black beret, or in Western suit and black homburg holding aloft a bolt-action rifle. His presence was everywhere. Art was used for political purposes and the statues, monuments and murals were a constant reminder to the population that he held them in his grip. Although Saddam was a Sunni, one of the most common paintings was of him astride a white horse, drawing a clear parallel with Hussein, grandson of the Holy Prophet and one of Shi'ite Islam's most revered figures, from whom Saddam considered himself to be directly descended. In his book *The Monument: Art and Vulgarity in Saddam Hussein's Iraq*, leading Iraqi dissident Kanan Makiya writes,

> The horse is a key symbol of Arab male pride, and whiteness signifies purity. But most importantly, as every Shi'ite knows, when Hussein the son of Ali was martyred on the plains of Karbala in AD 680, he was riding a white horse.[37]

The Kurds had taken particular pleasure in defacing these paintings by spraying them with bullets from their automatic weapons, paying particular attention to Saddam's head so that his headless torso was all that remained.

The wind was hot and dry; the countryside burnt yellow. *Echinops*, a teasel-like plant with silver-grey spiky leaves and pale lavender pompom flower heads often found in herbaceous borders in English country gardens, grew wild and in great profusion across the hillsides, creating a pale blue haze stretching for miles towards the distant mountains.

Such beauty, however, hid a crime so awful that it had been kept largely secret from the rest of the world. As we walked up the hillside through the waist-high grass, *echinops* and wild pink mallow, we were aware of an eerie stillness, an all-enveloping silence, save for the wind rustling through the dried grass. No birds sang and no human voices carried to us on the breeze. There were no buildings, no people and no animals. As we continued walking, the ground beneath our feet became increasingly uneven, causing Julian and me to stumble. In the grass we could see piles of huge stones, and twisted rusty metal rods protruding from lumps of concrete. This was all that remained of a village that had once stood in this remote mountainous valley, a stark reminder of Saddam's policy of forced clearance of people and habitation during the al-Anfal years.

We continued on through the beautiful and dramatic Barzan valley, birthplace of Mullah Mustafa Barzani, father of the region's current leader Masoud Barzani, following the course of the Khabur river, a turquoise-blue ribbon snaking below us through white limestone gorges. An impressive steel bridge was in the process of construction and I took shelter from the relentless sun under its metal frame. The construction workers invited us eat watermelon with them. The chief engineer, who had gained his experience building bridges at Basra during the Iran-Iraq war, explained that many of his construction workers, who were operating earth-moving machinery, were women. Noting my surprised expression, he asked, 'Why? Don't women do this work in your country?'

The sun was a white disc, the air like a furnace. At the village of Qandil we crossed the Zab al-Kabir river by ferry, accompanied by a large flock of sheep and goats. Heavy metal cables pulled us from one bank to the other. That afternoon we reached the city of Erbil. Our driver pointed out a river running parallel to the road.

'At this place last year, as the people walked towards Turkey, I saw women throw their babies into the water to drown them. They were exhausted and could not go on. They had no food for their babies.'

The KRO had arranged for us to stay overnight at the 'tourist resort' of Salahuddin built on the side of a mountain where, much to our relief, the air was appreciably cooler than on the plain.

With my project to find weavers uppermost in my mind, we made our way to the Kurdistan Women's Union (KWU), which ran literacy and income-generating programmes. The director, Khalima Hussein of the Barzani tribe, said it might be possible to find weavers amongst the widows at Khush Tepe widows' camp south of Erbil on the Kirkuk road, close to the border with Iraq. In fact, just to prove how close Saddam's forces were to Erbil, our driver insisted on taking us down the long straight road running towards Kirkuk through all the Peshmerga checkpoints until we reached the last one. Ahead of us lay the front line. Looking through binoculars, I could see clearly Saddam's tanks and infantry spread out across the plain guarding the oil wells.

Khush Tepe camp was a collection of depressing concrete huts in a flat, dusty plain. The women were widows of the followers of Mustafa Barzani, and were not Kurds at all but Tartars from Uzbekistan. The older women had met their husbands in Tashkent in the 1950s, when Barzani and his followers were in exile from Iraq. When Mustafa Barzani was invited back to Iraq in 1958, the women and children came too, but in 1983, after a Kurdish uprising against the Ba'athist regime, their husbands and sons were arrested, imprisoned and most likely executed. The women and children were forcibly removed from their villages and rehoused beside an Iraqi military barracks, which Julian and I could see a few hundred yards away, and were kept to be used by the soldiers. 'Just like the treatment of South Korean "comfort women" by the Japanese during the Second World War,' observed Julian. Their plight was truly sad. Marriage was out of the question for their grandchildren. Conceived as a result of rape, they were considered of mixed blood and therefore not acceptable to either Kurds or Arabs.

Depression hung heavy in the air. The women had little to do each day other than dwell on their misfortune, and I struggled to find anything positive to say that would alleviate their misery. They showed me the few pathetic, precious possessions they had brought with them from Uzbekistan, including a Russian sewing machine and a fur coat. I asked if any of them knew how to weave carpets and they showed me a few simple kilims, but it was hard to tell if they had woven them themselves or simply brought them from Central Asia. At that stage I did not want to say anything that would raise their hopes about employment on a rug-weaving programme, as I still had much research to do.

I was already having doubts. Obtaining wool was not the problem, as everywhere the countryside was dotted with flocks of sheep and goats. I had no doubts either about the availability of dyes. Although the hillsides were undergoing a massive programme of reforestation, dense oak woods still existed in areas that had escaped destruction. A deep black dye could be made using the tannin in oak galls and acorns, and rusty nails as a mordant. With Kurdistan's close proximity to Iran, I felt confident that other plants such as madder, walnut, buckthorn, weld and wild camomile were easily obtainable.

However, there was an embargo on exporting goods from Iraqi Kurdistan through Baghdad, part of Saddam's policy to subjugate and crush the Kurds to prevent them from forming a breakaway state. So all carpets and handicrafts would have to be transported north to the border with Syria or Turkey for export. Given the historical problems between the Turks and the Kurds, would the Turks accept carpets that they might consider unwelcome competition to their own carpet production? I had not yet had an opportunity to find out.

Above: Ian Cooke and members of Holy Trinity Brompton church pasting the Bosnia Family Aid logo on a lorry before setting off for Croatia.

Left: Making room to sleep in the back of the lorry.

Below: Crossing the pontoon bridge at Šibenik.

A war-damaged farmhouse in Croatia.

A picnic beside the Adriatic. The lorry boys Brian and Peter.

Croatian women and children, ethnically cleansed from villages in central Bosnia, living in railway carriages at Capljina.

The destruction of the road bridge spanning the Neretva river, north of Mostar was a deliberate attempt to stop aid reaching the Muslim enclaves.

The magnificent Austro-Hungarian buildings in east Mostar had been destroyed by incessant shelling, reducing many to rubble.

UN pontoon ferry operating on the Neretva river. It was the only way for vehicles transporting aid to reach the beleaguered towns of Jablanica and Konjic.

Departing Croydon with an ambulance donated by a Dutch charity and destined for the hospital at Jablanica, Bosnia.

Postman! Delivering a parcel from Bosnians living in London to their family near Konjic.

In Konjic, we parked our vehicles beneath a cliff for safety against incoming Serbian rockets.

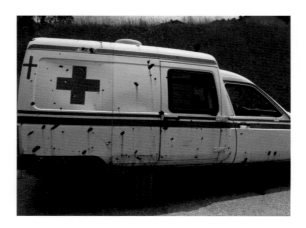

Jablanica hospital ambulance damaged during the fighting, 1992–93.

Peter Hunt hands over the ambulance to doctors and staff at Jablanica Hospital.

*A temporary rope and plank bridge replaced the Stare Most, Mostar's
16th-century Ottoman stone bridge which was destroyed by Serbian shells.*

With my husband Bryan, amongst the ruins of a Roman colannade in Palmyra.

With Saleh Mohammed and his children outside their home in Kabul, 2003.

CHAPTER 15

The Evil Eye

Julian and I left Khush Tepe and arrived late that night in Sulaimaniya. After booking into a hotel, we decided to stretch our legs, explore the town and get our bearings. We were later told that this was extremely dangerous and foolhardy. No foreigners working in Sulaimaniya at that time walked alone in the streets after dusk. It was widely believed that the Mukhabarat – Saddam Hussein's intelligence agency – was everywhere. On the way back to the hotel we passed the notorious Ba'ath Party detention centre, which had been liberated by the Peshmerga the year before. Beneath the concrete watchtowers that guarded the main entrance stood a huge and sinister metal sculpture of an evil eye, possibly a *nazar* or talisman. Whether it had existed during the Ba'ath regime or been placed there more recently by the Kurds to guard those entering the prison against evil, I could not be sure. Suffice to say, whatever its meaning, it made me feel ill at ease.

The Kurds in London had told me that I might well find weavers in the area surrounding Sulaimaniya, so in the morning we made our way to the KWU's offices; however, being a Friday, everything was closed. The Peshmerga guards gave us glasses of iced water and bottles of Pepsi, and eventually a smartly dressed, middle-aged lady appeared, introduced herself as Sirwa Hussein, and offered to take us to her home close by. We assumed that she must be the director of the Women's Union; however, it transpired that she was the headmistress of a girls' secondary school in Sulaimaniya.

Delightful, charming and speaking perfect English, Sirwa exuded an air of authority, no doubt developed over many years of running a school, that commanded respect. Her quiet reserve and dignified manner hid great personal suffering but, like so many of the women I met in Kurdistan, Sirwa possessed enormous inner strength and courage, a pride in being Kurdish and a no-nonsense approach to life's misfortunes. As a child she had grown up in the town of Halabja, 48 miles south-west of Sulaimaniya, close to the Iranian border. As she still had family living there, she suggested that Julian and I might like accompany her and her nine-year-old daughter Essrene to Halabja so that she could show us around and introduce us to her friends and relatives.

A Peshmerga guard from the Patriotic Union of Kurdistan (PUK) came with us for security. We boarded a local bus and rattled out of the city through countryside littered with minefields. Arriving in Halabja, once a thriving city with a population of 70,000, I was shocked by the devastation. It was as though an earthquake had struck. From the bus I could see the flat roof of a petrol station snapped in half and resting on the petrol pumps on the forecourt in a giant 'V' shape. As far as the eye could see, Halabja was one vast mass of concrete rubble and twisted metal. Not one building stood intact, and it looked as though no attempt had been made at reconstruction.

Poor Halabja! Once famed as a centre of political authority and cultural activity, home to poets, architects and intellectuals, Halabja was also home to Adela Khanum, the first woman in Kurdistan to promote women's rights. In his book *To Mesopotamia and Kurdistan in Disguise*, Major E.B. Soane, a British government agent who spent two years travelling disguised as a Persian merchant from Shiraz, described her as 'a lady unique in Islam'.[38] On his arrival in Halabja in 1912, Adela Khanum granted him an audience, and greeted him 'reclining on silken mattresses, smoking a cigarette'.[39] The daughter of an important Persian family, she married, in 1895, Uthman Pasha, ruler of Halabja, a member of the powerful Jaf tribe. Halabja was an insignificant village at that time, but Adela Khanum used her family's prestige to assert her position, an initiative not opposed by her husband. She built two houses finer than any in Sulaimaniya, importing Persian masons and craftsmen to do the work. Gradually official power came into her hands and, as her husband was so often called away on government business, Adela Khanum governed in his absence. She built a new prison and bazaar, and instituted a court of justice, of which she became president. 'Lady Adela so consolidated her own power, that the Pasha, when he was at Halabja, spent his time smoking a water pipe, building new baths and carrying out local improvements while his wife ruled,' wrote Soane.[40] I looked around to see if I could find her two fine houses. There were indeed the remains of some lovely old houses but, like everything else in the city, they lay in ruins.

Halabja had been bombed, first by the Iranians during the Iran-Iraq war, then by the Iraqi air force for three days in March 1988 as part of the al-Anfal campaign. Ali Hassan al-Majid ordered cluster bombs, mustard gas and the nerve agents sarin, tabun and VX to be dropped on its inhabitants. Within minutes, 5,000 of the 70,000 were dead, and a further 12,000 died in the days following.

As we picked our way across a wasteland of rubble, I asked Sirwa about her childhood. Growing up in Halabja surrounded by her extended family, Sirwa's early life had been happy. Over the years she had attended various schools, but they were all destroyed during the bombing and the chemical gas attack.

'I try and remember the happy times, but when I come to Halabja and see the ruins I become so sad that I cannot express my feelings to you,' she told me. 'I had many relatives living here – aunts, uncles – and many friends. Everyone I knew was living in Halabja, but thirty-five members of my family died from the gas.'

Sirwa went on to describe how, during the mass exodus in spring 1991, she and Essrene had walked for five days and nights from Sulaimaniya through Halabja to the Iranian border ten miles to the east.

'We were so afraid, as we didn't want to be at the mercy of Iraqi soldiers again. We knew what they were like. We were so afraid,' she repeated. Then she continued, 'We didn't know how to get to Halabja, or from there to the border. At night we slept in fields. We didn't even have a blanket to cover ourselves. We had no food, nothing ...'

'And Essrene?' I asked – she was only eight at the time. 'How did she manage?'

'She *had* to manage. Sometimes people carried her on their shoulders for a short distance and then put her down again, and she would continue to walk. Children even younger than Essrene were walking from here to the border. It was very, very terrible. I don't like to remember it.'

We stopped for a cup of tea at a chaikhana before visiting a clinic. The wards were filled with patients suffering from malaria and typhoid, but there was no medicine with which to treat them.

In a narrow street we stopped before a large sheet of hessian sacking stretched across a hole in the wall. Pulling it back, Sirwa indicated that we should enter the small courtyard, where an old lady in traditional clothing, seated on cushions and bolsters arranged along the wall, was busy rolling cigarettes. She lit one the size of a small cigar, inhaled and blew out a huge cloud of smoke. As soon as one cigarette was finished she would roll another. The house had been severely damaged at the time of the chemical attack and was only partially restored. At the sound of our voices several young women, all members of Sirwa's extended family, joined us in the courtyard. They greeted Sirwa and Essrene with great affection, and then insisted on preparing a simple meal, which we ate sitting cross-legged on cushions while the old lady complained loudly about Julian and me taking photographs. Many journalists had come to Halabja and taken pictures, but how did that help her? she grumbled as she started on another cigarette. She was right, of course. We would go home to our own comfortable, secure lives, and perhaps make money by writing a few articles on the suffering of the Kurds. Her direct comments put us both on the spot. As we left, I did not feel good about myself.

Back in Sulaimaniya, Sirwa brought us to the KWU's offices. The director, Nazarine Rasheed, welcomed us at her door with a warm smile. Tall and statuesque, Nazarine possessed a wonderfully quirky sense of humour that could turn the bleakest story of some ghastly event into something amusing. This habit of making a joke about their misfortunes was something that I noticed again and again amongst the Kurds. Their black sense of humour demonstrated to the outside world their refusal to be subjugated. Perhaps, too, it was their way of accepting and coping with the endless cycle of suffering perpetrated upon them throughout their history.

I hoped that Nazarine might know of some women weavers, and I discussed my mission with her. She ran Zhinan, a women's programme promoting literacy, dressmaking and sewing. She did not know of any weavers, but was open to the idea of further research.

My Kurdish contacts in London had told me that Kurdistan was a 'land of widows'. Adrian Quine had lent me his tape recorder, suggesting I interview widows of the al-Anfal whose stories might be of interest to the BBC Radio 4 programme 'Women's Hour'. As we journeyed through Kurdistan, I realised that the women of northern Iraq led a life quite unlike that of their Islamic sisters in neighbouring countries. In urban areas women dressed in smart suits, stockings and high-heeled shoes. Only in the countryside did we see women wearing the traditional Kurdish dress of voluminous trousers and headscarf. Nazarine confirmed my observations.

'Although some women cover their head and faces in the Islamic tradition, most women in Kurdistan dress like Europeans,' she said. 'Here women can receive guests even if their husbands or brothers or fathers are not in the home. This means that Kurdish women have more freedom than any other woman in the Middle East.'

As Soane wrote,

> The Kurd has a manlier treatment of his women than is seen among any other Mussulman. Among other Mohammedan nations, whose women are strictly secluded, marriages can only be matter of arrangement by third parties; but among the Kurds where women are practically as free as in any European country – except that they do not go to the bazaar – free intercourse between the sexes is the rule and the result is a large number of love marriages.[41]

Nazarine suggested that Julian and I might visit the PUK post at Chamchamal in order to see the Peshmerga in action. She arrived at our rendezvous outside the PUK's offices wearing trainers and armed with a stout walking stick.

Chamchamal lies about 45 miles south-west of Sulaimaniya on the road to Kirkuk. At that time the Iraqi government tanks and soldiers were stationed on the plain around the city of Kirkuk just a few miles away. We stopped at a checkpoint to pick up a Peshmerga bodyguard, who sat in the front seat of the

Toyota pick-up with his Kalashnikov. I was surprised to see women wearing Peshmerga uniform too, checked *keffiyehs* tightly wrapped around their faces. Saddam's Mukhabarat was active in the area and the women were not going to run any risk of being recognised. Nazarine told me there were many stories of famous women who risked their lives and shared the dangers of war with their menfolk. During the Kurdish uprising at the end of the Gulf War the previous year, women played an important role supporting the Peshmerga by nursing the wounded or carrying vital information between Peshmerga bases in the mountains and cities. Some took up arms, following in the footsteps of Margaret George Malik, a Christian Assyrian who, aged 20, joined the Peshmerga in 1960 in their struggles against the central government. She quickly rose up through the ranks, taking command and leading the Peshmerga in many difficult battles before she was assassinated at the age of just 29. Controversy surrounds her death. Some say it was at the hands of a jealous lover after she rejected his marriage proposal; others that she was killed by the Kurdish leadership, who saw her popularity and Assyrian nationalism as a threat to their own influence.

Once through the town of Chamchamal, our driver accelerated when we were in full view of Iraqi lookout posts on the mountain peaks far to our left, and slowed down as the road dipped into a valley and we became hidden from view. As we approached the Peshmerga camp, three Kurdish soldiers emerged from the undergrowth carrying bunches of the grapes that grew wild in the area. They were walking to Chamchamal after 15 days on duty, but agreed to come with us to show us the way to the rest of their group. We arrived at the 'post', a bombed, burnt-out mosque on the hillside. The young Peshmerga, armed with rocket launchers, Kalashnikovs and grenades, greeted us warmly. They said they would be happy to take us up the valley to the hilltop so we could view the Iraqi troops on the plain below through binoculars.

We set off in single file across rocky terrain covered in grass dried yellow by the August heat, the beautiful large lilac flower heads of echinops mingling with the wild grapevines. We regrouped in a bombed-out village while the soldiers explained that from this point on we should hug the mountainside so as not to be seen by the Iraqi troops and to give us some protection from incoming rockets. The sun was beginning to set, and the shadows were lengthening – it was nearly 7 pm by the time we reached a patch of open ground in full view of the Iraqi checkpoint. Suddenly, the Peshmerga raced off at speed, signalling for us to follow. We crouched low and ran for cover across open ground. The Kurds seemed intent on taking us as close as possible to the Iraqis, but Julian said he didn't want to go any nearer, thinking that they might fire some rockets at us. The earth and vegetation under our feet and the hillside around us had all been burnt black by a rocket attack only the week before.

I found the whole experience of walking across the hillsides of northern Iraq with a group of exceedingly handsome Kurdish guerrillas armed to the teeth with rocket launchers quite an exhilarating adventure. However, Julian, an experienced journalist and a veteran of many years with the Mujahideen, had in his time experienced some very hair-raising situations. He certainly did not view the situation in quite the same romantic way as I! With a wife and child back in Thailand, he had no intention of taking any unnecessary risks, so we retraced our steps down the hillside. Nazarine strode ahead with her walking stick, and gathered grapes that she handed to us all to eat. Back at the burnt-out mosque, the Peshmerga amused themselves by shooting at snakes in a well.

By now the sun had dipped below the peaks and it was time for us to return to Chamchamal. As darkness would soon be upon us, the driver took the precaution of removing the bulbs from the rear brake lights so they would not glow red in the dark should he need at any point to put his foot on the brake. With only the light of the moon illuminating the dirt road, and Nazarine leaning out of the passenger window giving instructions to the driver, we reached Chamchamal safely, undetected by the Iraqi forces.

The next morning, Julian at last received an invitation to interview Jalal Talabani, joint chairman with Masoud Barzani of the IKF, and departed early for the PUK office. Nazarine invited me to spend the day at her home. The floor of her courtyard was covered with tomatoes drying in the sun. The fruit and vegetable canning factories outside Sulaimaniya had once played an important part in the local economy, but Saddam Hussein, understanding their significance to the region, had had them destroyed. However, the Kurds, ever resourceful, had not allowed the closure of their factories to defeat them. With their typical humour, they laughed off this cruel act and simply turned to bottling and preserving fruit and vegetables in their own homes.

Over a simple lunch Nazarine talked about the aspirations of Kurdish women in the newly-liberated Kurdistan.

'In the future we want Kurdish women to be like any other women, to take their part in the building of Kurdistan, to go out into the world and to take their share in political appointments. We hope that we are not less than any other women in the world. Kurdish women are intelligent. They strive to go to university and get good degrees. They achieve doctoral degrees, so why should they not share in the building of Kurdistan? We Kurdish women can do anything in the world, just like other women. In our society you will see men and women working together even in the villages. We have a traditional dance called *rashbolaq*. It means literally "men and women dancing together".'

That evening, she suggested I interview Piri Khan, recently elected Minister for Health and Social Welfare in the new Kurdistan Regional Government. At her beautiful home, with views overlooking Sulaimaniya, Piri graciously offered us tea and began her story.

One night two years earlier, her husband had been arrested by Iraqi security forces at a checkpoint on the road to Kirkuk. Despite being pregnant with their first child, she went from house to house warning her husband's friends of his arrest. She knew that he would reveal their names under torture. Her worst moment was realising that not one member of her large extended family could hide her from the authorities for fear of attracting attention to themselves. Piri only received one telephone call from her husband, a ploy to entice her to the detention centre where she knew she would be threatened with rape to force him to reveal information. She did not go, and since that moment had neither seen nor heard from him. The shock of the ordeal caused her to miscarry her baby. It seemed that neither wealth nor status had protected Piri and her husband from Saddam's secret police.

The following day, while visiting the PUK's television station, Julian and I met Lydia, an attractive Russian journalist and television presenter in her late forties. She had plenty of stories to tell, and we promised to return later that day to interview her. In the meantime, she wanted to show us the detention centre where she had been held prisoner and interrogated by the Mukhabarat for having been the wife of a Kurdish guerrilla. Beneath the watchtowers, tangled electricity cables and barbed wire hung down from walls pockmarked by artillery and mortar fire. Outside, on a patch of waste ground now being used as a parking lot for UN vehicles, Lydia told us how Kurdish women had been herded into containers and gang-raped by Iraqi soldiers, their underwear nailed to the walls of the containers or tied to the aerials of lorries as trophies to flutter in the breeze as the vehicles were driven through the streets of Sulaimaniya.

In darkness, we cautiously felt our way down uneven steps littered with debris to the prison cells, with only the pale beam of Julian's torch to guide us. Set into the walls were small, open-fronted cubicles, their peeling cream-coloured plaster smeared and splattered with dark-brown streaks of dried blood. Cold, clammy stale air enveloped us.

Outside each cubicle was an electricity junction box, and tangles of electrical wires and cables hung down, ripped out by the Peshmerga when they liberated the prison. Just below the ceiling, thick pipes like those in the boiler room of the *Titanic* ran through each of the cubicles via a hole at the top of the connecting walls. From this dangled large butcher's meat hooks. 'These are the torture chambers,' said Lydia. 'Prisoners were hung up by their arms and given electric shocks from these wires.'

Descending another flight of stairs, we reached the bowels of the detention centre. As our eyes adjusted to the gloom, we could see huge metal cages like those used in zoos for keeping lions and tigers. The air was dank, and I shivered.

Inside each of the cages, our guide explained, 200 prisoners had been crowded together in darkness without sanitation and packed so tightly they could hardly lie or sit down. A tiny window about 20 feet up in the wall provided the only ventilation and a glimmer of light. In the heat of summer there would have been no air conditioning, and in winter no heating.

'Most of the prisoners were subjected to electric shocks, beatings and sexual assault,' Lydia told us. 'They were given only a small can of water each day.'

I couldn't even imagine the terrible fear the prisoners must have felt, as they waited to be taken upstairs to be tortured, beaten, raped or shot. During their incarceration, they tied small pieces of cloth around the bars of their cells, testimony to their desperate prayers for deliverance from an unutterable hell. I was overwhelmed by such a feeling of horror and fear that I couldn't stay in that dreadful place a moment longer. How Lydia could even take one step inside that prison after all she had experienced said much about her courage. We retraced our way up the stairs and emerged finally into the courtyard to bright sunshine and the sound of children's laughter. Fair-haired Kurdish children were playing amongst the rubble.

'They're refugees from Kirkuk,' said our Peshmerga guide. 'The town is controlled by Saddam Hussein, so they have come here to Sulaimaniya to find safety.'

The Peshmerga had rehoused the Kurdish families in the burnt-out remains of the detention centre, and the women were cooking the midday meal in torture chambers where the walls were smeared with dried blood. Later that evening, we interviewed Lydia.

'While I was studying English at Moscow University I met a Kurdish student studying journalism. We fell in love. In 1968, when I was in my fifth year of study, my Kurdish husband died leaving me with a child aged eighteen months. Despite being widowed I was determined to finish my final year and receive a degree. My husband's family said that, as my late husband had four brothers, I was free to choose one to marry – the traditional eastern approach to a young widow. One of the brothers spoke English and I had been corresponding with him for a long time, so he came to Moscow, married me and together we went back to Sulaimaniya. For ten years we enjoyed a very happy marriage, but my husband joined the Peshmerga to fight against Saddam Hussein and was killed in January 1978, leaving me once again a young widow, and a single parent with a twelve-year-old son.

On 4 April 1988, we were woken at dawn by the sound of helicopters, and announcements through loudspeakers that the day was to be a curfew in Sulaimaniya. The sun was rising and the day had all the promise of being glorious, but not for us. We were terrorised by fear because every second house in Sulaimaniya had something or somebody to hide and the question was whether there would be time for the necessary arrangements to be made. Fortunately we had only one army deserter to hide, and all the books and papers that could discredit us had been disposed of or hidden ages ago. We were ready to meet our uninvited guests, but how anxious, how worried, how troubled we were listening to every sound, every shot, every explosion, fervently wishing for this nightmare to be finished. But the minutes dragged. The clock hands seemed to have stopped, and so did our troubled and suffering hearts. We were waiting for them to come and search our house and take our loved ones away, fully aware that once they were taken we would never see them again. Only a miracle could save us, but we were sadly short of miracles in those days, living as we were in our cruel, hard and unmerciful world. A man can be so strong at times, otherwise how could he live that day and so many other similar and dreadful days and still stay sane? However, our nightmare existence is finished for the present, but it still haunts us in our never-ending dreams and in our still-insecure present daily life.

Lydia spent 18 days on the Iranian border, sitting and sleeping in a Datsun car with five other passengers and her 22-year-old son, a student at the University of Sulaimaniya. Had he been captured by government troops, he would have been considered a deserter from the Iraqi army. For his safety Lydia decided he should cross over the border into Iran with the rest of the group who were being guided by the Peshmerga through the mountains to safety. As they came closer to the border, the small group became more relaxed, although they had no idea where they were going, but Lydia was afraid to enter Iran because of Islamic fundamentalists and decided to remain in Iraq.

'The weather was terrible that morning at the border. It was like night, so dark you would never have thought it was morning. There were thunderstorms and lightning.' At the border she had to say goodbye to her son. 'I couldn't cry, and he couldn't cry, but there were tears in our eyes.' She said to him as they parted company, 'Believe me, we shall emerge, and you *will* see my smiling face again.'

I feel quite sure that Lydia did see her son again, because it was now safe for him to return, but she never told me and during the interview I forgot to ask.

As we were leaving her office, Lydia remarked, 'I should like to have a Bible, but there is not one to be found here in Sulaimaniya'.

That night in my hotel room I couldn't sleep. When I checked that I had securely bolted the bedroom door, I saw that at some point it had been forced open and crudely repaired. The brown carpet was heavily stained. I was frightened to turn off the light or close my eyes because, each time I did, bad images swirled through my head. I saw the sculpture of the evil eye, women's underwear fluttering from car aerials, the dried blood on the walls, the meat hooks. I thought of Piri's husband being tortured. My eyes kept being drawn to the forced lock and the stains on the carpet. Had someone been killed in my room? Such a feeling of evil was something I have never experienced before or since. I was overwhelmed by fear.

Just before I had left London, a friend had handed me a pocket-size travel Bible. I searched through my backpack until I found it, and pulled it out. I opened it at Psalm 23: 'Even though I walk through the valley of the shadow of death, I will fear no evil; your rod and your staff, they comfort me'. At last I fell asleep.

Julian was staying on in Iraq to complete some interviews, but I felt I had achieved all I could. For two weeks I had been out of communication with my family and, as my father wasn't well, I was keen to get home as soon as possible. As I prepared to leave, I put the Bible in an envelope and wrote Lydia's name on the outside. She was not in her office when I called by, so I simply left it on her desk.

The journey through Iraqi Kurdistan had been a fascinating insight into the extraordinary courage of the Kurds, a remarkable people who, despite all the terrible things that have happened to them, still manage to maintain a strong and positive outlook. Their territory has so much potential, if they could only be given the chance to develop it. But the journey highlighted, too, the difficulties of undertaking any craft project while Kurdistan remained virtually separated from the rest of Iraq. During my time there, I saw no carpet-weaving and, even if a training project had been set up, there would have been difficulties in exporting across the Turkish border, where the Turkish government was waging war against the PKK.

However, the land is beautiful, with snow-capped mountain ranges, plenty of natural resources and a plethora of archaeological sites, an attractive place for tourism in the future. The Kurds are warm, welcoming and very hospitable, and their great sense of humour in the face of adversity is something I shall never forget.

PART V
FORMER YUGOSLAVIA

CHAPTER 16

Bosnia-Herzegovina
October 1993–December 1994

'Loverly jubberly, 'Arry', came Peter's voice over the radio, as I carefully manoeuvred the 7.5-tonne truck, callsign Guinevere, down the ramp of the roll-on roll-off freight ferry at Dunkirk. I was driving one of four trucks transporting humanitarian aid to Bosnia-Herzegovina. This was my first convoy with the charity Bosnia Family Aid. Ahead of us lay a 1,500-mile journey across Europe to the Balkans, which would take four days and three nights with overnight stops, sleeping in our vehicles in autobahn lay-bys and service stations.

'Merlin to Guinevere, Arthur and Lancelot,' came Peter's voice again, 'we're taking the road to Lille. So watch out for overhead road signs marked E42 and, whatever you do, remember to drive on the right!'

Our leader, Peter Hunt, had been organising and taking aid convoys to Bosnia for over a year. An out-of-work builder, painter and decorator, he sported a solid gold ring in one ear, as 18th-century sailors did to pay for their funerals if they were drowned and washed ashore. I'd been introduced to Peter through Suzanne, who I had met on an Alpha evangelistic course at Holy Trinity Brompton church (HTB) in September 1993. She had recently travelled with Peter on a convoy to Split in Croatia, distributing aid to refugee camps. Now, she told me, she was about to embark on another convoy with a group of friends from HTB to deliver aid, this time to Medjugorje, a holy shrine and centre of Catholic pilgrimage in Bosnia.

I had just completed a year-long postgraduate diploma course in agricultural extension and rural development at the University of Reading. The university had offered me a place on the course, accepting my fieldwork in Afghanistan as my first degree. Back in a classroom environment after more than 20 years, I felt like a dry sponge suddenly dropped into water. I couldn't soak up the information quickly enough. Most of all, I enjoyed studying with men and women from places as diverse as Papua New Guinea, Ethiopia, Ghana, southern Sudan, Indonesia and the Caribbean. Many of the women came from patriarchal societies and had had to overcome enormous obstacles – gender prejudice, parental disapproval, war, poverty, and religious constraints – to get to Reading to study. From both men and women I heard about the prevalence of female genital mutilation, wife-beating and gender inequality. Their courage and personal stories were an inspiration. It was a wonderful, happy year and I loved every day of my time at Reading.

Having achieved a qualification, I hoped to be employed by an NGO working on rural women's programmes but, despite writing countless letters, I was only offered one interview, to work in a women's refuge in Zagreb. Most NGOs didn't bother to reply. My expectations had been too high. Graduates with better qualifications and more experience than me were applying for the same jobs. Aid agencies wanted people with skills in health, sanitation, engineering and logistics, not a degree in income generation. Elizabeth Winter's brother, Philip, who lived just outside Nairobi, told me there was a vacancy with Save the Children working with refugees from southern Sudan in Lokichokio near the Kenya–Sudan border, and suggested I apply, but I was concerned about my father's health and wanted to find something closer to home.

British radio and television channels were full of the horrors of ethnic cleansing taking place in the former Yugoslavia, yet governments seemed powerless to bring the war to an end. Yugoslavia, which means 'Land of the Southern Slavs', was formed at the end of the First World War when Croatia, Slovenia and Bosnia – territories that had been part of the Austro-Hungarian empire – united with the Kingdom of Serbia. During the Second World War Croatia broke away and became allied to Nazi Germany, but it was reunited at the end of the war by the communist partisan leader Josip Broz Tito, who in 1945 liberated the country and created a socialist government.

The Slavs had arrived in the Balkans (then part of the Roman Empire) in the sixth and seventh centuries from Poland and Russia. They came as marauders following the barbarian invasion of the Roman Empire in the second to fifth centuries by Huns, Goths and Visigoths. As they settled in the area and came into contact with existing Christian communities they gradually began to convert to Christianity, but to two very different branches – the Serbs to the Eastern Orthodox Church under the Byzantine Emperors, and the Croats (who were converted by priests from Rome) to Roman Catholicism. After the Great Schism in 1054 between the Byzantine east and Papal Rome over disputes about doctrine, especially the authority of the Pope, Serbia remained under Constantinople and Croatia under Rome.

Caught between the Serbs and the Croats was a third group – the Slavic Muslims, who belonged neither to Serbia nor to Croatia but had their own homeland called Bosnia-Herzegovina. For centuries the three groups had lived side by side in towns and villages, and intermarriage was not uncommon, but each group had evolved from very different traditions.

With Tito's death in 1980, European communism began to collapse. After the fall of the Berlin Wall in 1989, the reunification of Germany in 1990 and the collapse of the Soviet Union in 1991, countries previously held together by communism began to assert their independence. Slovenia was the first to declare formal independence, on 25 June 1991, closely followed by Croatia and Bosnia. Memories of the atrocities perpetrated during the Second World War had not been forgotten and, as Yugoslavia's political stability disintegrated, so began the rapid descent into war as the two great Balkan powers, Croatia and Serbia, emerged to settle old historical scores and to reassert ancient frontiers with modern weaponry.

I was at a loose end and restless. I wanted to get involved in doing something practical to help the people of Bosnia. When Suzanne suggested I join her group on the next convoy travelling to Bosnia-Herzegovina, I leapt at the opportunity.

Early in 1993, at the height of the Bosnia crisis, Peter Hunt had been the lorry driver on a fact-finding mission to Bosnia-Herzegovina with the Duchess of York and Theo Ellert, who were in the process of founding the non-profit organisation Children in Crisis. Peter had the quick wit and humour typical of a south Londoner, and over a cup of tea at his kitchen table in South Croydon he kept me entertained with anecdotes of his travels with the Duchess and her entourage in Split, where they were delivering aid. Back in Croydon, together with chartered accountant Michael Heathcote and a nun called Sister Valerie O'Donnell, he set up the charity Bosnia Family Aid Appeal.

So how could I help?

'We need to raise about £800 each month to hire a three-and-a-half-tonne lorry to transport aid to Bosnia,' he told me. 'Then there's the cost of the diesel. Usually there are three people in each lorry to share the driving. Even when the lorries are filled to seven and a half tonnes, you don't need an HGV licence.'

And how long would the journey take?

'It's three thousand miles there and back, and it takes about four days to reach Medjugorje. Once we reach Bosnia we spend four days delivering aid to homes and refugee camps in and around Medjugorje and Mostar before returning to the UK. So the whole journey takes roughly a fortnight. In Medjugorje we stay in a hotel, otherwise we sleep in the back of our lorries.'

'And what kind of things do you take to Bosnia? What do people really need?'

'Food is the priority, but also clothes and shoes. Many families have been forced out of their homes at gunpoint, or their homes have been set on fire, so they escape with just the clothes they stand up in. Shoes are a particular priority for children.'

He told me that the charity had contacted British supermarkets that were happy to let its people stand outside their main entrances with collecting tins. The system worked rather like a present-day food bank. As customers went in they were handed a leaflet, asking them to buy and donate one item from a list.

'We're doing a collection this weekend, if you want to join us,' Peter told me.

And that is how I found myself with Peter and Brian outside Safeway in Fulham Broadway one wet October weekend, rattling a collecting tin and handing out leaflets. Slight in build and quietly spoken, Brian, like Peter, was a south Londoner, with an incredibly quick wit and a wide range of knowledge about all manner of things. Despite the rain, there was never a dull moment as the boys kept me laughing with their inexhaustible supply of jokes. Although he was a jack of all trades, Brian had chosen to be on the dole because he needed the freedom and time to collect and make the monthly journeys to Bosnia from Coulsdon, where he lived.

By the end of the weekend, we had collected over £1,000 in cash and had filled 40 boxes. The system worked well. As soon as each trolley was full, I would wheel it across the car park to the Bosnia Family Aid lorry, a 3.5-tonne Mercedes donated by the non-profit organisation Feed the Children. The supermarket gave the charity empty cardboard banana and apple boxes free of charge, and Brian would immediately make up 'family boxes', containing flour, sugar, cooking oil, tinned food, rice, pasta, toothbrushes, toothpaste, shampoo and nappies.

The boxes were large, sturdy and of identical size, so they were easy to arrange into a level platform on the floor of the lorry. With inflatable mattresses laid over the top they provided a comfortable base on which to sleep. Following an article in the *Fulham Chronicle*, word spread quickly that I was collecting clothes for Bosnia, and the response was overwhelming. People knocked daily on my door with offerings. Within days the ground floor of Finlay Street resembled a charity shop, filled with black bin liners stuffed full of second-hand winter clothing. The manager of a children's clothes shop offered outgrown shoes left behind when children came to be fitted with new ones. She must have spread the word amongst the yummy mummies of Fulham, because soon I was collecting several bags of shoes a week, most of them hardly worn.

Using money raised from our supermarket collections, we bought food in bulk at wholesale prices. Tate and Lyle delivered a pallet of sugar, Rank Hovis a pallet of strong flour. Another company donated a pallet of cooking oil. From the Surrey and Guildford Hospital, which had been so generous in supplying the hospitals of Kabul, came boxes of medicines and equipment for the hospitals in Mostar and Jablanica. The charity Jacob's Well, run by Dr Beryl Beynon, the GP from Beverley in Yorkshire, delivered several boxes of bone saws, and both K Shoes of Kendal in Cumbria and Clarks of Street in

Somerset donated shoes. Envelopes began to drop through my letterbox from complete strangers, enclosing handwritten notes. 'I have heard about your work and would like to give this donation to help the people of Bosnia.' Or, with a crumpled £5 note, 'I am sorry I cannot give more, but I am a pensioner'.

By late October 1993 we were ready to leave for Bosnia. The day before we left I drove down the M4 to Reading with Suzanne and three of the group, Nick, Gavin and Christina, to hire three 3.5-tonne lorries from Adrian Truck Hire. There was a certain amount of paperwork to complete, including a disclaimer stating that we would not be taking the lorries anywhere near a war zone, which would invalidate the insurance. No doubt the company knew full well where their vehicles were going, but kindly turned a blind eye as we signed on the dotted line.

I was allocated an Iveco. It was my first experience of driving such a large vehicle, but its power steering made it easy to manoeuvre. As I drove cautiously through the narrow streets of Reading to pick up two tonnes of breakfast cereal from Feed the Children in Caversham Road, my main concern was that I might forget to observe the height restrictions of the Victorian railway bridges! Then I drove through the outskirts of London to Coulsdon. Peter had more items to load, so I left the lorry with him and caught the train home.

Just after dawn, Gavin arrived at Finlay Street. Into the back of his lorry went the numerous black bin liners of clothes and shoes, boxes of food for our journey and ten boxes of tangerines. Then we drove down to Coulsdon, where the rest of the group were busy pasting the Bosnia Family Aid logo onto the side of a hired lorry. With them were a Chinese girl called Margaret, and Ian Cooke, both from HTB. There would be 12 of us in all including Jamie, another south London friend of Peter and Brian. By the afternoon, CB radios had been fitted and all four lorries weighed at the weighbridge to make sure we did not exceed 7.5 tonnes. Each lorry was allocated a callsign. Peter and Brian's was Merlin, mine was Guinevere and the other two Arthur and Lancelot.

As we motored through the South Downs we noticed that the Iveco, now being driven by Margaret, seemed slower than the others in the convoy. It was losing power on the uphill gradients. Two and a half hours later, after a quick chAfghanaidl crossing by freight ferry, we disembarked in Calais. Leaving the harbour on the road for Lille, our lorry continued to be very slow, making only 25 mph on the gradients. We'd never make the mountain roads through Austria and Yugoslavia at that rate. Realising that the whole convoy would be held up, Peter made the decision to stop overnight in Lille so that we could arrange for mechanics to check the engine in the morning.

In cold, thick swirling fog, French mechanics delved into the engine, eventually pulling out two bent rods from the cam-shaft.

'Someone didn't change gear properly,' Peter remarked accusingly. Looking round the group, his eye finally alighted on Margaret. 'I think, Margaret, you might have changed from fifth gear into second instead of fourth?'

'Oh yes, I tink so,' said Margaret in her lilting Chinese accent, which made us all crack up with laughter. She would become one of the most popular characters on the convoy, liked by all and teased mercilessly by Peter, Brian and Jamie, the butt of their south London humour.

It was decided that the three lorries would proceed while Gavin, Christina and Ian stayed in Lille to wait for a mechanic from Adrian Truck Hire to bring a new Iveco from England. We agreed to rendezvous in Rijeka in Croatia a few days later.

From Lille we drove south-east, through mile after mile of flat, featureless fields of ploughed clay, the skyline broken by occasional avenues of poplar trees and red-brick villages. Recently harvested mangel-wurzels were piled high at the side of the road beside neatly stacked unexploded shells from the First World War. Being a tractor driver in this part of the world must be a risky occupation! Somewhere out in those cold grey fields lay the remains of my great-uncle Mervyn Sandys, my grandfather's identical twin. An officer in the York and Lancaster Regiment, he was killed aged 28, five days after arriving at the front line near Lille in October 1914. His body was never found. My father, born eight months later, was given his name.

Crossing into Germany at Aachen, we continued south to Würzburg, east of Frankfurt, before finally stopping shortly after midnight in a siding off the autobahn near Nuremburg. It was bitterly cold, and we were all very tired. Keeping our concentration while driving in the dark against the relentless glare of headlights, sometimes in blizzards, had stretched all our nerves. In addition, we had to cope with German and Italian drivers who flashed past us at terrifying speeds. They thought nothing of suddenly pulling in without indicating, or overtaking on the wrong side. When we applied the brakes, the fully loaded lorries took longer to slow down than we were used to. I often found myself narrowly missing the bumper of a car that had suddenly pulled in front of me.

Guinevere's cab had a bed just behind the driver's seat, with curtains that could be drawn for privacy. In this cosy space I settled down for the night, totally exhausted, and slept soundly, warm in my down sleeping bag that had accompanied me on so many journeys in India, Pakistan and Iraq.

The other members of the group did not fare so well. They had packed their lorries with no thought as to how they were going to rest at night. They crawled and burrowed in amongst the black bin liners filled with clothes, and as a consequence none of them had a good night's sleep. Furthermore, the boys were wearing only thin denim jeans and in the thick morning frost all were suffering from the cold. Peter and Brian's lorry, Merlin, contained a two-ring

Calor gas stove, mugs, cooking pots, a frying pan and plates. We carried our own water in two large white plastic jerrycans. It didn't take long for the kettle to boil, and we stood around warming our hands on mugs of scalding tea. I filled my thermos with boiling water so I could drink tea on the journey, but the flask had become so cold during the night in the cab that it cracked with a bang and I discarded it in a litter bin.

It was late in the afternoon by the time we arrived at the Austrian border, only to find that, for some inexplicable reason, it was closed to lorries for three days. While Suzanne, who spoke fluent German, went to the police post to argue that we were a humanitarian aid group carrying aid to Bosnia, I took the opportunity to stretch my legs. A line of assorted vehicles was backed up along the autobahn for a considerable distance. I stopped to talk with drivers in British-registered vehicles. Nearly all were volunteers. Some were young and unemployed, with dyed hair, tattoos and piercings; others were retired couples. They had travelled from all corners of the UK in vehicles crammed with food and clothes donated by church groups, the Women's Institute and Rotary groups. Suzanne's linguistic skills were successful, and we were given permission to proceed. Having cleared customs, we drove in the dark through the Alps under starlit skies with the moonlight shining on snowy peaks and reflecting off drifts.

We spent that night in the car park of an autobahn restaurant at Villach, close to Klagenfurt. In the months ahead, when I drove with Peter and Brian on other convoys, this was without doubt one of our favourite stopping places. Not only did the restaurant serve delicious food and hot chocolate, but for a few deutschmarks it was possible to have a hot shower and the use of a hairdryer, always much appreciated by the girls.

The Slovenian border lay deep within a massive tunnel cut through the Karawanken mountain range. A plaque at the entrance was dedicated to the thousands of concentration-camp victims who died working on the construction of the tunnel during the Third Reich. An extraordinary feat of engineering, the narrow *Karawankentunnel* burrowed for five miles through the Alps and seemed to go on forever. In fact, it seemed to take us only about five minutes to drive through it from entrance to exit; however, I found it a scary experience as oncoming tankers and other lorries passed too close for comfort. When we emerged into daylight and resumed radio contact, we were in Slovenia proper.

On first impression, Slovenia seemed affluent and unscathed by the fighting that was tearing apart the rest of Yugoslavia. Shiny Mercedes-Benzes and BMWs, some towing smart luxury yachts, whizzed past us at speed. The countryside was dotted with neat whitewashed farmhouses with red-tiled roofs and in the fields hung hay, drying in the sunshine from high wooden frames called *kozolci*.

'We'll stop for lunch at the fish restaurant just before we cross the border to Croatia at Rupa,' Peter announced. This simple family-run roadside tavern was a popular stopping venue for convoys, as it served excellent fish and chips. Over the coming months we would visit it many times.

At the attractive Adriatic port of Rijeka in Croatia, we were reunited with the others who had remained behind in Lille awaiting a replacement lorry. They must have driven day and night to catch us up. We found them chatting to a group of evangelicals from South Wales who, like us, were on their way to Bosnia to deliver aid. Ian suggested a group session of prayer and a singalong to Nick's guitar before entering the war zone, but it was all a bit much for me. My faith was something personal and private. As I needed some quiet time alone, I retired to my bunk bed in Guinevere and curled up in my sleeping bag.

Our lorries were parked on the quayside, surrounded by magnificent buildings with ornate wrought-iron verandas and doors and windows adorned with curvilinear scrolls and pediments. Rijeka's architecture reflected its history. It had once been part of the Austro-Hungarian Empire and its beauty was in stark contrast to the regimented rows of pale-yellow Soviet-style high-rise flats that we had seen dominating Ljubljana's skyline earlier in the day.

Peter wanted to make an early start and reach a good overnight stop on the beach at Omiš, south of Split. He had arranged a rendezvous at the Feed the Children depot in Split to drop off the breakfast cereal, and we still had a long way to go if we wanted to reach Medjugorje the following day.

We followed the winding coastal road with dramatic views over steep cliffs to the waves of the Adriatic several thousand feet below. On our left, the inhospitable jagged Dinaric Alps rose up. Just a few miles further east, behind the mountains, war was raging. Within half an hour or so it was clear that fierce fighting between Croats and Serbs had taken place over the previous year in the area through which we were now driving. Mile after mile of burnt-out farmhouses dotted the landscape, their lovely terracotta roofs and wrought-iron balconies nothing but piles of rubble. Orchards and woods once carefully tended stood burnt and charred, and whole hillsides were blackened by fire. We steered around shallow, star-shaped craters caused by shells and mortar bombs.

Far out to our right, islands in the blue Adriatic shimmered in the morning light. We turned off the coast road and stopped for a picnic lunch. After the bitter cold of Austria, the sun was positively hot, and Brian, Peter and Jamie stripped off to shorts and tee shirts. Nick dived into the sea. The water was crystal clear, and spherical purple sea urchins clung to the rocks. As I paddled in the water I thought I saw a body, but to my relief it was only a shirt held down by a tyre!

At Šibenik, just north of Split, we came to a pontoon bridge over a river estuary. The original bridge had been destroyed. Peter's voice came over the radio.

'Merlin to Guinevere, Lancelot and Arthur. We are going to drive the lorries across one at a time. As soon as one lorry reaches the far bank, the next lorry moves on to the bridge. Everyone got that?'

'Roger, Merlin. Out.'

This was the first moment on the journey in which I experienced fear. Up to this point it had all been a bit of a jolly, but now we had no way of knowing whether or not the Serbs were still in the mountains overlooking us. If they were, they would have a bird's-eye view of our white vehicles, so Peter didn't want us all on the bridge at the same time in case they chose to open fire. I sat in Guinevere awaiting my turn. The first lorry seemed to take an eternity to cross and I willed it to go faster. We maintained radio silence until we heard Gavin say, 'We've made it!' and we all cheered.

'OK, Guinevere, you're next.' I changed into first gear and moved off down the hill. It took only a couple of minutes to cross the pontoon bridge, but it seemed like a lifetime.

That night we parked amongst pine trees and sand dunes on the beach at Omiš, overlooking the islands of Brac and Hvar. Across the small inlet alongside us, white UN vehicles were lined up in rows. Peter suggested that we walk into town to find a restaurant, but it was the same old story. Once we were seated around the table drinking beer, we were told our deutschmarks were not acceptable. I volunteered to go back to Merlin to start cooking supper and Brian offered to come with me. I was grateful for his company, as the road was very dark as it passed through the pine forest.

Just as the water for the spaghetti came to the boil, Gavin appeared.

'Come on back. The restaurant owners have changed their minds and have agreed to make us all pizzas.'

As we began walking back, a car with headlights on full beam appeared out of the dark. It accelerated and came straight at us, forcing us to scatter left and right. At first we thought it had nothing to do with us, but when the car stopped and then reversed at speed, engine whining and tyres screeching, it dawned on us that the driver didn't like us very much and again we dived out of the way. The car stopped. Three Croatian soldiers, all very large and very drunk, tumbled out and stood blocking our way. We had already noticed on our journey through Croatia how exceptionally tall the Croatian people are as a race. The men towered over Brian, shouting and threatening him and accusing us of being members of UNPROFOR, the United Nations peacekeeping force. Brian stood his ground, insisting that we were humanitarian aid workers from England, not UN personnel.

''Arry, you'd better leg it to the restaurant and bring reinforcements,' he said quietly.

When I burst into the restaurant, Jamie and Peter jumped up and rushed out, closely followed by the Holy Trinity boys. Half an hour later, they all returned to the restaurant safely.

It seemed to have been a case of mistaken identity, but none of us could understand why UNPROFOR personnel should be so disliked. While no one was hurt in the altercation with the Croatian soldiers that night, things could have turned out very differently had the soldiers been armed.

Horrific atrocities were taking place at this time in central Bosnia – mass rape, torture, massacres, forced removal of people from their homes and cases of neighbour killing neighbour. Notorious internment camps had been established where men and boys over 15 were taken for interrogation, and often never seen again. Thousands disappeared without trace. There were reports of people being shot and thrown down mineshafts, and bodies being bulldozed into mass graves. The incident that night was a salutary reminder that we were now in a war zone, and that men deeply affected by horrors experienced in the war were mentally unstable, frequently drunk and often on drugs.

The road inland to Medjugorje led across an extraordinary plateau of limestone known as karst. Over millennia, the chemical reaction of rainwater falling on the Dinaric limestone range had eroded the rock, which was deeply etched by fissures and grooves. In winter the landscape was grey and bleak without a hint of vegetation, yet humans had attempted to farm on the karst by clearing stones by hand and using them to construct drystone walls. The effect was an extraordinary honeycomb of tiny, round fields. They reminded me of the small stone enclosures built by crofters on the Perthshire moors to corral their sheep.

We crossed the Croatia–Bosnia-Herzegovina border at Vrgorac without a hitch. Now, driving further east, we began to see evidence of the destruction of ethnic cleansing that had taken place in 1992–3 when Croat forces forced Serbs and Muslims out of their homes – mile upon mile of ruined farmhouses with mangled wrought-iron verandas and smashed terracotta roofs.

It was late in the afternoon by the time we drove down the main street of Medjugorje and parked outside a small family-run hotel. Peter knew the family well, having stayed many times on previous convoys, and we were given a warm welcome. In the past, the family had helped him distribute aid to needy families and refugees 'cleansed' from areas under Serbian control, who were now sheltering in schools, hotels and railway carriages in the small towns around Medjugorje.

Roman Catholics consider Medjugorje the third most important pilgrimage site after Lourdes and Assisi. It was said that, since June 1981, when the Virgin Mary first appeared to six local children (known as the Visionaries), she had been giving them messages on an almost daily basis, and on occasions actually appearing. Having been brought up an Anglican, this was my first visit to a Catholic shrine. Peter and Brian enlightened me.

'People claim to have seen the sun spinning in the sky or seeing shapes of hearts and crosses in the clouds,' they explained.

Before the sun set, we were all keen to visit the Catholic church of St James at the top of the high street, to say a prayer and to stretch our legs by climbing up Apparition Hill to visit the 14 Stations of the Cross. As we climbed the steep, rocky path we all gazed earnestly at the sky hoping to see an apparition or the sun spinning, but everything seemed very normal.

The war, it appeared, had not deterred pilgrims, who continued to arrive in Medjugorje from all over the world. Making our way back down the rocky track, we met a group of elderly Americans on their way up to the giant cross at the summit. We had seen them earlier alighting from coaches outside St James's church, wearing sun hats, checked shirts and white shoes, before heading off as a group towards the numerous souvenir shops selling rosaries and white statuettes of the Virgin. They seemed totally unperturbed by the fact that war was raging in the next valley.

Medjugorje, like Peshawar, had something of the Wild West atmosphere of a frontier town. Only eight miles to the south, the Muslims in the city of Mostar were under heavy bombardment from Croats and Serbs. At the church of St James, Croat soldiers in camouflage fatigues deposited their weapons at the door before entering to attend Mass. In the high street they drove by in stolen Italian and German cars with tinted-glass windows and false number plates, leaning out to give us a Churchillian two-finger salute as they swept past. The soldiers would loiter in bars, restaurants and cafes, getting drunk on *šljivovica* before jumping into vehicles and roaring off to the front line to fire rockets down on the Muslims of East Mostar.

Peter had formed an extensive network of friends and contacts in the area, and they were able to advise where the aid was most needed. The Holy Trinity group were keen to deliver toys and clothes to children living in hostels run by the Franciscans. Karolina, the hotel owners' daughter, had identified some needy families out in the countryside. We decided to go there first, offload some of the family boxes and return via the hostels. Karolina's father would come with us as guide.

Rural Bosnia-Herzegovina was like stepping back in time a hundred years. We wound our way up rutted mountain tracks to remote farms. The land was bleak and desolate, and the people in this agricultural community were very poor. In cold, sleeting rain we offloaded the apple and banana boxes and handed them out, but the people had their pride, and understandably didn't want to be on the receiving end of charity without reciprocating in some way. From their homes they produced bottles of homemade wine and šljivovica, a fiery brandy made from a variety of fermented fruits – plums, grapes, apples, quince and wild berries. We came away with several white plastic jerrycans filled with the stuff and bottles of wine that was really undrinkable, almost vinegar. The šljivovica was so powerful that, in Brian's words, it was 'only good for cleaning the toilet'. Nevertheless, I noticed that he quite enjoyed it and never refused a glass when offered.

At the Franciscan-run hostels we spent a happy afternoon with the children. Nick strummed his guitar and taught the children songs in English. We made Christmas decorations, paper chains from coloured paper, and distributed toys and crayons while the mothers received warm clothing, shoes and family boxes.

Peter had heard about 250 Croatian refugees, mostly women and children, living in 15 carriages in a railway siding in the town of Čapljina, and wanted to deliver food parcels and clothing to them. Just a few months before, Čapljina had been the scene of horrific ethnic cleansing. The town had been badly shelled and the large modern Soviet-style concrete bridge over the Neretva river had been completely broken in half. One end rose up to the sky, with twisted metal rods hanging from it; the other end lay partly submerged under the water.

The refugees were penned in behind a high wire security fence. Dark-green railway carriages were lined up on the tracks with rows of wet washing strung between them. As soon as we turned in at the main gates of the railway siding, we were surrounded by women and children. Human nature being as it is, the women all wanted to be first to get hold of whatever we had to offer. The fair distribution of aid amongst large numbers of refugees always presented us with a problem – the strongest members of the group would shout, barge, elbow, push and grab. Try as we might to get them to form an orderly queue, this was impossible. It was like the first day of a department store sale. As soon as we opened up the lorries and attempted to hand out a box of food or a bin liner of clothes, the women fought over the bags, tearing them so that the clothes fell out into the mud. All of us were concerned that the weakest and neediest at the back of the crowd would not get a look-in, so we had no alternative but to resort to throwing the bags over the heads of those in front. It was degrading and humiliating for all concerned to see human beings behave in such a way. We needed a better strategy. In the months ahead, we would refine our methods of offloading, which proved to be fairer, but these were early days and we learnt by our mistakes.

Over the next 15 months, I drove on a further eight convoys. Money and food collected each month from supermarkets all over London and the suburbs, and generous donations of money and humanitarian aid from the British public, meant that we were able to fund and fill three to five vehicles and drive to Bosnia every four to six weeks. Any group could join the convoy providing they could fund their own vehicle. This meant we had a cocktail of people from many walks of life and backgrounds: Polish aristocrats driving on behalf of the Knights of Malta with the Maltese cross emblazoned on their lorry, an Irish tinker and reformed alcoholic, an Amway salesman, police dog handlers, plain-clothes police, a BBC camera crew and evangelical Christians.

Peter proved to be a natural leader. Teamwork was essential to the smooth running of the convoy, and prior to every departure he briefed us all on the importance of working together as a cohesive unit. He was responsible for the safety of the convoy, and made all the decisions on starting and stopping, when to refuel and when to stop for meals. But with so many diverse backgrounds and personalities, each with their own agenda of where they wanted their aid delivered and to whom, tensions could arise. Add to this the long hours driving a large vehicle on unfamiliar roads through blizzards, followed by cold, uncomfortable nights in the back of lorries curled up like mice amongst plastic bags filled with clothes and toys, and these tensions were understandable. Crossing Germany and Austria in the winter, the weather was always bitterly cold. One night as we slept at Villach, our breath condensed and froze, forming a layer of ice inside Merlin's fibreglass body. In the morning, as the sun rose, the warmth melted the ice and we were showered with large drops of water. Merlin was the only lorry with a cooker, fuelled by a large blue gas cylinder, so everyone gravitated to Merlin for cups of tea, toast and eggs. This annoyed Peter and Brian.

'It's not right, 'Arry. They should all be self-sufficient. Instead they come to us to make them breakfast, then leave us to wash up their bloody tea mugs, plates and greasy pans.'

We would start on the road at around 7.30 am, taking it in turns to drive three-hour shifts, and would only stop when we reached a good place to park. On one journey we stopped as usual at Karlobag harbour on the Adriatic coast, a popular overnight resting place for HGV drivers plying the coast road between Rijeka and Dubrovnik. Except for a brief stop at the fish restaurant, our convoy of four lorries and one ambulance destined for the hospital at Jablanica had been on the road since crossing the Austrian-Slovenian border earlier in the day. Now it was 1 am, and we were all deeply weary and desperate to get some sleep, but our entrance to the harbour car park was blocked by a badly parked juggernaut. There was no way that our convoy could squeeze between it and a mobile cement mixer, and we were faced with motoring further along the coast road to find another stopping place.

I jumped out of the cab to ask the driver if he could move his vehicle just a little to the right to allow us to enter. When I tapped on his window, I was greeted by a grunt. Moving round to the passenger window, I tapped again and succeeded in waking the fat, now angry, Croatian driver. I pointed to our convoy and with much miming explained that we just wanted him to move a little to allow us through. He began to manoeuvre the enormous vehicle but unfortunately he managed to jam it between the harbour wall and the quayside. After much reversing, he finally turned the juggernaut around, allowing enough space for our convoy to enter the harbour. I thanked him for his trouble and gave him two packets of Silk Cut cigarettes and a bottle of champagne that we had been keeping as a birthday present for one of our group. But, annoyed at having been so rudely awakened, he decided to hit the road, and off he sped in a cloud of diesel fumes without a word of thanks!

'Well, 'Arry, you've got about as much front as 'Arrods,' Peter remarked.

We parked that night with the rear of the lorries facing out across the Adriatic to prevent theft. Exhausted, I fell asleep in the back of Merlin, lulled by the sound of waves lapping against the harbour wall. The boys, however, decided to go in search of Karlobag's nightlife in the bars and cafes along the seafront. They returned at about 3 am. Brian had been on a bender. He collapsed on his mattress fully clothed, and I awoke to find his boots in my face. In the morning he seemed none the worse, just a little quieter than normal, his eyes bloodshot.

For many, joining the convoys was their first experience of driving through a war zone. Once, as we were offloading aid at the hospital in Mostar, we came under fire. With no warning, the big guns positioned in the hills above the hospital commenced shelling the east bank of the Neretva. We had no alternative but to abandon our delivery and drive back to the safety of Medjugorje. On another occasion, in the town of Konjic, a Bosnian soldier on the far side of the road swayed drunkenly towards an oncoming car that – like so many – had no number plates. Waving his rifle at the windscreen, he moved around to the driver's window and greeted friends, four young soldiers back from night duty on the front line. The soldier accepted a glass of šljivovica from his friends, swallowed the contents in one gulp, dropped his rifle with a clatter, retrieved it and inadvertently pressed the trigger. Four shots rang out. The bullets narrowly missed us.

Passing through checkpoints often presented problems, especially if the Croats thought we were delivering aid to Muslims. Young men, frequently drunk and belligerent, sought to intimidate us by waving their automatic weapons and demanding that we give them some of our aid. If we remonstrated with them, they would climb aboard anyway and throw things around until they found something they wanted before grudgingly allowing us to continue. It was at moments like this that Peter would remain calm and unflappable. His wit and humour always raised a laugh and helped defuse the tension.

In the spring, our convoy coincided with Easter week. Church bells rang out in the towns and villages on the Adriatic coast, and women and children dressed in traditional Croatian costume carried brightly coloured decorated eggs called *pisanice* in wicker baskets, an old Slavic custom dating back to pagan times. On Easter Sunday children played a traditional game of tapping their opponent's egg to see which would be the first to crack. I'd seen an almost identical game played in Afghanistan and wondered if there was some connection, although I couldn't imagine how, as thousands of miles separate the two countries.

In the valley approaching Mostar, the fruit trees standing untended amongst derelict farms had burst into blossom; even the karst had adopted a mantle of green. For months we had been delivering aid to refugee centres around Medjugorje, but we all felt that our aid would be more welcome and needed further east amongst the Bosniaks (Slavic Muslims) of central Bosnia, who made up 40% of the population. Of the three groups, they were least able to fend for themselves and had suffered appallingly during the process of ethnic cleansing. The Bosniaks traced their ancestry back to a heretical sect called the Bogomils, who distanced themselves from both the Catholic and Orthodox religions. Their beliefs had certain similarities with Islam. They rejected the crucifixion and the sanctity of the Virgin Mary, and considered it idolatrous to bow down before icons. As a result they were persecuted for their beliefs and oppressed by Catholics and Serbs. With the arrival of the Ottoman Empire, they converted and embraced the new religion of Islam and were rewarded by the Turkish rulers with advantages and privileges. During Ottoman rule, the new converts gained economic and social status, education and opportunities to inherit land and property. Converting to Islam gave merchants greater freedom of movement to buy and sell goods, and rapid promotion for soldiers. By the 20th century, many of Bosnia's doctors, musicians, academics and scientists were Muslim.

Since October 1993 humanitarian convoys from the Dalmatian coast into Bosnia had been suspended by UN Secretary-General Boutros Boutros-Ghali after a convoy had been attacked near Novi Travnik, killing a civilian driver and wounding eight UNPROFOR soldiers. With winter then not far off, the US Department of State estimated that 2.7 million people in Bosnia were at risk from fighting, disease, malnutrition and lack of adequate shelter. In central Bosnia, temperatures could drop as low as –25°C. Without adequate aid the most vulnerable – the elderly, sick, wounded, handicapped and small children – would die. Continuing attacks on civilians, the destruction of the aid routes into central Bosnia, and bureaucratic obstacles created by both Serbs and Croats to hamper aid convoys, meant there was a strong possibility that cold and starvation would finish off the Muslims. Bosnia Winter Watch, a newsletter compiled every fortnight by Refugees International to provide information to governments, relief agencies and the press reported that:

> Without firing a single bullet, the Serbs and Croats hope to finish their conquest of Bosnia by tying up humanitarian aid in so much red tape that it never reaches the cold and hungry people who need it.[42]

To overcome these obstacles and to get aid through to where it was desperately needed, UNPROFOR had made great efforts to open up the major all-weather highway connecting Metković on the Dalmatian coast to Sarajevo and Tuzla. The highway was suitable for carrying heavy traffic through central Bosnia and followed the Neretva River through Mostar, but it had been impassable for months since a major bridge in the north of the city had been destroyed. Furthermore, sections of the road that followed the course of the Neretva north to Jablanica and Sarajevo, passing through numerous tunnels cut into the mountains, had collapsed through sustained shelling. In 1993 engineers replaced the bridge in Mostar with a Bailey bridge and a UN pontoon ferry now operated on the Neretva east of Mostar, transporting UN humanitarian aid convoys and military vehicles upriver towards the beleaguered Muslim towns of Jablanica and Konjic. For some time Peter had been talking about getting aid to these towns and, now that the bridge had been rebuilt, this was the route that he proposed to take on our next journey. Bosnia Family Aid had been donated an ambulance by a Dutch charity, and Peter intended delivering it to the hospital at Jablanica.

'The ambulance is really needed as so many of their own have been destroyed in the war. You might like to drive it on our next convoy, 'Arry,' Peter said as we collected money outside a supermarket.

I felt honoured to be asked. As the postal system in the former Yugoslavia had been disrupted by the war, Peter came up with the idea of offering to carry parcels and letters from Bosnian Muslims living in the UK and delivering them personally to their families living between Mostar and Konjic. Finlay Street became the drop-off point, and it wasn't long before Bosnians were arriving on my doorstep with parcels that we would deliver to their families within five days of leaving London.

The wheels of the ambulance rumbled over the wooden planks of the UN-built Bailey bridge spanning the Neretva. East Mostar, where the Bosniaks lived, was a scene of utter devastation. Incessant shelling by Serbs and Croats had destroyed the magnificent Austro-Hungarian buildings, and those that had not been reduced to rubble stood as forlorn shells of their former glory, the sky visible through glassless windows and charred roof timbers.

As we navigated the flyover that took us east out of the city, we looked down on miles of Soviet-style high-rise apartment blocks. Mortar shells had punched great gaping holes in the buildings, splattering the walls with shrapnel and blackening them with smoke. At the height of the shelling, residents had taken refuge in the cellars or left for refugee camps but, judging by the amount of washing hanging from windows to dry, many still appeared to be living there.

Children shouted and waved to us from the roadside. Brian threw sweets and toys out of the window, and I watched in the wing mirror as they scrabbled in the road behind us. Ideally it would have been better to stop and hand them some food – they were quite obviously in desperate need, living as they were in the flats below the flyover – but it was just too dangerous for us to stop. In the circumstances, it was the best we could do.

Like the residential area, the industrial complexes on the outskirts of Mostar had also been destroyed. In a marshalling yard, Roma gypsies were living in squalor in empty shipping containers. Out in the countryside, we could see the effect of the UN aerial humanitarian aid drops during the previous winter; smashed wooden pallets littered the wooded hillsides and valleys.

We stopped by the river to await the arrival of the UN pontoon ferry.

'I think I'll just catch some rays,' said Peter, climbing onto the roof of the ambulance, donning his dark glasses and turning his face to the sun.

The rest of us joined him for a spot of sunbathing until the ferry docked below us. With our vehicles securely anchored to the deck by chains, UN soldiers from the Slovenian battalion towed us upriver by motor launch through a spectacular limestone gorge. Above the pine forests, the mountain peaks were still covered in snow. From the ferry we surveyed the destruction of pretty villages of whitewashed houses and red tiles and Turkish-style mosques with octagonal basilicas and elegant, thin fluted minarets with pointed conical roofs.

Close to Jablanica we turned off the main road and bumped down rutted tracks in search of the addresses on the parcels and letters given to us by young Bosnians in London. For me personally, delivering these parcels was one of the most rewarding aspects of our work. The parents were not only overjoyed to receive them, but almost more important to them was hearing first-hand news of their children.

The Muslim town of Konjic lay on the main Sarajevo road, at the eastern end of Lake Jablanica. Before we left London, Peter had been given the address of a family who might be able to help us with distributing the aid. The only problem was that we had absolutely no idea where they lived in the town! After many requests for directions, we turned off down a road, the right side of which was piled high for several miles with the twisted wreckage of buses and cars placed as a barrier to protect pedestrians and motorists from snipers. A large wooden sign, hand-painted with the words '*Pazi Snyper*' ('Beware of sniper'), hung at an angle from a tree. It was difficult not to feel anxious as I drove the white ambulance down the road, wondering whether the sniper was still operating in the area.

We were advised to park in the lee of a cliff that local residents said would afford us protection from Serb shells fired from the mountains, which from time to time still landed in the town. The family's teenage daughters met us at the door holding cylindrical brass coffee mills that they turned incessantly, grinding coffee beans. Their father agreed that the fairest way to distribute our aid would be to appoint the elders of the community to oversee the operation. A room in an empty building nearby was set aside for the purpose, and the elders conducted the distribution in a calm, dignified and well-ordered way.

Bosniaks are not considered by the rest of the Muslim world to be true followers of the faith. Most of them didn't pray or even visit the mosque. They smoked and drank heavily. While the older women covered their heads with scarves and wore the traditional Turkish baggy trousers, for the most part their daughters wore jeans and tee shirts and moved around town with their heads uncovered. The only thing they had in common with other Muslims was their extraordinary warm and generous hospitality. From the moment we arrived in Konjic, families plied us with coffee, cigarettes and šljivovica, and offered us accommodation in their homes. However, I preferred to sleep in the cab of the lorry parked in the lee of the cliff. Around 2 am, a Russian rocket fired from Serb positions above the town passed directly over the top of the lorry. The explosion was utterly deafening and I woke with a jolt, heart racing. In the morning I went to see where it had landed. Just across the river behind where we were parked, eight homes had been destroyed. The force of the blast had torn the plaster off the exterior walls revealing the brickwork beneath, roof beams lay open to the elements, and the ground was littered with fragments of red tile. The cabbages in the vegetable gardens had been shredded, leaving only the veins in the leaves.

In my wanderings I came across a Serbian church and stepped inside but, like all the other buildings, it had been severely damaged. Pages from religious manuscripts littered the floor. Many were beautifully illuminated, and I bent down to pick up a few, thinking to salvage them and take them home. But then the thought came into my mind that it would be sacrilege to remove them from this holy place; it would be stealing. So I let them drop to the floor. It was then that I noticed piles of human excrement. The church had been deliberately desecrated, used as a latrine, and the pages of the Bible and other religious books used as lavatory paper.

One hot afternoon, Mustafa and Jadranka Alikadic invited us for a picnic by the lake. They owned a small summerhouse on the shore and Jadranka prepared a stew for us, demonstrating an age-old cooking method. First she heated stones in a fire and dropped them one by one to the bottom of a deep pit dug into the ground, then lowered the pot into the hole, placing it carefully on the hot stones. She piled more hot stones on the lid and sealed the heat in by packing turf on top. While we were waiting for the stew to cook, the boys suggested a swim in the lake. The water looked inviting and I waded in. We swam for a while in the warm water until I noticed raw sewage bobbing just inches from my face. I alerted the boys and they were out of that lake in the blink of an eye.

Our work completed in Konjic, it was time for us to head home to England. All that remained was to drop off the ambulance at the hospital in Jablanica. Children offered to clean it for us and they set to with soap, sponges, buckets and a hosepipe. Much of the water was aimed at each other rather than the vehicle but, by the end of the afternoon, the ambulance was gleaming. The town of Jablanica had seen heavy shelling during the previous year and so many ambulances had been destroyed during the fighting that staff assured us it would be put to use straightaway. The ambulance and I had shared a long journey together and, while I was sorry to say goodbye to it, I was happy that it would be doing what it was designed to do, helping to save lives. I joined Peter and Brian in Merlin for the journey home.

It was early evening as we crossed the karst. Just before we joined the coast road and turned north towards Croatia, the sun was beginning to set above the Adriatic. No words can do justice to the beauty of that sunset – the mackerel clouds streaked salmon pink, pale and dark grey, orange, purple and magenta. Peter pulled Merlin over and parked in a lay-by.

'Let's just stop here and watch the sun set. They say that the very second it dips below the horizon, you see a flash.'

Brian rolled a cigarette, and we sat in companionable silence watching the sun, now an enormous orange disc, slowly descend towards the sea.

'It's going. It's going. Watch out for the flash,' said Peter, breaking the silence, as the sun touched the horizon and began to disappear from sight. Just a few more seconds and it disappeared altogether.

'I didn't see any flash. Did you?' I asked Brian and Peter, and they had to agree that they hadn't seen it either.

Over the next few months we made many more journeys to Konjic, and frequently transported items for other NGOs. It was Bosnia Family Aid's aim to deliver aid wherever it was most needed, regardless of religious, ethnic or cultural background and, while the amount of aid we were able to transport was a pathetic drop in the ocean, it was, we all felt, a way of showing concern for those who were suffering. When the charity Marie Stopes International (MSI) asked if we could transport four sets of snow chains for their vehicles in Bosnia we were happy to do so. With offices throughout former Yugoslavia, MSI reached thousands of displaced and refugee women through their counselling and social programmes. The rape of women and young girls was just one of many brutal crimes being committed in the war, and the chains would enable MSI vehicles to reach remote areas currently affected by appalling winter weather. On behalf of the charity War Child we carried £25,000-worth of drugs to hospitals at Jablanica and Konjic. And as Christmas approached, we took hundreds of shoeboxes containing small gifts for the children donated by churches and school pupils all over London.

From Konjic we went north to the towns of Prozor and Gornji Vakuf where, during 1992 and 1993, some of the worst ethnic cleansing of Muslims had taken place. During the winter of 1993, this route was selected by UNPROFOR as the main supply line to bring desperately needed aid to the packed towns of Tuzla, Zenica and Travnik. However, the problem was that this route passed through Prozor, Gornji Vakuf, Novi Travnik and Vitez, the 'corridor of conflict'.

The road snaked up into the mountains through dramatic scenery. Above fast-flowing rivers soared majestic jagged peaks. On the lower slopes, wild pomegranate trees grew in the rocky limestone outcrops, their ochre-yellow leaves bright against the dark-green pine forests. It was Sunday, and in Prozor women dressed in distinctive white dresses and black scarves and aprons were walking with their children to Mass.

At the height of the ethnic cleansing, the Muslim population had been forced out of their homes during four days of house burnings. Between Prozor and Gornji Vakuf, derelict homes stood on the hillside amid vines left untended. Gornji Vakuf remains as a testament to some of the most extreme acts of barbarity that took place during the war between Muslims and Croats. The main high street became the front line, with ferocious street battles between neighbours.

At the entrance to the town, we came across the memorial to Wayne Edwards from Wrexham. A lance corporal with the Cheshire Regiment, he was shot dead by a sniper at a crossroad just 30 yards from the main hospital, when he stuck his head out of a Warrior armoured vehicle while helping to clear a route through Gornji Vakuf.

As we moved slowly down the high street, we were shocked by the enormity of the destruction of houses, restaurants, cafes, offices and shops. It was difficult to comprehend the depth of hatred that had overcome this mixed community who had lived in harmony during the days of Tito. Street signs were so riddled with bullets that it was a wonder they still stood upright. Piles of empty tin cans and heaps of twisted metal, broken glass, shell casings and rubble lay amongst the weeds. At one end of town the mosque lay in ruins, while at the other the church was gradually being rebuilt.

We left Konjic a few days later. A shell had landed earlier in the centre of town and the main bank was a blazing, raging inferno, papers fluttering down from windows like ticker tape. Ancient and battered fire engines were trying unsuccessfully to quell the blaze.

Some Bosnian girls in London had asked if Peter could deliver a box of food to an elderly relative who lived alone in the Soviet-style housing complex beneath the flyover on the outskirts of Mostar. It was dark by the time we reached the turn-off to the housing complex. Leaving the flyover, we descended into an underworld.

'Shit happens,' remarked Brian laconically, observing the bomb-damaged buildings in the beam of Merlin's headlights. It was pitch-black. No lights of any description appeared in the street, not even the glow from a lighted cigarette or the flicker of a candle in the windows of the forbidding concrete buildings. Only when the moon emerged for a few seconds from behind clouds could we detect people flitting silently through the streets like wraiths.

'Switch off the engines and headlights,' instructed Peter over the radio.

I wanted to help Peter and Brian deliver the boxes of food.

'No, 'Arry, you stay here and look after Merlin.'

They returned about an hour later, having located the elderly man living in the cold darkness of what remained of his flat. Great gaping holes had left the staircase open to the elements.

'We could smell the cordite,' Peter said as he climbed back into Merlin's cab.

I made one final journey to Konjic in December 1994. From there Brian and Peter were leaving the convoy with Merlin to take much-needed aid to Sarajevo, which was under siege and constant bombardment by the Serbs. Some of us wanted to go with them, but Peter was adamant that only he and Brian would make the journey.

'It's just too dangerous for you to come with us, 'Arry. We'll be going over Mount Igman in the dark.'

Mount Igman was the only supply route into the city, and it was in the control of General Mladic's Chetniks. The boys would have to drive on mountain roads without headlights. As I helped to stick black tape over Merlin's brake lights, I felt anxious for their safety.

During the past year we had driven 32,000 miles together and shared some extraordinary experiences. For me it had been a privilege to travel with Brian and Peter on the convoys. They had accepted me unconditionally, making me feel part of the team and 'one of the boys'. Now they were about to undertake the most dangerous of journeys. We stood in the lee of the cliff in Konjic, said our goodbyes and watched them depart down Sniper's Alley before turning east on the Sarajevo road. I too was parting company with the group. While the rest were driving back to England, I planned to stay in Mostar to see if I could find a job with an NGO. Karen Locke, a friend from London, was working for St David's Foundation in Medjugorje, teaching English to schoolgirls in Grabovica. She had offered me a room in her house at the foot of Ascension Hill. On my first night there I appreciated the comfort of a proper bed after many spent sleeping in the back of the lorry.

In the villages around Medjugorje, pigs were being slaughtered to provide food for the winter. Below my bedroom window a large sow stood in her sty awaiting her fate. The farmer and his wife were busy laying out knives, meat cleavers and bowls of hot water on the stone butcher's slab in the orchard. They placed a rope around the pig's neck and as they began to haul the reluctant animal out of its sty towards the stone slab, it struggled violently, emitting blood-curdling screams. Poor creature; it must have known it was going to its death. I watched in morbid fascination as they slit its throat, butchered it and then used a blowtorch to remove the bristles from the skin. Every part of the animal was used, even the intestines. After washing them in a bucket of water, the farmer's wife attached them to a machine. As meat was fed in one end, sausages shot out of the other. Nothing went to waste. Finally, the slab was scrubbed and sluiced down, the knives packed away and the remains of the pig carried back to the house.

Every morning, the UN peacekeepers based in Medjugorje offered me a lift in their vehicle on their daily journey to their office in Mostar. They would drop me on the Croat west bank and I would walk across the Bailey bridge to the Muslim east bank to visit various NGO offices before returning to Medjugorje in the evening with the peacekeepers.

One morning, as I was crossing a street in the Muslim quarter, a man wearing a grey Chitrali hat and shalwar kameez emerged from a bombed building, picking his way carefully through the fallen masonry. I was intrigued by his clothing and I was quite sure he came from either the North-West Frontier or Afghanistan. I followed him at a distance, and when he stopped to talk to someone he obviously knew I overheard them speaking in Dari. It confirmed my suspicion that the man was an Afghan, but what was he doing in Mostar?

As early as 1992 Muslim volunteers from Indonesia, Iraq, Syria, Chechnya, Afghanistan, Saudi Arabia and North Africa had been arriving in Bosnia-

Herzegovina. Initially they came with humanitarian aid organisations and to help protect the local Bosnian Muslim population, but gradually they began actively recruiting young local men and introducing them to their more radical form of Islam – Wahhabism. The American historian Carl Savich writes in *Al-Qaeda on Trial* that a senior al-Qaeda recruiter and veteran of the Mujahideen in Afghanistan, Abu Abdel Aziz, was made military commander of the Muslim unit Al Mujahid, comprising Saudi Arabian and Afghan Mujahideen in Bosnia. These foreign mercenaries were recruited, financed and organised by Osama bin Laden and were particularly active around the town of Zenica, where they fought alongside the Muslim army. Their goal was 'to re-create a Muslim Caliphate that would include Bosnia and Kosovo'.[43] In 2003, in the war crimes trial at the International Criminal Tribunal for the former Yugoslavia in The Hague, it was stated that Al Mujahid was involved in ritual beheadings, executions and torture of Serbs and Croats. Two of the 9/11 hijackers were Saudis who had trained and fought in Bosnia.

My wanderings brought me to the old Ottoman quarter with its narrow, cobbled streets and ancient souq overlooked by Turkish-style houses with latticed wooden verandas. Here, before the war, in tiny open-fronted shops now closed and boarded up, Bessarabian kilims and beaten copper artefacts were sold to tourists. At the end of the souq, the cobbled street led to the beautiful and famous Ottoman bridge, the Stari Most. Ever since it was built by the architect Mimar Hajruddin in 1557–66, the Stari Most had come to represent the beauty of Mostar, one of the most cosmopolitan and ethnically intermingled cities in the former Yugoslavia. In happier times, young men would show off their prowess by diving from its walls into the swirling waters of the Neretva.

After its destruction in November 1993 the bridge became a symbol of the violence and barbarity of the war in Bosnia-Herzegovina. Despite the best efforts of residents to protect it by hanging rubber tyres along its walls, repeated shelling so pulverised the limestone blocks that they finally succumbed to the sustained onslaught and fell into the river. A temporary rope suspension bridge now replaced the Stari Most. All that remained of the original bridge was a steep, wide limestone ramp, the stone polished over the centuries by the feet and hooves of human and animal traffic. I made my way up the ramp and onto the suspension bridge clutching hold of the thick ropes on either side, willing myself to look ahead and not down, where I could see the river through wide gaps in the wooden slats. When I reached the middle, the bridge swayed alarmingly. Years earlier when trekking through Zanskar in Ladakh, I had experienced similar rope bridges when crossing river gorges. I hated them then and I hated this one now! The fear came back to me as I stood completely frozen in the centre of the bridge, unable to move forwards or backwards. Some locals crossing the bridge gave me encouragement and I reached the west bank, where I heard children's laughter coming from inside a small damaged building. The building backed onto a wide boulevard several miles in length that had comprised some of the most beautiful buildings in Mostar. Just a few months before, the boulevard had been on the front line. Now it resembled Dresden after the Allied bombing. I clambered over the rubble and ducked through a shell hole in a wall to find five or six little boys and girls playing happily. This was their den and they had decorated the walls with murals. Taking me by the hand, they showed me around their 'home' and invited me to join in their games.

On my journey back to Medjugorje that evening, the UN peacekeepers told me that the Hollywood actor Harvey Keitel was in Mostar with a film director and crew, filming *Ulysses' Gaze*. He particularly wanted to meet children affected by the war, so I suggested to the peacekeepers that I might show him around the Ottoman quarter and introduce him to the children. The meeting was arranged and a few days later, in brilliant sunshine, Harvey and I walked across the Stari Most. The children were rather bemused by such an entourage of adults descending upon their 'den', but their shyness soon wore off.

One afternoon I climbed up the steep hillside from the Muslim quarter to the Christian cemetery and walked amongst the enormous white limestone crosses and gravestones. I sat for a while enjoying the panoramic view over Mostar, but I felt ill at ease alone on the exposed hillside – an easy target for a sniper – so I wasted no time in retracing my steps down the slope and scrambled back to the relative safety of the streets.

Back in the Muslim quarter, I made my way through cobbled streets largely untouched by conflict, to the other end of town where MSI ran a drop-in centre for women. Here, in a small, warm, cosy house, Muslim women sat around talking, drinking coffee, knitting and crocheting. All were victims of ethnic cleansing and some had suffered rape and torture. In the safe, comfortable environment of MSI they could share their experiences, receive counselling and learn English – a passport, the women told me, to a better life. Their teacher was a young German girl, and listening to her teaching a language that was not her mother tongue gave me the idea of doing a Teaching English as a Foreign Language (TEFL) course in the UK. I had watched how Karen taught English to the schoolgirls in Grabovica, and felt sure that, with some training, I could do the same. The German girl confided that she was shortly leaving MSI to return home, and the manager agreed I could come back in few months later and take her place. In London I made enquiries about TEFL, but the course was expensive and more than I could afford. However, a friend, Mark Hopkins, invited me to speak at his church during a Sunday family service about the work of Bosnia Family Aid and my plans to return to Mostar. Ken Costa, an investment banker in the City of London who owned a number of language schools, approached me and generously offered me a TEFL course free of charge at one of his language schools in High Street Kensington. After an intensive month of study and achieving the qualification, I began to prepare for my return to Mostar. However, my life was about to change, and in the event I never did return.

The previous summer in London, Elizabeth Winter had invited me to speak about the UNESCO *ikat* silk-weaving project at a conference she had organised on Afghanistan. The invitation extended to drinks that evening on the third floor of the offices of Christian Aid near Waterloo Station, followed by dinner in a Spanish tapas restaurant on the South Bank. The first person I saw as I entered the room was a tall, elegant man in a smart grey pinstriped suit sipping fruit cocktail from a plastic cup and talking to the Iranian Ambassador. He looked rather incongruous amongst the more casually dressed aid workers in open-necked shirts, socks and sandals. As we walked to the restaurant, I knew that he was the only person I wanted to sit next to during dinner.

Bryan Ray had been an infantry officer in the British Army, serving in Africa, the Middle East, the Near East and Northern Ireland. He later commanded the Northern Frontier Regiment of the Sultan of Oman's army during the Dhofar War. During dinner we discovered we had much in common: a great interest in Afghanistan, and a love of travel, horses and the countryside. Usually when I spoke to men about my life, a glazed look would come over their faces and they would look over my shoulder for someone else to talk to. However, that evening Bryan was not at all fazed by my exploits because he had achieved so many extraordinary things in his own life, which he later wrote about in his fascinating book *Dangerous Frontiers*.

No sooner had I completed the TEFL course than my father died suddenly of a heart attack. After his funeral in Cumbria I needed to get away, and Bryan suggested we travel together around Syria. We both wanted to see the Crusader castle Krak des Chevaliers and the Græco-Roman city of Palmyra. With a copy of the Lonely Planet *Guide to Syria and the Lebanon* in our backpacks, we set out for Damascus.

PART VI

SYRIA

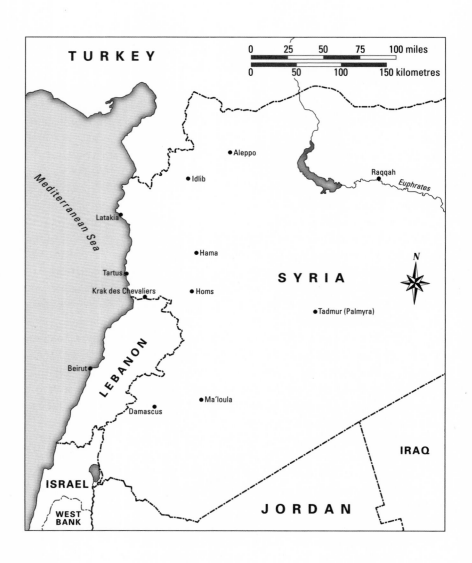

Chapter 17
Syria – the calm before the storm
April 1995

Travelling through Syria by local bus, there was no indication of discontent or the unrest that was to spark the Arab Spring in 2011. Seeing Syria for the first time through tourists' eyes, it appeared, on the surface, to be calm, prosperous and westernised – very similar in many ways to Iraqi Kurdistan. Syrian society was a melting pot of different ethnic groups and religions: Shia, Alawites, Kurds, Druze, Sunnis and Yazidis, as well as numerous different Christian communities living in harmony alongside one another. In the towns, women wore a variety of clothing according to their class and religion. Some wore European-style jackets and skirts and did not cover their heads. Others completely shrouded themselves in the billowing black abaya, while in the countryside women wore the traditional Syrian costume called *Syriaci*, an ankle-length black dress heavily embroidered in maroon cross stitch down the front and around the cuffs.

Only when we reached the town of Hama to view the famous water wheels constructed for irrigation during Ottoman rule did we become aware of Syria's troubled past, and the iron hold that President Hafez al-Assad wielded over his own people through torture, imprisonment and massacres. In 1982, he savagely crushed a rebellion by the Sunni Islamist group, the Muslim Brotherhood, against the secular and nationalist Ba'ath Party. The old city of Hama was bombed from the air and buildings demolished by heavy artillery and tank fire. Diesel was pumped into tunnels under the old city and set ablaze to flush out civilians who had taken cover. The Syrian Human Rights Committee estimated that possibly 40,000 of Hama's citizens had died in the fighting.[44] Following the massacre, the five-star Apame Cham Palace Hotel, complete with tennis courts and swimming pool, was built over the ruins.

Late one evening we decided to go for a drink in the hotel's bar. Crystal chandeliers hung from the ceiling and water cascaded from a fountain in the centre of the foyer, the floor of which was made from different sections of highly polished coloured marble. Neither of us felt comfortable sipping our gin and tonics, knowing that beneath our feet lay buried the remains of thousands of Assad's victims. We left through a side exit near the hotel kitchen and emerged directly on to a dusty, rubble-strewn lane. As we stumbled in the dark with only the beams from our torches to light our way, we could see all around us the ruins of bombed-out houses. The fact that such a vulgar and ostentatious building had been deliberately constructed over the ruins of the old city in order to disguise such a barbarous crime affected both of us, and we walked home subdued.

For travellers visiting Aleppo, the legendary Baron Hotel had been *the* place to stay. T. E. Lawrence, Freya Stark and Kemal Ataturk had all been guests there. But at reception we realised the hotel had definitely seen better days, and that its romantic reputation far exceeded the deplorable state of its decor, which appeared untouched since the 1920s. Our bathroom was a relic from the Edwardian era; a deep bath stood on ball-and-claw feet and the walls were tiled with white tiles from floor to ceiling like a public convenience. It was impossible to draw the curtains in our bedroom as they hung in shreds from the curtain pole, and when I mislaid a shoe and bent down to retrieve it from under the bed, I rather wished I hadn't. No broom had visited the space beneath the bed for decades and the dust and fluff of ages had found refuge there. When the author William Dalrymple had stayed in the Baron a year before us, he summed up the experience:

> the inexplicably horrible food, the decaying neo-gothic architecture, the deep baths and the uncomfortable beds; no wonder Lawrence and his contemporaries felt so much at home here – the Baron is the perfect replica of some particularly Spartan English public school strangely displaced to the deserts of the Middle East.[45]

It was Easter Sunday and church bells were pealing out across the city.

Ten percent of Syria's population is Christian, the religion having been brought to Damascus by Saint Peter the Apostle. However, it was the arrival of Armenians, driven out of Turkey at the end of the First World War, that made Aleppo's population 'one of the largest Christian populations anywhere in the Middle East'.[46]

I very much wanted to go to church to celebrate Easter, but we found the many Christian sects quite bewildering – which should we choose? There were Syrian Protestants, Maronites, the Greek Orthodox Church of Antioch, the Greek Catholic Church, the Oriental Syriac Orthodox Church, the Chaldean Catholic Church (who sang hymns in Aramaic) and the Assyrian Church of the East. Fortunately our taxi driver informed us that those of the Eastern Orthodox persuasion were celebrating Easter on a different day altogether, which narrowed down the choice. He brought us to the Greek Catholic church, referred to as the Latin cathedral, where we joined Syrian families dressed in their Sunday best, queuing to enter for Mass.

As we inched forward towards the altar, Bryan asked me to marry him and I accepted. He wanted to buy me an engagement ring, so we looked for one in the jewellery shops in the Armenian quarter after the service, but they were too bright and gaudy, like something one might find in a Christmas cracker. I politely declined to wear any of them!

We set out to explore Aleppo's 12th-century covered souq, the largest historic market in the world and a UNESCO World Heritage Site. In its labyrinth of narrow vaulted passageways and medieval cobbled streets leading to the citadel, a huge stone fortress built on a hill dominating Aleppo, the souk was a hive of activity. Shops were selling everything – spices, vegetables, carpets, ladies' underwear, marquetry backgammon boards, copper pots and fine silk gauze scarves for which Syria is renowned. Behind giant fortified wooden doors inlaid with metal studs, merchants unloaded their goods in inner courtyards surrounded by carved wood lattice balconies, a scene unchanged for hundreds of years.

Silk scarves of traditional Syrian design but in a variety of colours hung from shop doorways and I bought several dozen to take home as gifts and to sell. Having experienced so many problems when dyeing silk in Peshawar, I was interested to discover what method the Syrians used. A flight of ancient stone steps led to the dye house, once the hammam, and here we found men working in Dickensian conditions, screen-printing lengths of silk cloth. They were producing not the colourful scarves that I had hoped to find, but the traditional black-and-white silk headcloths worn by widows, and the maroon-and-black scarves favoured by rural women.

Tragically, in 2012 the war in Syria spread to Aleppo. The fighting set the souk ablaze. Fire swept through the wood caravanserais and shops that had been a place of trade for 800 years, burning it to the ground.

Both Bryan and I wanted to visit the Græco-Roman city of Palmyra, one of the most important archaeological sites in the world. From Homs we took a bus across the Syrian desert towards the Euphrates, a long, hot and dusty journey. Arriving at nightfall on the outskirts of the modern town of Tadmur, we were greeted by the magnificent sight of floodlit colonnades and temples. Seeing Palmyra for the first time, I experienced the same feelings of wonder and awe as I did when I first set eyes on the Taj Mahal. The sheer magnitude of the site, which stretches far out in to the desert, the beauty and sophistication of the architecture and the fact that so many buildings were still standing, gave the impression that the Romans had only left a century or so before.

Ancient Tadmur, an oasis on the caravan route dating from the second millennium BC, was renamed by the Romans 'Palmyra' because of the palm trees growing close by. Palmyra flourished under Roman rule, becoming wealthy and important as a trade route linking Egypt, Babylon, Persia, India and Central Asia. The city was a fusion of cultures, with its own language and style of dress. Together with the Greeks and the Judeans, the Palmyrenes were great traders; the city was ideally situated to receive goods from India transported up the Persian Gulf and Euphrates and from China via the overland route through Bactria and Persia. In the third century AD, Palmyra was ruled by Queen Zenobia after the assassination of her husband. The Romans, concerned by her increasing power and reputation in the east of their empire, sent an army to overthrow her but she defeated them in battle in 269 AD.

For two days we wandered amongst the well-preserved ruins admiring the beautifully paved roads lined with columns, the drainage and water systems, the Roman aqueduct and the great temple of Bel with its entablatures and porticos.

In August 2015 Palmyra became a place of execution. I was at home in Somerset when I heard the shocking news of the beheading by ISIS of the retired chief archaeologist and curator of the museum, Khalidad al-Asaad, followed a fortnight later by the destruction of the Temple of Bel, the great sanctuary of the Palmyrene gods and one of the most important buildings of the first century AD.

Back in Damascus, Bryan and I walked in the footsteps of Saint Paul along the Street called 'Straight', and on the recommendation of a Lebanese friend took a bus to Ma'loula, an almost entirely Christian town clinging to a rocky escarpment close to the Lebanese border. Nearly all the houses were painted pale blue, which reminded me of the Jain houses in Jodhpur, but it was the fact that the inhabitants still spoke Aramaic, the language of Jesus Christ, that we found so fascinating. In a Byzantine convent an inner courtyard led us into a beautiful chapel carved out of the rock face, the entrance to which was accessible only by bending double to squeeze through the tiny door. Candlelight flickered in the gold leaf of the icons hanging from the hewn rock walls. We were welcomed by a priest who recited the Lord's Prayer in Aramaic. We seriously contemplated getting married in the chapel, but then came to the conclusion that it was probably too far and too expensive for friends to travel.

In the event, we married three months later in the church in Hawkshead, where I was christened and where my father had been buried three months before, high up on the hillside with views of the mountains and countryside he loved.

Tying up loose threads

In January 2001 I received a letter from a remarkable American woman called Mary MacMakin. She had started an NGO in Kabul called Physiotherapy and Rehabilitation Support for Afghanistan (PARSA), opening her office in the very month the Taliban occupied the city. However, Mary courageously remained in Kabul, organising and running many diverse projects – motor-repair training for Afghan orphans, home schools where girls could continue their education, and wool-spinning classes so that poor women could support themselves by supplying carpet-weavers with well-spun knotting yarn. But after several years, she had to leave.

> Since the Taliban kicked me out of Kabul last July, I have been setting up an office here in Peshawar ... With the expert help of Saleh Mohammed, Ali Tarshi's brother-in-law, PARSA has a nice little silk weaving project up and running. He has eight women trained and their production keeps going up. But we need markets. Could you do some selling for us?

In 2003 Bryan and I flew to Kabul to meet Mary and Saleh. I took with me Ciba-Geigy acid dyes for Saleh, as he had found it impossible to procure good dyes in Kabul.

After the bombing of the Tora Bora Mountains by ISAF (International Security Assistance Force), the Taliban and Osama bin Laden had fled the country and crossed into the tribal territories of Pakistan. Now, after 32 years of war, Afghanistan was at last looking forward to peace and stability. There was a feeling of euphoria and the arrivals hall at Kabul airport was a scene of happy chaos as Afghans returning from all over the world heaved huge suitcases off the broken and stationary carousel. There was a party atmosphere as people welcomed friends and family arriving on the Ariana flight from Sharjah. Amongst the crowd we recognised good friends – Sandy Gall's daughter Michaela, our Cumbrian neighbour Anthony Fitzherbert, who worked for the FAO in Afghanistan, and Helen Saberi, who had been a committee member of

ARIN. Helen and her Afghan husband, Nasir, were now back in Kabul for the first time since leaving the country in 1980 after the Soviet invasion.

Saleh was waiting for us in the gardens of PARSA. Ten years had passed since we'd last met and now he was a married man of 27 with a young family. Apart from the fact that he had grown a long black beard, he was just the same cool, reserved young man that I remembered. He simply shook Bryan by the hand, then turned to me and said, 'Oriot, you want to see women weavers? Come.' And he strode off to hail a taxi.

Kabul had suffered during the Taliban years. As we motored down the traffic-choked Daraluman Road I was shocked to see the ruined buildings, trees stripped of their leaves, tangled wires hanging from telegraph poles and piles of rubbish lining the road. The imposing Daraluman Palace had been so mortared and fought over that all that remained was an empty shell. Soon we were on the outskirts of Kabul in an area untouched by fighting and far from the noise and mayhem of the city centre. There Saleh paid off the taxi driver, and led us along dusty lanes hemmed in by high mud walls. Suddenly I heard the familiar *clack-clack* of flying shuttle looms, and I felt a lump in my throat. When I left Peshawar in 1990 I assumed that the silk project would collapse and cease to operate. How wrong I had been. I had underestimated Saleh. All through the Taliban years he had worked secretly with numerous families, providing them with silk yarn and taking the finished product to Mary MacMakin to sell through PARSA, thus providing the women with an income during that terrible time. We entered the walled compound, and Saleh introduced me to the women weavers. Over the next four years I bought many of Saleh's scarves and sold them through my business in Somerset.

Before leaving Kabul, Bryan and I wanted to buy presents to take home. As we wandered down Chicken Street, Afghans appeared at their shop doors, shouting out, 'Oriot! Oriot! Oriot jan – remember me?'

The merchants from Shinwari Plaza and Murad market had all returned home from years of exile in Peshawar. Now I was reunited with the Makoo brothers and Qayum. They knew that I understood all that they had endured during those long years and now they wanted to share their happiness in being home in Kabul, and their appreciation of our long friendship. It was a joyous moment. But while the merchants were doing well out of trade with ISAF, the UN and humanitarian aid workers, there were still many who had little or no money and were on the brink of starvation.

There is one image Bryan and I will never forget. As we drove out to Kabul airport to catch our flight home, we saw a woman in a lilac chador suddenly throw herself down on the ground, beating her head and hands in the dust in utter desolation and despair.

In September 2002, I received an email from John Jennings, the freelance journalist from 10 Canal Bank Road, telling me that Mumtaz, my Pakistani pi-dog, had died in America.

The Mumtaz you remember changed little as she aged; though she grew more sedate by temperament, she remained physically fit and energetic. The vet had trouble believing she was 12. It was never hard to provoke her into a game of chase. She remained a swift and deadly foe of cats and squirrels until this summer – until just about the time I realised her limp wasn't 'arthritis'.

To the end, she loved to ride around in trucks. I took her on a long drive to the mountains of West Virginia, in the first week of September. She was still able to walk a few hundred yards at a stretch then. Before she got sick, she usually 'stood' on the window sill of my pick-up – rather than the dashboard – because she liked to hang out the window, which I always left down for her. Like you I have a picture of her and myself sitting together on a cot – the one on which I used to sleep outdoors in Kabul's fine summer weather. She often joined me, curling up at my feet. The picture dates from 1992, right before Gulbuddin's rocketing of Kabul began.

I still remember on Canal Bank Road, she had a swollen haunch and a big bruise, presumably from Afghans kicking her or beating her while we weren't around (I can't imagine it was Mohamed Gul or Wadood because she liked both of them). As a result, till the end she distrusted men.

Here in NYC, every morning I used to walk her to the corner store, tie her leash to a parking meter, and duck inside for coffee. She was very sweet-natured and friendly under most circumstances – yet whenever anybody went into the store behind me, she'd snap, snarl and lunge at them. She saw herself first and foremost as my bodyguard. She used to howl piteously whenever I left town and greet me joyously whenever I returned. Perfect love and loyalty ain't to be taken lightly. It was clear she felt the same about you. What a wonderful gift you gave when you entrusted her to me. (As you recall, I wasn't immediately grateful.) I am sure that if we are good, we'll see her again someday, but in the meantime a lot of sparkle has gone outta my world.

In 1974 Bryan had been Christopher Barnes's commanding officer during the Dhofar War, fighting communist insurgents in southern Oman. Now Christopher and his wife Katherine were celebrating their 25th wedding anniversary, and invited us to fly out to California to stay with them for a few days at their beautiful home in Point Reyes National Park, just north of San Francisco. As I sat beside their pool shaded from the hot Californian sun by a large umbrella, watching pelicans fly down the lake and deer grazing in the land below their house, I chatted to fellow guest Vivian Rowe. A Royal Marine, Viv had also served in Dhofar and shared some hair-raising moments with Bryan and Christopher before going on to serve in the Falklands War and in Iraqi Kurdistan at the end of the first Gulf War.

'I was in Kurdistan around the same time,' I said. 'I knew someone called Charlie Maxwell who was murdered there.'

'I found his body,' Viv said grimly.

As second-in-command of 40 Commando Royal Marines, Viv was given the task of finding and retrieving the bodies of Charlie Maxwell, Nick and Rosanna della Casa from the mountains of Kurdistan. On 19 May 1991, a PKK guerrilla called Hashem Ciftci reported to a US Army Special Forces team at a refugee camp close to the Turkish border that he had seen the journalists, but refused to divulge more information except to a British officer. The following morning he was taken by helicopter to the headquarters of 3 Commando Brigade where, Viv said, 'he nervously and hesitantly described where he had seen the journalists but wouldn't say whether they were alive, held hostage or dead'. An immediate aerial reconnaissance by Sea King helicopter was conducted but, although Ciftci pointed to a general area, nothing was seen to prove he was telling the truth. However, by the following morning he had revealed that the journalists were dead and that he had seen the bodies once in late March and again shortly before contacting the coalition forces. He had been very upset on religious grounds to find the bodies still unburied and had decided to report his evidence to the authorities. So Viv took him in a smaller, Lynx helicopter; despite turbulent air and steep-sided terrain, the pilot, Rob Wilsey, skilfully managed to position the helicopter low enough to enable Viv to get a good view of the land below. Something caught his eye in a dry stream bed. 'It was a faded yellow shirt,' he told me. On 23 and 24 May a ground search was launched, and Viv took a search party down a steep valley to the suspected site, where they found two bodies in the dry stream bed. The painstaking gathering of evidence was carried out by a military Scene of Crime team and the bodies were later identified as Charlie and Nick. Buried a foot beneath the ashes of an old campfire they found Rosanna's diary together with the journalists' passports, a trick Nick had learnt while travelling in Cambodia. An AK-47 cartridge case was also found nearby. Hashem Ciftci later confessed to the murder of the two men, but not of Rosanna. He was found guilty at a trial in the town of Erbil. A further search of the area by a patrol on 15 June found a boot, sock and hairgrip belonging to Rosanna, near the track but nearly four miles from where Viv found Nick and Charlie. Her body was never found.

On a hot, sultry, airless July evening in 2011, I was on my way to a charity fundraising event in London, an Afghan fashion show being held at the 20th Century Theatre in Westbourne Grove. As I walked through the streets of Notting Hill, the buildings and pavements radiated heat like a night storage heater, and I began to regret wearing the pale-blue silk Pushtun nomad's dress with its heavy purple velvet bodice embroidered with gold thread that I had put on especially for the occasion. Sweat trickled down my back, my face was the colour of a setting sun, and I wondered how the nomad women coped wearing such garments in the summer heat of Afghanistan.

By the time I arrived, a long queue of Afghans was waiting for the doors to open. I eagerly searched the faces in the crowd, but the majority were young and sophisticated, quite a different generation from the Afghans that I used to know. Yet, like me, they had come to lend their support to various charities working inside Afghanistan.

Was it really 20 years since I had lived in Peshawar? The years had passed so quickly that it seemed but a moment ago. I quietly observed the young Afghan men and women speaking English with London accents. It occurred to me that, having been born and educated in Britain after their parents fled their homeland during the Soviet occupation, they had probably never had an opportunity to visit the land of their forefathers.

Upstairs, the theatre was lined with stalls selling antique and contemporary Afghan clothes, jewellery and textiles. The room was crowded with diplomats, journalists, politicians, members of the Afghan royal family and humanitarian aid workers. As the guests took their seats, the lights dimmed and the haunting beautiful music of Afghanistan filled the auditorium, bringing back a flood of memories.

One by one, elegant models emerged from behind a black curtain and descended the catwalk wearing the traditional dresses and clothing of the different tribal groups of Afghanistan. Then the music changed, becoming more vibrant, dramatic and exciting, heralding the next part of the show. To the beat of the *dahria*, *rebab* and *tabla*, the models emerged a second time. This time they were dressed in smart designer suits, jackets and skirts made from tweed and wool, all expertly tailored and incorporating traditional Afghan embroidery and beadwork; everything had been designed by young Afghan women educated in Britain who had returned to work with poor women in Kabul. The clothes on display that evening were stunning, and a tribute to a generation of young Afghans determined to play a part in their country's regeneration.

Suddenly a model appeared from behind the black curtain wearing a beautiful full-length dark-green shot-silk evening dress decorated with calligraphy. She stopped for a moment to twirl in front of the audience. The silk dress billowed out, shimmering under the spotlight. My heart skipped a beat, and I was transported back in time to the small concrete yard in Shaheen Town, where 17-year-old Saleh and I would crouch side by side dyeing skeins of silk in the large metal cauldron balanced over a gas burner, before rinsing and hanging them on his sister's washing line to dry. I cast my mind back to the North-West Frontier, to the weeks, months and years I spent travelling through Pakistan, researching and setting up the silk-weaving project. I remembered all the obstacles, problems, fears and setbacks. I thought of the courage of Saleh who, after I left Peshawar, took the project to Afghanistan and worked secretly with women weavers during the Taliban occupation of Kabul. Saleh was now an *Ustad*, a master weaver, employed by Turquoise Mountain, a charity set up in Kabul by President Hamid Karzai, Prince Charles and Rory Stewart to preserve traditional Afghan handicrafts. I was only glad that in the darkness no one could see the tears running down my cheeks and that the Afghan music drowned out my voice as I said out loud, 'Well done, Saleh, well done. I am *so* proud of you!' I had sown the seed all those years ago, but Saleh had taken that seed, nurtured it and grown it into a thriving tree.

In the summer of 2014, my childhood friend Adam Naylor invited me to his 60th birthday party in the grounds of my old school, Blackwell, now an arts-and-crafts museum. It was a glorious and perfect summer's evening. From the playground – now a neat lawn – where I had once played tig, hopscotch and lacrosse, I looked out across Windermere and the fells, enjoying the stillness and beauty. Adam came up and said, 'Do go and speak with Mary Burkett. She's sitting at a table over there in the shade.' Mary, a few weeks short of her 90th birthday, was frail and not in good health but was delighted to see me. I took the opportunity to thank her for all the support she had given me over many years. In a gable above us was a garret window and behind it the room where, 50 years earlier, Mary had shown me pottery shards brought back from her archaeological dig at Gonbad-e Qabus. I was prompted to ask something that I had wanted to ask her for years.

'Why did you ask me, out of all the other little girls, to come with you to Galava? That day really influenced the course of my life.'

She replied simply, 'Because you were interested'.

A few months later, Mary invited me to her home, Isel Hall, a peel tower near Cockermouth, to celebrate her 90th birthday, but I was unable to make the journey from Somerset to West Cumbria. I sent her some flowers and, a few weeks later, on 5 November, I received a postcard from her.

> The scent of the lilies and roses was filling the hall for several weeks – I hated to see them go. Thank you so much, dear Harriet – I thought of you each time I passed near them and thought of our long friendship – something I treasure.

A week later, on 12 November, she died peacefully at Isel.

In 2014, my mother told me that, while carrying out some family research, my sister had discovered that we had Huguenot forebears, French Protestants who had left their homeland to escape persecution and settled in Spitalfields.

'And what did they do there? I asked

'They were silk-weavers,' my mother replied.

My mother's five times great-grandfather, John Nash, wanted to marry a Huguenot girl called Jeanne Loi, but her father, Sebastien Loi, a wealthy master silk-weaver who lived with his family in an elegant house in London's Spital Square, refused to allow it on the grounds that John spoke no French and wasn't a weaver. Master silk-weavers at that time imported silk cocoons from Italy and produced woven silk of high quality – brocades, damasks, tabby and floral silk fabric incorporating silver and gold thread, which was made into gowns and waistcoats for London's high society. In order to satisfy Jeanne's tyrannical father and obtain his permission to marry her, John took himself off for several months, learnt French and worked as a journeyman until he was able to produce a piece of satin of excellent workmanship, every bit as fine as that woven by Sebastien Loi. Finally, permission was given and they married at Spitalfields church. Their great-grandson was General Joseph Nash, who was given the ruby by Shah Shuja in Afghanistan.

Little did I realise, when I started the silk-weaving project in Pubbi Jalozai refugee camp, that my own forebears were both refugees and silk-weavers!

Endnotes

[1] Ben Macintyre, *Josiah the Great: The True Story of The Man Who Would Be King*, p. 22.

[2] Peter Hopkirk, *The Great Game: On Secret Service in High Asia*, p. 192.

[3] James Atkinson, Superintending Surgeon of the Army of the Indus, Bengal Establishment, *The Expedition into Afghanistan. Notes and Sketches*, p. 189.

[4] Ibid.

[5] Ibid.

[6] Nancy Hatch Dupree, *An Historical Guide to Afghanistan*, p. 165.

[7] Mohammad Yousaf & Mark Adkin, *Afghanistan: The Bear Trap – The Defeat of a Superpower*, p. 32.

[8] Macintyre, op. cit., p. 159.

[9] Louis Dupree, *Afghanistan* (Oxford Pakistan Paperbacks), p. 198.

[10] Letter from Gertrude Bell to her parents, May 1917, in Georgina Howell, *Queen of the Desert: The Extraordinary Life of Gertrude Bell*, p. 297.

[11] Arminius Vámbéry, *Travels in Central Asia. Being the Account of a Journey from Teheran across the Turkoman desert on the eastern shore of the Caspian to Khiva, Bokhara, and Samarcand*, p. 140.

[12] Ibid.

[13] 'No 10 Canal Bank Road', in Joss Graham and Harriet Sandys, 'The Decorative Arts of Central Asia' exhibition catalogue (Ikat weavings), Zamana Gallery, London, May 1988.

[14] Roland and Sabrina Michaud, *Caravans to Tartary*.

[15] Vámbéry, op. cit., p. 172.

[16] David Loyn, *Frontline: The True Story of the British Mavericks Who Changed the Face of War Reporting*.

[17] John Tulloch Nash, 'Fighting with the Bengal Yeomanry Cavalry', p. 106.

[18] Ibid., p. 69.

[19] Tariq Alam and Farooq Khattak, *The Times of Peshawar*, 1989

[20] Captain H.L. Nevill DSO RFA, *North-West Frontier: British and Indian Army Campaigns on the North-West Frontier of India 1849–1908*, pp. 274–5.

[21] Colonel Sir Robert Warburton, 'The Afridi lad from his earliest childhood' in Warburton, *Eighteen Years in the Khyber 1879–1898*. Quoted in Nevill, *North-West Frontier*, p.274.

[22] Loyn, op. cit., p. 26.

[23] Susan Maria Farrington, *Peshawar Monumental Inscriptions II*, British Association for Cemeteries in South Asia, 1991, p. 7.

[24] Ibid., p. 100.

[25] Ibid., p. 74.

[26] Kathy Evans, 'Afghan cleric tells women how to dress', *The Guardian*, 23 June 1990.

[27] Robert Abdul Hayy Darr, *The Spy of the Heart*, p. 181.

[28] Erwin Knoll, 'Journalistic Jihad. Holes in the coverage of a holy war', *The Progressive*, May 1990, pp. 17–22.

[29] Ibid.

[30] Nancy Hatch Dupree, *Afghanistan*, p. 392.

[31] Vámbéry, *Travels in Central Asia*, p. 174.

[32] Wilfred Thesiger, *Desert, Marsh and Mountain*, 1979, p. 125.

[33] Human Rights Watch/Yale University Press, *Iraq's Crime of Genocide: The Anfal Campaign against the Kurds*, 1994, pp. 96 and 170.

[34] Wikipedia.

[35] Diary of Rosanna della Casa, cited in Loyn, *Frontline*, p. 152.

[36] Human Rights Watch/YaleUniversity Press, *Iraq's Crime of Genocide*, pp. 143–5.

[37] Kanan Makiya, *The Monument: Art and Vulgarity in Saddam Hussein's Iraq*, I.B. Tauris, 2003, p. 11.

[38] Ely Banister Soane, *To Mesopotamia and Kurdistan in Disguise*, Cosimo Classics, 2007 [John Murray, 1912].

[39] Ibid.

[40] Ibid.

[41] Ibid.

[42] Refugees International, 'Bosnia Winter Watch' newsletter, 15 November 1993, p. 3.

[43] Carl K. Savich, 'Al-Qaeda on Trial: The Hague and Bosnian Muslim War Crimes (Part 2)', Balkanalysis.com, 17 March 2005.

[44] Syrian Human Rights Committee report, quoted in Wikipedia, '1982 Hama massacre'.

[45] William Dalrymple, *From the Holy Mountain*, p. 134.

[46] Ibid., p. 154.

Glossary

Angrez (Urdu)   English

Ashak   Small parcels of pasta filled with leek and served with a minced meat
                sauce on a bed of yoghurt

Aujakh   Large metal cauldron used as a dye vat

Azan   The Muslim call to prayer five times a day

Balla Hissar   A fort or castle on a hill

Ba ma nekhoda (Dari)   Goodbye

Bismillah ir-Rahman ir-Rahim   In God's name, the Most Gracious, the Most Merciful

Bolesht   Woven camel or donkey bag used for carrying grain; also a large cushion
                or pillow for people to lean against, when sitting on the floor

Boulanee   Fried pastries stuffed with chopped leeks or mashed potato with chopped
                spring onion

Bukhari (Dari) Stove

Buzkashi   Literally, 'goat dragging' or 'catch goat'. A traditional horseback game
                played by the Turkic-speaking peoples of Central Asia

Chador   The traditional Afghan 'shuttlecock' pleated covering with crocheted
                headpiece, worn by women to cover themselves when going outside the
                home

Chai khanna   Tea house

Chai sabz   Green tea

Chai sia   Black tea

Chaparkat   Low wooden three-sided seat used throughout northern Afghanistan
                in homes and chai khannas; can also mean a bed with four legs like a
                charpoy

Chappals   Leather or plastic sandals

Chapan   Traditional long overcoat made from woven camel's wool, silk ikat or
                gaily-coloured striped silk worn by men throughout Afghanistan in the
                19th and 20th centuries until the Soviet invasion. They are now being
                worn once more in Afghanistan.

Chitor asti? (Farsi) How are you?

Chopendoz   Rider taking part in the traditional game of Buzkashi

Dashtarkhan   A cloth or thin mat used to protect a carpet at mealtimes. In the bazaar,
                merchants would often refer to the long narrow carpets or kilims made by
                Sunni Hazaras of the Qala-i-Nau as a dashtarkhan. These were frequently
                used in carpet shops at mealtimes in lieu of a cloth.

Dervish   Muslim Holy man dedicated to a life of extreme poverty

Dhurrie   Flat woven cotton floor covering

Dogh   Refreshing drink made from yoghurt, mint and cucumber

Dopiaza (Farsi) Literally, 'two onions'. An Afghan dish of boiled lamb cooked with onions
                and split peas, then garnished with raw vinegared sliced white
                onions

Dupatta   Large scarf worn by Muslim women to cover their heads

Ell   A measurement for woollen and linen cloth used in Europe from the
                Middle Ages but abolished in 1835. One ell is approximately 45 inches.

Fallahi	Cross stitch, usually of maroon silk thread, used to decorate the front and sleeves of traditional black Palestinian women's dresses
Feringee	Foreigner
Firni	Cold milk pudding made with either cornflour or ground rice, flavoured with cardamom and frequently decorated with ground or finely chopped pistachio and almonds
GAZ	Russian lorry marque
Ghazzals	Persian and Urdu love songs
Jelabi	Sticky sweetmeat sold in the bazaar
Hadji Bibi	An honorific term to describe a venerable lady or grandmother who has undertaken the *Haj*
Hindko	Language spoken by various tribes in the North-West Frontier, particularly in Peshawar, the Khyber Agency and parts of the Punjab
Iftar	The meal eaten at the end of the day to break the fast during the holy month of Ramadan
Ikat (Indonesian)	The tying or binding of yarn in certain places before it is placed in the dye vat. Referred to as *Abr* ('cloudy') in Afghanistan because of the soft blurring between the colours caused by this method of resist-dyeing.
Jezail	Long-barrelled matchlock musket with a fixed rest. A formidable weapon used by Baluch and Pathan tribesmen against the British and Indian sepoys in Afghanistan in the 19th and early 20th centuries. In the hands of a skilled marksman, its six-foot barrel meant the jezail was extremely accurate. The bullet could travel 800 yards.
Jihad	To strive in the way of Allah
Kaffir	Infidel or unbeliever. A derogatory term for non-Muslims
Karai	Cast-iron metal cooking dish with handles (similar to a wok) for frying fish, lamb kebab and chicken
Kariz/karez	An ancient form of irrigation used for centuries to transport snow-melt or spring water from the mountains to villages through underground tunnels dug deep beneath the desert. Water is accessed through a succession of wells constructed at some distance from each other. On a clear day these wells can be seen from the air, stretching in a straight line for miles like anthills across the inhospitable and barren desert that exists in much of Afghanistan.
Keffiyeh	Checked cotton headcloths introduced to Afghanistan by Arab jihadists and worn by the Afghan Mujahideen
Khalat	Overcoats padded with cotton worn by Turkmen and Uzbeks
Kishmish	Raisins. In Chitral they were often sold mixed with almonds, walnuts and mulberries as a snack
Lunghi	Cotton sarong
Naan	Bread made from wheat flour
Naswar	Narcotic snuff produced from tobacco; placed under the tongue or inside the lower lip
Noql-e-badomi	Sugared almonds
Nullah	A deep watercourse with steep sides caused by erosion
Paratha	Bread similar to a chapati but deep-fried in oil
Pattu	Woven woollen shawl, usually grey or brown, worn on the North-West Frontier and in Afghanistan. The Mujahideen used their pattus for

	camouflage, as prayer mats and tablecloths, and as stretchers to carry the wounded.
Peshmerga	Kurdish militia. Literally, 'Those who face death'
Phiran	Traditional Kashmiri tweed wool cape
Pisanice	Hard-boiled eggs coloured and decorated to celebrate Easter in Croatia
Qabuli pilau	Yellow rice cooked with meat (usually lamb) and meat juices. The pilau is served with the lamb (often an entire sheep's head) buried in the centre and topped with carrots and raisins. Sour oranges (*naranj*) are often served with the rice and it is the custom to sprinkle the juice over the pilau.
Qaleb	Revolving wooden frame used by ikat silk-weavers to wind on the silk threads to form skeins. Once the skeins are in place, the frame is removed and laid flat on the floor so that the design can be marked out on the skeins, which are then tightly bound with cotton cloth prior to dyeing.
Qurut	Hard dried Central Asian cheese made from fermented yoghurt and formed into small round balls
Rabab	A lute-like musical instrument originating from Central Afghanistan
Salaam Aleikum	Peace be upon you
Saag Jaanghi	Dog fight
Sarwan	Camel handler
Segosha	V-shaped embroidered hanging used by nomads to cover and disguise bedding rolls stored during daytime around the walls of yurts
Sherwa	An Afghan soup of meat or vegetables. Naan is often broken up and dropped into the soup to soak up the broth and then eaten using the fingers.
Shippens	North Country word for a cow byre.
Shuravi (Dari)	Russian. Afghans frequently referred to black tea imported from the Soviet Union as '*chai shuravi*'
Talib (Arabic)	Student, or 'one who seeks knowledge'
Taliban (pl.)	Young men born in the Afghan refugee camps of Pakistan during the time of jihad and educated in Pakistani madrassas. Many developed their fighting skills with the Mujahideen, who they idealised. After the Soviet withdrawal from Afghanistan, they became disillusioned with, and distanced themselves from, the power struggle between the different factions. The Taliban wanted to become a party that would purify the Islamic way of life, which they felt had become corrupted.
Tarshoumar	An embroidery stitch from eastern Afghanistan. The skill is passed down from mother to daughter.
Thali	A variety of food, usually vegetarian, served on a large circular metal platter in India and Pakistan
Zere zamin (Dari)	Literally 'under the ground'. Merchants in the bazaar referred to artefacts dug up from archaeological sites in Afghanistan and then sold to foreign art dealers in the bazaars of Peshawar as 'zere zamin'.

Bibliography

Afghan Refugee Information Network (ARIN). Newsletter No. 9, March/April 1983.

Atkinson, James. *The Expedition into Afghanistan. Notes and Sketches descriptive of the country contained in a personal narrative during the campaign of 1839 and 1840, up to the surrender of Dost Mohammed Khan*. London, 1842.

Biggs, Robert D. (ed.) *Discoveries from Kurdish Looms*. Exhibition catalogue. Evantson, Ill.: Mary and Leigh Block Gallery, Northwestern University, 1983.

Boden, Mark (ed.) *Furness Iron. The Physical Remains of the Iron Industry and Related Woodland Industries of Furness and Southern Lakeland*. Swindon: English Heritage at the National Monuments Record Centre, 2000.

Boulnois, Luce. *The Silk Road: Monks, Warriors and Merchants*. George Allen & Unwin Ltd, 1966.

Burkett, M.E. Catalogue for travelling exhibition *The Art of the Felt Maker*. Abbot Hall Art Gallery, Kendal, Cumbria. Sponsored by Crafts Advisory Committee, Northern Arts and Sotheby's, 1979.

Clements, Jonathan. *An Armchair Traveller's History of the Silk Road*. London: The Armchair Traveller at The bookHaus, 2013.

Dalrymple, William. *From the Holy Mountain. A journey in the shadow of Byzantium*. Flamingo (HarperCollins), 1998.

Dalrymple, William. *Return of a King. The Battle for Afghanistan 1839–42*. New York, Alfred A. Knopf, and London: Bloomsbury Publishing, 2013.

Darr, Robert Abdul Hayy. *The Spy of the Heart*. Fons Vitae, 2006.

Dawood, N.J. *The Koran*. Penguin Books Limited, 1974.

Derry, Douglas L. *Making it Big in Canada: The Life of William Ramsay of Bowland*. Caledon, ON: Poplar Lane Press, 2010. www.poplarlane.net

Dupeigne, Bernard (tr. Helena Beattie). *Ikats d'Afghanistan*, Bulletin du Centre International d'Étude des Textiles Anciens, 1976, I et II, 43–44, pp. 137–8.

Dupree, Louis. *Afghanistan*. Princeton University Press, 1973.

Dupree, Nancy Hatch. *An Historical Guide to Afghanistan* No. 5 (2nd ed.). Kabul: Afghan Tourist Organisation, 1977.

Elphinstone, Mountstuart. *An account of the Kingdom of Caubul, and its Dependencies in Persia, Tartary and India*. London, 1843.

Elroy Flecker, James. *Hassan*. London: Heineman Educational Books Ltd.

Farrington, Susan Maria. *Peshawar Monumental Inscriptions II*. London: BACSA, 1991.

Gibb, Lorna. *Lady Hester, Queen of the East*. London: Faber and Faber, 2005.

Giradet, Edward and Walter, Jonathan. *Afghanistan* (CROSSLINES Essential Field Guides to humanitarian and conflict zones). Media ActionInternational. Geneva: CROSSLINES Publications, 1998 and 2004.

Hopkirk, Peter. *The Great Game: On Secret Service in High Asia*. London: Oxford University Press, 1990.

Howell, Georgina. *The Extraordinary Life of Gertrude Bell*. London: Macmillan, 2006.

Human Rights Watch/Yale University Press. *Iraq's Crime of Genocide: The Anfal Campaign against the Kurds*. 1994

Kalter, Johannes. *The Arts and Crafts of Turkestan*. London: Thames and Hudson, 1984.

Kalter, Johannes. *The Arts and Crafts of the Swat Valley.* London: Thames and Hudson, 1991.

Klimburg, Max. 'The Ikats of Central Asia', in *Tessuti Ikat dell'Asia Centrale,* exhibition catalogue. Turin, Italy, 1986.

Knoll, Erwin. 'Journalistic Jihad. Holes in the coverage of a holy war.' *The Progressive,* May 1990, pp. 17–22.

Lonely Planet: *Pakistan & the Karakoram Highway.* 1981

Loyn, David. *Frontline. The true story of the British mavericks who changed the face of war reporting.* London: Michael Joseph/Penguin Books, 2005.

Macintyre, Ben. *Josiah the Great. The True Story of the Man Who Would Be King.* HarperCollins, 2004.

Makiya, Kanan. *The Monument: Art and Vulgarity in Saddam Hussein's Iraq.*

Martakies, Robin. *Ambleside Roman Fort. 'Galava'.* Privately published, 2007.

Nash, John Tulloch. *Fighting with the Bengal Yeomanry Cavalry.* First published in 1893 as *Volunteering in India.* Oakpast Limited, 2009.

Nevill, Captain H.L. *British and Indian Army Campaigns on the North-West Frontier of India, 1849–1908.* First published 1912. London: Tom Donovan Publishing Limited, 1992.

Parsons, R.D. *Oriental Rugs Volume 3: The Carpets of Afghanistan.* Suffolk: Antique Collectors Club Limited, 1983.

Rashid, Ahmed. *Taliban, Islam, oil and the New Great Game in Central Asia.* London and New York: I.B. Tauris & Co Ltd, 2000.

Russell, Gerald. *Heir to Forgotten Kingdoms. Journeys into the Disappearing Religions of the Middle East.* London: Simon and Schuster UK Ltd, 2014.

Saberi, Helen. *Noshe Djan: Afghan Food & Cookery.* Totnes, Devon: Prospect Books, 1986. (New revised edition, 2000.)

Savich, Carl K. 'Al-Qaeda on Trial: The Hague and Bosnian Muslim War Crimes (Part 2)' Balkanalysis.com, 17 March 2005.

Soane, E.B. *To Mesopotamia and Kurdistan in Disguise: with Historical Notices of the Kurdish Tribes and the Chaldeans of Kurdistan.* London: John Murray, 1912.

Summerson, Henry. *Edward I at Carlisle: King and Parliament in 1307.* Cumberland and Westmorland Antiquarian and Archaeological Society. Kendal: Titus Wilson & Son, 2011.

Thesiger, Wilfred. *Desert, Marsh and Mountain: The World of the Nomad.* London: William Collins Sons and Co. Ltd, 1979.

UN Economic and Social Council. *Report on the situation of human rights in Iraq, submitted by the Special Rapporteur of the Commission on Human Rights, Mr. Max van der Stoel, pursuant to Commission resolution 1996/72.* February 1997.

Vámbéry, Arminius. *Travels in Central Asia. Being the account of a journey from Teheran across the Turkoman desert on the eastern shore of the Caspian, to Khiva, Bokhara and Samarcand.* London: John Murray, 1863.

Vender, Ben. *I felt like an adventure. A life of Mary Burkett.* Durham: The Memoir Club, 2008.

Victoria and Albert Museum. *Ikats* (The Victoria and Albert Colour Books). Webb and Bower, 1989.

Vulliamy, Ed. *Seasons in Hell: Understanding Bosnia's War.* Simon &Schuster Ltd, 1994.

Yousaf, Mohammad and Adkin, Mark. *Afghanistan – The Bear Trap: The Defeat of a Superpower.* Pen & Sword Books, 2001.

Zorz, Annie (tr. Helena Beattie). *Ikats d'Afghanistan* (1971). Film commentary. CNRS-SERDDAV, 1975.

Index